The Norton Scores

An Anthology for Listening

Fifth Edition

VOLUME I

The Norton Scores

An Anthology for Listening

Fifth Edition
in Two Volumes

VOLUME I:
Gregorian Chant to Beethoven

Edited by
Roger Kamien
Professor of Music,
Hebrew University, Jerusalem, Israel

W · W · Norton & Company
New York London

Acknowledgments

The text translation for item 4 is by Martin Best. Reprinted by permission of Nimbus Records.
The text translation for item 7 is by Dr. Yvette Louria.
The text translation for item 9 is by Howard Garey.
The text translation for item 14 is by Alejandro Planchart.
Item 35: Translation of the libretto © 1968 by Lionel Salter. Reprinted by kind permission of Deutsche Grammophon GmbH, Hamburg.

ISBN 0-393-95745-4

W. W. Norton & Company, Inc., 500 Fifth Avenue, New York, N.Y. 10110
W. W. Norton & Company, Ltd., 37 Great Russell Street, London WC1B 3NU

1 2 3 4 5 6 7 8 9 0

Contents

Preface

This anthology is designed for use in introductory music courses, where the ability to read music is not a prerequisite. The unique system of highlighting employed in this book enables students to follow full orchestral scores after about one hour of instruction. This system also has the advantage of permitting students who *can* read music to perceive every aspect of the score. It is felt that our system of highlighting will be of greater pedagogical value than artificially condensed scores, which restrict the student's vision to pre-selected elements of the music. The use of scores in introductory courses makes the student's listening experience more intense and meaningful, and permits the instructor to discuss music in greater depth.

The works included in this Fifth Edition have been chosen from among those most frequently studied in introductory courses. The selections range from Gregorian chant to the present day, and represent a wide variety of forms, genres, and performing media. To make this Fifth Edition reflect today's concert repertory more closely, increased emphasis has been placed on instrumental and secular music of earlier periods and on music of the present century. A majority of the pieces are given in their entirety, while the others are represented by complete movements or sections particularly suitable for classroom study. Scenes from operas and some choral works are presented in vocal score, while all others are reprinted in their full original form. In the case of a few recent works, obstacles of copyright or practicality prevented inclusion of a complete score. This anthology may be used independently, or along with any introductory text. The publishers have prepared a set of recordings to accompany *The Norton Scores*.

A few words about the highlighting system employed in the full scores: Each system of score is covered with a light gray screen, and the most prominent line in the music at any given point is spotlighted by a white band (see No. 1 in sample on page *x*). In cases where two or more simultaneous lines are equally prominent, they are each highlighted. When a musical line continues from one system or page to the next, the white highlighting band ends with a wedge shape at the right-hand margin, and its continuation begins with a reverse wedge shape (see No. 2 in sample). By following these white bands in sequence through the score, the listener will perceive the notes corresponding to the most audible lines. Naturally, the highlighting will not *always* correspond with the most prominent instruments in a specific recording, for performances differ in their emphasis of particular lines. In such cases, we have highlighted those parts that, in our opinion, *should* emerge most clearly. (There are occasional passages in complex twentieth-century works where no single line represents the musical continuity. In such passages we have drawn the listener's attention to the most audible musical events while endeavoring to keep the highlighting as simple as possible.) To facilitate the following of highlighted scores, a narrow white band running the full width of the page has been placed between systems when there is more than one on a page.

It must be emphasized that we do not seek here to *analyze* melodic structure, contrapuntal texture, or any other aspect of the music. The highlighting may break off before the end of a phrase when the entrance of another part is more audible, and during long-held notes the attention will usually be drawn to more rhythmically active parts. The highlighting technique has been used primarily for instrumental music; in vocal works, the text printed under the music provides a firm guideline for the novice score-reader.

A few suggestions for the use of this anthology may be found useful:

1. The rudiments of musical notation should be introduced with a view to preparing the student to associate audible melodic contours with their written equivalents. It is more important for beginning students to recognize rising and falling lines, and long and short notes, than to identify specific pitches or rhythms. It is helpful to explain the function of a tie, and the layout of a full score.
2. Before listening to a work, it is best for students to familiarize themselves with the names and abbreviations for instruments used in that particular score (a glossary of instrumental names and abbreviations will be found at the conclusion of the book). We have retained the Italian, German, French, and English names used in the scores reproduced in this anthology. This exposure to a wide range of terminology will prepare students for later encounters with scores.
3. Students should be careful to notice whether there is more than one system on a page of score. They should be alerted for tempo changes, repeat signs, and *da capo* indications. Since performances often differ, it is helpful for the instructor to forewarn the class about the specific repeats made or not made in the recordings used for listening.
4. When a piece is very fast or difficult, it is helpful to listen once without a score.

5. It is best to begin with music that is relatively simple to follow: e.g. (in approximate order of difficulty) Handel, "Comfort ye" from *Messiah;* the first and third movements of Mozart's *Eine kleine Nachtmusik;* and the second movement of Haydn's Symphony No. 104 in D major *(London).*
6. Important thematic material and passages that are difficult to follow should be pointed out in advance and played either on the recording or at the piano. (We have found that rapid sections featuring two simultaneously highlighted instruments sometimes present difficulties for the students—e.g. Beethoven, Symphony No. 5, first movement, m. 65 ff.)

We have attempted to keep the highlighted bands simple in shape while showing as much of the essential slurs and dynamic indication as possible. Occasionally, because of the layout of the original score, stray stems and slurs will intrude upon the white area and instrumental directions will be excluded from the highlighting. (Naturally, the beginning of a highlighted area will not always carry a dynamic or similar indication, as the indication may have occurred measures earlier when the instrument in question was not the most prominent.) As students become more experienced in following the scores, they can be encouraged to direct their attention outside the highlighted areas, and with practice should eventually develop the skill to read conventional scores.

I should like to record here my great debt to the late Nathan Broder, who originated the system of highlighting employed here and whose advice and counsel were invaluable. My thanks go also to Mr. David Hamilton, and to Claire Brook and Juli Goldfein of W. W. Norton, for many helpful suggestions. I am most grateful to my wife, Anita, who worked with me on every aspect of the book. She is truly the co-editor of this anthology.

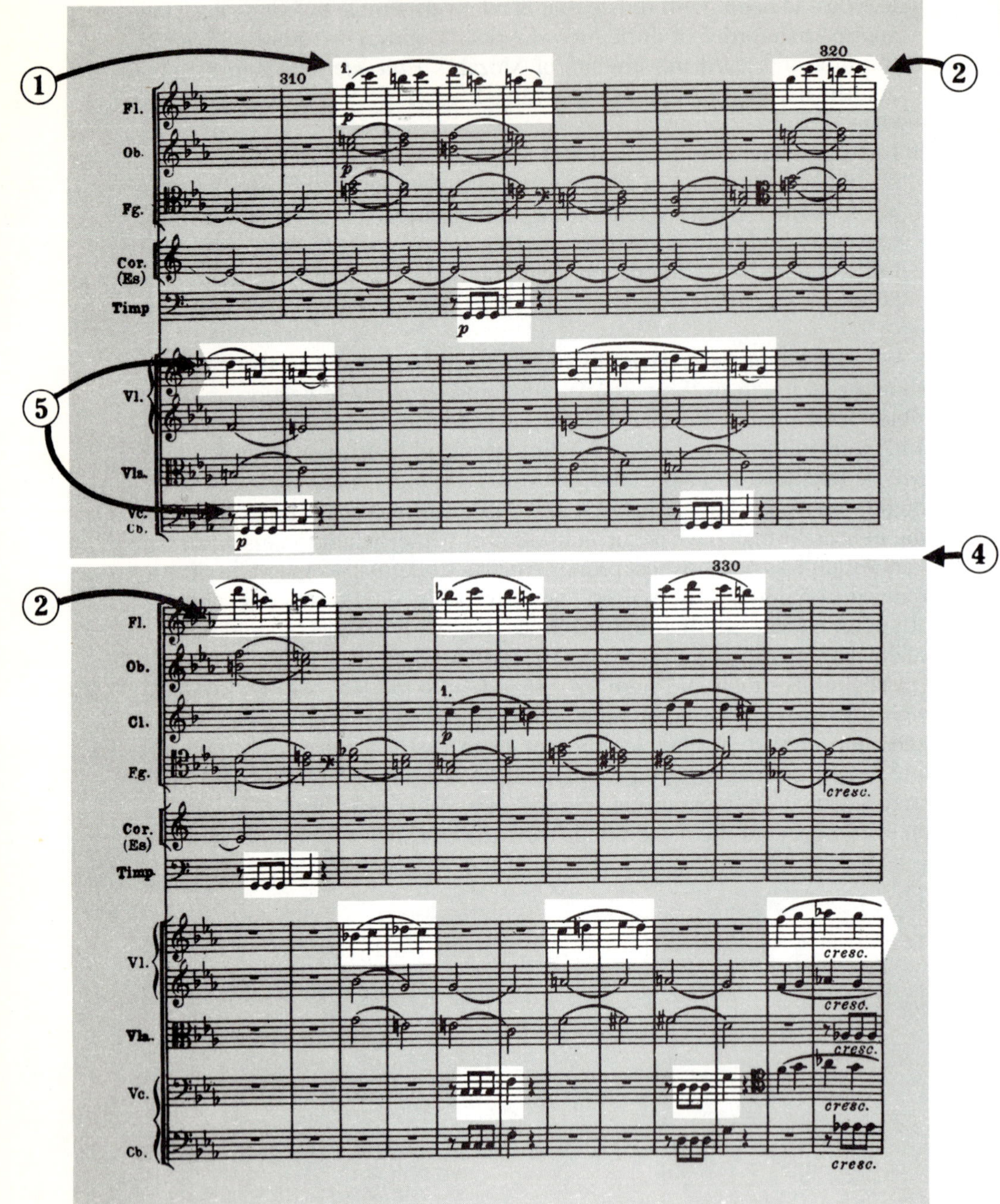

1
2
310
320
1.
Fl.
Ob.
Fg.
Cor.
(Es)
Timp
p
5
Vl.
Vla.
Vc.
Cb.
4
330
Cl.
cresc.

HOW TO FOLLOW THE HIGHLIGHTED SCORES

1. The most prominent line in the music at any given time is highlighted by a white band.
2. When a musical line continues from one system (group of staffs) or page to the next, the white highlighted band ends with a wedge shape, and its continuation begins with a reverse wedge shape.
3. By following the highlighted bands in sequence through the score, the listener will perceive the notes corresponding to the most audible lines.
4. A narrow white band running the full width of the page separates one system from another when there is more than one on a page. It is very important to be alert for these separating bands.
5. When two or more lines are equally prominent, they are each highlighted. When encountering such passages for the first time, it is sometimes best to focus on only one of the lines.

A NOTE ON PERFORMANCE PRACTICE

In performances and recordings of earlier music, certain variations from the printed scores will frequently be observed. These are not arbitrary alterations of the music, but are based upon current knowledge concerning the performance practice of the period. In earlier times, the written notes often represented a kind of shorthand, an outline for performers, rather than a set of rigid instructions. The following specific practices may be noted:

1. Ornaments are frequently added to melodic lines, particularly at cadences and in repetitions of musical material.
2. During the Middle Ages and Renaissance, performers were often expected to supply sharps, flats, and naturals that were not written in the music. Some modern editors indicate these accidentals above the

notes, while others do not. Moreover, modern editors and performers often differ in their interpretation of the conventions governing the use of accidentals in early music.

3. In many early sources, the placement of words in relation to notes is not clearly indicated, or shown only in part; thus, modern editions and performances may differ.
4. In music before about 1600, the choice of voices or instruments and the choice of specific instruments was a matter of some freedom. Thus, in performance, some parts of a piece may be played rather than sung, or alternate between voices and instruments.
5. Since, at certain times and places in the past, pitch was higher or lower than it is today, modern performers sometimes transpose music to a key lower or higher than written, in order to avoid performance difficulties.
6. In Baroque music, the figured bass part, consisting of a bass line and numbers indicating harmonies, will be "realized" in different ways by different performers. In some editions included here (e.g. Purcell, *Dido and Aeneas*), there is a suggested realization by the modern editor—but it is only a suggestion, and will not necessarily be followed in a given performance.

1. Gregorian Chant,

Gradual, *Haec dies*

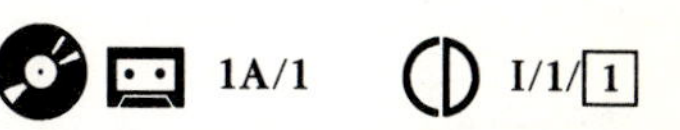

Grad.
2

HÆC dí- es, * quam fé- cit Dó-

mi- nus : exsulté- mus,

et lae- té- mur in é- a.

℣. Confi-témi-ni Dó- mi- no, quó-

ni- am bó- nus : quó-ni- am in saé-

culum mi-se-ri-cór- di- a * é- jus.

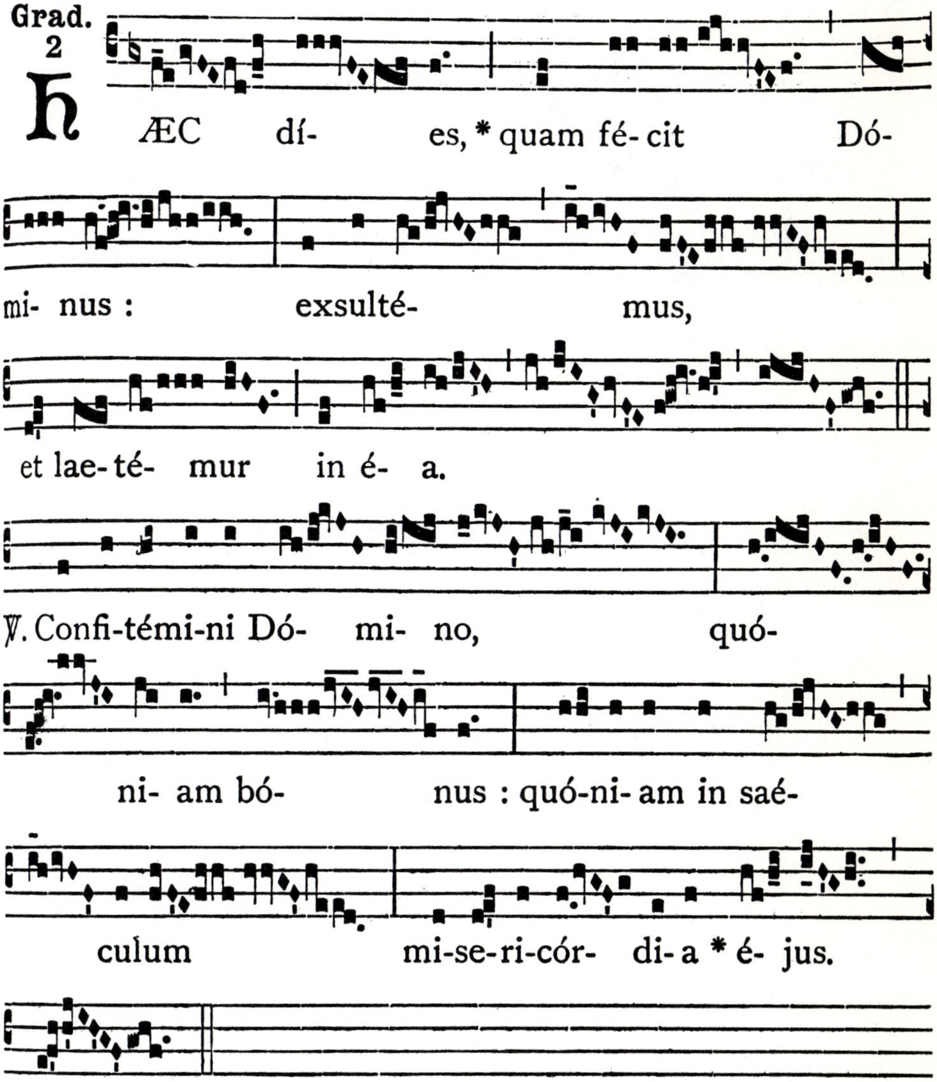

* = *choral response*

Adapted from Willi Apel's transcription in The Historical Anthology of Music, *Vol. I (Cambridge, Mass.: Harvard University Press, 1962).*

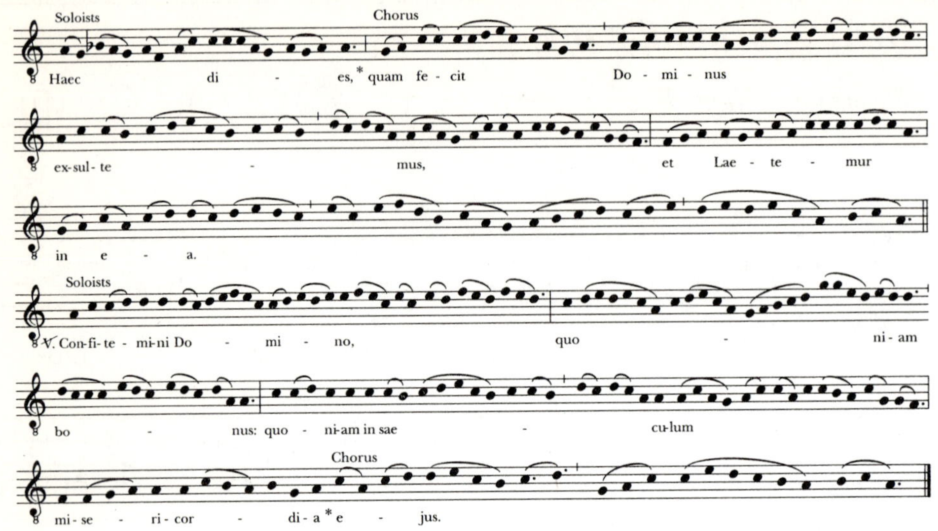

Translation

Haec dies
quam fecit Dominus
exsultemus et
laetemur in ea.
Confitemini Domino,
quoniam bonus:
quoniam in saeculum
misericordia
ejus.

This is the day
which the Lord hath made;
we will rejoice and be
glad in it.
O give thanks to the
Lord, for he is good:
for his mercy
endureth
forever.

2. Notre Dame School,

Organum, *haec dies,* Excerpt (c. 1175)

For a translation of the text, see page 2.

Adapted from Waite, The Rhythm of Twelfth Century Polyphony *(New Haven: Yale Univ. Press), 1954. Reprinted by permission of Yale University Press.*

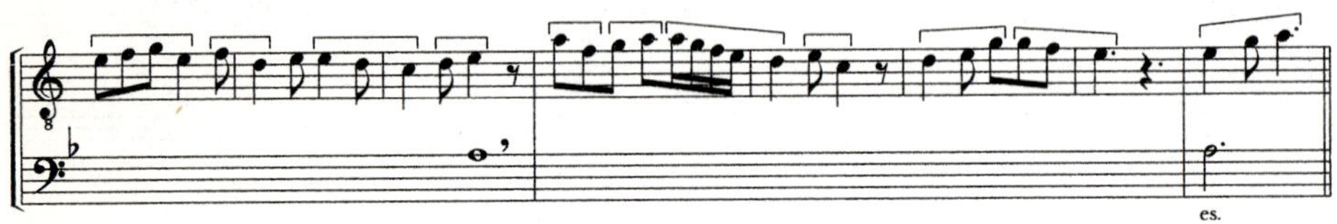
es.

Chorus
quam fe - cit Do - mi - nus:

ex - sul - te - mus

et lae - te - mur in e - a.

V. Confitemini.
Con - fi -

f. 31'
te - mi -

ni do -

mi - no

quo
ni
am
bo
nus

3. Anonymous (13th century),

Motet, *O Mitissima—Virgo—Haec dies*

Adapted from Willi Apel's transcription in The Historical Anthology of Music, *Vol. I (Cambridge, Mass.: Harvard University Press, 1962).*

Translation

TOP VOICE:
O mitissima Virgo Maria,
Posce tuum filium,
Ut nobis auxilium
Det et remedium
Contra demonum
Fallibiles astucias
Et horum nequicias.

O sweetest Virgin Mary,
beg thy son
to give us help
and resources
against the Demon's
deceptions and
their iniquities.

MIDDLE VOICE:
Virgo virginum,
Lumen luminum,
Reformatrix hominum,
Que portasti Dominum,
Perte Maria,
Detur venia,
Angelo nunciante,
Virgo es post et ante.

Virgin of virgins,
light of lights,
reformer of men,
who bore the Lord,
through thee, Mary,
let grace be given
as the Angel announced:
Thou art a Virgin before and after.

BOTTOM VOICE:
Haec dies . . .

This is the day . . .

4. Moniot d'Arras (fl. 1213–1239),

Ce fut en mai

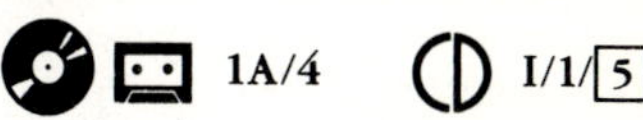

1A/4
I/1/5

A
1.
2.
Ce fut en mai Au douz tens gai, Que la se-son est be-le;
Main me le-vai Jü-er m'a-lai Lez
u-ne fon-te-ne-le.

B
1.
2.
En un ver-ger Clos d'es-glen-tier O-i u-ne vi-e-le;
La vi dan-cier Un che-va-lier Et
u-ne de-moi-se-le.

Translation

I Ce fut en mai
Au douz tens gai
Que la saisons est bele,
Main me levai,
Joer m'alai
Lez une fontenele.
En un vergier
Clos d'aiglentier
Oi une viele;

In early May
When skies are gay
And green the plains and mountains
At break of day
I rose to play
Beside a little fountain
In garden close
Where shone the rose
I heard a fiddle played, then:

La vi dancier
Un chevalier
Et une damoisele.

A handsome knight
That charmed my sight
Was dancing with a maiden.

II Cors orent gent
Et avenant
Et molt très bien dançoient;
En acolant
Et en baisant
Molt biau se deduisoient.
Au chief du tor,
En un destor,
Doi et doi s'en aloient;
Le jeu d'amor
Desus la flor
A lor plaisir faisoient.

Both fair of face,
They turned with grace
To tread their Maytime measure;
The flowering place,
Their close embrace,
Their kisses brought them pleasure.
Yet shortly they
Had slipped away
And strolled among the bowers;
To ease their heart
Each played his part
In love's games on the flowers.

III J'alai avant.
Molt redoutant
Que nus d'aus ne me voie,
Maz et pensant
Et desirrant
D'avoir ausi grant joie.
Lors vi lever
Un de lor per
De si loing com j'estoie
Por apeler
Et demander
Qui sui ni que queroie.

I crept ahead
All chill with dread
Lest someone there should see me,
Bemused and sad
Because I had
No joy like theirs to please me.
Then one of those
I'd seen there, rose
And from afar off speaking
He questioned me
Who I might be
And what I came there seeking.

IV J'alai vers aus,
Dis lor mes maus,
Que une dame amoie,
A cui loiaus
Sanz estre faus
Tot mon vivant seroie,
Por cui plus trai
Peine et esmai
Que dire ne porroie.
Et bien le sai,
Que je morrai,
S'ele ne mi ravoie.

I stepped their way
To sadly say
How long I'd loved a lady
Whom, all my days
My heart obeys
Full faithfully and steady.
Though still I bore
A grief so sore
In losing one so lovely
That surely I
Would come to die
Unless she deigned to love me.

V Tot belement
Et doucement
Chascuns d'aus me ravoie.
Et dient tant
Que Dieus briement
M'envoit de celi joie
Por qui je sent
Paine et torment:
Et je lor en rendoie
Merci molt grant
Et en plorant
A Dé les comandoie.

With wisdom rare,
With tactful air,
They counselled and relieved me;
They said their prayer
Was God might spare
Some joy in love that grieved me
Where all my gain
Was loss and pain
So I, in turn, extended
My thanks sincere
With many a tear
And them to God commended.

5. Guillaume Machaut (c. 1300-1377),

Hareu! hareu! le feu—Helas! ou sera pris confors—Obediens usque ad mortem

1A/5 I/1/6

Adapted from Leo Schrade's transcription in Polyphonic Music of the Fourteenth Century: Guillaume de Machaut © *Editions de l'Oiseau-Lyre, Les Remparts, Monaco.*

spoir que de-vi-ez yert, eins Que bonne A-mour de mer-ci l'as-se-u-re
— plus, Pour ce que je l'aim plus que nulz,

Par la ver-tu d'e-spe-ran-ce se-u-re. Car pour li seul, qui en-du-re mal meint; Pi-tié def-faut, ou
Et Sou-ve-nir pour en-a-sprir L'ar-

tou-te biau-té meint; Dur-tés y regne et Dan-giers y re-meint, Des-deins y vit et Loy-au-tez s'i feint
-dour de mon tri-ste de-sir Me moustre a-

Et A-mours n'a de li ne de moy cu-re. Joi-e le het, ma da-me li est du-re,
dés sa grant bon-té Et

Et, pour croi-stre mes do-le-reus mes-chiés, Met de-dens moy A-mours,
sa fi-ne vrai-e biau-té Qui dou-ble-ment me fait ar-doir.

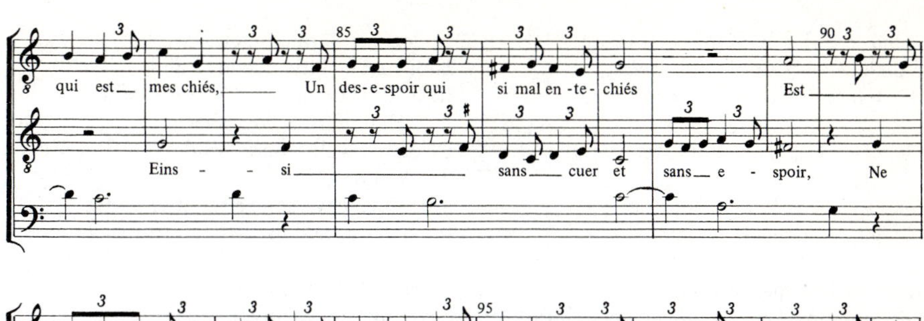

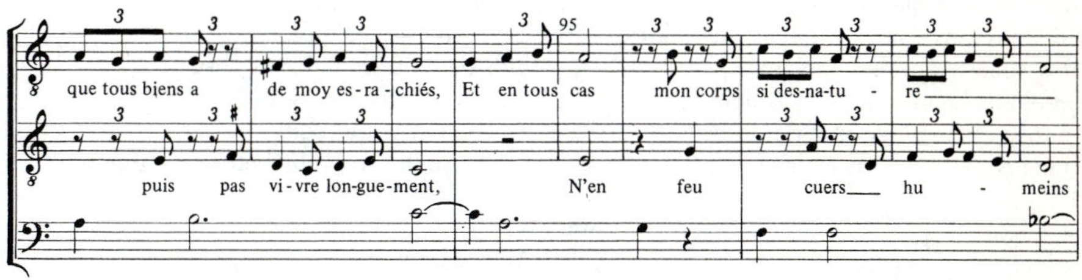

Translation

TRIPLUM

Hareu! hareu! le feu, le feu, le feu
D'ardant desir, qu'einc si ardant ne fu,
Qu'en mon cuer a espris et soustenu
Amours, et s'a la joie retenu
D'espoir qui doit attemprer telle ardure.

Las! se le feu qui ensement l'art dure,
Mes cuers sera tous bruis et esteins,
Qui de ce feu est ja nercis et teins,
Pour ce qu'il est fins, loyaus et certeins;
Si que j'espoir que deviez yert, eins
Que bonne Amour de merci l'asseure
Par la vertu d'esperance seure.

Help! Help! Fire! Fire! Fire!
My heart is on fire with burning desire
Such as was never seen before.
Love, having started it, fans the flames,
Withholding all hope of joy which might put out such a blaze.
Alas, if this fire keeps on burning,
My heart, already blackened and shriveled,
Will be burnt to ashes.
For it is true, loyal, and sincere.
I expect I shall be mad with grief
Before gentle Love consoles it
With sound hope.

Car pour li seul, qui endure mal meint;
Pitié deffaut, ou toute biauté meint;
Durtés y regne et Dangiers y remeint,

Desdeins y vit et Loyautez s'i feint

Et Amours n'a de li ne de moy cure.
Joie le het, ma dame li est dure.

Et, pour croistre mes dolereus meschiés,
Met dedens moy Amours, qui est mes chiés,
Un desespoir qui si mal entechiés,
Est que tous biens a de moy esrachiés,
Et en tous cas mon corps si desnature
Qu'il me convient morir malgré Nature.

It alone, suffering much Hardship,
Is devoid of Pity, abode of all beauty.
Instead, Harshness rules over it and
    Haughtiness flourishes.
Disdain dwells there, while Loyalty is a rare
    visitor
And Love pays no heed to it or to me.
Joy hates it, and my lady is cruel to it.

To complete my sad misfortune,
Love, my sovereign lord,
Fills me with such bitter despair
That I am left penniless,
And so wasted in body
That I shall surely die before my time.

DUPLUM

Helas! ou sera pris confors
Pour moy qui ne vail nés que mors?
Quant riens garentir ne me puet
Fors ma dame chiere qui wet
Qu'en desespoir muire, sans plus,
Pour ce que je l'aim plus que nulz,
Et Souvenir pour enasprir
L'ardour de mon triste desir
Me moustre adés sa grant bonté

Et sa fine vraie biauté
Qui doublement me fait ardoir.
Einssi sans cuer et sans espoir,
Ne puis pas vivre longuement,
N'en feu cuers humeins nullement
Ne puet longue duree avoir.

Alas, where can I find consolation
Who am as good as dead?
When my one salvation
Is my dear lady,
Who gladly lets me die in despair,
Simply because I love her as no other could,
And Memory, in order to keep
My unhappy desire alive,
Reminds me all the while of her great goodness

And her delicate beauty,
Thereby making me want her all the more.
Deprived thus of heart and hope
I cannot live for long.
No man's heart can long survive
When once aflame.

TENOR

Obediens usque ad mortem

Obedient unto death

6. Anonymous (14th century),

Saltarello

  1A/7  I/1/7

Primo pars.

Secunda pars.

Prima pars is repeated

Tertia pars.

Quarta pars.

Tertia pars is repeated

Adapted from transcription in *Archiv für Musikwissenschaft.*

7. Guillaume Dufay (c. 1397?-1474),

Alma redemptoris mater

 1A/6 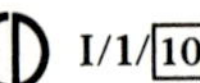 I/1/10

The chant *Alma redemptoris mater,* on which the top voice is based

Al - - - - ma re-demp - to - ris ma - ter, quae

per - vi - a cae - li por - ta ma - nes, Et stel - la ma - ris,

suc - cur - re ca - den - ti, sur - ge - re qui cu - rat po - pu - lo.

Tu quae ge - nu - i - sti, na - tu - ra mi - ran - te,

tu - um san - ctum Ge - ni - to - rem, Vir - go pri - - us

ac pos - te - ri - us, Ga - bri - e - lis ab - o - re

su - mens il - lud A - ve, pec - ca - to - rum mi - se - re - re.

Superius

Contra-Tenor

Tenor

5

Al - - - - - -

10
15
- - - - - - ma
20
re - demp - to - ris ma - - - ter,
25
30
quae per - - - vi - - - - - - a
35
cae - - - li por - - - ta ma -

40
45
- - - - nes, Et stel -
50
- - - la ma -
55
- - - - ris, suc - cur - re ca - - - den -
60
65
ti, sur - ge - re qui cu - rat po - pu - lo.

70
Tu quae ge - nu - i - - sti,
75
na - tu - ra mi - ran - te, tu-um
80
san - ctum Ge - ni - to - rem,
85
Vir - - - - - -

90
go pri - - - us ac po - - ste -
95
100
ri - us, Ga - bri - e - lis ab o -
105
re su - mens
110
115
il - lud A - ve, pec ca -

Translation

Alma redemptoris mater,
quae pervia caeli porta manes,
Et stella maris, succurre cadenti,
surgere qui curat populo.

Tu quae genuisti, natura mirante,
tuum sanctum Genitorem,
Virgo prius ac posterius,
Gabrielis ab ore sumens illud Ave,
peccatorum miserere.

Gracious mother of the Redeemer,
Abiding at the doors of Heaven,
Star of the sea, aid the falling,
Rescue the people who struggle.

Thou who, astonishing nature,
Has borne thy holy Creator,
Virgin before and after,
Who heard the Ave from the mouth of Gabriel,
Be merciful to sinners.

DR. YVETTE LOURIA

8. Anonymous (15th century),

Carol, *Deo gratias, Anglia* S1A/1 S1/1

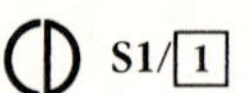

2 He set a siege, forsooth to say,
To Harflu town with royal array;
That town he won and made affray
That France shall rue till Domesday:
Deo gracias.

3 Then went him forth our king comely;
In Agincourt field he fought manly;
Through grace of God most marvellously
He had both field and victory:
Deo gracias.

Translation

Deo gratias, Anglia redde pro victoria.	England, give thanks to God for the victory.

Stainer & Bell Limited and the Trustees of Musica Brittanica Trust. From MUSICA BRITTANICA, vol. IV, Medieval Carols, John Stevens, ed.

9. Johannes Ockeghem (c. 1410–1497),

L'autre d'antan

Cantus:
Tenor:
Contratenor:

Par tel façon me fricassa
Que de ses gaiges me cassa;
Mais, par Dieu, elle fist son dan.

L'autre d'antan . . . a Melan.

Puis aprés nostre amour cessa,
Car, oncques puis qu'elle dansa,
L'autre d'antan, l'autre d'antan,
Je n'eus ne bon jour ne bon an,
Tant de mal enuy amassa.
L'autre d'antan, l'autrier passa.

L'autre d'antan . . . l'autrier passa.

From The Mellon Chansonnier, *vol. I, edited by Leeman Perkins and Howard Garey (New Haven: Yale Univ. Press), 1979, no. 20 (p. 87); translation from vol. II (p. 268). Reprinted by permission of Yale University Press.*

Translation

L'autre d'antan, l'autrier passa,
Et en passant me trespercha
D'ung regard forgié a Melan
Qui me mist en l'arriere ban,
Tant malvais brassin me brassa.
L'autre d'antan, l'autrier passa.
Par tel fachon me fricassa
Que de ses gaiges me cassa;
Mais, par Dieu, elle fist son dan.

L'autre d'antan, l'autrier passa,
Et en passant me trespercha
D'ung regard forgié a Melan.

Puis apres nostre amour cessa,
Car, oncques puis qu'elle dansa
L'autre d'antan, l'autre d'antan
Je n'eus ne bon jour ne bon an,
Tout de mal enuy amassa.
L'autre d'antan, 1'autrier passa,

L'autre d'antan, l'autrier passa,
Et en passant me trespercha
D'ung regard forgié a Melan
Qui me mist en l'arriere ban,
Tant malvais brassin me brassa.
L'autre d'antan, l'autrier passa.

The other year, the other day, she passed by
And, in passing, pierced me through
With a glance forged in Milan
That knocked me into the rear ranks
So rude a blow she dealt me.
The other year, the other day, she passed by.
She destroyed me so thoroughly
That she dismissed me from her troops;
But, by God, she did her damage.

The other year, the other day, she passed by
And, in passing, pierced me through
With a glance forged in Milan.

And then our love ended,
For, ever since she did her dance,
The other year, the other year,
I've had neither good day nor good year,
So much bad luck has piled up.
The other year, the other day, she passed.

The other year, the other day, she passed by
And, in passing, pierced me through
With a glance forged in Milan
That knocked me into the rear ranks
So rude a blow she dealt me.
The other year, the other day, she passed by.

HOWARD GAREY

10. Josquin Desprez (c. 1440–1521),

Missa La sol fa re mi, Agnus Dei   1A/9  I/1/12

Agnus Dei I

Superius
Agnus De-i
A - - gnus De -

Altus
A - gnus De-i
A - - gnus De - - i,

Tenor
A - gnus De-i
A - - gnus De - - i, a - - gnus

Bassus
A-gnus De-i
A - gnus De - i, a - gnus De - -

5

i, a - gnus De - - i, a - gnus De -

De - i, De - - - i, De -

De - - i, a - gnus De - - i, a - gnus

10

- i, qui tol - lis pec - ca - ta mun - - - -

- - i, qui tol - lis pec - ca - ta mun - -

De - - - i,

- - i, qui tol - lis pec - ca - ta mun - - -

Edited by Prof. Dr. A. Smijers. Reprinted by permission of Vereniging voor Nederlandse Muziekgeschiedenis.

* = In Agnus Dei III, *miserere nobis* becomes *donna nobis pacem.*

Agnus Dei II

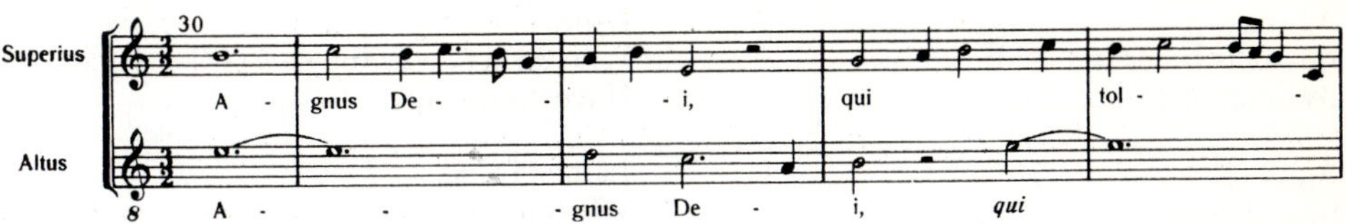

Agnus Dei III = literal repeat of Agnus Dei I

TRANSLATION

Agnus Dei
qui tollis peccata mundi,
miserere nobis,

Lamb of God,
Who takest away the sins of the world,
Have mercy upon us.

Agnus Dei
qui tollis peccata mundi,
miserere nobis,

Lamb of God,
Who takest away the sins of the world,
Have mercy upon us.

Agnus Dei,
qui tollis peccata mundi,
dona nobis pacem.

Lamb of God,
Who takest away the sins of the world,
Grant us peace.

11. Tielman Susato (c. 1515–1567),

Three Dances (publ. 1551)  1B/1 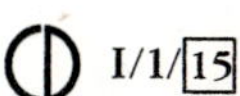 I/1/15

I

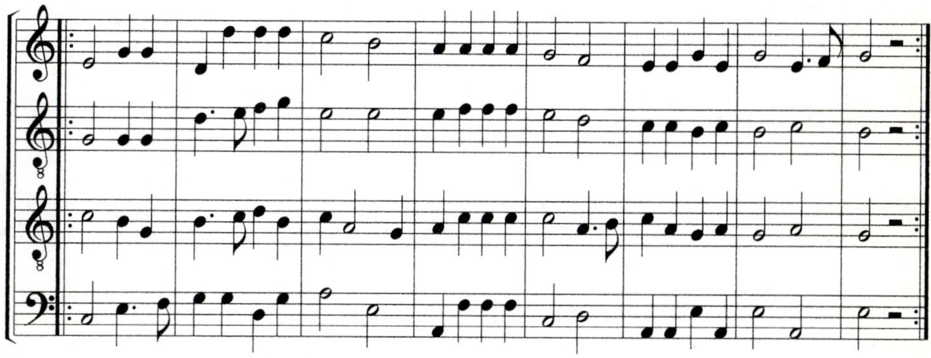

II

III

12. Giovanni Pierluigi da Palestrina (c. 1525–1594),

Missa Papae Marcelli, Gloria
(publ. 1567)

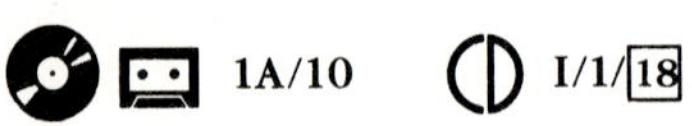

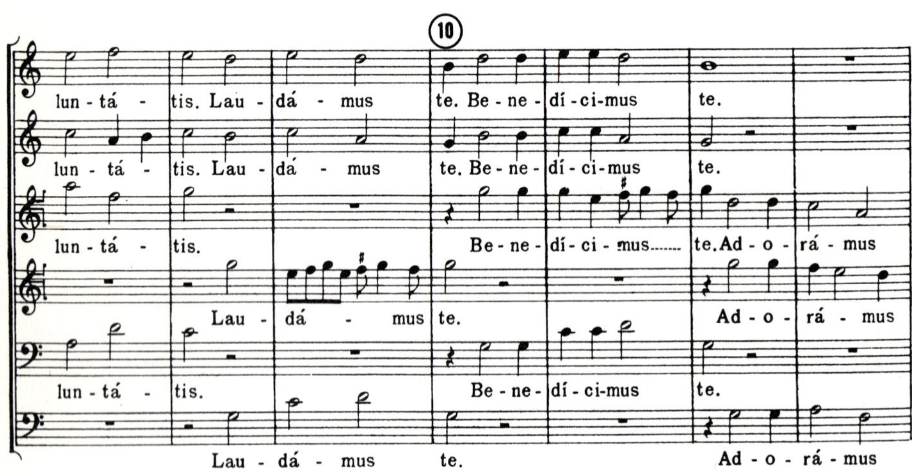

15
20
Glo-ri-fi - cá - mus te. Grá - ti-as á - gi - mus ti- -bi pro-
Glo-ri-fi - cá - mus te. Grá - ti-as á - gi - mus ti- -bi
te. Grá - ti-as á - gi mus ti - bi
te. Glo-ri-fi - cá - mus te. Grá - ti-as á - gi - mus ti - bi pro-
Glo-ri-fi - cá - mus te. pro-
te. Grá - ti-as á - gi - mus ti- -bi
25
- pter ma - - gnam gló-ri-am tu- - am.
tu- -am. Dó- mi-ne De - us, Rex cæ - lé -
Dó- mi-ne De - us, Rex cæ-lé -
- pter ma - gnam gló - ri - am tu - am.
- pter ma - gnam gló-ri-am tu - am. Dó- mi-ne De - us, Rex
Dó - mi-ne De - us, Rex cæ-lé -
30
De - us Pa - ter o - mní-po - tens. Dó - mi - ne Fi - li, Dó - mi-ne
stis, Dó - mi - ne Fi - li, Dó - mi-ne
stis, Dó - mi - ne Fi - li, Dó - mi-ne
De - us Pa - ter o - mní-po - tens. Dó - mi-ne
De - us Pa - ter o - mní- po - tens. Dó - mi-ne
stis, Dó - mi - ne Fi - li, Dó - mi-ne

35
40
Fi - li u - ni - gé-ni-te, u - ni-gé-ni - te, Je - - su
Fi - li u-ni-gé - ni-te, u - ni-gé-ni - te, Je- - su
Fi - li u - ni - gé- - -ni - te, Je- - su
Fi - li u - ni - gé-ni-te, Je- - su
Fi-li u - ni-gé-ni - te,
Fi - li u - ni - gé-ni-te, Je- - su
45
Chri - ste, Je- - su Chri - ste.
Chri - ste, Je- - su Chri-ste. Dó-mi-ne De-us, A- gnus De- -
Chri - ste, Je- - su Chri - ste. Dó-mi-ne De-us, A - gnus De -
Chri - ste, Je- - su Chri - ste. A - gnus De -
Je- - su Chri-ste. Dó-mi-ne De-us, A - gnus De -
Chri - ste, Je- - su Chri - ste.
50
Dó - mi-ne De - us, A - gnus De - i, Fí - li-us Pa- -
- -i, Fí - li-us Pa- -
- -i, A - gnus De - i, Fí - li - us
i, Dó - mi-ne De - us, A-gnus De - i,
- -i, Fí - li-us Pa-
Dó - mi-ne De - us, A - gnus De - i,

55
60
- - tris, Fí - li - us Pa - - tris.
tris, Fí - li - us Pa - tris, Fí - li-us Pa - tris.
Pa - tris, Fí - li-us Pa - - tris,[Pa- - tris.]
Fí - li - us Pa - tris, Fí - li - us Pa - tris.
- - tris, Fí - li - us Pa- - tris.
Fí - li - us Pa - tris, Fí - li - us Pa - tris.
65
Qui tol - lis pec - cá-ta mun- -di, mi - se-ré-re
Qui tol - lis pec - cá-ta mun- -di, mi - se-ré-re no- -bis, no-
Qui tol - lis pec - cá-ta mun- -di, no - bis, mi - se-ré-re
mi - se-ré-re no - bis.
Qui tol - lis pec - cá-ta mun-di, mi - se-ré-re
mi - se-ré-re no - bis.
70
no - bis. Qui tol - lis pec-cá - ta mun - di, sú - sci - pe, sú- -
- -bis. Qui tol - lis pec-cá - ta mun - di, sú - sci - pe,
no - bis. Qui tol - lis pec - cá - ta mun - di, sú - sci - pe, sú - sci -
Qui tol- lis pec-cá - ta mun - di, sú - sci - pe, sú- -
no - bis. sú - sci - pe, sú -
Qui tol - lis pec-cá - ta mun - di, sú - sci - pe, sú -

- sci - pe de - pre - ca - ti - ó - nem no - stram, de - pre - ca - ti - ó - nem
sú - sci - pe de - pre - ca - ti - ó - nem no - stram, de - pre - ca - ti - ó - nem
pe de - pre - ca - ti - ó - nem no - stram.
- sci - pe de - pre - ca - ti - ó - nem no -
- sci - pe de - pre - ca - ti - ó - nem no - stram.
- sci - pe de - pre - ca - ti - ó - nem

no - stram. Qui se - des ad déx - te - ram Pa - tris,
no - stram. mi - se - ré - re no -
Qui se - des ad déx - te - ram Pa - tris,
- stram. mi - se - ré - re no -
Qui se - des ad déx - te - ram Pa - tris,
no - stram. mi - se - ré - re

mi - se - ré - re no - bis. Quó - ni - am tu
- bis, no - bis. Quó - ni - am tu
mi - se - ré - re no - bis.
- bis. Quó - ni - am tu
mi - se - ré - re no - bis.
no - bis. Quó - ni - am tu

95

so - lus san - ctus. Tu so-lus Dó- - mi - nus.
so-lus san - ctus. Tu so - lus Al -
Tu so - lus Dó- mi - nus.......... Al -
so - lus san - ctus. Tu so - lus Dó- mi-nus. Tu so - lus Al -
Tu so - lus Dó- mi - nus..........
so - lus san - ctus. Tu so - lus Al -

100 105

Je - su Chri - ste, *Je - su Chri-* -
tís - si - mus, Je - su Chri - ste, *Je - su Chri-* -
- tís - si - mus, Je - su Chri - ste, Je - su Chri - -
- tís - si - mus, Je - su Chri - ste, Je- - su Chri- -
Je - su Chri - ste, Je - su Chri - -
- tís-si - mus, Je - su Chri - ste, *Je - su Chri -* -

110

ste. Cum San-cto Spí - ri - tu in gló-ri - a,
ste. Cum San-cto Spí-ri-tu De - i Pa - tris. A- -
ste. Cum San-cto Spí-ri-tu in gló-ri-a De - i Pa - tris. A- -
ste. Cum San-cto Spí - ri - tu, *cum San-cto Spí-ri-tu*
ste. Cum San-cto Spí - ri - tu in gló-ri-a De - i Pa - tris. A- -
ste. Cum San-cto Spí-ri-tu

Translation

Gloria in excelsis Deo
et in terra pax hominibus
bonae voluntatis.
Laudamus te,
Benedicimus te.
Adoramus te.
Glorificamus te.
Gratias agimus tibi propter
magnam gloriam tuam.
Domine Deus, Rex caelestis,
Deus Pater omnipotens.
Domini Fili

Gloria be to God on high,
And on earth peace to men
of goodwill.
We praise Thee.
We bless Thee.
We adore Thee.
We glorify Thee.
We give Thee thanks for
Thy great glory.
Lord God, heavenly King,
God the Father Almighty.
O Lord, the only-begotten Son,

unigenite, Jesu Christe.
Domine Deus, Agnus Dei,
Diliua Patris.
Qui tollis
peccata mundi,
miserere nobis,

Qui tollis peccata mundi,
suscipe deprecationem nostrum.
Qui sedes ad dexteram Patris,
miserere nobis.
Quoniam tu solus sanctus.
Tu solus Dominus.
Tu solus Altissimus.
Jesu Christe, cum Sancto Spiritu
in gloria Dei Patris.
Amen.

Jesus Christ.
Lord God, Lamb of God,
Son of the Father.
Thou that takest
away the sins of the world,
have mercy on us,
have mercy on us,
Thou that takest away the sins
of the world, receive our prayer.
Thou that sittest at the right hand,
of the Father, have mercy on us.
For thou alone art holy.
Thou only art the Lord.
Thou alone art most high.
Jesus Christ, along with the Holy Ghost
in the glory of God the Father
Amen.

13. Roland de Lassus (1532–1594),

Bon jour mon coeur

 1B/2 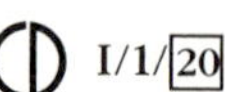 I/1/20

From The Sixteenth-Century Chanson, *edited by Jane Bernstein, 1987, Vol. 11, "Orlande de Lassus." Reprinted by permission of Garland Publishing Inc.*

20
doux prin- tems Ma dou- ce fleur nou- vel- le Mon doux plai- sir Ma dou- ce co- lom- bel-
doux prin- tems Ma dou- ce fleur nou- vel- le Mon doux plai- sir Ma dou- ce co- lom- bel-
doux prin- tems Ma dou- ce fleur nou- vel- le Mon doux plai- sir Ma dou- ce co- lom- bel-
doux prin- tems Ma dou- ce fleur nou- vel- le Mon doux plai- sir Ma dou- ce co- lom- bel-

25
le, Mon pas- se- reau Ma gen- te tour- te- rel- le, Bon jour ma dou-
le, Mon pas- se- reau Ma gen- te tour- te- rel- le, Bon jour ma dou-
le, Mon pas- se- reau Ma gen- te tour- te- rel le, Bon jour ma dou- ce
le, Mon pas- se- reau Ma gen- te tour- te- rel- le, Bon jour ma dou-

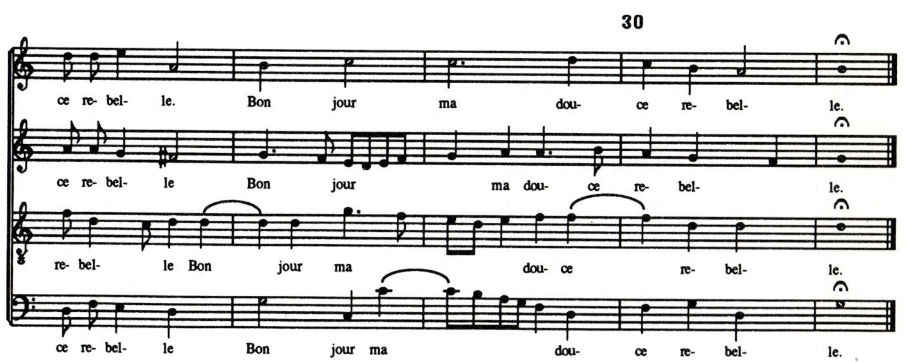
30
ce re- bel- le. Bon jour ma dou- ce re- bel- le.
ce re- bel- le Bon jour ma dou- ce re- bel- le.
re- bel- le Bon jour ma dou- ce re- bel- le.
ce re- bel- le Bon jour ma dou- ce re- bel- le.

TRANSLATION

Bon jour mon coeur, Bon jour ma douce vie.	Good day my heart, good day my sweet life.
Bon jour mon oeil, Bon jour ma chère amie,	Good day my eye, good day my dear friend,
Hé bon jour ma toute belle,	ah, good day, my beauty,
Ma mignardise, bon jour,	my darling one, good day,
Mes délices, mon amour,	my delight, my love,
Mon doux printemps, Ma douce fleur nouvelle,	my sweet spring, my sweet fresh flower,
Mon doux plaisir, Ma douce columbelle,	my sweet pleasure, my sweet young dove,
Mon passereau, Ma gente tourterelle,	my sparrow, my gentle turtle dove,
Bon jour, ma douce rebelle.	good day, my sweet rebel.

14. Giovanni Gabrieli (c. 1557-1612),

Plaudite, psallite (publ. 1597)  S1A/2  S1/5

From Opera Omnia, *edited by Denis Arnold, vol. II. Reprinted by permission of Hänssler-Verlag.*

10
-nis ter- -ra: al - le - lu - ja, al - le - lu - ja, al -
ter- -ra: al - le - lu - ja, al - le-lu - ja,
om - nis ter - ra: al - le - lu - ja, al - le - lu- -ja,
ter- -ra: al - le - lu - ja, al - le - lu- -ja, alter - -ra: al - le - lu - ja, al -
ter- -ra: al - le - lu - ja, al -
ter- -ra: al - le - lu - ja, al -
ter- -ra: al - le - lu - ja, al -
ter- -ra: al - le - lu - ja, al -
- nis ter- -ra: al - le - lu - ja, al -
ter- -ra: al - le - lu - ja,
ter- -ra: al - le - lu - ja, al-

-le- -lu - ja, be - ne - di-cant Do- -mi-num, om-nes gen - tes,
al - le - lu- -ja, be - ne - di- -cant Do- -mi - num,
al - le - lu - ja, be - ne - di-cant Do- -mi-num, om-nes gen - tes,
-le- -lu- -ja, be - ne - di-cant Do- -mi-num, om-nes gen - tes,
-le- -lu - ja, om-nes gen - tes,
8 -le- -lu - ja, om-nes gen - tes,
-le- -lu - ja, om-nes gen - tes,
-le- -lu - ja, om-nes gen - tes,
-le- -lu - ja, om-nes gen- tes, be - ne - di - cant Do-
-le- -lu - ja, om-nes gen - tes, be - ne - di - cant Do-
al - le - lu - ja, be - ne - di- -cant Do-
-le- -lu - ja, om-nes gen - tes, be - ne - di - cant Do-

20
be - ne - di-cant Do- -mi - num, om-nes gen-tes, col- lau - dan-tes e - um:
be - ne - di-cant Do- -mi-num,omnes gen-tes, col- lau - dan-tes e- - um:
be - ne - di-cant Do. - mi-num, om-nes gen-tes, col- lau - dan-tes e - um:
be - ne - di-cant Do- -mi - num, om-nes gen - tes, col - lau - dan-tes e - um:
be - ne - di- cant Do- - mi - num, om-nes gen - tes, col-lau-
8
be - ne - di-cant Do- - mi - num, om-nes gen - tes, col-lau-
be - ne - di-cant Do- -mi- -num, om-nes gen - tes, col-lau-
be - ne - di-cant Do- - mi - num, om-nes gen - tes, col-lau-
- mi-num, om-nes gen - tes, col-lau-dan-tes e-
- mi-num, om-nes gen - tes, col-lau-dan-tes e-
- mi-num, om-nes gen - tes, col-lau-dan-tes e-
- mi-num, om-nes gen - tes, col-lau-dan-tes e-

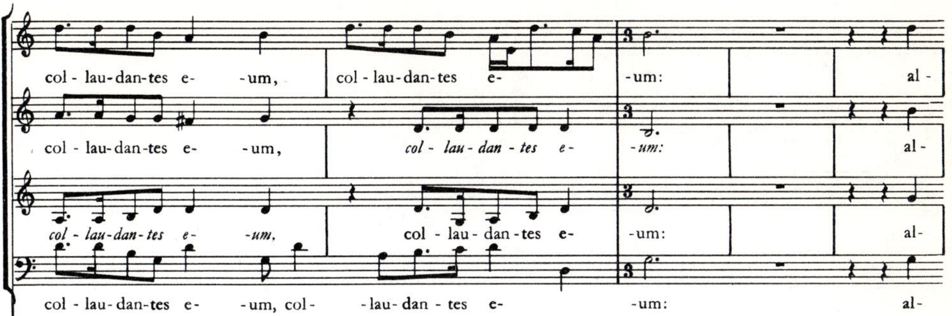
col - lau-dan-tes e- -um, col - lau-dan-tes e- -um: al -
col - lau-dan-tes e- -um, col - lau - dan - tes e - -um: al -
col - lau-dan- tes e- -um, col - lau - dan - tes e- -um: al-
col - lau-dan-tes e- -um, col- -lau- dan - tes e- -um: al-

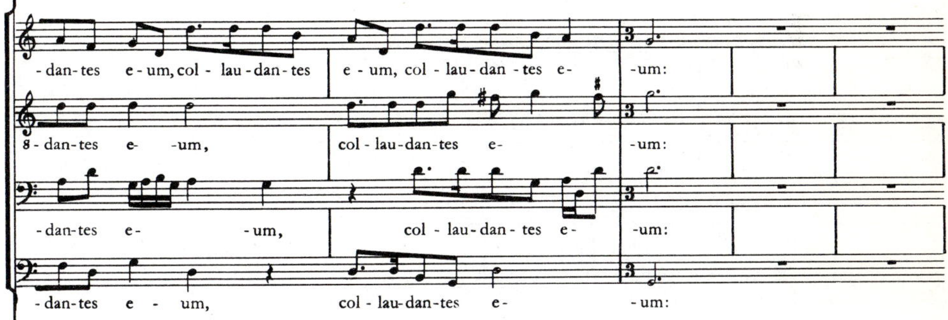
- dan- tes e - um, col - lau - dan- tes e - um, col - lau - dan - tes e- -um:
8 - dan- tes e- -um, col - lau- dan- tes e- -um:
- dan- tes e- -um, col - lau- dan - tes e- -um:
- dan- tes e - um, col - lau- dan- tes e- -um:

-um, col - lau-dan-tes e- -um: al - le - lu - ja,
-um, col - lau-dan-tes e- -um: al - le - lu - ja,
-um, col - lau-dan-tes e- -um: al - le - lu - ja,
-um, col - lau-dan-tes e- -um: al - le - lu - ja,

30
-le - lu - ja, al - le - lu - ja, al - le- -lu - ja:
-le - lu - ja, al - le - lu - ja, al - le - lu - ja:
-le - lu - ja, al - le - lu- -ja, al - le - lu - ja:
-le - lu - ja, al - le - lu - ja, al - le- -lu - ja:

al - le - lu - ja, al - le - lu - ja: qui- -a fe - cit no - bis-
al - le - lu - ja, al - le - lu - ja: qui- -a fe - cit no - bis-
al - le - lu - ja, al - le - lu - ja: qui - a fe - cit no - bis-
al - le - lu - ja, al - le - lu - ja: qui - a fe - cit no - bis-

al - le - lu - ja:
al - le - lu - ja:
al - le - lu - ja:
al - le- -lu - ja:

40
qui - a fe- - cit no - bis- -cum Do
qui - a fe- - cit no - bis- -cum
qui - a fe- - cit no - bis- -cum
qui - a fe- - cit no - bis- - cum
-cum Do- - mi - nus
8
- cum Do - mi - nus
- cum Do- - mi - nus
- cum Do- -mi - nus
qui- - a fe - cit no - bis- -cum Do- - mi - nus
qui- - a fe - cit no - bis - cum Do- - mi - nus
qui- - a fe- - cit no - bis- - cum Do- - mi - nus
qui- - a fe- -cit no - bis- - cum Do- - mi - nus

-mi - nus mi- -se-ri-cor- -di-am, mi-se-ri-cor- -di-am
Do- -mi - nus mi- -se-ri-cor- -di-am, mi-se-ri-cor- -di-am mi-se-ri-cor-
Do- -mi-nus mi - se-ri - cor- -di-am, mi - se-ri-
Do- -mi - nus mi - se-ri-cor- -di - am, mi-se-ri-cor- -di-
mi - se-ri - cor- -di-am, mi-se-ri - cor- -di-am
mi - se-ri-cor- -di - am, mi-se-ri-cor - di-
mi - se-ri - cor- -di-am, mi-se-ri - cor - di - am
mi - se-ri - cor- -di-am, mi-se-ri - cor- -di-am
mi - se-ri - cor- -di-am, mi-se-ri - cor- -di-am
mi-se-ri-cor- -di - am, mi-se-ri-cor - di- -am
mi-se-ri - cor - di-am, mi - se-ri - cor - di - am
mi-se-ri-cor- -di - am, mi-se-ri-cor- -di- -am

50
su- -am: al - le - lu - ja, al - le - lu -
-di - am su.- -am: al - le - lu - ja, al - le - lu
cor - di - am su - am: al - le - lu - ja, al - le - lu -
- am su- - am: al - le - lu - ja, al - le- -lu-
su- - am: al - le- -lu -
8 - am su- -am: al - le- -lu-
su- -am: al - le- -lu-
su - - am: al - le- -lu -
su- -am: al - le - lu - ja,
su- -am: al - le - lu - ja,
su- -am: al - le - lu - ja,
su- -am: al - le - lu - ja,

-ja, al - le- - lu- -ja.
-ja, al - le - lu- -ja.
-ja. al - le- -lu- -ja,
-ja, al - le- -lu- -ja.
-ja, al - le- - lu - ja, cap - ti - vi-
-ja, al - le- - lu - ja, cap - ti - vi-
-ja, al - le- - lu - ja, cap - ti - vi-
-ja, al - le- - lu - ja, cap - ti - vi-
al - le- -lu- -ja, et cap - ti - vam du - xit cap - ti - vi - ta - tem,
al - le- -lu- -ja, et cap - ti - vam du - xit cap - ti - vi - ta - tem,
al - le - lu- -ja, et cap - tivam du- -xit cap- -ti - vi - ta - tem,
al - le- - lu- -ja. et cap- ti - vam du - xit cap - ti - vi - ta - tem,

60
et cap - ti - vam du - xit cap - ti - vi - ta - tem, ad-
et cap - ti - vam du - xit cap - ti - vi - ta - tem, ad-
et cap - tivamdu- -xit cap - ti - vi - ta - tem, ad-
et cap - ti - vam du - xit cap - ti - vi - ta - tem, ad-
-ta - tem, cap - ti - vi - ta - tem, cap - ti - vi - ta - tem, ad-
8 -ta - tem, cap - ti - vi - ta - tem, cap - ti - vi - ta - tem,
-ta - tem, cap - ti - vi - ta - tem, cap - ti - vi - ta - tem, ad-
-ta - tem, cap - ti - vi - ta - tem, cap - ti - vi - ta - tem, ad-
cap - ti - vi - ta - tem, ad-
cap - ti - vi - ta - tem, ad-
cap - ti - vi - ta - tem, ad-
cap - ti - vi - ta - tem, ad-

-mi - ra- -bi - lis et glo - ri - o - sus, et glo - ri-
-mi - ra - bi - lis et glo - ri - o - sus, et glo - ri-
mi - ra- -bi - lis et glo - ri - o - sus, et glo - ri-
-mi - ra - bi - lis et glo - ri - o - sus, et glo - ri-
-mi - ra- -bi - lis et glo - ri - o - sus, et glo - ri-
8 ad- -mi - ra - bi - lis et glo - ri - o - sus, et glo - ri-
mi-ra - bi - lis et glo - ri - o- -sus, et glo - ri-
-mi - ra- -bi - lis et glo - ri - o - sus, et glo - ri-
-mi - ra- -bi - lis et glo - ri - o- -sus, et glo - ri - o-sus in sae - cu - la,
-mi - ra - bi - lis et glo - ri - o- -sus, et glo - ri - o-sus in sae - cu - la,
-mi - ra- -bi - lis et glo- ri - o- -sus, et glo - ri - o-sus in sae - cu - la,
mi - ra- -bi - lis et glo-ri - o- -sus, et glo - ri - o-sus in sae - cu - la,

70
-o-sus in saec-cu-la, et glo-ri-o-sus in sae-cu-la, in sae-cu-la, in sae-cu-la, et glo-ri-
-o-sus in sae-cu-la, in sae-cu-la, in sae-cu-la, et glo-ri-
-o-sus in sae-cu-la, et glo-ri-o-sus in sae-cu-la, in sae-cu-la, in sae-cu-la, et glo-ri-
-o-sus in sae-cu-la, et glo-ri-o-sus in sae-cu-la, in sae-cu-la, in sae-cu-la, et glo-ri-

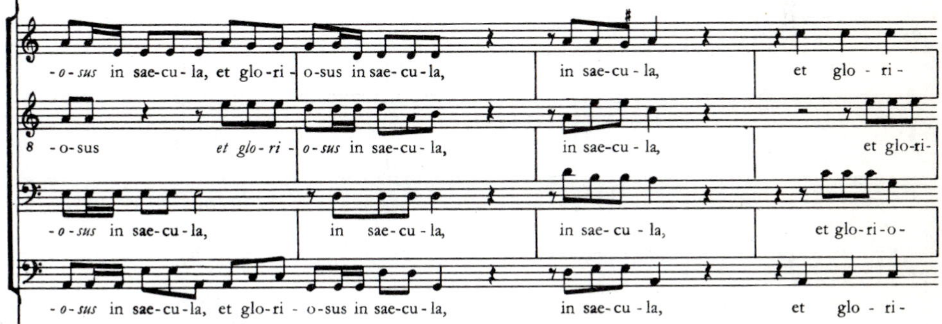
-o-sus in sae-cu-la, et glo-ri-o-sus in sae-cu-la, in sae-cu-la, et glo-ri-
8 -o-sus et glo-ri-o-sus in sae-cu-la, in sae-cu-la, et glo-ri-
-o-sus in sae-cu-la, in sae-cu-la, in sae-cu-la, et glo-ri-o-
-o-sus in sae-cu-la, et glo-ri-o-sus in sae-cu-la, in sae-cu-la, et glo-ri-

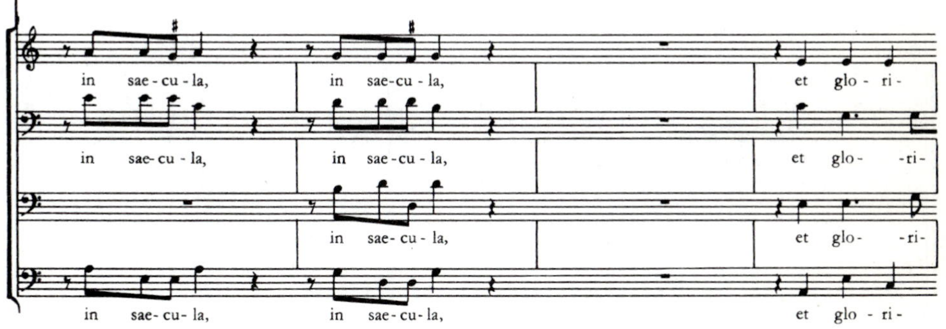
in sae-cu-la, in sae-cu-la, et glo-ri-
in sae-cu-la, in sae-cu-la, et glo-ri-
in sae-cu-la, et glo-ri-
in sae-cu-la, in sae-cu-la, et glo-ri-

-o- -sus in sae - cu- -la: al - le - lu - ja, al - le - lu - ja, al-
-o- -sus in sae - cu- -la: al - le - lu - ja, al - le - lu - ja,
-o-sus in sae - cu - la: al - le - lu - ja, al - le - lu- -ja,
-o- -sus in sae - cu - la: al - le - lu - ja, al- - le- -lu - ja, al -
-o- -sus in sae - cu- -la: al - le - lu - ja, al-
8 -o- -sus in sae - cu - la: al - le - lu - ja, al -
-sus in sae- -cu- -la: al - le - lu - ja, al-
-o - sus in sae - cu- -la: al - le - lu - ja, al -
-o- -sus in sae - cu- -la: al - le - lu - ja, al-
-o-sus in sae - cu- -la: al - le - lu - ja, al-
-o - sus: al - le - lu - ja,
-o- -sus in sae - cu- -la: al - le - lu - ja, al-

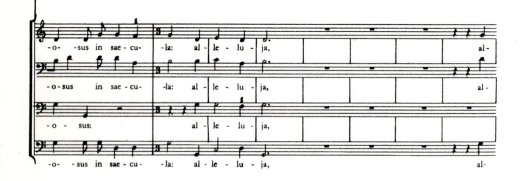

Translation

Plaudite, psallite,
Jubilate Deo,
Omnis terra:
Alleluia.
Benedicant Dominum,
Omnes gentes
Collaudantes eum:
Alleluia.
Quia fecit nobiscum
Dominus misericordiam:
Alleluia.
Et captivam duxit,
Captivitatem, admirailis
Et gloriosus in saecula:
Alleluia.

Oh, clap your hands and sing
Rejoice in the Lord
All the earth
Alleluia.
Let all the nations
Bless the Lord,
Praising him:
Alleluia.
For the Lord has shown
His mercy to us:
Alleluia.
And led the captive woman
To her freedom, admirable
And glorious forever:
Alleluia.

15. Claudio Monteverdi (1567–1643),

Ohimè! se tanto amate (publ. 1603)  1B/3 

From Instituta et Monumenta, Serie I: Monumenta, Vol. 5. Reprinted by permission of Fondazione Claudio Monteverdi.

deh, per-ché fa - te deh, per-ché fa - te Chi di - -
deh, per-ché fa - te Chi di - -
deh, per-ché fa - te deh, per - ché fa - te Chi di - ce «oi -
deh, per - ché fa - te deh, per-ché fa - te Chi di - ce «oi -
deh, per - ché fa - te deh, per - ché fa - te Chi di - ce «oi - mè»

- ce «oi - mè» mo - ri - re? S'io mo - ro, un
- ce «oi - me» mo - ri - - re?
mè, oi - mè» mo - ri - re? S'io mo - ro, un
mè» mo - ri - - re? S'io mo - ro, un
mo - ri - - re?

sol po - tre - te Lan - gui - do e do - lo - ro - so e
sol po - tre - te Lan - gui - do e do - lo - ro - so e
sol po - tre - te Lan - gui - do e do - lo - ro - - so e do - lo - ro -

30

do - lo - ro - so «oi - mè» sen - ti - re; S'io mo - ro, un sol po -

S'io mo - ro, un sol po -

do - lo - ro - so «oi - mè» sen - ti - re; S'io mo - ro, un sol po -

- so «oi - mè» sen - ti - re; S'io mo - ro, un sol po -

S'io mo - ro, un sol po -

35

tre - te Lan - gui - do e do - lo -

tre - te Lan - gui - do e do - lo -

tre - te Lan - gui - do e do - lo - ro - so «oi - mè»

tre - te Lan - gui - do e do - lo - ro - so e do - lo - ro - - -

tre - te Lan - gui - do e do - lo - ro - so e do - lo - ro - so «oi -

40

ro - so «oi - mè» sen - ti - re; Ma se, cor mio, vo - le - te Che vi - ta ab - bia da

ro - so «oi - mè» sen - ti - re; Ma se, cor mio, vo - le - te Che vi - ta ab - bia da

sen - ti - re; Ma se, cor

so «oi mè» sen - ti - re; Ma se, cor mio, vo - le - te Che

mè» sen - ti - re; Ma se, cor mio, vo -

Ma se,

voi, e voi da me,

voi, e voi da me,

mio, vo - le - te Che vi - ta ab - bia da voi, e voi da me,

vi - ta ab - bia da voi, e voi da me,

le - te Che vi - ta ab - bia da voi, e voi da me,

45

A - vre - te A - vre - te A - vre - te mil - l'e

A - vre - te A - vre - te A - vre - te mil - l'e mil - le

A - vre - te A - vre - te

A - vre - te A - vre - te

(♭)

A - vre - te A - vre - te A - vre - te mil - l'e mil - le

(♭)

♯ ♯ ♮ ♭ ♮

50

mil - le dol - ci «oi - mè, oi - mè, oi - mè, oi - mè, oi - mè».

dol - ci «oi - mè, oi - mè, oi - mè, oi - mè, oi - mè, oi - mè».

A - vre - te

(♭)

A - vre - te

♮

dol - ci «oi - mè, oi - mè, oi - mè, oi - mè, oi - mè, oi - mè».

♮ ♮ ♯

55
A - vre - te
A - vre - te
mil - l'e mil - le dol - ci «oi - mè, oi - mè, oi - mè, oi - mè». A - vre - te A -
mil - l'e mil - le dol - ci «oi - mè, oi - mè, oi - mè, oi - mè». A - vre - te A -
A - vre - - te A - vre - te A -
60
A - vre - te mil - l'e
A - vre - te mil - l'e
vre - te mil - l'e mil - le dol - ci «oi - mè, oi - mè, oi - mè, oi - mè». A - vre - te mil - l'e
vre - te mil - l'e mil - le dol - ci «oi - mè, oi - mè, oi - mè, oi - mè». A - vre - te mil - l'e
vre - te mil - l'e mil - le dol - ci «oi - mè, oi - mè, oi - mè, oi - mè,
65
mil - le dol - ci «oi - mè, oi - mè, oi - mè, oi - mè, oi - mè».
mil - le dol - ci «oi - mè, oi - mè, oi - mè, oi - mè, oi - mè».
mil - le dol - ci «oi - mè, oi - mè».
mil - le dol - ci «oi - mè, oi - mè, oi - mè».
oi - mè».

Translation

Ohimè! se tanto amate
di sentir dir Ohimè, deh, perché fate
chi dice Ohimè morire?
S'io moro, un sol potrete
languido e doloroso Ohimè sentire;
Ma se, cor mio, volete
che vita abbia da voi, e voi da me,
avrete mille e mille dolci Ohimè.

Alas! If you so love
to hear me say alas, then why do you slay
the one who says it?
If I die, you will hear only
a single, languid, sorrowful alas;
but if, my love, you wish
to let me live and wish to live for me,
you will have a thousand times a sweet alas.

16. Monteverdi

L'incoronazione di Poppea,
Act III, scene 7 (1642)

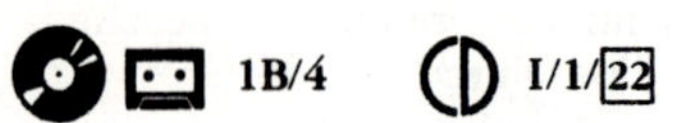

1) N: *Ritornello si piace*, but lacking and no space was left for copying it. V: A later hand (Cavalli's?) has crossed out the entire piece. The first bar in 3 parts and the rest bass only follow the Sinfonia p.241-2 (bass only) and precede a 2-bar coda, forming the (untitled) overture to Sacrati's *La finta pazza* in a MS recently discovered by Prof. L. Bianconi in the private Borromeo library on Isola Bella (IB). See Preface.

133
136
IB:
139
142

CONSOLI E TRIBUNI 1)
145
[CONSOLI]
A te, a te so - vra - - - na au - gu - - - - - - - - sta,
O hail to thee our emp - - ress, our rul - - - - - - - - er
6 — 5 6
150 [TRIBUNI]
Con il con - sen - so u - ni - ver - sal, u - ni - ver - sal di Ro - - ma,
By our u - na - ni - mous con - sent, and that of all the Ro - - mans.
Con il con - sen so u - ni - ver - sal, u - ni - ver - sal di Ro - ma, di Ro - - ma,
By our u - na - ni - mous con - sent, by the con - sent of all loy - al Ro - - mans.
153
In - dia - de - miam, in - dia - de - miam la chio - - ma.
Now with this crown, now with this crown we crown thee.
N: b♭
In - dia - de - miam, in - dia - de - miam la chio - - - - ma.
Now with this crown, now with this crown we crown thee.
N: 6 6 4 3
157
A te l'Eu - ro - pa, a te l'Eu -
And now let Eur - ope, and now let
A te l'A - sia, a te l'A - fri - ca s'at - ter - ra, s'at - ter - ra;
Now shall A - sia, now shall A - fri - ca be hum - ble be - fore thee.

1) N seems to imply that the Consuls are the tenors, the Tribunes the basses; however, the reverse would make more sense, since the Consuls should have the privilege of speaking first.

160
ro - pa, e'l mar che cin - ge e ser - ra Que - st'im - pe - ro fe - li - - - - ce,
Eur - ope, and all the seas which be - long to This most for - tu - nate em - - - pire
Que - st'im - pe - ro fe - li - - - - ce,
This most for - tu - nate em - - - pire
163
O - ra con - sac - ra e do - na, e do - na Que - sta del mon - do im - per - ri - al co - -
Of - fer and con - se - crate, of - fer in hon - our, This the fair crown of the migh - ty Ro - man
166
O - ra con - sa - cra e do - na, e do - na Que - sta del mon - do im - pe - ri - al co - -
Of - fer and con - se - crate, of - fer in hon - our, This the fair crown of the migh - ty Ro - - man
ro - - - - - - - - - - - - na, o - ra con - - sa - cra e do - na, e do - - na
em - - - - - - - - - - - pire, of - fer and con - se - crate, of - fer in hon - - our,
169
ro - na,
em - pire.
que - - sta del mon - do im - pe - ri - al co - - ro - - - - - - - - - - - - - - - na,
this the crown of the migh - ty Ro - man em - - - - - - - - - - - - - - pire.
N&V: ♯
N: 6 5
V: ♭
V: ♮
V: ♯

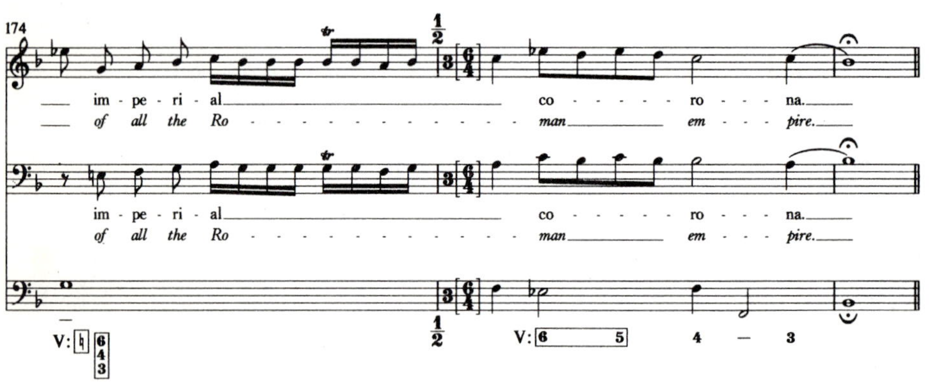

1) N: *Ritornello,* but lacking and not enough space was left for copying it. V: A later hand (Cavalli's?) has crossed it out, as it has also bars 265-305, which follow immediately afterwards and lead to the final duet (b. 344), *not* crossed out. Preceded by a breve *d,* the entire bass of this Sinfonia, with 2 blank treble clef staves above, opens IB (see note 1, p.237).

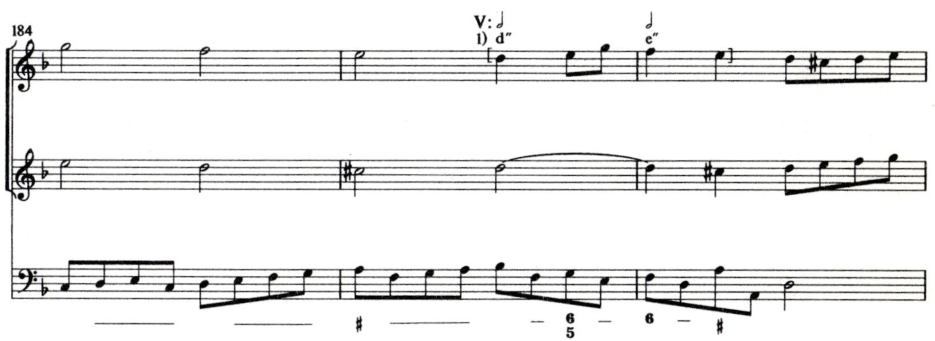

1) Upper parts do not fit with bass here. Since IB has same bass (but no upper parts) it is the top line I have chosen to alter; one could also leave that line as it is in V and alter last 3 bass notes of 185 and first 2 of 186 to: g a f g e.

2) IB: [♮], but only because the overture continues, with bar 126 (see note 1, p.237)

No. 24
339 Ritornello
[Violin I]
[Violin II]
[Adagio][1)]
POPPEA
Pur ti mi - ro, pur ti mi - ro,
I a - dore you, I a - dore you,
NERONE
Pur ti go - do, pur ti
I de - sire you, I de -
Pur ti strin - go, pur ti strin - go, Pur t'an -
I em - brace you, I em - brace you, I en -
go - do, Pur t'an - no - do, Pur ti strin
sire you, I en - chain you, I em - brace
no - do, Più non pe - no, non pe -
chain you, no more griev - ing, no griev -
go, pur ti strin - go, Più non mo -
you, I em - brace you, no more sor -

1) Since the reprise, bar 392, is marked **Adagio** (in V, but not in N) it is possible, by analogy with the final duet of II. iv, that the middle section should be marked **Presto**. However, these indications must not be taken in the modern sense of extremes, but only as subtle variations of the basic pulse.

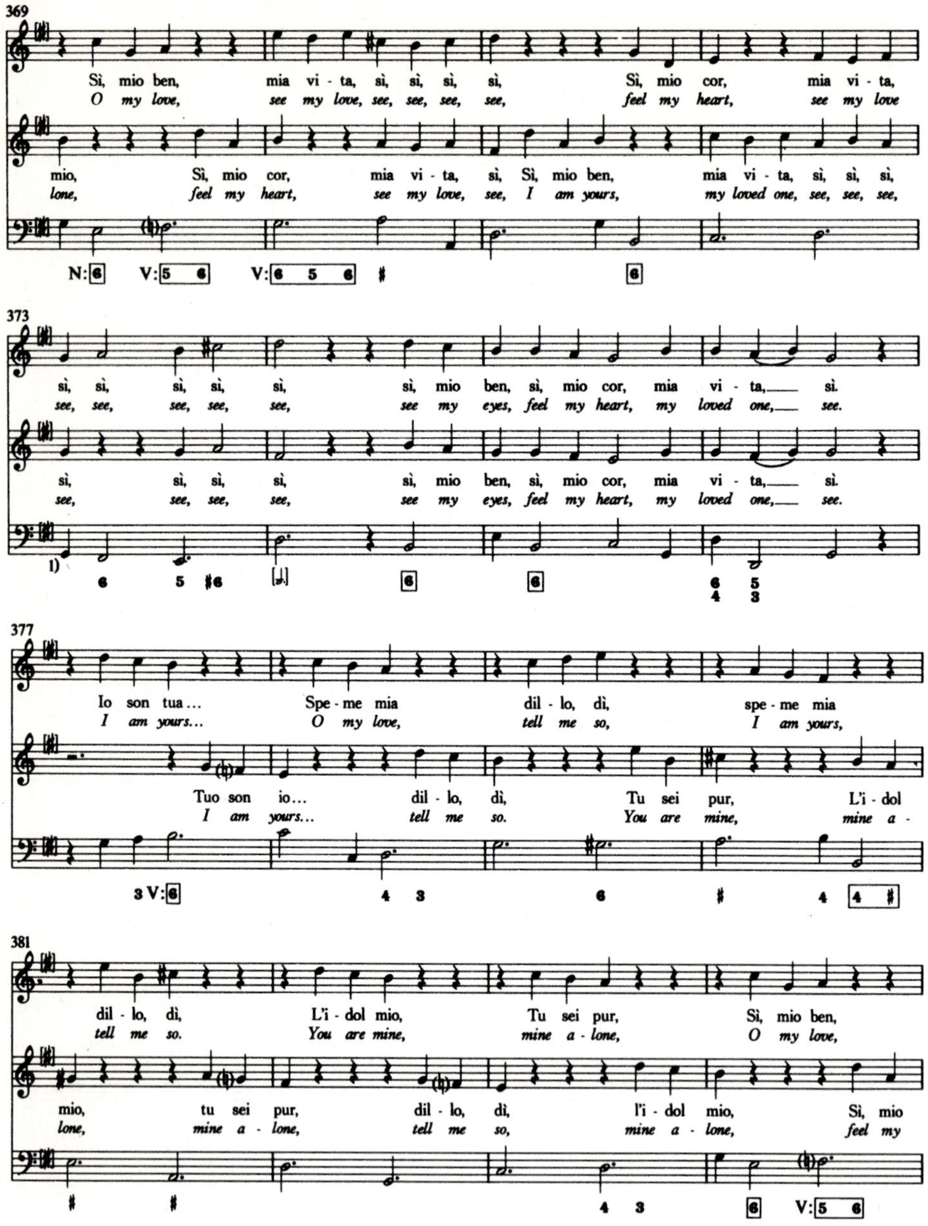
369
Sì, mio ben, mia vi - ta, sì, sì, sì, sì, Sì, mio cor, mia vi - ta,
O my love, see my love, see, see, see, see, feel my heart, see my love
mio, Sì, mio cor, mia vi - ta, sì, Sì, mio ben, mia vi - ta, sì, sì, sì,
lone, feel my heart, see my love, see, I am yours, my loved one, see, see, see,
N: 6 V: 5 6 V: 6 5 6 # 6
373
sì, sì, sì, sì, sì, sì, mio ben, sì, mio cor, mia vi - ta, sì.
see, see, see, see, see, see my eyes, feel my heart, my loved one, see.
sì, sì, sì, sì, sì, mio ben, sì, mio cor, mia vi - ta, sì.
see, see, see, see, see my eyes, feel my heart, my loved one, see.
1)
6 5 #6 6 6 6 5 4 3
377
Io son tua… Spe - me mia dil - lo, dì, spe - me mia
I am yours… O my love, tell me so, I am yours,
Tuo son io… dil - lo, dì, Tu sei pur, L'i - dol
I am yours… tell me so. You are mine, mine a -
3 V: 6 4 3 6 # 4 4 #
381
dil - lo, dì, L'i - dol mio, Tu sei pur, Sì, mio ben,
tell me so. You are mine, mine a - lone, O my love,
mio, tu sei pur, dil - lo, dì, l'i - dol mio, Sì, mio
lone, mine a - lone, tell me so, mine a - lone, feel my
4 3 6 V: 5 6

1) *sic* in both N and V, but cf. bar 388, which would seem preferable.

1) N: cf. also bar 370.

2) *sic* in both N and V, but cf. bar 376.

399
- - no, non pe - - - - no, Più non mo - - - - - - - ro, non mo - - ro, O mia vi - ta,
ing, no griev - - - ing, no more sor - - - - - row, no sor - - row, o my dear - est,
mo - - - - - - - - - - - ro, Più non pe - - - - - - - no, O mia
sor - - - - - - - - - - row, no more griev - - - - - - - ing o my
4 ♯ — 6 7 6
403
V:
o mio te - so - ro, o mia vi - ta, o mio te - so - - ro.
o my be - lov - ed, o my dear - est, o my be - lov - - ed.
vi - ta, o mio te - so - ro, o mia vi - ta, o mio te - so - - ro.
dear - est, o my be - lov - ed, o my dear - est, o my be - lov - - ed.
4 ♯ 6 5
4 — ♯

17. John Farmer (fl. 1597–1601),

Fair Phyllis (publ. 1599)

S: Fair Phyl - lis I saw sit - ting all a - lone, Feed - ing
A: Feed - ing
T: Feed - ing
B: Feed - ing

5

S: her flock near to the mount - ain side; side. The
A: her flock near to the mount - ain side; side.
T: her flock near to the mount - ain side; side.
B: her flock near to the mount - ain side; side.

10

S: shep - herds knew not, they knew not whi - ther she was
A: The shep - herds knew not, whi - ther she was
T: The shep - herds
B: The

"Fair Phyllis" by John Farmer, from THE PENGUIN BOOK OF ENGLISH MADRIGALS FOR FOUR VOICES edited by Denis Stevens (Penguin Books, 1967), copyright © Denis Stevens, 1967, pp. 54–57.

gone,
gone, But
knew not, they knew not whi - ther she was gone,
shep - herds knew not whi - ther she was gone,
But af - ter her lov - er, her lov - er, but af - ter her
af ter her lov - er, her lov - er, but af - ter her
But af - ter her lov - er, her lov - er,
But af - ter her lov - er,
15
lov - er A - myn - tas hied.
lov - er A - myn - tas hied.
but af - ter her lov - er A - myn - tas hied. Up and down he
but af - ter her lov - er A - myn - tas hied. Up and
20
Up and down he wan - dered,
Up and down up and down he
wan - dered, up and down up and
down he wan - - - dered, he

up and down he wan - dered.
wan - dered, up and down he wan - -
down he wan - dered, up and down he
wan - - - - - dered,
25
up and down he wan - dered, up and down he
- dered, up ___ and down he wan - dered, up and
wan - dered, up and down he wan - dered,
up and down
wan - dered, up and down he wan - - -
down he wan - - dered, he wan - -
up and down he wan - dered, up and down he wan - -
he wan - - - - -
30
- dered, whilst she was miss - ing; When
- dered, whilst she was miss - ing; When ___
- dered, whilst she was miss - ing; When
- dered, whilst she was miss - ing; When

he found her,
he found her, O, then they fell a -
he found her, O, then they fell a -
he found her, O, then they fell a -
35
O, then they fell a - kiss - ing, a - kiss - ing, O,
- kiss - ing, O, then they fell a - kiss - ing, a - kiss - ing, O,
- kiss - ing, O, then they fell a - kiss - ing, a - kiss - ing, O,
- kiss - ing, O, then they fell a - kiss - ing, a - kiss - ing, O,
40
1
2
then they fell a - kiss - ing; kiss - ing.
then they fell a - kiss - ing; kiss - ing.
then they fell a - kiss - ing; Up and down he kiss - ing.
then they fell a - kiss - ing; Up and kiss - ing.

18. Thomas Tomkins (1572-1656), *When David Heard That Absalom Was Slain* (publ. 1622)

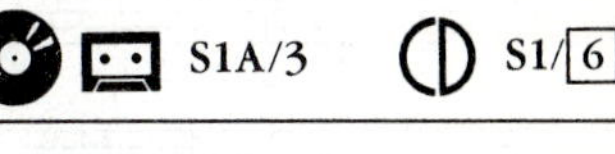

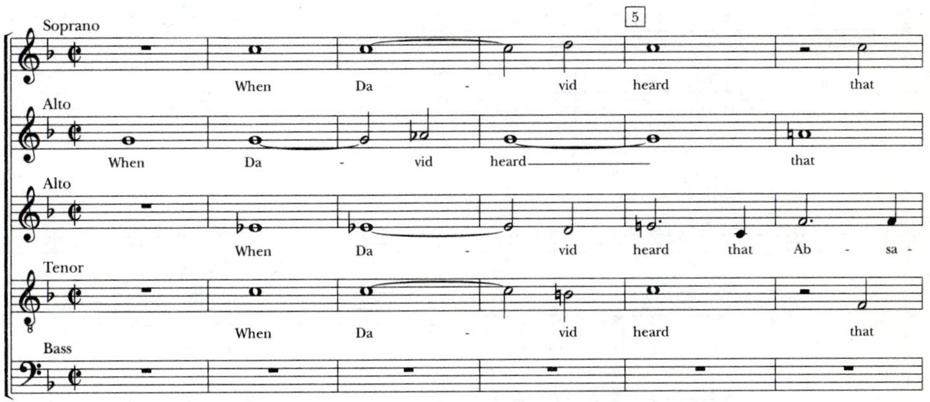

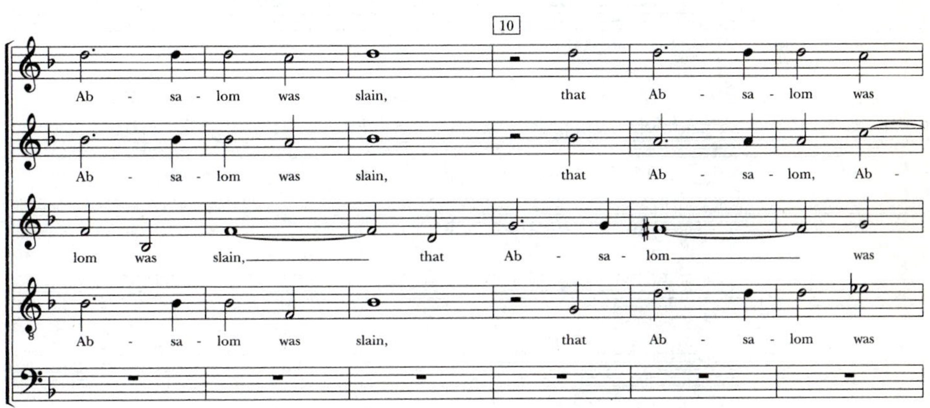

15
slain, He went up to his Cham - ber,
sa lom was slain, He went up to his Cham - ber,
slain, was slain,
slain, was slain, He up to his Cham - ber,
20
ov - er the gate, the
he went up to his Cham - ber ov - er the gate, the
He went up to his Cham - ber ov - er the gate, the
ov - er the gate, the
He went up to his Cham - ber ov - er the
25
30
gate, and wept, and wept, and
gate, and wept, and wept, and
gate, and wept, and wept, and wept, and
gate, and wept, and wept, and
gate, and wept, and wept, and

35
wept, And thus he said, and
wept, And thus he said, and thus he said,
wept, And thus he said, and thus he said,
And thus he said, and thus he said,
wept, And thus he said, and thus he said, and
40
thus he said, and thus he
and thus he said, and thus he said, thus
and thus he said, and thus he
and thus he said, he
thus he said, and thus he said, and thus he
45
said:
he said: O my son,
said: O my
said: O my son, my
said:

50
O my son, my son,
my son, O my son, my
son, O my son,
son, my son, O my son,
O my son, my
55
60
my son, O my son, my
son, O my son, my
O my son, my son, my son, my
my son, O my
son, O my son, my son, my son, my son, my
65
son, Ab - sa - lom my son, Ab - sa - lom my
son, Ab - sa - lom my son, O my
son, Ab - sa - lom my son, my son,
son, Ab - sa - lom my son, my
son,

70
son, Ab - sa - lom my son, my— son, Ab -
son, my son, Ab - sa - lom my son,
O Ab - sa - lom my son, O my son, Ab - sa - lom
son, Ab - sa - lom my son, my son,
Ab - sa - lom my son, Ab - sa - lom,

75
sa - lom my son, my son, my son, Ab -
O my son, O my son,
my son, Ab - sa - lom my son,
Ab - sa - lom my son, my son,
Ab - sa - lom my son, my son,

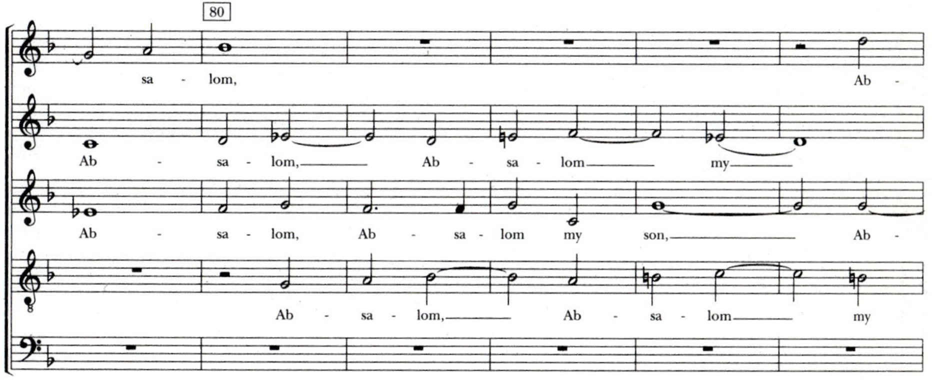
80
sa - lom, Ab -
Ab - sa - lom, Ab - sa - lom my
Ab - sa - lom, Ab - sa - lom my son, Ab -
Ab - sa - lom, Ab - sa - lom my

85
90
sa - lom, Ab - sa - lom my son, O Ab - sa - lom
son, Ab - sa - lom, Ab - sa - lom my
sa - lom, O my son, O Ab - sa -
son, O Ab - sa - lom, O my son,
Ab - sa - lom, Ab -

95
my son,
son, Ab - sa - lom my son, Would God I had
lom my son, Ab - sa - lom my son, my son,
O Ab - sa - lom my son, Would
sa - lom my son, my son,

100
Would God I had died for thee, for
died for thee, for thee,
Would God I had died for
God I had died for thee, for thee,
O my son, my son, Would

105

thee, would God I had died, I had

would God I had died, died— for thee,

thee, would God I had died for

would God— I had died for—

God I had died, I— had died for thee, would

110

died for— thee,—

would God I had died for thee, for

thee, for— thee, Ab -

— thee, would God I had died for thee,—

God I had died for thee,— Ab - sa -

115 120

Ab - sa - lom my son, my—

thee, Ab - sa - lom my son, my son, O

sa - lom my son,— Ab - sa - lom

— Ab - sa - lom, Ab - sa - lom— my son,

lom my son, my son, O

125

son, Ab - sa - lom my son,

Ab - sa - lom, Ab - sa - lom, Ab - sa - lom

my son, my son, Ab - sa -

O Ab - sa - lom my son, my son, Ab -

my son, Ab - sa - lom my

130

O Ab - sa - lom my son, O my son,

my son, O Ab - sa -

lom my son, O Ab - sa - lom my son,

sa - lom my son, O Ab - sa - lom my son, O

son, my son,

135

Ab - sa - lom my son.

lom my son, O Ab - sa - lom, Ab - sa - lom my son.

O Ab - sa - lom my son.

Ab - sa - lom my son, my son.

O Ab - sa - lom my son.

19. Henry Purcell (1659–1695),

Dido and Aeneas, End of Act III (1689)

37

DIDO

Grave [♩ = 𝅗𝅥]

Thy hand, Be-lin - da; dark - ness shades me, On thy bo - som let me rest; More I would, but Death in-vades me; Death is now a wel - come guest.

38

Violin I

Violin II

Viola

Larghetto [𝅝. = 𝅗𝅥]

very soft

very soft

pp sempre

When I am

pp sempre

pp

10
laid, — am laid — in earth, may my wrongs — cre - ate No
2nd time
1st time
1
1
trou - ble, no trou-ble in — thy breast,
When I am
2
2
20
Re - mem - ber me! re - mem - ber me! but
ah! — for-get my fate, re - mem-ber me! but ah! —

for - get my — fate. Re - mem - ber me! re - mem - ber me! but

ah! ——— for-get my fate, re - mem - ber me! but ah! ———

RITOR.

for - get my — fate.

39 {*Cupids appear in the clouds o'er her tomb*}

Violin I

Violin II

Viola

CHORUS

SOPRANO

With droop - ing wings ye Cu - pids come, with droop - ing wings, with

ALTO

With droop - ing wings ye

TENOR

With droop - ing wings ye Cu - pids come, with droop - ing,

BASS

With droop - ing wings ye Cu - pids come,

Larghetto [♩ = 𝅗𝅥]

C *p*

10

droop - ing wings, with droop - ing wings ye Cu-pids come, And

Cu - pids come, with droop - ing wings ye Cu - pids come, And

droop-ing wings, with droop-ing wings, with droop-ing wings, with droop-ing wings ye Cu-pids come,

with droop - ing wings ye Cu - pids come, ye Cu-pids come,

scat - ter ro - ses, scat - ter, scat - ter_ ro - ses_ on_ her tomb,
scat - ter ro - ses, scat - ter, scat - ter_ ro - ses on her tomb, Soft, soft ___ and
And scat - ter, scat - ter_ ro - ses on her tomb, Soft, soft,_
And scat - ter_ ro - ses, scat - ter_ ro - ses_ on her tomb,
[pp]
20
Soft,_ soft ___ and gen - tle, soft,_ soft,_ soft,_ soft ___ and
gen - tle as_ her heart, gen - tle as her_ heart, soft,_ soft ___ and gen - tle,
soft and gen - tle as her heart, soft,_ soft ___ and
Soft,_ soft ___ and gen - tle, soft,_ soft,_ soft,_ soft,_ soft ___ and
pp

gen-tle as_ her heart; Keep here, here your watch, keep here, here, keep here your watch, and
gen-tle_as her heart; Keep here, here_ your watch, keep here, here, keep here your watch, and
gen-tle_as her heart; Keep here, here your watch, keep here, here, keep here your watch, and
gen - tleas her heart; Keep here, here your watch, keep here, here, keep here your watch, and
p
mp
mf
f
30
1
2
nev-er, nev-er, nev - er part, and never, nev-er, nev - er, nev - er part. With droop - part.
nev-er, nev-er, nev - er part, and nev-er, nev-er, nev - er, nev - er part. part.
nev-er, nev-er, nev - er part, and nev-er, nev-er, nev - er, nev - er part. With part.
nev-er, nev-er, nev - er part, and nev-er, nev-er, nev - er, nev - er part. part.
dim.
p

20. Antonio Vivaldi (1678–1741),

The Four Seasons, "La Primavera" (c. 1725)

7
Vl. solo
I
Vl.
II
Vla.
B.C.

B
Solo
10
Vl. solo
Il canto
I
Vl.
II
Vla.
B.C.

14
Vl. solo
de gl' Ucelli
Solo
I
Vl.
II
Solo

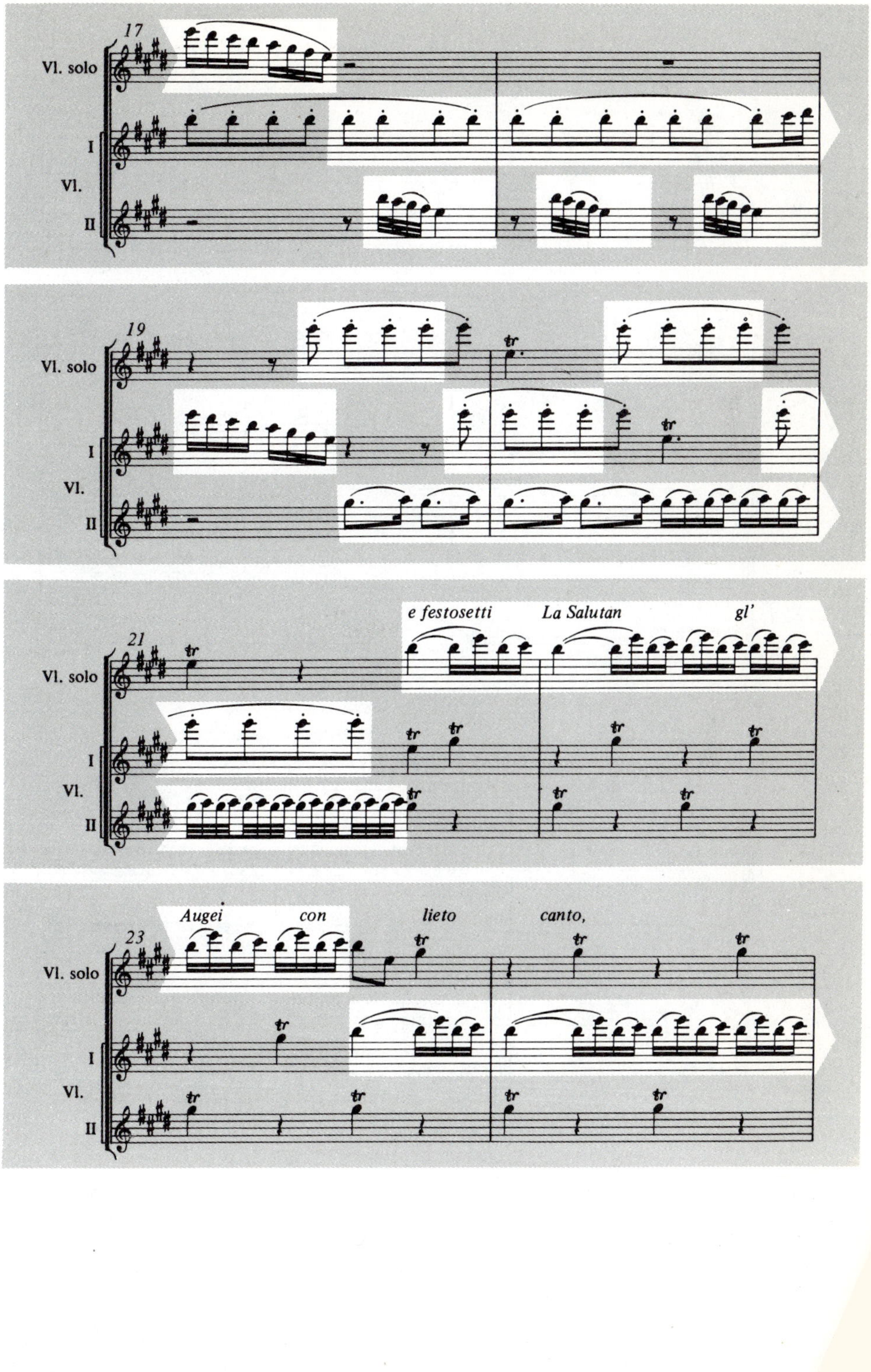

17
Vl. solo
I
Vl.
II
19
Vl. solo
I
Vl.
II
e festosetti
La Salutan
gl'
21
Vl. solo
I
Vl.
II
Augei
con
lieto
canto,
23
Vl. solo
I
Vl.
II

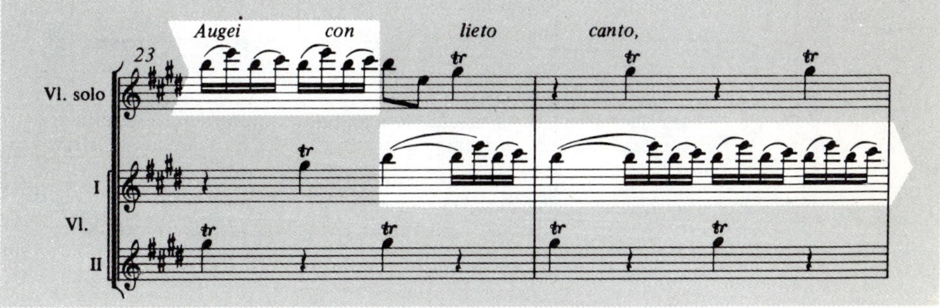

25
Vl. solo
I
Vl.
II
tr

27
Vl. solo
Tutti
I
Vl.
II
Vla.
B.C.
tr

30
C
Ei fonti allo Spirar de' Zeffiretti Con dolce mormoria
Vl. solo
I
Vl.
II
Vla.
B.C.
p

33
Scorrono intanto:
Vl. solo
I
Vl.
II
Vla.
B.C.

35
Vl. solo
I
Vl.
II
Vla.
B.C.

37
Vl. solo
I
Vl.
II
Vla.
B.C.
6
5

39
Vl. solo
I
Vl.
II
Vla.
B.C.
f
[f]
D
[Tuoni]venzon' coprendo L'aer di
nero an amanto
42
E Lampi, e tuoni ad annuntiarla
eletti
45

47
Solo
Vl. solo
I
Vl.
II
Vla.
B.C.
6
5

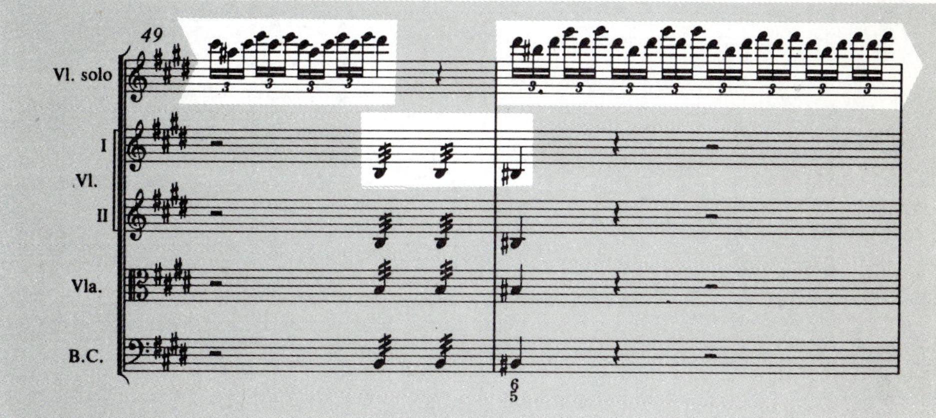
49
Vl. solo
I
Vl.
II
Vla.
B.C.
6
5

51
Vl. solo
I
Vl.
II
Vla.
B.C.

53
Vl. solo
I
Vl.
II
Vla.
B.C.

Tutti
Vl. solo
I
Vl.
II
Vla.
B.C.

Indi tacendo questi, gl' Angeletti, Tornan' di nuoro allor
58
E
Vl. solo
Canto d' Ucelli
Solo
I
Vl.
II
Vla.
B.C.
Tasto solo

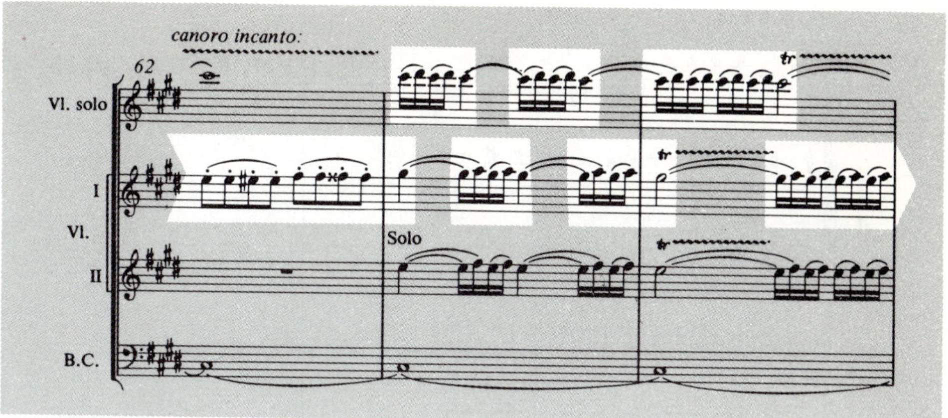
canoro incanto:
62
Vl. solo
I
Vl.
II
Solo
B.C.

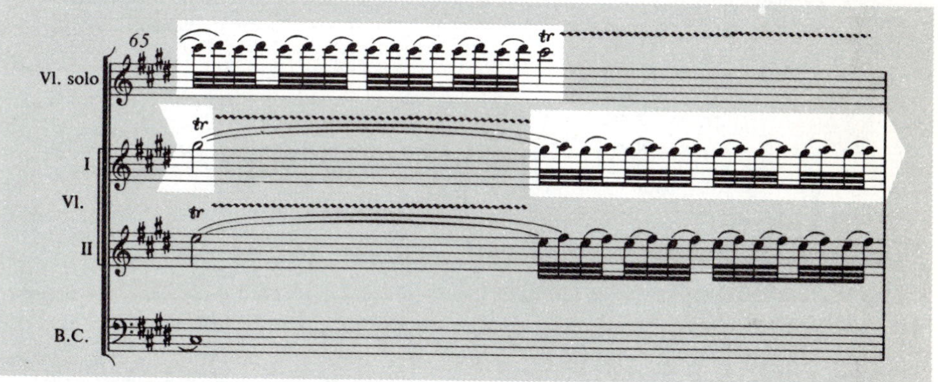
65
Vl. solo
I
Vl.
II
B.C.

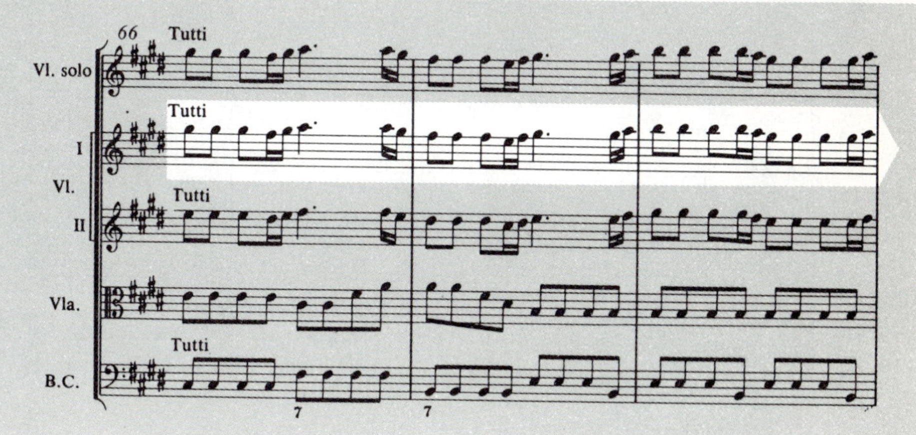
66
Tutti
Vl. solo
Tutti
I
Vl.
Tutti
II
Vla.
Tutti
B.C.

69
Solo
Vl. solo
I
Vl.
II
Vla.
B.C.
Tasto solo

72
Vl. solo
B.C.

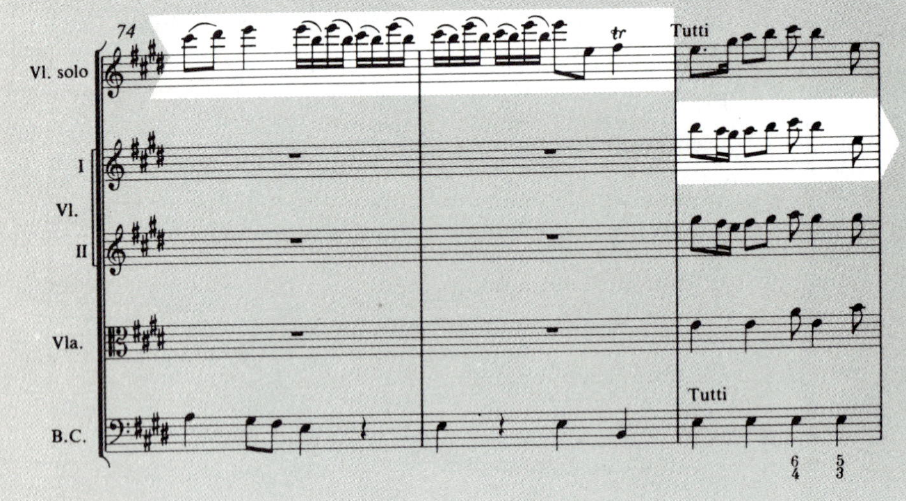
74
tr
Tutti
Vl. solo
I
Vl.
II
Vla.
Tutti
B.C.
6
4
5
3

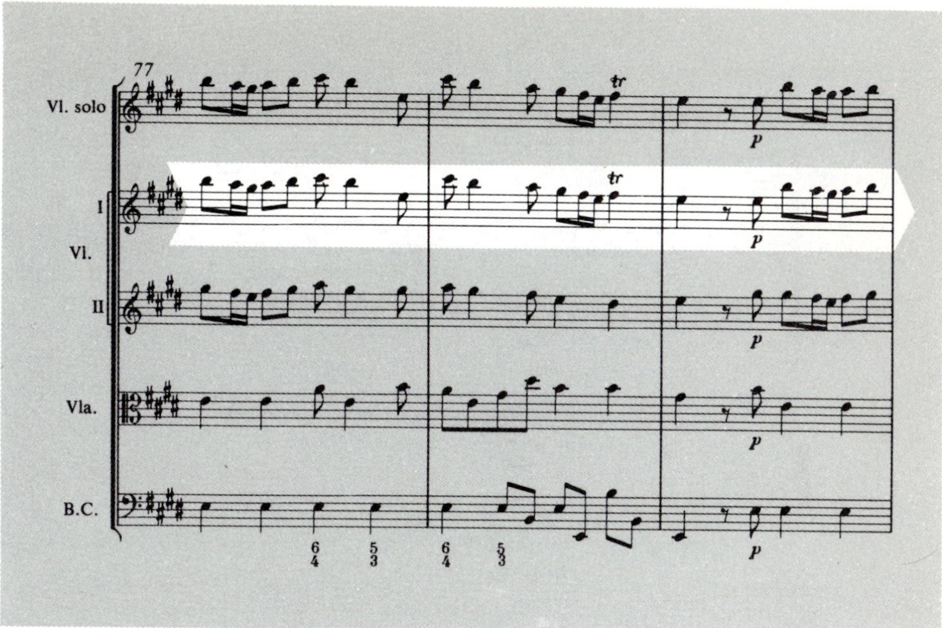
77
Vl. solo
tr
p
I
Vl.
II
Vla.
B.C.
6
4
5
3

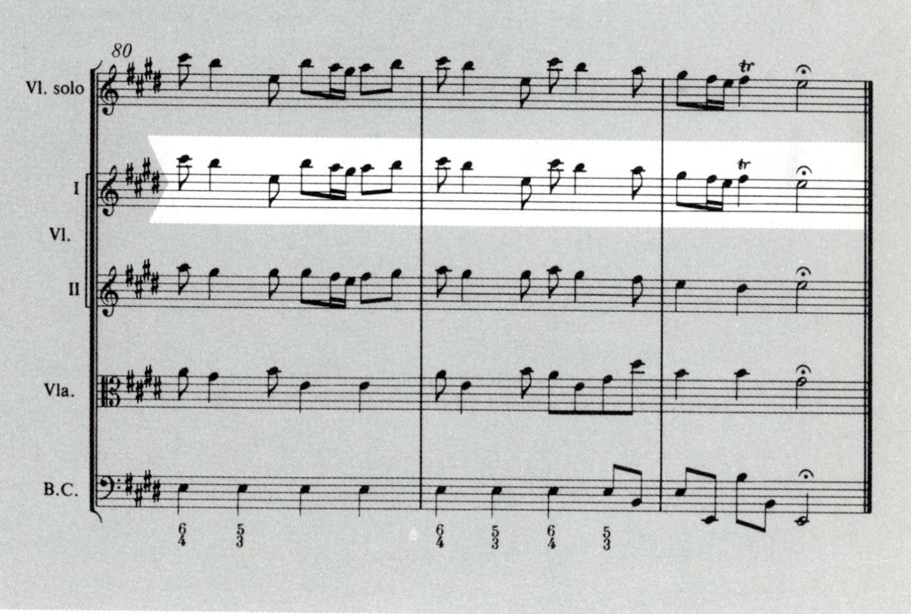
80
Vl. solo
tr
I
Vl.
II
Vla.
B.C.
6
4
5
3

II
F
E quindi Sul fiorito ameno prato Al caro mormorio
Largo e pianissimo sempre
Il capraro che dorme
Violino solo
Violino I
Violino II
Il cane che grida
Viola
si deve suonare sempre molto forte, a strappato

di fronde e piante Dorme 'l Caprar col fido can'à lato.
4
Vl. solo
I
Vl.
II
Vla.

8
Vl. solo
I
Vl.
II
Vla.

12
Vl. solo
I
Vl.
II
Vla.

15
Vl. solo
tr
I
Vl.
II
Vla.

18
Vl. solo
I
Vl.
II
Vla.

21
Vl. solo
I
Vl.
II
Vla.

24
Vl. solo
I
Vl.
II
Vla.

27
Vl. solo
I
Vl.
II
Vla.

30
Vl. solo
I
Vl.
II
Vla.
tr

33
Vl. solo
I
Vl.
II
Vla.

36
Vl. solo
I
Vl.
II
Vla.
tr

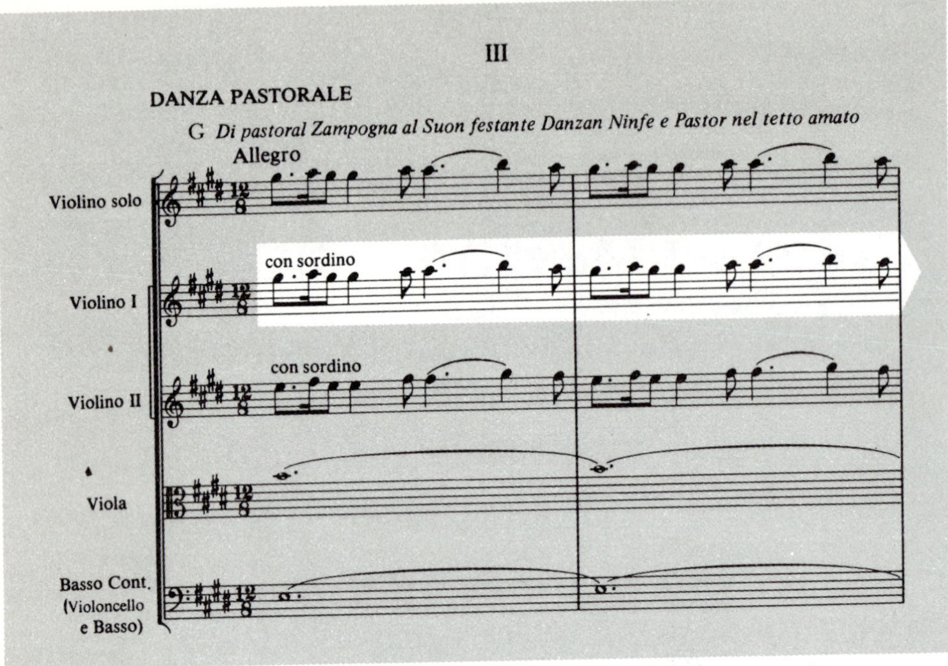
III
DANZA PASTORALE
G Di pastoral Zampogna al Suon festante Danzan Ninfe e Pastor nel tetto amato
Allegro
Violino solo
con sordino
Violino I
con sordino
Violino II
Viola
Basso Cont.
(Violoncello
e Basso)

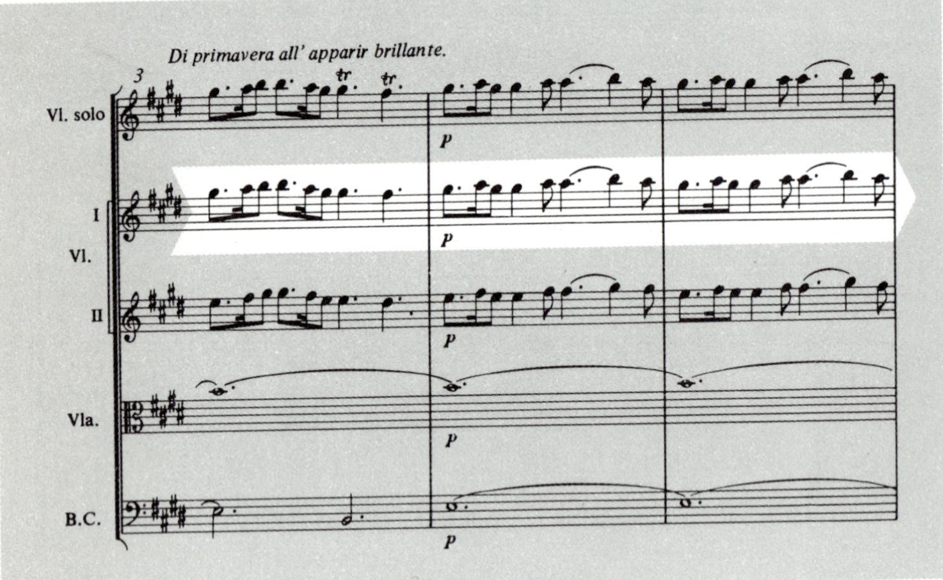
Di primavera all' apparir brillante.
3
Vl. solo
I
Vl.
II
Vla.
B.C.
p

6
Vl. solo
I
Vl.
II
Vla.
Tasto solo
B.C.

9
Vl. solo
I
Vl.
II
Vla.
B.C.

12
Solo
Vl. solo
I
Vl.
II
Vla.
B.C.

15
Vl. solo
[Tutti]
B.C.
6
6

17
Vl. solo
6
B.C.

19
Vl. solo
B.C.
7 5
6 4
5 ♯

22
Vl. solo
Tutti
I
Vl.
II
Vla.
B.C.
Tasto solo

25
Vl. solo
I
Vl.
II
Vla.
B.C.

29
Vl. solo
I
Vl.
II
Vla.
B.C.
f
6

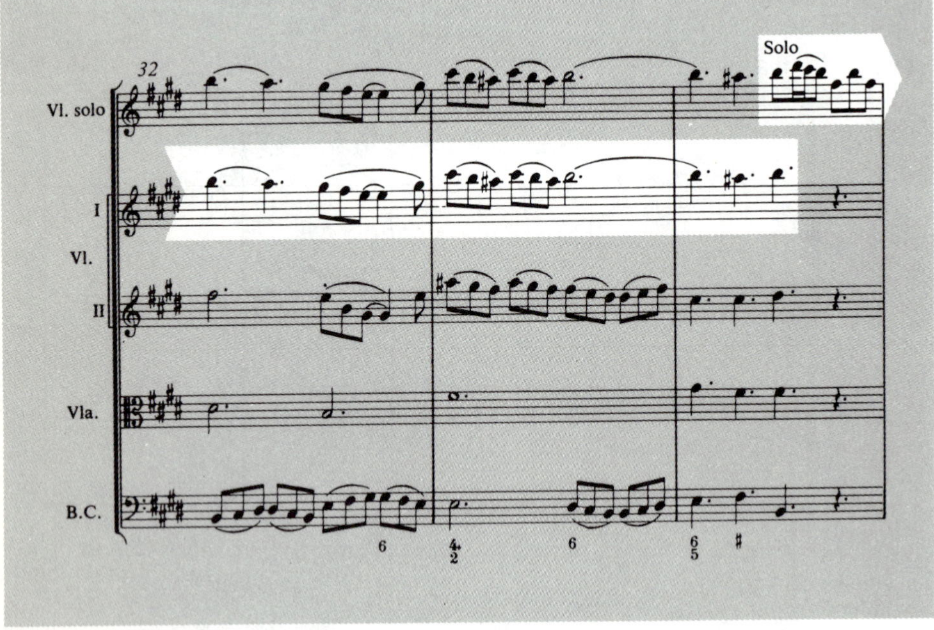
32
Solo
Vl. solo
I
Vl.
II
Vla.
B.C.
6
4+
2
6
6
5
♯

35
Vl. solo
Vl. I
Solo
B.C.
6
5♮
7♭

38
Vl. solo
Vl. I
B.C.
Tasto solo
6
5♮
7
6
5
7

41
Vl. solo
Vl. I
B.C.

45
Vl. solo
I
Vl.
II
B.C.
Tutti
p
p

49
Vl. solo
I
Vl.
II

51
Vl. solo
I
Vl.
II

53
Vl. solo
I
Vl.
II
Vla.
p

55
Vl. solo
I
Vl.
II
Vla.

57
Tutti
Vl. solo
f
I
Vl.
f
II
f
Vla.
f
B.C.
f Tasto solo

59
Vl. solo
I
Vl.
II
Vla.
B.C.

61
Vl. solo
I
Vl.
II
Vla.
B.C.
6
4
5
♯
6
4
5
♯

64
Vl. solo
I
Vl.
II
Vla.
B.C.

67
Vl. solo
I
Vl.
II
Vla.
B.C.

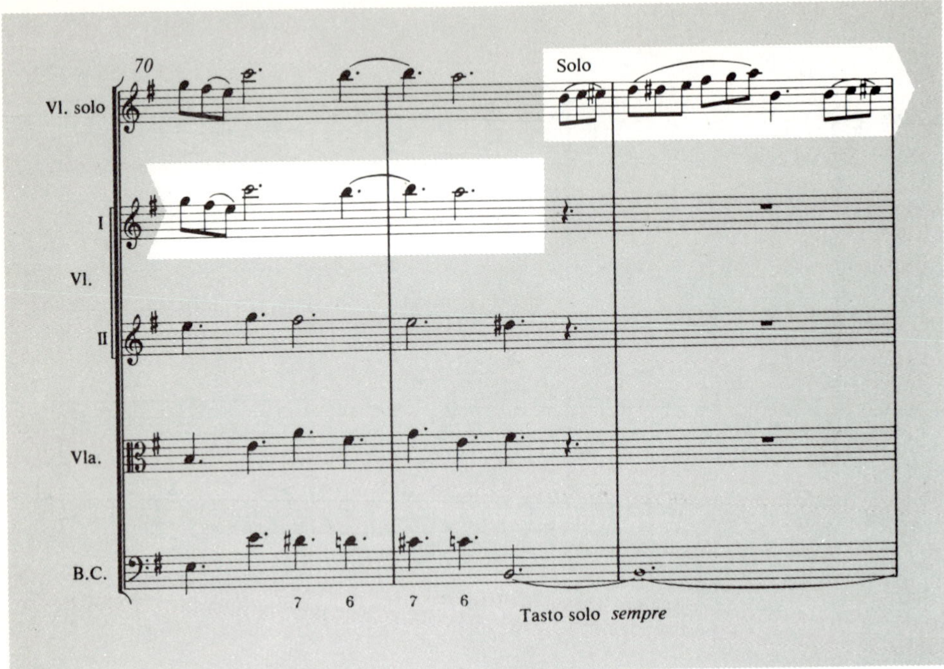
70
Vl. solo
Solo
I
Vl.
II
Vla.
B.C.
7
6
7
6
Tasto solo *sempre*

73
Vl. solo
B.C.

76
Vl. solo
B.C.

79
Vl. solo
tr
Tutti
I
Vl.
II
f
Vla.
f
f
Tutti
B.C.
f

81
Vl. solo
I
Vl.
II
Vla.
Tasto solo
B.C.

83
Vl. solo
I
Vl.
II
Vla.
B.C.

86
Vl. solo
I
Vl.
II
Vla.
B.C.
tr
p
Tutti
Tasto solo
Tutti

Translation

I ALLEGRO	
Giunt è la Primavera e festosetti	Joyful Spring has arrived,
La salutan gl'Augei con lieto canto,	The birds greet it with their cheerful song,
E i fonti allo spirar de' Zeffiretti	And the brooks in the gentle breezes
Con dolce mormorio scorrono intanto:	flow with a sweet murmur.
Vengon' coprendo l'aer di nero amanto	The sky is covered with a black mantle
E Lampi, e tuoni ad annuntiarla eletti	And lightning and thunder announce a storm.
Indì tacendo questi, gl'Augelletti;	When they fall silent, the birds
Tornan' di nuovo allor canoro incanto:	Take up again their melodious song.
II LARGO	
E quindi sul fiorito ameno prato	And in the flower-rich meadow,
Al caro mormorio di fronde e piante	To the gentle murmur of bushes and trees
Dorme'l Caprar col fido can' à lato.	The goatherd sleeps, with his faithful dog at his side.
III ALLEGRO (Rustic Dance)	
Di pastoral Zampogna al Suon festante	To the festive sounds of a rustic bagpipe
Danzan Ninfe e Pastor nel tetto amato	Nymphs and shepherds dance in their favorite spot
Di primavera all'apparir brillante.	When spring appears in its brilliance.

21. George Frideric Handel (1685-1759),

Water Music, Nos. 3, 4, 5, and 6
(1717)

 S1A/4 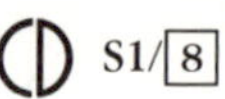 S1/8

3

Corno I.
Corno II.
Oboe I.
Oboe II.
Bassons.
Violino I.
Violino II.
Viola.
Violoncello, e Cembalo.
Contrabasso.

tr
tr
tr
tr
6
6

tr
tr
tr
tr
tr
tr
tr

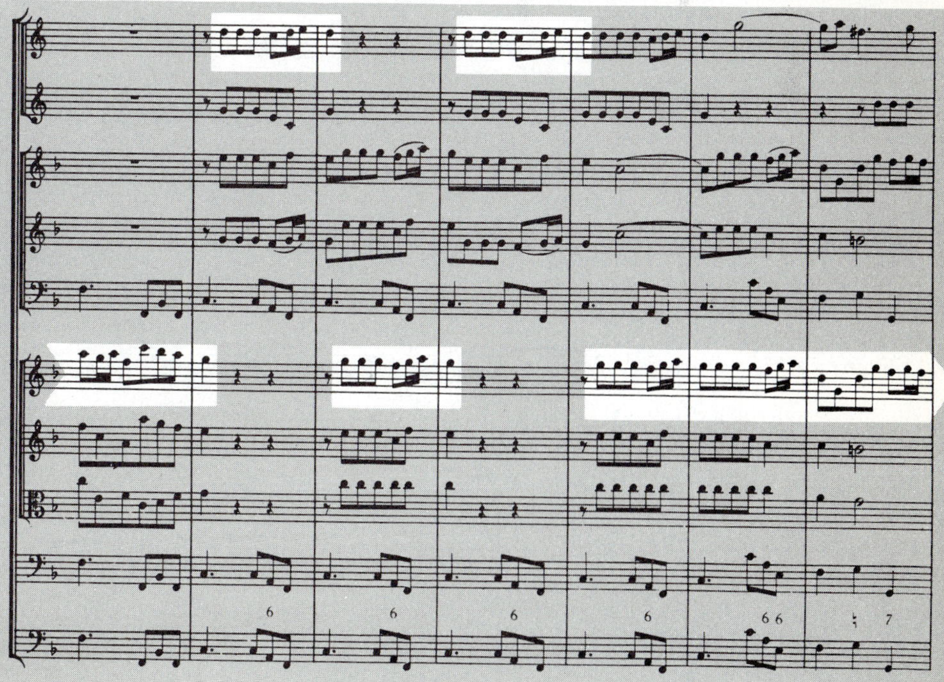

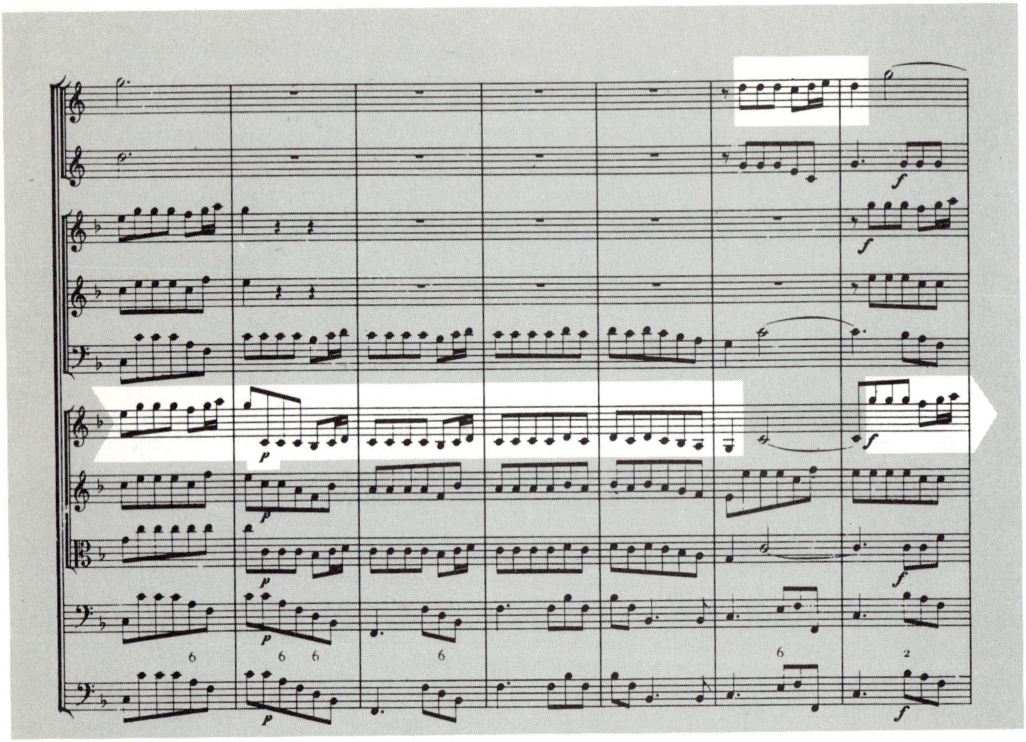

Fine.

4

Andante.

tr

tr

unis.

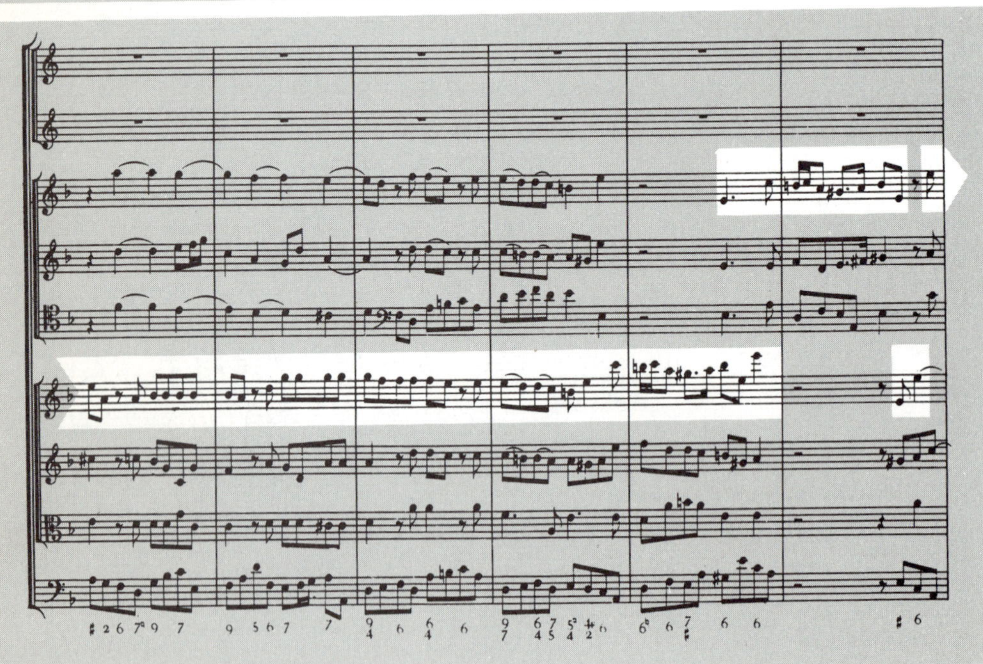

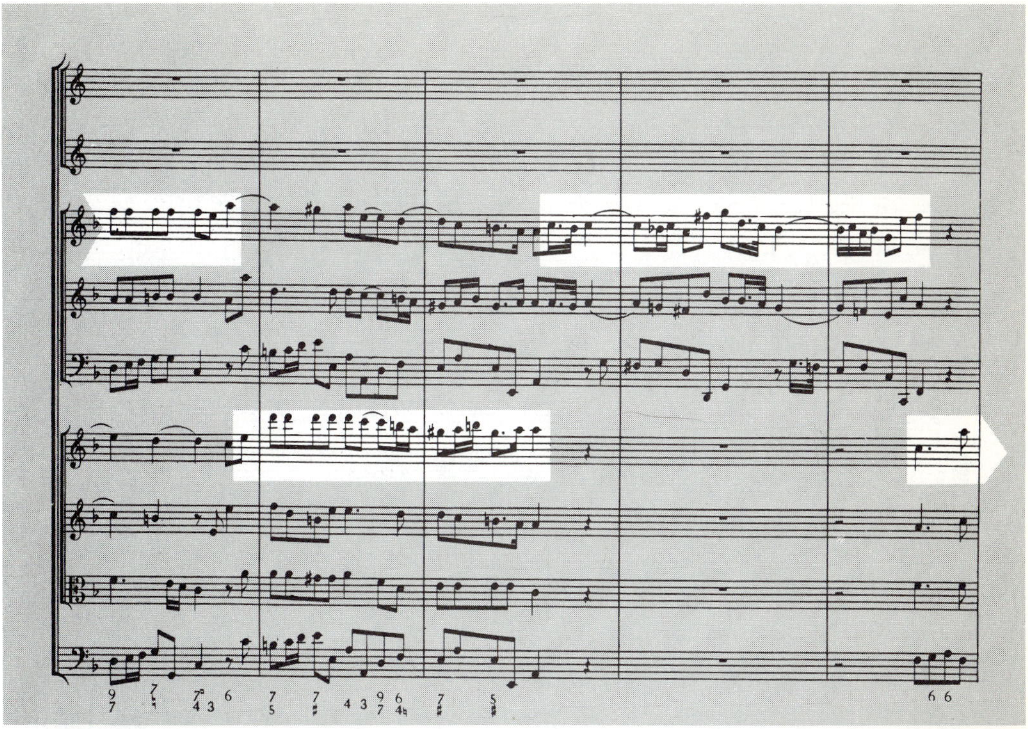

9
7
7
5
9
7
(7)
7
7
♯
4 3 6
7
3
7
3
7
♯
7
7 6
♯
6
5

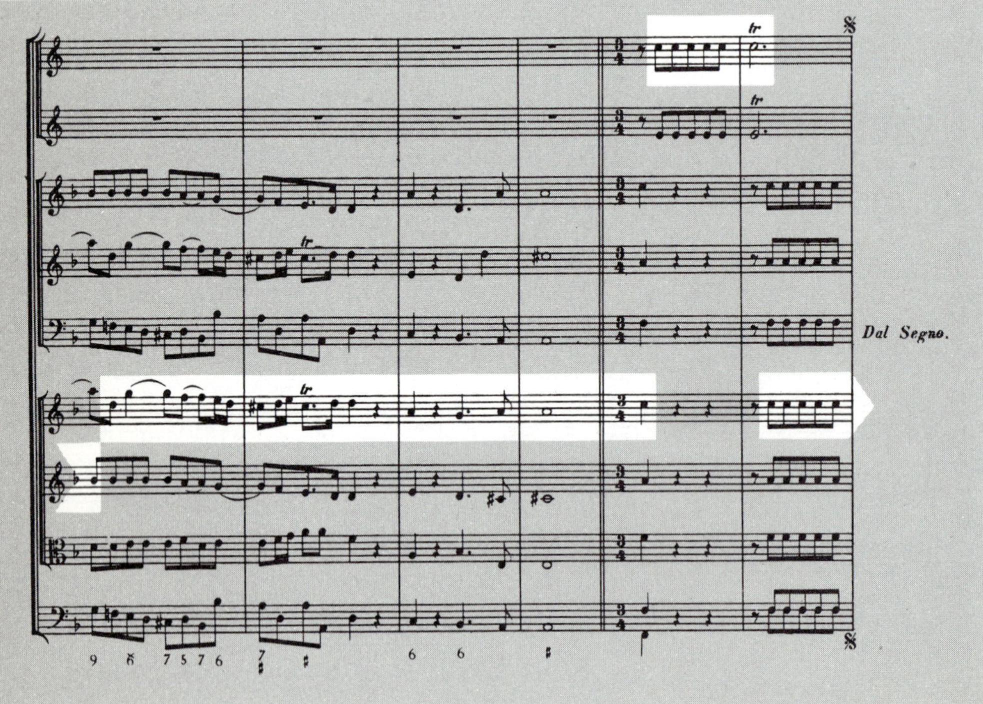
tr
tr
tr
tr
Dal Segno.
9
7 5 7 6
7
♯
♯
6
6
♯

#7 Stokowski
#6
5
(Violino I. Tutti Oboe.)
(Violino II.)
(Viola.)
(Bassi.)
tr
Corno I.
Corno II.
Viol. I, e tutti Oboe.
Violino II.
Viola.
(Tutti) Bassi.

6
tr
9 8
7 6
6 7 6
6
4
♮
6
5♭
6
5♭
6
5♭
6 5
4 3
6
5
4 3
6 4
7 7 7
6 5
4 3
9 8
7 6
6
6
4 3
#1
Stokowski
#7
Corno I.
Corno II.
Oboe I.
Oboe II.
Bassons.
Violino I.
Violino II.
Viola.
(Bassi.)

1.
2.
6
4
6
6
6
6
6
6
1.
2.
6
7
7
6
6
7
8
6
7
5

1.
2.
1.
2.

22. Handel

Giulio Cesare in Egitto,
"V'adoro, pupille" (1724)

Largo.

Oboe, e Violino I. — Oboe. — unis.
Sordini. — Viol.
Violino II.
Viola.
Viola da Gamba.
Teorba, Harpe, Bassons e Violoncelli.
CLEOPATRA.

V'a - do - ro, pu - pil - le, sa - et - te — d'A - mo - re, le vo - stre fa - vil - le son

Orchestra.
Violino I.
Sordini.
Violino II.
Viola.
Bassi.

gra - te nel sen; v'a - do - ro, pu - pil - le, le vo - stre fa - vil - le son gra - te, son

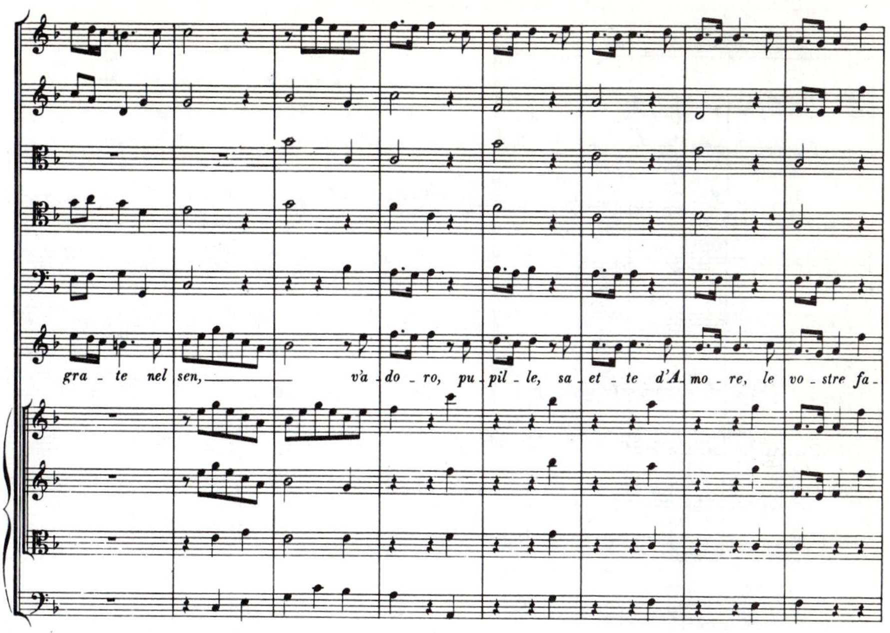
gra - te nel sen, v'a - do - ro, pu - pil - le, sa - et - te d'A - mo - re, le vo - stre fa -

- vil - le son gra - te nel sen, le vo - stre fa - vil - le son gra - te nel sen.

Translation

V'adoro, pupille, saette d'amore,
le vostre faville son grate nel sen.
Pietose vi brama il mesto mio core,
ch'ogn'ora vi chiama l'amato suo ben.

I adore you, O eyes, arrows of love,
Your sparks are pleasing to my heart.
My sad heart begs for your mercy,
Never ceasing to call you its belowed.

23. Handel

Excerpts from *Messiah* (1742)   S1B/1 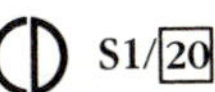 S1/20

No. 1: Overture

Sinfony

Grave

2 Oboi

2 Fagotti

Grave [con rip]

Violino I

Violino II

Viola

Basso continuo

Ob.

Fag.

Viol. I

Viol. II

Viola

Basso cont.

[p]

Allegro moderato

Ob. I

Ob. II

Allegro moderato

Viol. I

Viol. II

21
I
Ob.
II
Fag.
[tr]
[f]
21
I
Viol.
II
Viola
[f]
[tr]
Vc.
Basso cont.
[f]
29
I
Ob.
II
Fag.
[tr]
29
I
Viol.
II
Viola
Basso cont.
[tr]
88
I
Ob.
II
Fag.
88
I
Viol.
II
Viola
Basso cont.

46
Ob. I
II
Fag.
Viol. I
II
Viola
Basso cont.
[tr]
55
68

71
I
Ob.
II
Fag.
71
I
Viol.
II
Viola
Basso cont.
81
I
Ob.
II
Fag.
[tr]
81
I
Viol.
II
Viola
Basso cont.
[tr]
89
I
Ob.
II
Fag.
[tr]
89
I
Viol.
II
Viola
Basso cont.
[tr]

No. 2: "Comfort ye"

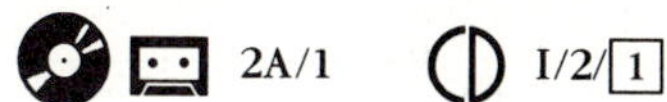

2A/1 I/2/1

Larghetto e piano
p
Tenor Solo
Com-fort ye, com - - - fort ye my people,
fp
p
ad lib.
com - fort ye,
fp
a tempo
com - - fort ye my peo-ple,
a tempo
p
fp

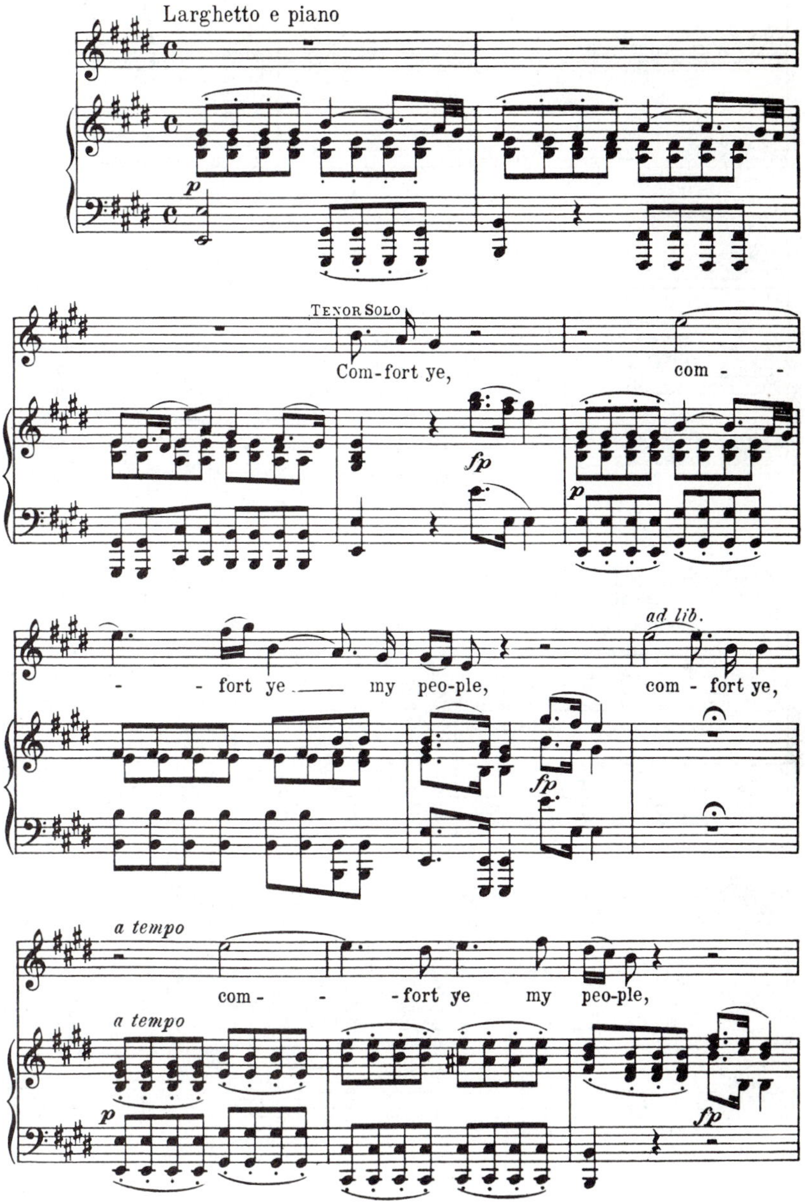

saith your God, saith your God;
fp
mf
speak ye com-fort-a-bly to Je - ru - sa-lem, speak ye
p simile
com - fort-a - bly to Je - ru - sa-lem, and cry un - to her that her
mf
war - fare, her war - fare is ac-complished, that her in -
p

i - qui - ty is par-don'd, that her in - i - qui - ty is par - -
don'd.
mf
The voice of him that crieth in the wilderness, Pre-pare ye the way of the
Lord, make straight in the desert a high-way for our God.

No. 3: "Ev'ry valley"

ex-alt - - - - - - - - - - - - - - - -

- - - - - - - - ed, shall be ex - alt - - - ed,

shall be ex-alt - - - - - - - - - - - - - -

- ed, and ev-'ry moun - tain and hill made low;

the crook-ed straight,
and the rough plac-es
plain,
the crook-ed
straight, the crook - ed straight, and rough plac-es
plain,
cresc.
p
simile

— and the rough plac-es plain.
p
mf
Ev-'ry val-ley,
ev-'ry val-ley —
p
f
p
— shall be ex-alt - - - - - - - - - - - - - -
- - - - - - - - - - - - - ed,
f

ev - 'ry val-ley, ev - 'ry val - ley shall be ex-alt - - - - - - - - - - - - - ed, and ev-'ry moun-tain and
hill made low; the crook-ed straight, the
crook-ed straight, the crook-ed straight, and the rough plac-es plain,
p
f
p
p
tr

and the rough plac-es plain, and the rough plac-es
plain,
the crook-ed straight,
f
ad lib.
and the rough plac - es plain.
colla voce
senza Ped.
f a tempo
tr
p
f
p
cresc.
f

No. 4: "And the glory of the Lord"

*) According to the original score.

Lord. shall be re -
Lord
Lord shall be re - - veal - - - ed,
Lord shall be re - - veal - - -
veal - - - ed, and the glo - ry, the glo-ry of the
shall be re - veal-ed,
and the glo - ry, the glo-ry of the Lord
- ed, shall be re - veal-ed,
Lord shall be re - veal'd, and the
be re - - veal - - - - - - - - ed, and the
shall be re - veal - - ed, and the
and the

glo - ry, the glo-ry of the Lord shall be re - veal - ed,
glo - ry, the glo-ry of the Lord shall be re-veal - ed,
glo - ry, the glo-ry of the Lord shall be re-veal - ed,
glo - ry, the glo-ry of the Lord shall be re-veal - ed,
mf
and all flesh shall
see it to - geth-er,
mf
and all flesh shall see it to - geth-er;

B
and all flesh shall see it to-geth-
and all flesh shall see it to-geth-
for the mouth of the Lord hath spok-en
For the mouth of the Lord hath spok-en
B
er; for the mouth of the Lord hath spok-en
er, and all flesh shall see it to-geth-
it; and all flesh shall see it to-geth-
it; and all flesh shall see it to-geth-
it;
er, and all flesh, and all flesh shall see it to-geth-er;
er, and all flesh shall see it to-geth-er; the
er; for the
C
C

and all flesh — shall see it to - geth - - er;
and all flesh — shall see it to - geth - er;
mouth of the Lord hath spok - en it.
mouth of the Lord hath spok - en it.

And the glo - ry, the glo-ry of the Lord, and all
And the glo - ry, the glo-ry of the Lord, and all flesh — shall
And the glo - ry, the glo-ry of the Lord, and all flesh — shall
And the glo - ry, the glo-ry of the Lord, and all

D

flesh — shall see it to - geth - er; the mouth of the Lord hath
see it to - geth - er; and the glo - ry, the glo-ry of the
see it, shall see it to - geth - er;
flesh — shall see it to - geth - er;

D

spok - en it,
Lord shall be re - - veal - ed, and all
and all flesh —
and all flesh —
for the mouth of the Lord hath
flesh — shall see it to - geth - er; for the
shall see it to - geth - er; the glo - ry, the glo - ry of the
shall see it to - geth - er;
E
spok - en it, hath — spok - - - - en it;
mouth of the Lord hath spok - en it; and all
Lord shall be re - - veal - - ed,
and the glo - ry, the glo-ry of the Lord shall be re - veal - ed,
E

ff
and the glo-ry, the glo-ry, the
flesh shall see it to-geth-er;
and all flesh shall see it to-geth-er;
and all flesh shall see it to-geth-er;
glo-ry of the Lord shall be re-veal-ed,
ff
and the glo-ry, the glo-ry of the Lord shall be re-
ff
and the glo-ry, the glo-ry of the Lord
ff
and the glo-ry, the glo-ry of the Lord shall
and all flesh shall
veal-ed, re-veal-ed, and all flesh shall
shall be re-veal-ed, and all flesh shall
be re-veal-ed, re-veal-ed; for the mouth

F
see it to - geth - er, to - geth - - er; for the mouth of the
see it to - geth - er, to - geth - - er; for the mouth of the
see it to - geth - er, to - geth - - er; for the mouth of the
of the Lord hath spok - en it, for the mouth of the
F
Lord hath spok - en it, for the mouth of the
Lord hath spok - en it, for the mouth of the
Lord hath spok-en it, for the mouth of the Lord, the
Lord hath spok - en it, for the mouth of the Lord, the
Adagio
Lord hath spok - - en it
Lord hath spok - - en it.
mouth of the Lord hath spok - - en it.
mouth of the Lord hath spok - - en it.
Adagio

No. 12: "For unto us a Child is born"

us a Child is born:
un-to us a Son is giv-en, un-to
us a Son is giv-en:
For un-to us a Child is born,
For un-to
un-to us a Son is giv-en, un-to
us a Child is born,

us a Son is giv-en, un-to us a Son is
un-to us a Son is giv-en:
mf
and the gov-ern-ment shall
giv-en:
mf
and the gov-ern-ment shall be up-on His shoul -
mf
mf
cresc.
be up-on His shoul - - der, up-on His shoul-der; and His
mf
cresc.
and the gov-ern-ment shall be up-on His shoul-der; and His
cresc.
der; and His
mf
cresc.
and the gov-ern-ment shall be up-on His shoul-der; and His
cresc.

Name shall be call-ed Won - der-ful, Coun - sel-lor,
Name shall be call-ed Won - der-ful, Coun - sel-lor,
Name shall be call-ed Won - der-ful, Coun - sel-lor,
Name shall be call-ed Won - der-ful, Coun - sel-lor,
The might-y God, The ev - er - last - ing Fa - ther, The Prince of Peace.
The might-y God, The ev - er - last - ing Fa - ther, The Prince of Peace. Un- to
The might-y God, The ev - er - last - ing Fa - ther, The Prince of Peace.
The might-y God, The ev - er - last - ing Fa - ther, The Prince of Peace.
us a Child is born, un- to us a Son is
For un-to us a Child is born,

p
Un-to us a Child is born,

giv-en: mf and the gov-ern-ment shall

p
un-to us a Son is giv-en:

be up-on His shoul - - - - - - - - - - - -

mf
and the gov-ern-ment shall be up on His shoul - -

cresc. ff
and His Name shall be call-ed Won - der-ful,

cresc. ff
- der; and His Name shall be call-ed Won - der-ful,

cresc. ff
and His Name shall be call-ed Won - der-ful,

cresc. ff
- der; and His Name shall be call-ed Won - der-ful,

cresc.

ff

Coun - sel-lor, The might - y God, The

Coun - sel-lor, The might - y God, The

Coun - sel-lor, The might - y God, The

Coun - sel-lor, The might - y God, The

ev - er-last-ing Fa-ther, The Prince of Peace. For un-to

ev - er-last-ing Fa-ther, The Prince of Peace.

ev - er-last-ing Fa-ther, The Prince of Peace. Un-to us a Child is born,

ev - er-last-ing Fa-ther, The Prince of Peace.

us a Child is born,

For un-to us a Child is born,

For un-to us a Child is born, un-to

p
un-to us a Son is
p
un-to us a Son is
us a Son is giv-en:
giv-en:
mf
and the gov-ern-ment shall
mf
giv-en: and the gov-ern-ment shall be up-on His shoul - - - der;
mf
be up-on His shoul - - - der;
cresc.
and His
mf
and the gov-ern-ment shall be up-on His shoul-der; and His
cresc.
and His
mf
and the gov-ern-ment shall be up-on His shoul-der; and His

Name shall be call - ed
Won - - der - ful,
Coun - - sel - lor,
The might - y God,
The
ev - er - last - ing Fa - - ther,
Prince of Peace.
For un-to
Un - to
us a Child is born, un-to

us a Child is born,
us a Child is born,
us a Child is born, un - to us a Son is
us a Child is born, un - to us a Son is
giv - en, un - to us a Son is
giv - en, un - to us a Son is
un-to us a Son is giv-en: and the gov-ern-ment, the gov-ern-ment shall
un-to us a Son is giv-en: and the gov-ern-ment shall
giv-en, un-to us a Son is giv-en:
giv-en, un-to us a Son is giv-en:

be up-on His shoul - - - - der, and the gov-ern-ment shall
be up-on His shoul - der, and the gov-ern-ment shall
and the gov-ern-ment, the gov-ern-ment shall
and the gov-ern-ment, the gov-ern-ment shall
be up-on His shoul-der; and His Name shall be call-ed
be up-on His shoul-der; and His Name shall be call-ed
be up-on His shoul-der; and His Name shall be call-ed
be up-on His shoul-der; and His Name shall be call-ed
ff
Won - der-ful, Coun - sel-lor,
Won - der-ful, Coun - sel-lor,
Won - der-ful, Coun - sel-lor,
Won - der-ful, Coun - sel-lor,

The might-y God, The ev-er-last-ing Fa-ther, The Prince of Peace, The
The might-y God, The ev-er-last-ing Fa-ther, The Prince of Peace, The
The might-y God, The ev-er-last-ing Fa-ther, The Prince of Peace, The
The might-y God, The ev-er-last-ing Fa-ther, The Prince of Peace, The
ev-er-last-ing Fa-ther, The Prince of Peace.
ev-er-last-ing Fa-ther, The Prince of Peace.
ev-er-last-ing Fa-ther, The Prince of Peace.
ev-er-last-ing Fa-ther, The Prince of Peace.
f

No. 44: "Hallelujah"

lu - jah! Hal-le - lu - jah! Hal - le - lu - jah! for the Lord
lu - jah! Hal-le - lu - jah! Hal - le - - lu - jah! for the Lord
lu - jah! Hal-le - lu - jah! Hal - le - - lu - jah! for the Lord
lu - jah! Hal-le - lu - jah! Hal - le - lu - jah! for the Lord
God Om - ni - po - tent reign - eth. Hal-le - lu - jah! Hal-le - lu - jah! Hal-le -
God Om - ni - po - tent reign - eth. Hal-le - lu - jah! Hal-le - lu - jah! Hal-le -
God Om - ni - po - tent reign - eth. Hal-le - lu - jah! Hal-le - lu - jah! Hal-le -
God Om - ni - po - tent reign - eth. Hal-le - lu - jah! Hal-le - lu - jah! Hal-le -
lu - jah! Hal-le - lu - jah! Hal-le -
lu - jah! Hal-le - lu - jah! for the Lord God Om - ni - po - tent reign - eth. Hal-le -
lu - jah! Hal-le - lu - jah! for the Lord God Om - ni - po - tent reign - eth. Hal-le -
lu - jah! Hal-le - lu - jah! for the Lord God Om - ni - po - tent reign - eth. Hal-le -

lu - jah! Hal - le - lu - jah! Hal - le - lu - jah! Hal - le - lu - jah!
lu - jah! Hal - le - lu - jah! Hal - le - lu - jah! Hal - le - lu - jah!
lu - jah! Hal - le - lu - jah! Hal - le - lu - jah! Hal - le - lu - jah!
lu - jah! Hal - le - lu - jah! Hal - le - lu - jah! Hal - le - lu - jah!
for the Lord God Om - ni - - po - tent
Hal - le -
Hal - le - lu - jah! Hal - le - lu - jah! Hal - le - lu - jah! Hal -
reign - - - eth. Hal - le - lu - jah! Hal - le - lu - jah! Hal - le - lu -
lu-jah! Hal - le - lu - jah! Hal - le - lu - jah! Hal - le - lu - jah! Hal - le - lu -
le - - lu - - jah! Hal - le - lu - jah! for the Lord
Hal - le - lu - jah! for the Lord

jah! Hal-le-lu-jah! Hal - le - lu - jah! Hal-le-lu-jah!
jah! Hal-le-lu-jah! Hal - le - lu - jah! Hal-le-
God Om - ni - po - tent reign - eth. Hal-le-lu-jah!
God Om - ni - po - tent reign - eth. Hal-le-
Hal-le-lu-jah! Hal-le-lu-jah! Hal-le-lu-jah! Hal-le-lu-jah!
lu-jah! Hal-le-lu-jah! for the Lord
Hal-le-lu-jah! Hal-le-lu-jah! for the Lord
lu-jah! Hal-le-lu-jah! Hal-le-lu-jah! Hal-le-
Hal-le-lu-jah! Hal-le-lu-jah! Hal - le - lu - jah! Hal-
God Om - ni - po - tent reign - eth. Hal-le-lu-jah!
God Om - ni - po - tent reign - eth. Hal-
*)
lu-jah! Hal-le-lu-jah! Hal-le - lu-jah! Hal-le - lu-jah! Hal-le-

(p)
le - - lu - - jah! The king-dom of this
Hal - le - lu - jah! The king-dom of this
le - - - lu - jah! The king-dom of this
lu - jah! Hal-le - lu - jah! The king-dom of this
(p)
mf
f
world is be - - come the King - dom of our
world is be - - come the King - dom of our
world is be - - come the King - dom of our
world is be - - come the King - dom of our
Lord and of His Christ, and of His Christ;
Lord and of His Christ, and of His Christ;
Lord and of His Christ, and of His Christ;
Lord and of His Christ, and of His Christ; and He shall reign for ev - er and

and He shall reign for ev - - er and ev - - - -
ev - er, for ev - er and ev - - er, and He shall
and He shall reign for ev - - er and
er, and He shall reign for ev - - er and
reign, and He shall reign for ev - er, for
and He shall reign for ev - er and ev - -
ev - - er, for ev-er and ev-er, for ev - er and
ev - - er. and He shall reign for ev-er and
ev-er, for ev-er, for ev-er and ev-er, for ev - er, for ev-er and

er. King of Kings,
ev - er. King of Kings,
ev - er, for ev - er and ev - er. Hal-le-lu-jah! Hal-le-
ev - er, for ev - er and ev - er. Hal-le-lu-jah! Hal-le-
and Lord of Lords.
and Lord of Lords.
lu-jah! For ev-er and ev-er. Hal-le-lu-jah! Hal-le-
lu-jah! For ev-er and ev-er. Hal-le-lu-jah! Hal-le-
King of Kings,
For ev-er and ev-er. Hal-le-lu-jah! Hal-le-
lu-jah! For ev-er and ev-er. Hal-le-lu-jah! Hal-le-
lu-jah! For ev-er and ev-er. Hal-le-lu-jah! Hal-le-

and Lord of Lords,
lu-jah! For ev-er and ev-er. Hal-le-lu-jah! Hal-le-
lu-jah! For ev-er and ev-er. Hal-le-lu-jah! Hal-le-
lu-jah! For ev-er and ev-er. Hal-le-lu-jah! Hal-le-
King of Kings,
lu-jah! For ev-er and ev-er. Hal-le-lu-jah! Hal-le-
lu-jah! For ev-er and ev-er. Hal-le-lu-jah! Hal-le-
lu-jah! For ev-er and ev-er. Hal-le-lu-jah! Hal-le-
ff
and Lord of Lords, and Lord of Lords, and He shall
lu-jah! King of Kings, and Lord of Lords,
lu-jah! King of Kings, and Lord of Lords,
lu-jah! King of Kings, and Lord of Lords, and He shall
f

reign, and
and He shall reign, and He shall
and He shall reign, and He shall reign,
reign for ev - - er and ev - - er,
He shall reign for ev - er and ev - - er,
reign for ev - er and ev - - er, King of
and He shall reign for ev - er and ev - - er, King of
and He shall reign for ev - er and ev - er, King of
for ev - er and ev - er. Hal - le - lu - jah! Hal - le -
Kings, for ev - er and ev - er, and Lord of Lords. Hal - le - lu - jah! Hal - le -
Kings, and Lord of Lords,
Kings, for ev - er and ev - er, and Lord of Lords. Hal - le - lu - jah! Hal - le -

lu - jah! and He shall reign for ev - - er, for
lu - jah! and He shall reign for
and He shall reign for ev - - er, for
lu - jah! and He shall reign for ev - - er, for
ev - er and ev - - er, King of Kings, and Lord of
ev - er and ev - - er, King of Kings, and Lord of
ev - er and ev - - er, King of Kings, and Lord of
ev - er and ev - - er, King of Kings, and Lord of
Lords, King of Kings, and Lord of Lords, and
Lords, King of Kings, and Lord of Lords, and
Lords, King of Kings, and Lord of Lords, and
Lords, King of Kings, and Lord of Lords, and He shall

He shall reign for ev-er and ev - - er, King of
He shall reign for ev-er and ev - - er, for ev-er and
He shall reign for ev-er and ev - - er, for ev-er and
reign for ev - er, for ev-er and ev - - er, for ev-er and

Kings, and Lord of Lords. Hal-le-lu-jah! Hal-le-
ev - er, for ev - er and ev - er. Hal-le-lu-jah! Hal-le-
ev - er, for ev - er and ev - er. Hal-le-lu-jah! Hal-le-
ev - er, for ev - er and ev - er. Hal-le-lu-jah! Hal-le-

lu-jah! Hal-le-lu-jah! Hal-le - lu-jah! Hal - le - lu - jah!
lu-jah! Hal-le-lu-jah! Hal-le - lu-jah! Hal - le - lu - jah!
lu-jah! Hal-le-lu-jah! Hal-le - lu-jah! Hal - le - lu - jah!
lu-jah! Hal-le-lu-jah! Hal-le - lu-jah! Hal - le - lu - jah!

No. 45: "I know that my Redeemer liveth"

— at the lat - - - ter — day — up - on the*)

earth.

B

I know that my Re -

deem - er liv - eth, and that He shall — stand —

— at the lat - - ter day up - on the earth, — up - on the

C

earth. I know — that my Re - deem - er liv - eth, and He shall

*) This appoggiatura is not in Händel's score

stand at the lat - - - ter day up - on the earth,
up - on the earth:
cresc.
D
And though worms de - stroy this bod - y,
yet in my flesh shall I see

God, yet in my flesh shall I_ see God.
E
I know that my Re-
deem-er liv-eth. And though worms de - stroy this
bod-y, yet in my flesh shall I see God, yet in my
flesh _______ shall I see God, shall I see God. I

know that my Re - deem - er liv - eth.
f
F
For now is Christ ris - en from the dead,
p
pp
the first - - fruits of them that
sleep, of them that sleep, the
first - - fruits of them that sleep.
G
p

cresc.
For now is Christ ris-en, for now is Christ
p
cresc.
ris-en from the dead,
the
p
Adagio
first-fruits of them, of them that sleep.
f

24. Johann Sebastian Bach (1685–1750),

Brandenberg Concerto No. 2 in F major,
First movement (1717–18)

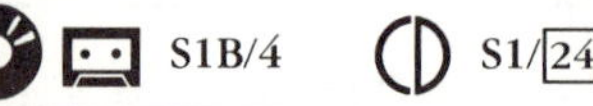

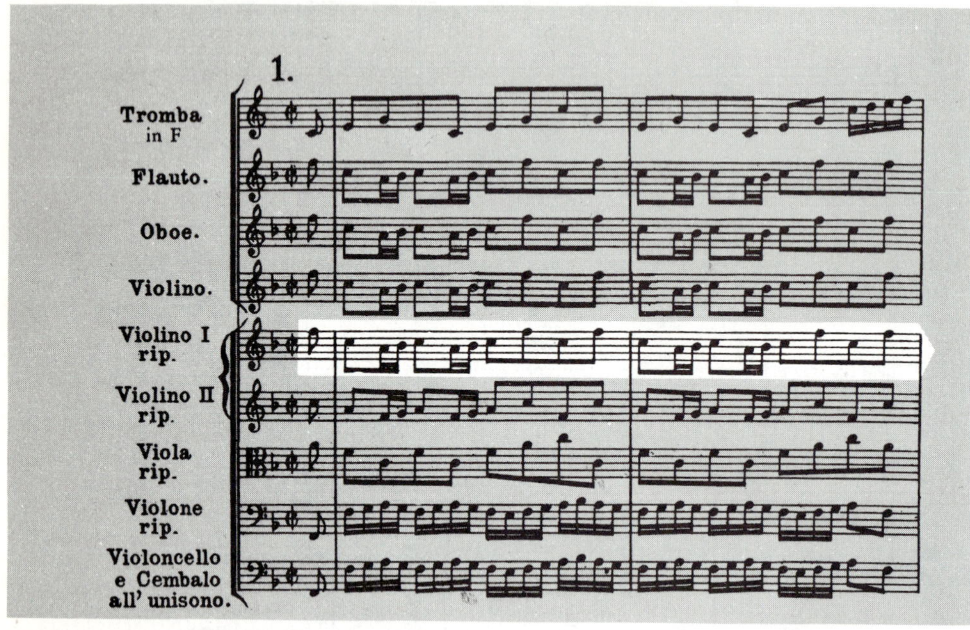

Tr. (F)
Fl.
Ob.
Vl.
Vl.
Vla.
V.
Vcl. Cont.
tr

Tr. (F)
Fl.
Ob.
Vl.
Vl.
Vla.
V.
Vcl. Cont.
10
tr.

Tr. (F)
Fl.
Ob.
Vl.
Vl.
Vla.
V.
Vcl. Cont.

Tr. (F)
Fl.
Ob.
Vl.
Vl.
Vla.
V.
Vcl. Cont.

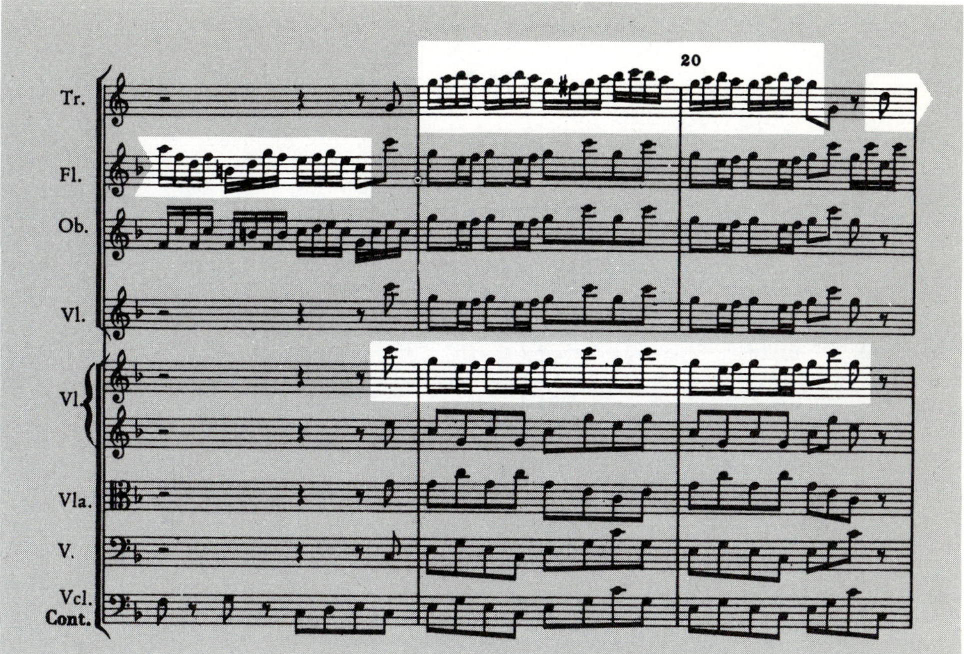
20
Tr.
Fl.
Ob.
Vl.
Vl.
Vla.
V.
Vcl.
Cont.

Tr.
tr
Fl.
Ob.
Vl.
Vl.
Vla.
V.
Vcl.
Cont.

Tr. (F)
Fl.
Ob.
Vl.
Vl.
Vla.
V.
Vcl. Cont.
Tr. (F)
Fl.
Ob.
Vl.
Vl.
Vla.
V.
Vcl. Cont.
tr

80
Tr. (F)
Fl.
Ob.
Vl.
Vl.
Vla.
V.
Vcl. Cont.
tr
p
f
Tr. (F)
Fl.
Ob.
Vl.
Vl.
Vla.
V.
Vcl. Cont.

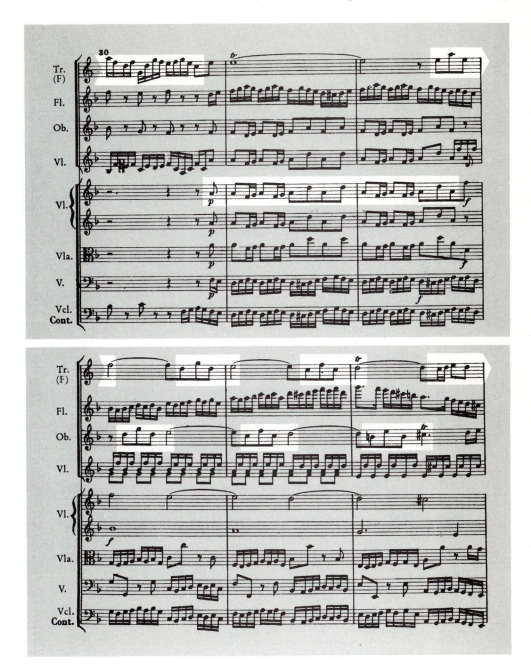

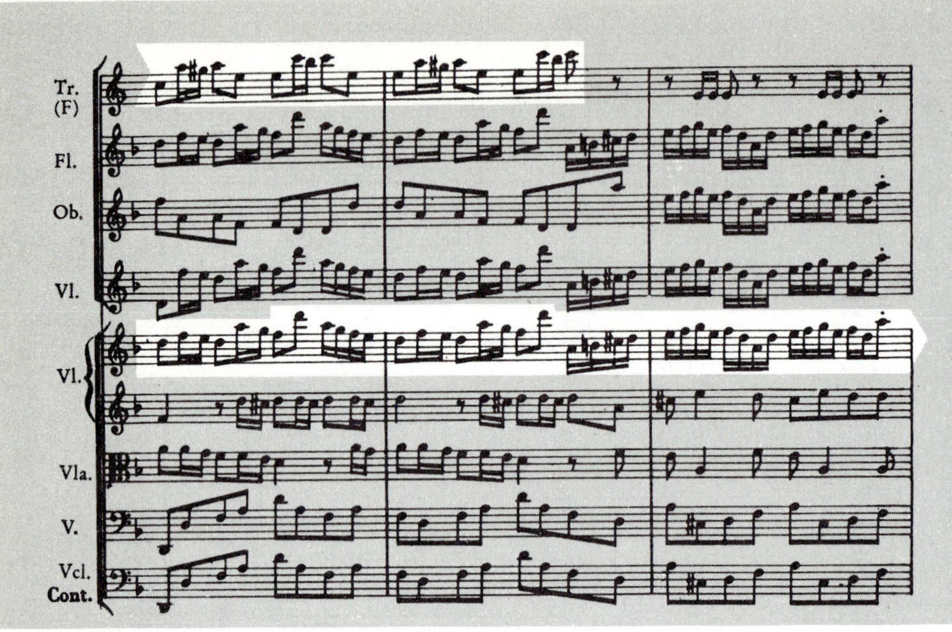
Tr.
(F)
Fl.
Ob.
Vl.
Vl.
Vla.
V.
Vcl.
Cont.

40
Tr.
(F)
Fl.
Ob.
Vl.
Vl.
p
piu Piano
pp
Vla.
V.
Vcl.
Cont.

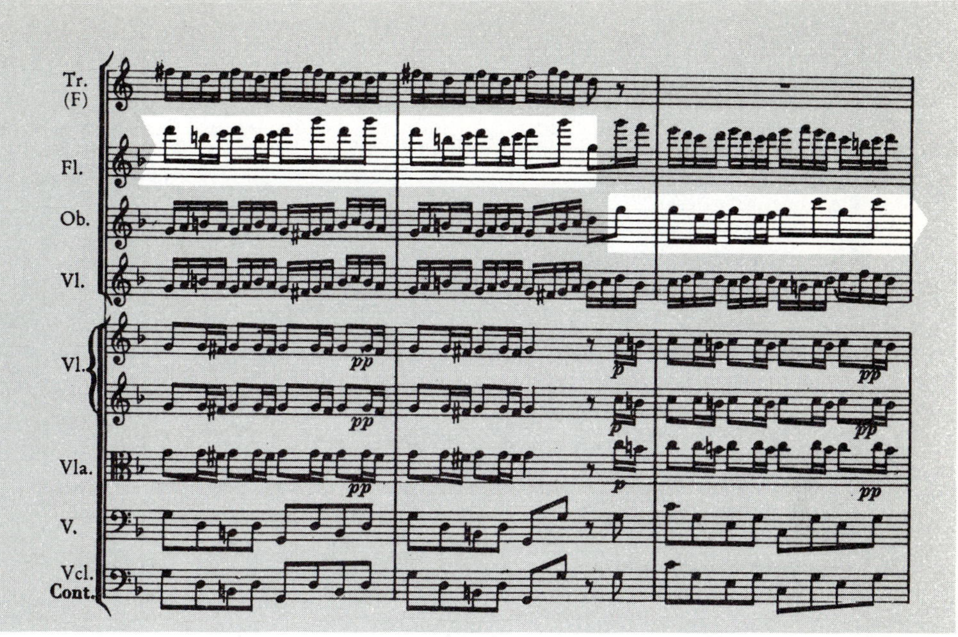
Tr.
(F)
Fl.
Ob.
Vl.
Vl.
pp
p
Vla.
V.
Vcl.
Cont.

Tr.
(F)
Fl.
Ob.
Vl.
Vl.
p
pp
f
Vla.
V.
Vcl.
Cont.

50
Tr.
(F)
Fl.
Ob.
Vl.
Vl.
Vla.
V.
Vcl.
Cont.
p
f

Tr. (F)
Fl.
Ob.
Vl.
Vl.
Vla.
V.
Vcl. Cont.

Tr. (F)
Fl.
Ob.
Vl.
Vl.
Vla.
V.
Vcl. Cont.

60
Tr. (F)
Fl.
Ob.
Vl.
Vl.
Vla.
V.
Vcl. Cont.
tr
Tr. (F)
Fl.
Ob.
Vl.
Vl.
Vla.
V.
Vcl. Cont.
tr

Tr. (F)
Fl.
Ob.
Vl.
Vl.
Vla.
V.
Vcl. Cont.

70
Tr. (F)
Fl.
Ob.
Vl.
Vl.
Vla.
V.
Vcl. Cont.

Tr.
(F)
Fl.
Ob.
Vl.
Vl.
Vla.
V.
Vcl.
Cont.

Tr.
(F)
Fl.
Ob.
Vl.
Vl.
Vla.
V.
Vcl.
Cont.

80
Tr.
(F)
Fl.
Ob.
Vl.
Vl.
Vla.
Vl.
Vcl.
Cont.

Tr.
(F)
Fl.
Ob.
Vl.
Vl.
Vla.
Vl.
Vcl.
Cont.

Tr. (F)
Fl.
Ob.
Vl.
Vl.
Vla.
V.
Vcl. Cont.

Tr. (F)
Fl.
Ob.
Vl.
Vl.
Vla.
V.
Vcl. Cont.

90
Tr. (F)
Fl.
Ob.
Vl.
Vl.
Vla.
V.
Vcl. Cont.

Tr. (F)
Fl.
Ob.
Vl.
Vl.
Vla.
V.
Vcl. Cont.

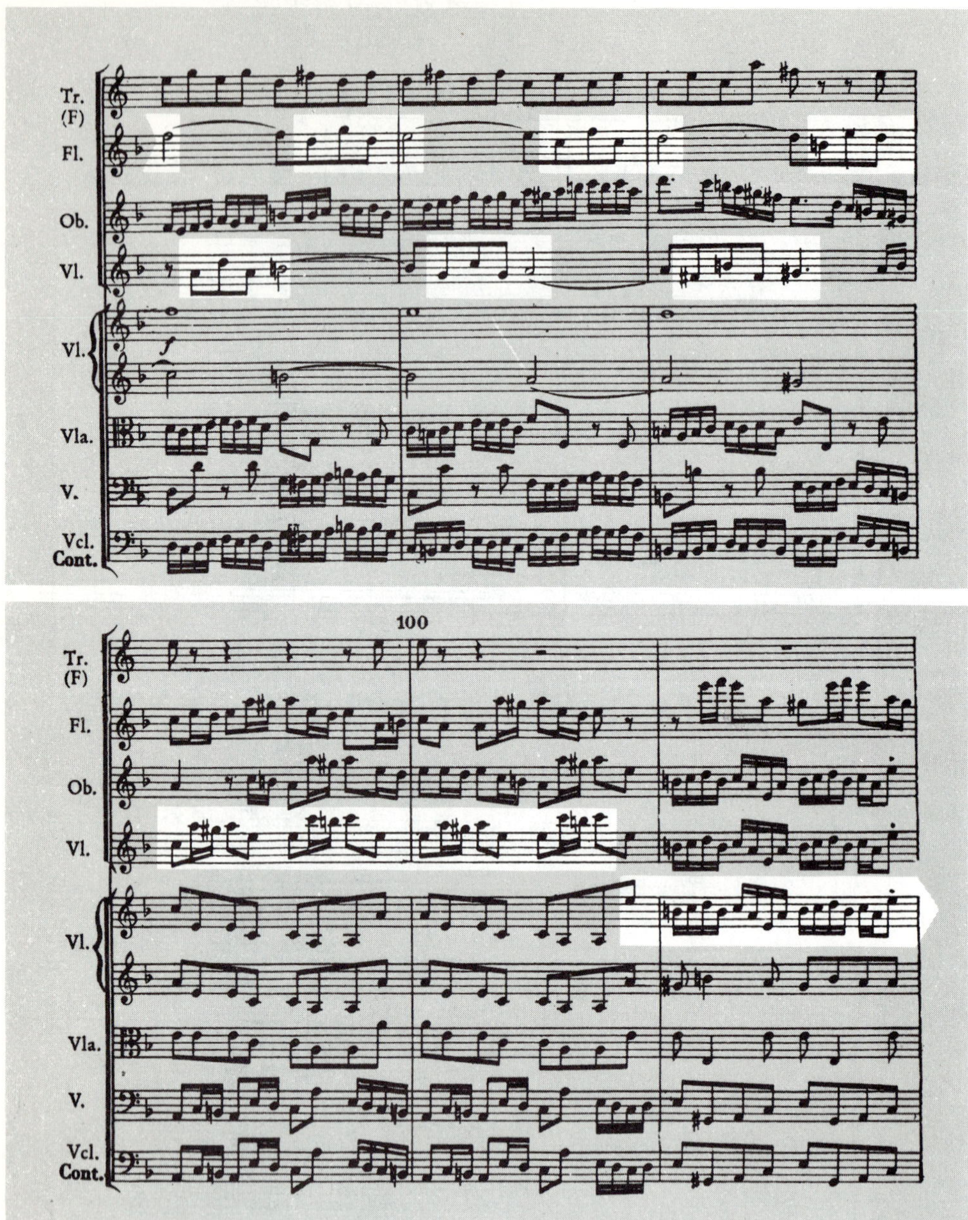
Tr. (F)
Fl.
Ob.
Vl.
Vl.
Vla.
V.
Vcl. Cont.
100

Tr.
(F)
Fl.
Ob.
Vl.
Vl.
Vla.
V.
Vcl.
Cont.
tasto solo
accomp.

Tr.
(F)
Fl.
Ob.
Vl.
Vl.
Vla.
V.
Vcl.
Cont.

110
Tr.
(F)
Fl.
Ob.
Vl.
Vl.
Vla.
V.
Vcl.
Cont.
Tr.
(F)
Fl.
Ob.
Vl.
Vl.
Vla.
V.
Vcl.
Cont.

Tr. (F)
Fl.
Ob.
Vl.
Vl.
Vla.
V.
Vcl. Cont.

Tr. (F)
Fl.
Ob.
Vl.
Vl.
Vla.
V.
Vcl. Cont.

25. Bach

The Well-Tempered Clavier, Book I, Prelude and Fugue in C minor (1722)

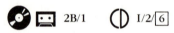

 2B/1 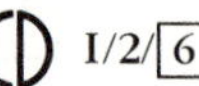

Presto.
Adagio.
Allegro.

26. Bach

Cantata No. 80, *Ein feste Burg ist unser Gott* (1724; revised before 1744)

  2B/2 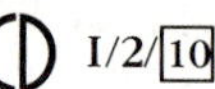

I

Tromba I in D

Tromba II III in D

Timpani in D-A

Oboe I II

Violino I

Violino II

Viola

Soprano

Alto

Tenore

Ein fe - - - - - - - ste Burg ist un - ser

Basso

(Manual)

Violoncello
ed Organo
Violone

(Pedal mit Posaune 16 Fuß)

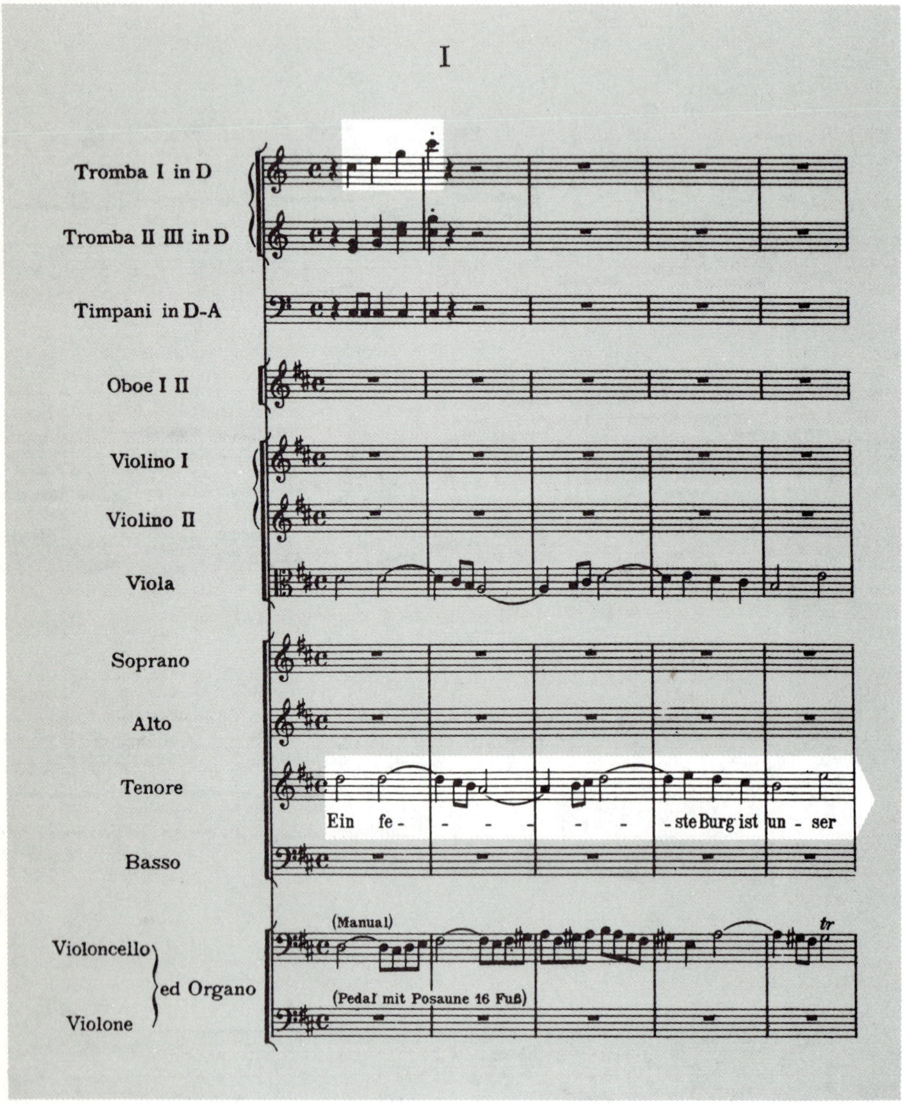

6
Vl. II
Vla.
A.
Ein fe - - - - - - - ste Burg ist un - ser
T.
Gott, ein gu - te Wehr und Waf - - - - - - -
Vc. ed Org.
11
Vl.
Vla.
S.
Ein fe - - - - - - - ste Burg ist un - ser
A.
Gott, ein gu - te Wehr und Waf - - - - - - -
T.
- - - - fen, ein gu - te Wehr und Waf - - -
Vc. ed Org.
16
Vl.
Vla.
S.
Gott, ein gu - te Wehr und Waf - - - - - - -
A.
- - - - fen, ein gu-te Wehr und Waf - -
T.
- - - - fen, ein fe - ste Burg ist un-ser
B.
Ein fe - - - - - - - ste Burg ist un - ser
Vc. ed Org.

(Melodie: „Ein feste Burg")
21
Tba. I
Tba. II III
Timp.
Ob. I II
zu 2
Vl.
Vla.
S.
- - - - - - - - fen, ein fe-ste Burg ist un-ser
A.
- fen, ein gu-te Wehr und Waf -
T.
Gott, ein gu - te Wehr und Waf - - - - - - - -
B.
Gott, ein gu - te Wehr und Waf - fen,
Vc. ed Org.
Vlne.

26
Tba.I
Tba.II III
Timp.
Ob.I II
Vl.
Vla.
S.
Gott, ein gu - te Wehr und Waf - - - - - - -
A.
- fen; ein fe - - - - - - - - - ste Burg ist
T.
- - fen, ein gu - te Wehr und Waf - -
B.
ein gu - te Wehr · und Waf - fen;
tr
Vc.
ed Org.
Vlne.

31
Tba. I
Tba. II III
Timp.
Vl.
Vla.
S.
A.
T.
Vc.
ed Org.
Vlne.
- fen; ein fe - - - - - - - ste Burg ist
un - ser Gott, ist un-ser Gott, ein gu - te Wehr und
- - - - - fen;
4 3

36
Tba. I
Tba. II III
Timp.
Vl.
S.
A.
B.
Vc.
ed Org.
un - ser Gott, ist un-ser Gott, ein gu - te Wehr und
Waf - - fen; ein fe-ste Burg, ein fe - ste Burg ist un -
ein fe - - - - - - - - - ste Burg ist

41
tr
Vl.
Vla.
S.
Waf - fen, ein gu - te Wehr und
A.
- ser Gott, ein gu-te Wehr
T.
ein fe - - - - - - - - ste Burg ist
B.
un - ser Gott, ein fe-ste Burg, ein fe - ste, fe-ste Burg
Vc.
ed Org.

46
Tba.I
Ob.I II
zu 2
tr
Vl.
Vla.
S.
Waf - fen, ein gu - te Wehr;
ein fe -
A.
und Waf-fen;
T.
un - ser Gott, ein fe - - - - - - ste Burg ist
B.
ist un - - - ser Gott, ein gu - te Wehr
Vc.
ed Org.
Vlne.
4
3
7 6 7

51
Tba. I
Ob. I II
Vl.
Vla.
S.
- - - - - - - ste Burg ist un - ser Gott,
A.
ein fe - - - - - - - ste Burg ist un - ser
T.
un - ser Gott, ein gu - te Wehr und Waf - fen, ein gu - te
B.
und Waf - fen, ein
Vc.
d Org.
Vlne.

56
Tba. I
Tba. II III
zu 2
Timp.
Vl.
Vla.
S.
ein gu-te Wehr und Waf - fen;
A.
Gott, ein gu - - te Wehr und Waf - fen;
T.
Wehr, ein gu-te Wehr und Waf - - - fen; er
B.
gu - te Wehr und Waf - - fen;
Vc. ed Org.
Vlne.
tr

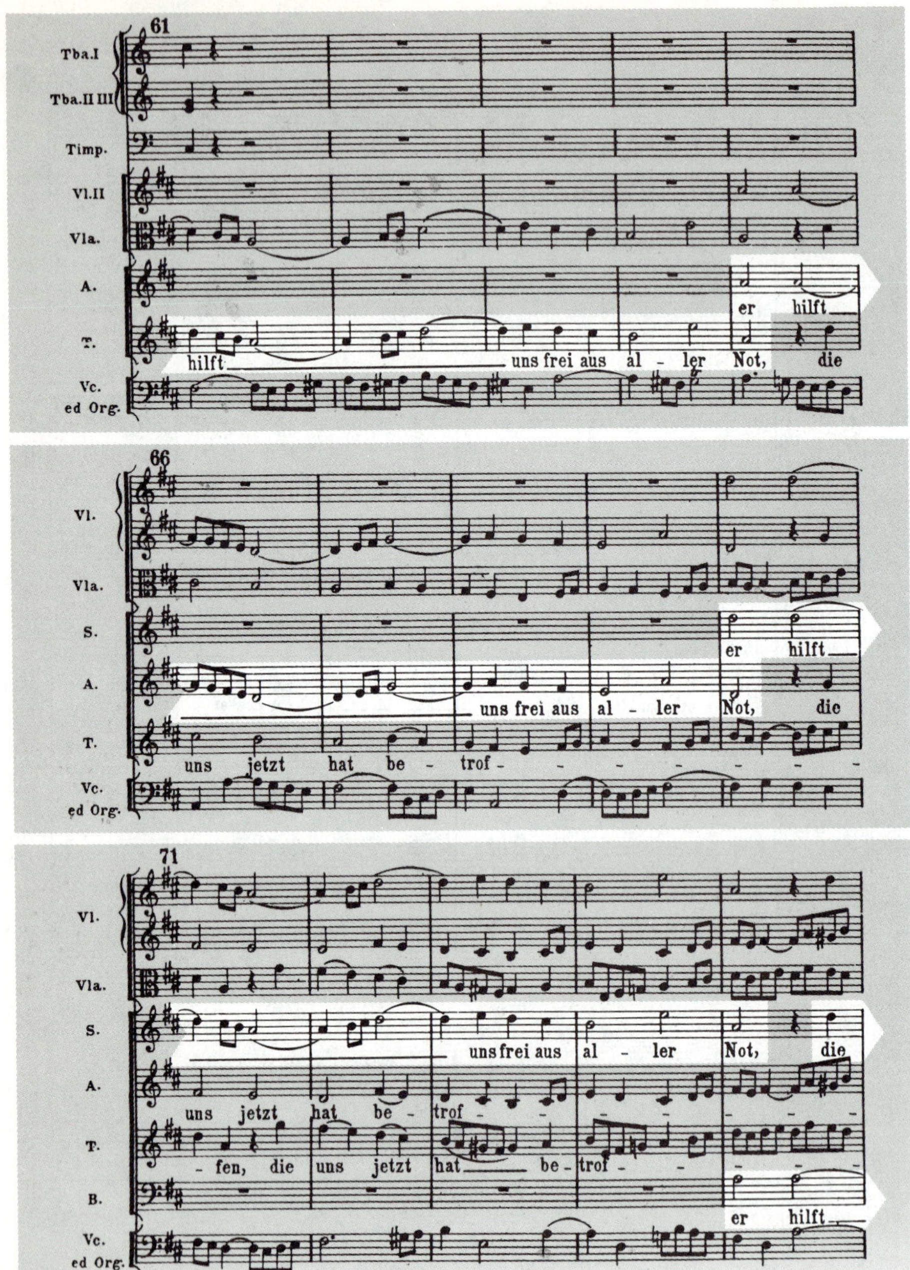
61
Tba.I
Tba.II III
Timp.
Vl.II
Vla.
A.
er hilft
T.
hilft uns frei aus al - ler Not, die
Vc. ed Org.
66
Vl.
Vla.
S.
er hilft
A.
uns frei aus al - ler Not, die
T.
uns jetzt hat be - trof -
Vc. ed Org.
71
Vl.
Vla.
S.
uns frei aus al - ler Not, die
A.
uns jetzt hat be - trof -
T.
- fen, die uns jetzt hat be - trof -
B.
er hilft
Vc. ed Org.

76
Vl.
Vla.
S.
uns jetzt hat be - trof - - - - - - - - -
A.
- fen, die uns jetzt hat be - trof - - - fen,
T.
- fen, er hilft uns frei aus al - ler Not, die uns
B.
uns frei aus al - ler Not, die
Vc. ed Org.
81
Tba. I
Tba. II III
Timp.
Ob. I II
zu 2
Vl.
Vla
S.
- - - fen, er hilft uns frei aus al - ler Not, aus
A.
die uns jetzt hat be - trof - fen, be - trof - - fen; er
T.
jetzt hat be - trof - - - - - fen,
B.
uns jetzt hat be - trof - - - - - fen, die uns jetzt
Vc. ed Org.
Vlne.

86
Tba.I
Tba.II III
Timp.
Ob. I II
Vl.
Vla.
S.
al - ler Not, die uns jetzt hat be - trof - - - - - - fen;
A.
hilft uns frei aus al - ler
T.
die uns jetzt hat be - trof - - - - -
B.
hat be - trof - - - - - - - - fen;
Vc.
ed Org.
Vlne.

91
Tba.I
Tba.II III
Timp.
Vl.
Vla.
S.
er hilft uns frei aus al - ler
A.
Not, aus al-ler Not, die uns jetzt hat be - trof - - -
T.
- fen;
Vc. ed Org.

96
Tba.I
Tba.II III
Timp.
Vl.
S.
Not, aus al-ler Not, die uns jetzt hat be - trof -
A.
fen, er hilft uns frei aus al - ler Not, aus al - - ler
B.
er hilft uns frei aus al - ler
Vc. ed Org.

101
Vl.
Vla.
S.
fen, die uns jetzt hat be - trof - -
A.
Not, die uns jetzt hat be - trof - - - - - - -
T.
er hilft uns frei aus al - ler
B.
Not, er hilft uns frei, er hilft uns frei aus al -
Vc.
ed Org.

106
Tba. I
Ob. I II
zu 2
Vl.
Vla.
S.
fen: er hilft uns frei aus al - ler Not, er hilft
A.
- - - - - fen er hilft
T.
Not, er hilft uns frei aus al - ler
B.
- - ler Not, die uns jetzt hat be - trof - - -
Vc.
ed Org.
Vlne.

111
Tba.I
Tba.II III
zu 2
Timp.
Ob.I II
Vl.
Vla.
S.
uns frei aus al - ler Not, dieunsjetzt
A.
uns frei aus al - ler Not, die uns
T.
Not, aus al - - - - - ler Not, aus al-ler Not,
B.
fen, die uns jetzt
Vc.
ed Org.
Vlne.

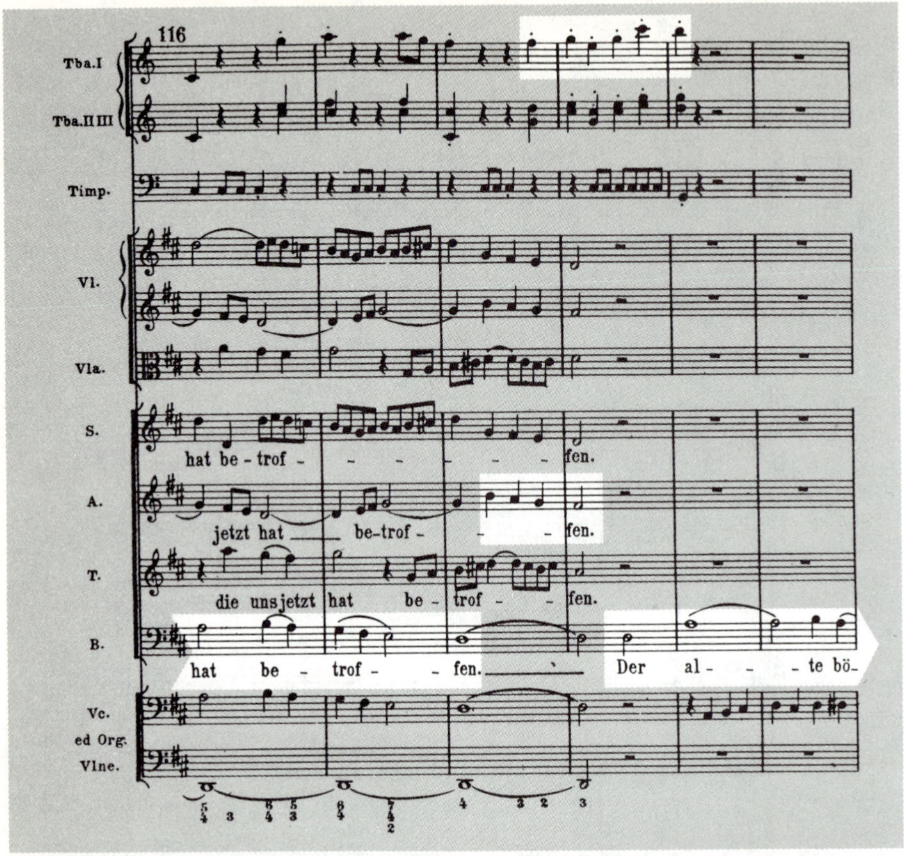

116
Tba.I
Tba.II III
Timp.
Vl.
Vla.
S.
hat be-trof - - - - - fen.
A.
jetzt hat be-trof - - - fen.
T.
die uns jetzt hat be - trof - - fen.
B.
hat be - trof - - fen. Der al - - - te bö-
Vc. ed Org.
Vlne.

199
Vl. II
Vla.
A.
Der
T.
Der al - - - te bö - - se Feind,
B.
- - se Feind, der al-te bö - se Feind, der
Vc. ed Org.

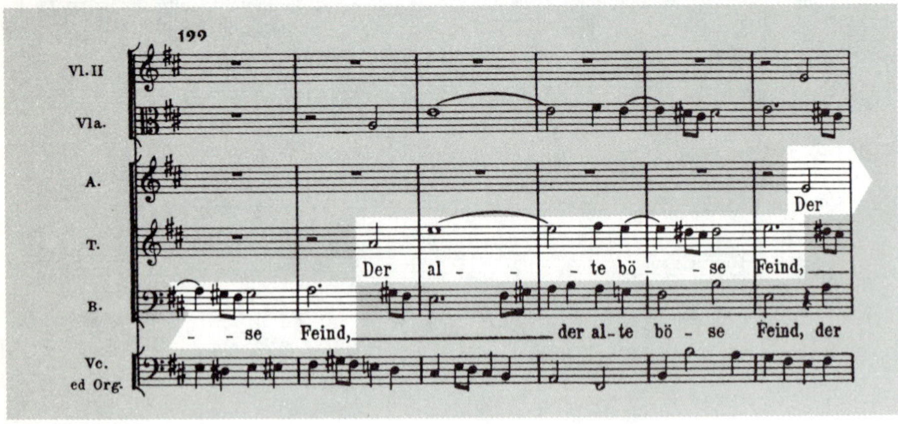

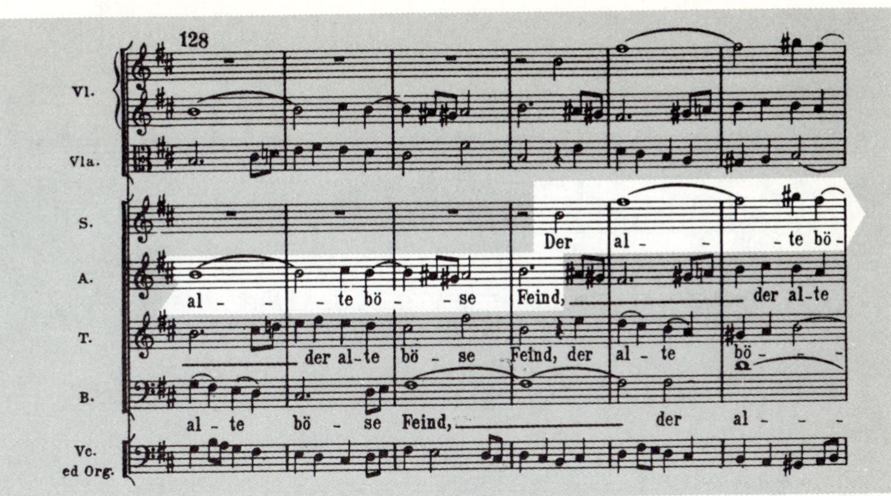
128
Vl.
Vla.
S.
Der al - - te bö-
A.
al - - te bö - se Feind, der al-te
T.
der al-te bö - se Feind, der al - te bö-
B.
al - te bö - se Feind, der al - - -
Vc. ed Org.

134
Tba. I
Tba. II III
zu 2
Timp.
Ob. I II
zu 2
Vl.
Vla.
S.
- se Feind, der al-te
A.
bö - se Feind, der al-te bö-se Feind, der al -
T.
- se Feind, der al - te bö-se Feind. der
B.
- te bö-se Feind, der al - te bö - se Feind. der al-te bö - se
Vc. ed Org.
Vlne.

139
Tba. I
Tba. II III
Timp.
Ob. I II
Vl.
Vla.
S.
bö-se Feind, der al - te bö - se Feind,
A.
- - te bö - - se Feind, mit
T.
al - - te bö - se, der al-te bö-se Feind,
B.
Feind, der al - - te bö-se Feind,
Vc.
ed Org.
Vlne.

144
Tba. I
Tba. II III
Timp.
Vl.
Vla.
S.
mit Ernst er's jetzt meint, mit Ernst
A.
Ernst er's jetzt meint, mit Ernst er's jetzt
T.
mit
Vc. ed Org.

150
Vl.
Vla.
S.
er's jetzt meint, mit Ernst er's jetzt
A.
meint, mit Ernst er's jetzt meint, mit Ernst
T.
Ernst er's jetzt meint, mit Ernst er's jetzt
B.
mit Ernst er's jetzt
Vc. ed Org.

155
Tba. I
Tba. II III
zu 2
Timp.
Ob. I II
zu 2
Vl.
Vla.
S.
meint, mit Ernst er's jetzt meint, mit
A.
er's jetzt meint, mit Ernst er's jetzt meint, mit Ernst er's jetzt meint,
T.
meint, mit Ernst er's jetzt meint, mit Ernst er's jetzt meint, mit Ernst
B.
meint, mit Ernst er's jetzt meint, mit Ernst er's jetzt
Vc. ed Org.
Vlne.

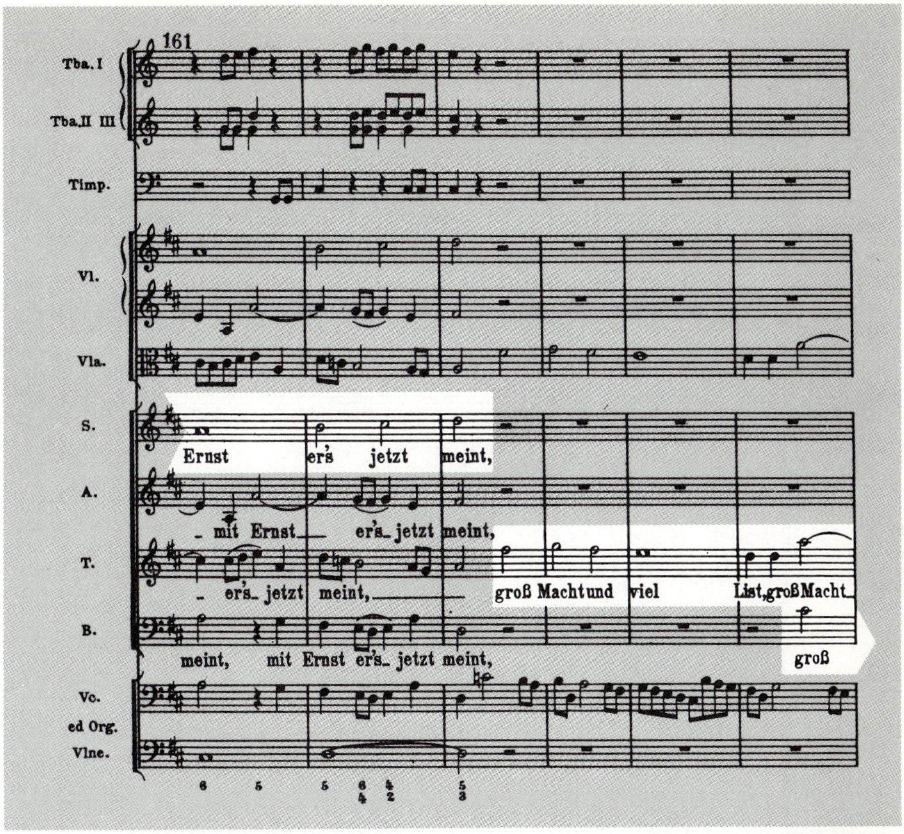

161
Tba. I
Tba. II III
Timp.
Vl.
Vla.
S.
Ernst er's jetzt meint,
A.
mit Ernst er's jetzt meint,
T.
er's jetzt meint, groß Macht und viel List, groß Macht
B.
meint, mit Ernst er's jetzt meint, groß
Vc. ed Org.
Vlne.
6 5 5 6 4 4 2 5 3

172
Tba. I
Tba. II III
zu 2
Timp.
Ob. I II
zu 2
Vl.
Vla.
S.
groß Macht und viel List, groß Macht
A.
List, groß Macht und viel List, groß Macht
T.
viel List, groß Macht und viel List, groß Macht und
B.
und viel List, groß Macht
Vc. ed Org.
Vlne.
6

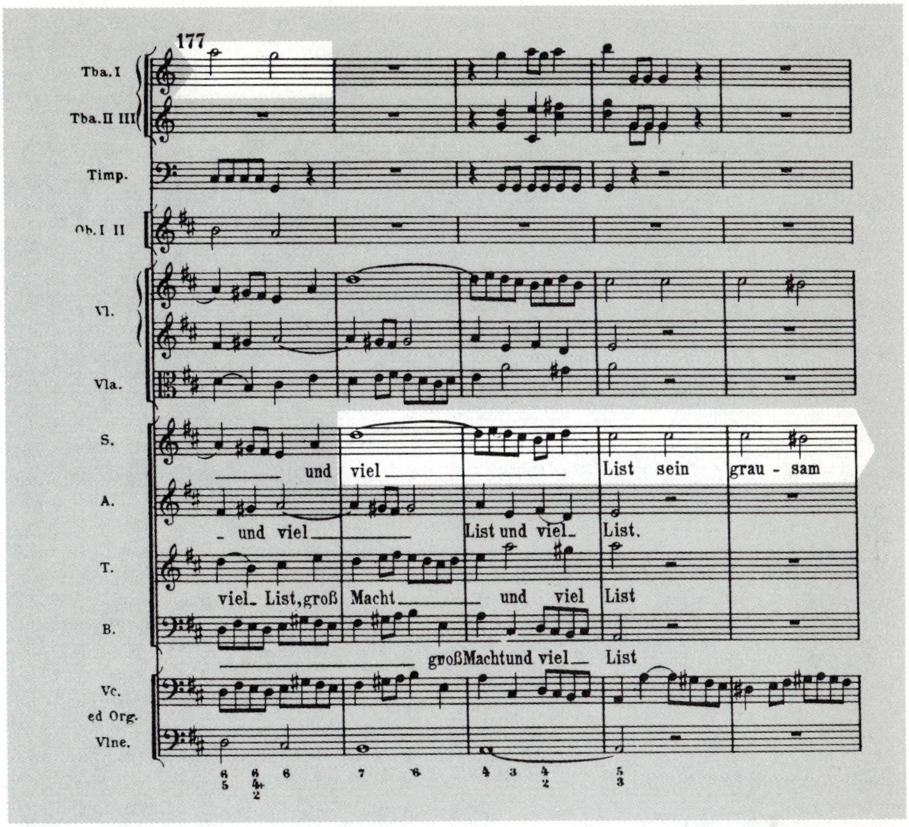

177
Tba. I
Tba. II III
Timp.
Ob. I II
Vl.
Vla.
S.
und viel List sein grau - sam
A.
- und viel List und viel List.
T.
viel List, groß Macht und viel List
B.
großMachtund viel List
Vc. ed Org.
Vlne.
6 5 6 4+ 2 6 7 6 4 3 4 2 5 3

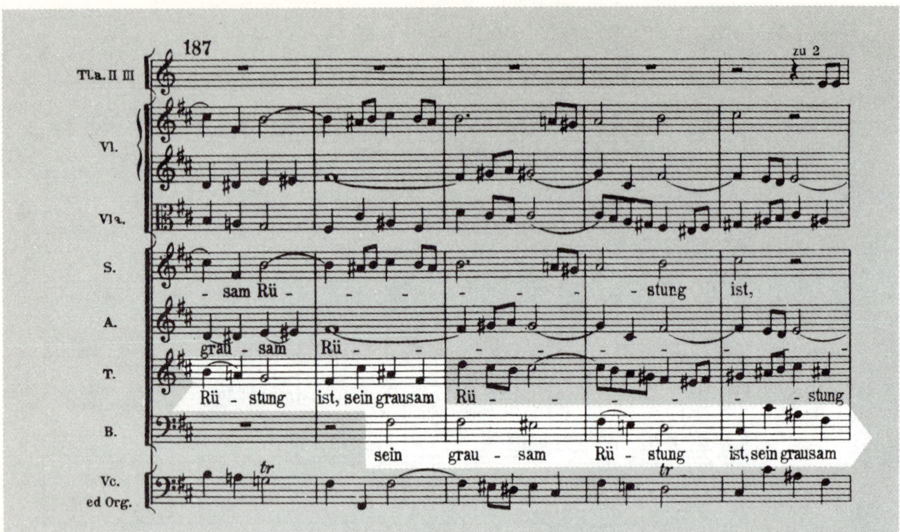
187
Tba. II III
zu 2
Vl.
Vla.
S.
- sam Rü - - - - - - stung ist,
A.
grau - sam Rü -
T.
Rü - stung ist, sein grausam Rü - - - - stung
B.
sein grau - sam Rü - stung ist, sein grausam
Vc.
ed Org.
tr

192
Tba. I
Tba. II III
zu 2
Ob. I II
Vl.
Vla.
S.
sein grau - sam Rü - stung,
A.
- stung ist, sein grau - - sam Rü - stung ist, sein
T.
ist, sein grau - sam Rü - stung ist, sein grau-sam
B.
Rü - stung ist, sein grau-sam Rü - stung ist,
Vc.
ed Org.
Vlne.

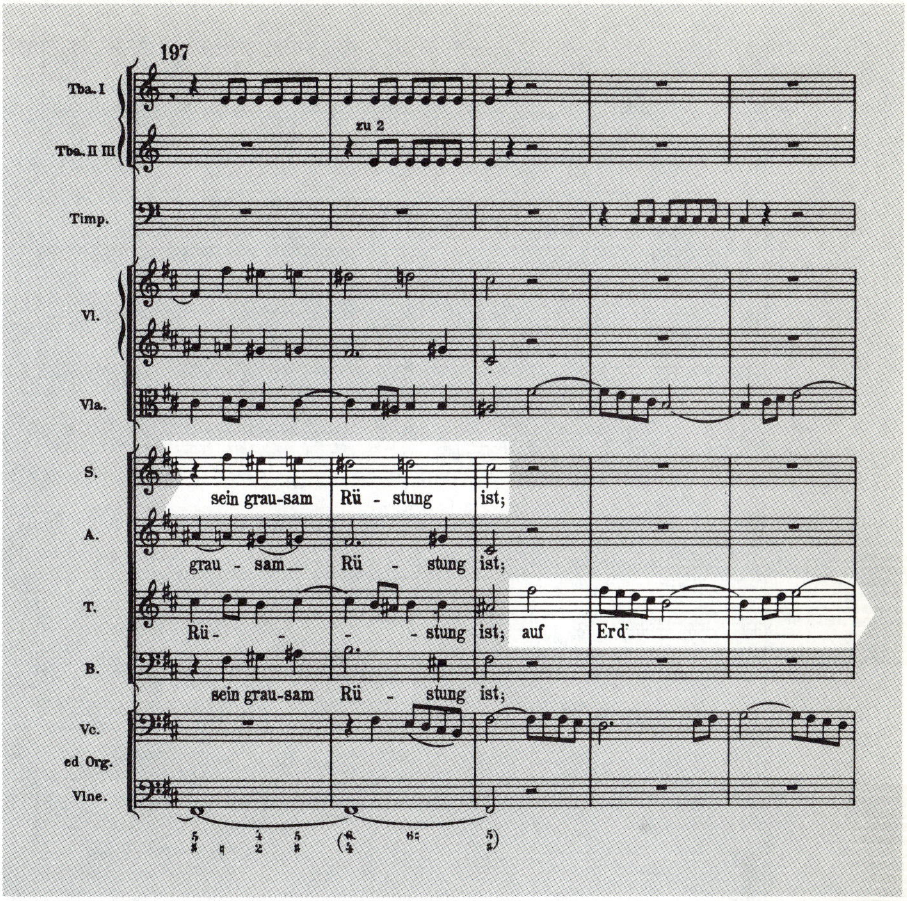

197
Tba. I
Tba. II III
zu 2
Timp.
Vl.
Vla.
S.
sein grau-sam Rü - stung ist;
A.
grau - sam Rü - stung ist;
T.
Rü- - - stung ist; auf Erd'
B.
sein grau-sam Rü - stung ist;
Vc.
ed Org.
Vlne.

202
Vla.
T.
ist nicht seins - glei - chen, ist nicht seins - glei - - chen. nicht seins-
B.
auf Erd' ist nicht seins-
Vc.
ed Org.

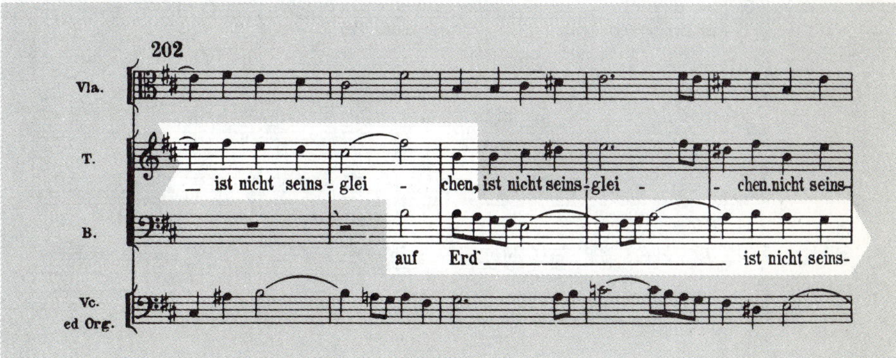

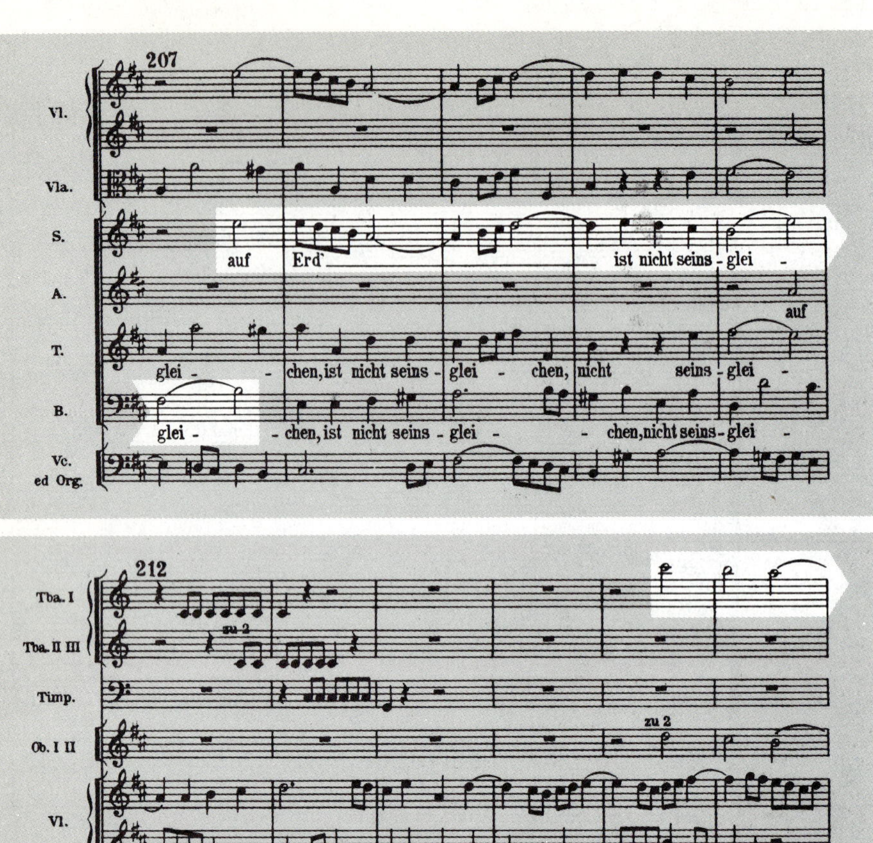
207
Vl.
Vla.
S.
auf Erd' ist nicht seins - glei -
A.
auf
T.
glei - chen, ist nicht seins - glei - chen, nicht seins - glei -
B.
glei - chen, ist nicht seins - glei - chen, nicht seins - glei -
Vc. ed Org.
212
Tba. I
Tba. II III
zu 2
Timp.
Ob. I II
zu 2
Vl.
Vla.
S.
chen, ist nicht seins-glei - chen, nicht seins-glei - - - -
A.
Erd' ist nicht seins-glei - - - chen,
T.
chen, auf Erd'
B.
chen, ist nicht seins-glei - chen, nicht, ist nicht seinsglei - chen, ist nicht seins-
Vc. ed Org.
Vlne.

218
Tba. I
Ob. I II
Vl.
Vla.
S.
- chen, auf Erd' ist nicht seins - glei - -
A.
auf Erd' ist nicht seins-
T.
— ist nicht seins - glei - chen, seins - glei - - - -
B.
glei - - - - chen,
Vc.
ed Org.
Vlne.

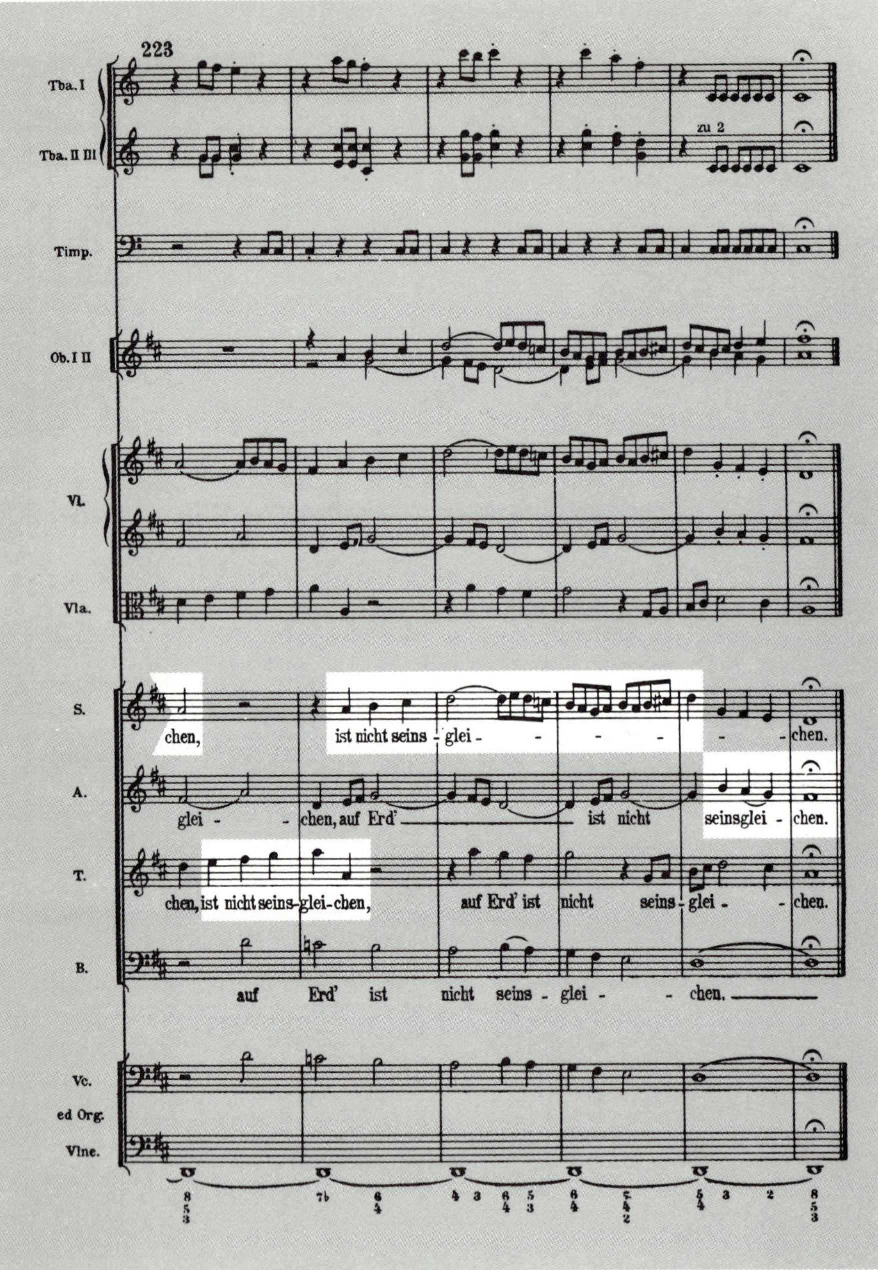
223
Tba. I
Tba. II III
zu 2
Timp.
Ob. I II
Vl.
Vla.
S.
chen, ist nicht seins - glei - - - - - chen.
A.
glei - chen, auf Erd' ist nicht seinsglei - chen.
T.
chen, ist nicht seins- glei- chen, auf Erd' ist nicht seins - glei - chen.
B.
auf Erd' ist nicht seins - glei - - chen.
Vc.
ed Org.
Vlne.

II
Oboe
Violino I II e Viola
in unisono
Soprano
Basso
Continuo
3
Vl.
e Vla.
Cont.
6
Vl.
e Vla.
Cont.
9
Ob.
Vl.
e Vla.
S.
B.
Cont.
Mit uns - rer Macht
Al - - - - - - - les, al - - -

12
tr
Ob.
Vl.
e Vla.
S.
— ist nichts ge - tan,
B
- - -les, was von Gott ge - bo - ren, al - les, was von Gott ge -
Cont.

14
Ob.
Vl.
e Vla.
S.
wir
B.
bo - ren, ist zum Sie - gen aus - er - ko - - - - -
Cont.

16
Ob.
Vl.
e Vla.
S.
sind gar bald ver - lo - - - - - -
B.
- - - - - - ren, zum Sie - gen aus - er-ko -
Cont.

18
Ob.
Vl. e Vla.
S.
ren.
B.
ren, ist zum Sie-gen aus-er-ko
Cont.
20
ren, zum Sie-gen
23
Es streit für uns der rech-
aus-erko-ren.
Al les, al
26
tr
te, der rech te Mann,
les, was von Gott ge-bo-ren, al-les, was von Gott ge-

28
Ob.
Vl. e Vla.
S.
den
B.
bo - ren, ist zum Sie - gen aus - er - ko - - - - - - - -
Cont.

30
Ob.
Vl. e Vla.
S.
Gott selbst hat er - ko - - - - - - - - - -
B.
- - - - - - - - - - ren, zum Sie - gen aus - er - ko - -
Cont.

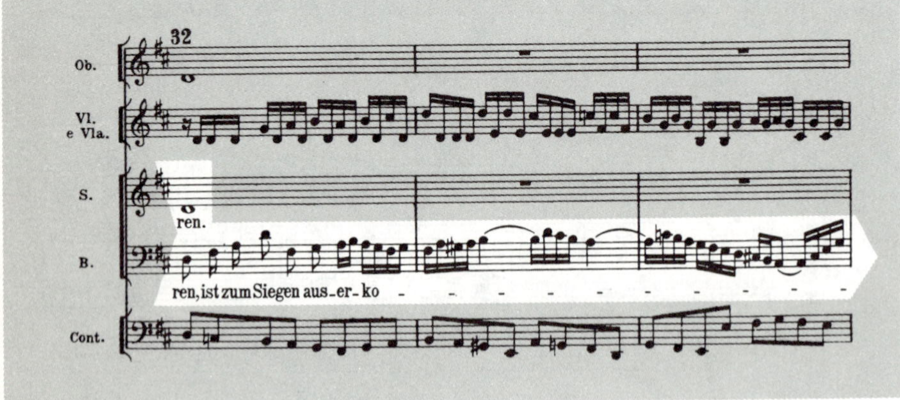
32
Ob.
Vl. e Vla.
S.
ren.
B.
ren, ist zum Siegen aus - er - ko - - - - - - - - - - - -
Cont.

35
Ob.
Vl. e Vla.
S.
B.
Cont.
Fragst
- - - - - - - - ren, zum Sie-gen aus-er-ko-ren.
38
tr
du, wer er ist?
Wer bei Chri-sti Blut-pa-nier, bei Chri-sti Blut- -
Cont
41
- - pa-nier in der Tau-fe Treu ge-schwo-ren, in der Tau-
44
Er heißt Je - sus
- fe, in der Tau - fe Treu ge - schwo - - - - - - -

46
Ob.
Vl. e Vla.
S.
Christ,
B.
- ren, in der Tau - fe Treu ge - schwo - ren. siegt im Gei - ste für und
Cont.

48
Ob.
tr
Vl. e Vla.
S.
der Her - re Ze - ba -
B.
für, siegt im Gei - - - - ste für und
Cont.

50
Ob.
Vl. e Vla.
S.
oth,
B.
für, siegt im Gei - ste für und für. Wer bei Chri - sti
Cont.

53
Ob.
Vl. e Vla.
S.
B.
Cont.
tr
und ist kein and - rer
Blut - pa - nier, bei Chri - sti Blut - pa - nier in der Tau - fe Treu ge -
56
Gott,
schwo-ren, Treu ge-schworen, siegt im Gei-ste für und für, siegt im Gei - -
59
- ste für und für.
62
das Feld muß
Al - - les, was von Gott ge -

65
Ob.
Vl. e Vla.
S.
B.
Cont.
er be - hal - - - -
bo-ren, al-les, was von Gott ge-bo-ren, ist zum Siegen auser-ko - - - -
68
ten.
ren, zum Sie-gen aus-er-ko - ren.
71
74

III
Basso
Er - wä - ge doch, Kind Got - tes, die so gro - ße Lie - be, da
Continuo
B.
Je - sus sich mit sei - nem Blu - te dir ver - schrie - be, wo -
Cont.
B.
mit er dich zum Krie - ge wi - der Sa - tans Heer und wi - der Welt und Sün - de ge -
Cont.
B.
wor - ben hat. Gib nicht in dei - ner See - le dem
Cont.
B.
Sa - tan und den La - stern statt! Laß nicht dein Herz, den Him - mel Got - tes auf der
Cont.

11
B.
Er-den, zur Wü - ste wer-den! Be-reu-e dei-ne Schuld mit Schmerz, daß
Cont.
14 Arioso
B.
Chri-sti Geist mit dir sich fest ver-bin - - de, daß
Cont.
17
B.
Chri-sti Geist mit dir sich fest ver-bin - - - de, mit
Cont.
20
B.
dir sich fest ver-bin - - - de, sich fest ver-bin -
Cont.
23
B.
de.
Cont.

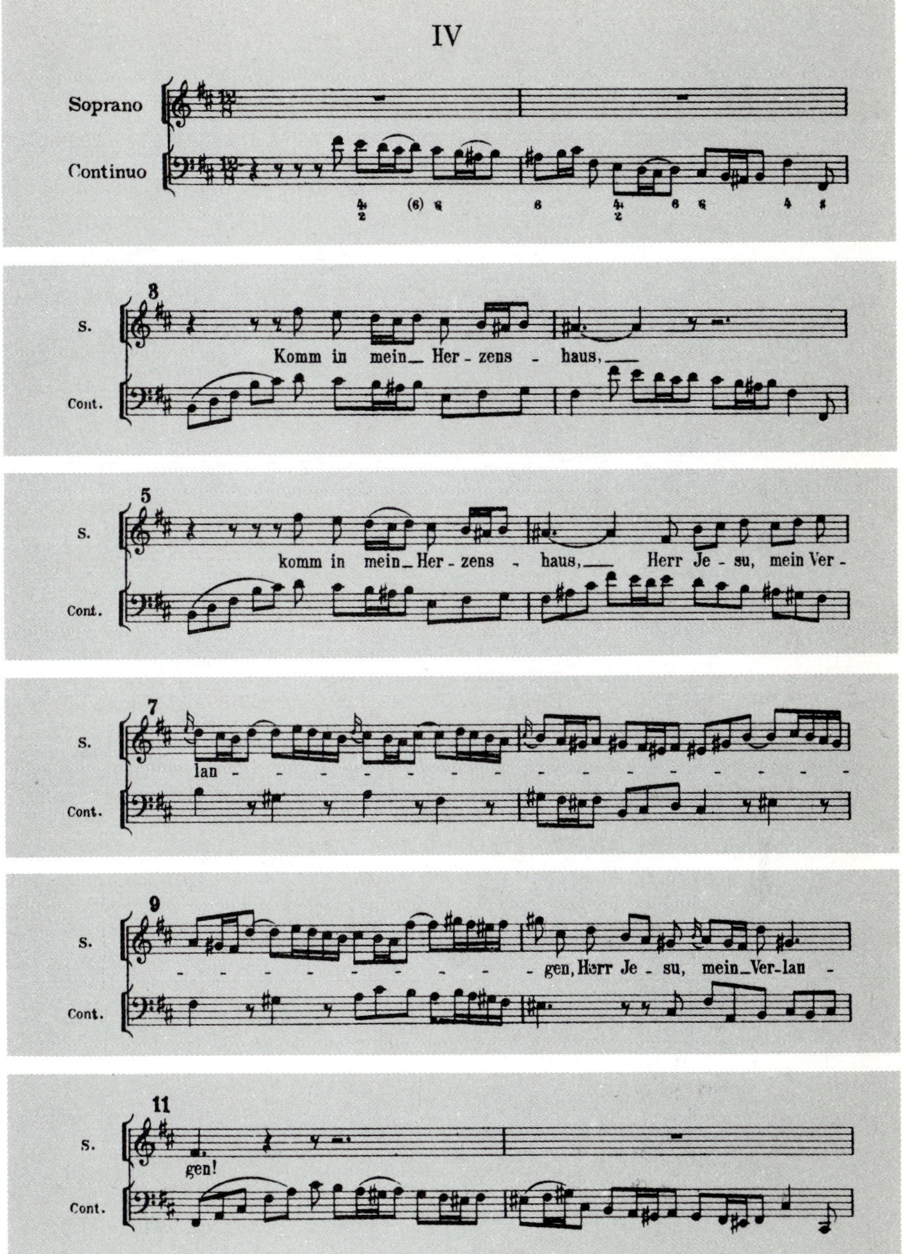
IV
Soprano
Continuo
S.
Cont.
Komm in mein_ Her-zens - haus,__
komm in mein_ Her-zens - haus,__ Herr Je - su, mein Ver -
lan - - - - - - - - - - - - - - - - -
- - - - - - - - - - - - gen, Herr Je - su, mein_ Ver-lan -
gen!

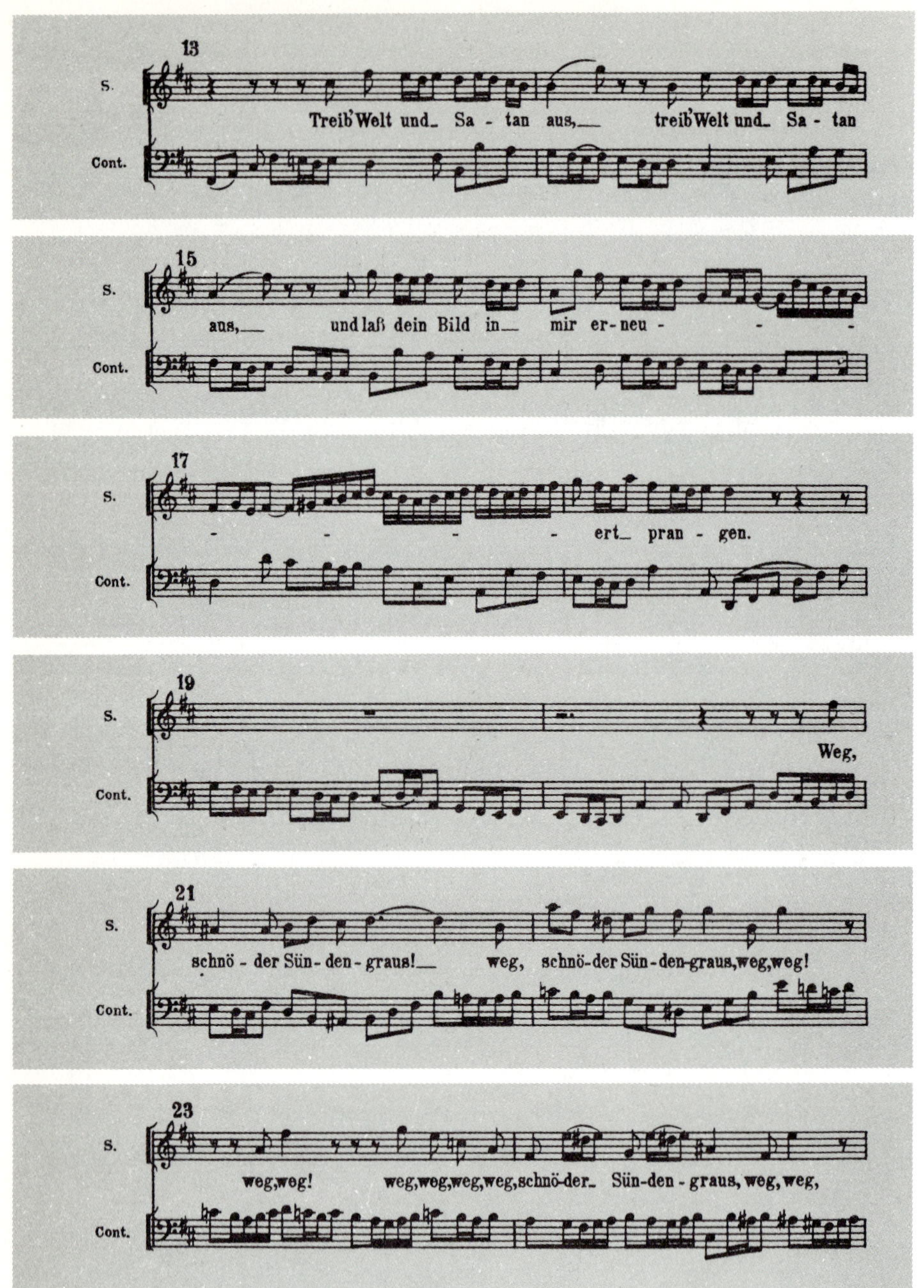
13
S.
Treib' Welt und Sa - tan aus, treib' Welt und Sa - tan
Cont.
15
S.
aus, und laß dein Bild in mir er-neu - - -
Cont.
17
S.
- - - - ert pran - gen.
Cont.
19
S.
Weg,
Cont.
21
S.
schnö - der Sün-den-graus! weg, schnö-der Sün-den-graus, weg, weg!
Cont.
23
S.
weg, weg! weg, weg, weg, weg, schnö-der Sün-den - graus, weg, weg,
Cont.

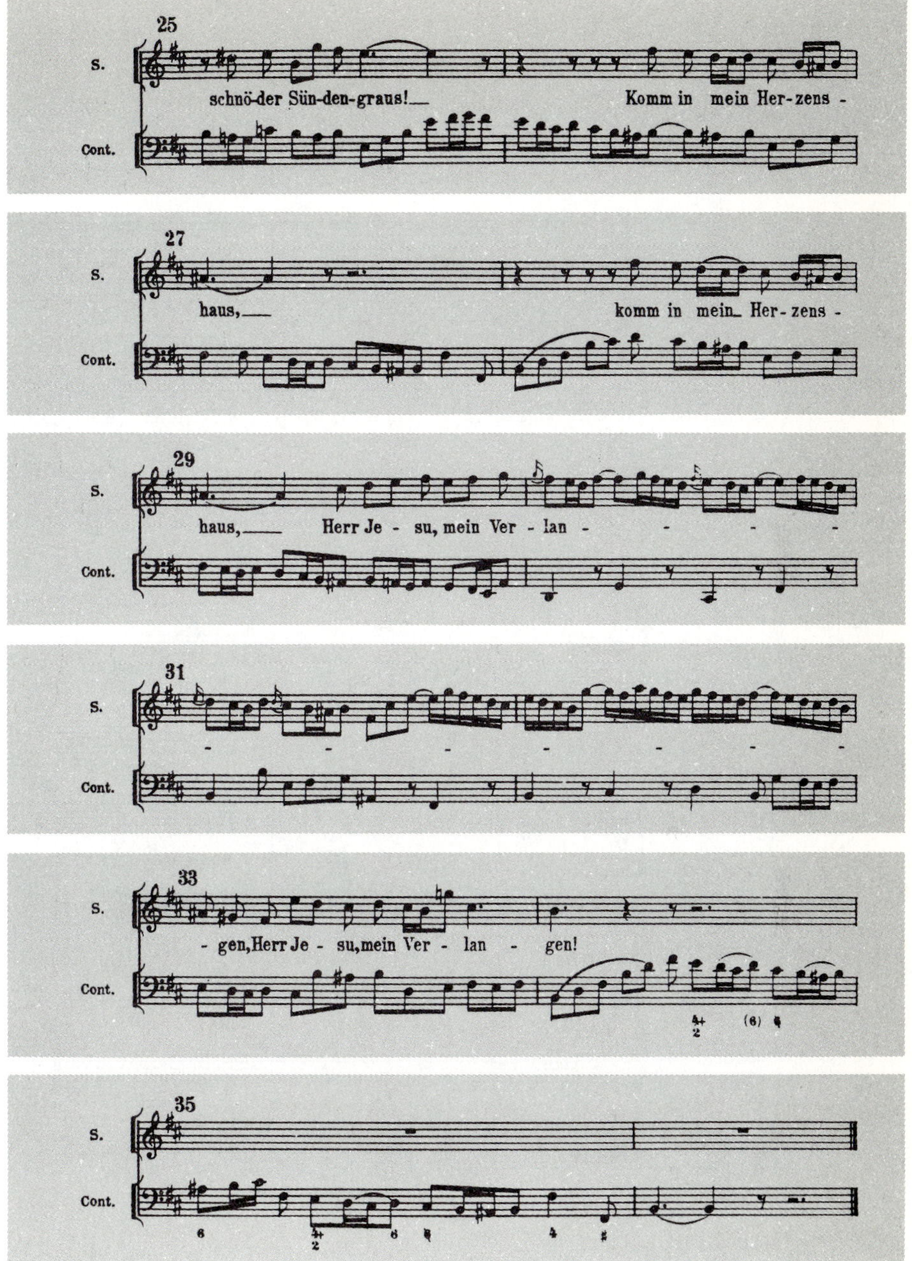
25
S.
schnö-der Sün-den-graus!
Komm in mein Her-zens-
Cont.
27
S.
haus,
komm in mein Her-zens-
Cont.
29
S.
haus, Herr Je-su, mein Ver-lan-
Cont.
31
S.
Cont.
33
S.
-gen, Herr Je-su, mein Ver-lan-gen!
Cont.
35
S.
Cont.

V
Tromba I in D
Tromba II III in D
Timpani in D-A
Oboe d'amore I
Oboe d'amore II
Taille
Violino I
Violino II
Viola
Soprano e Alto
Tenore e Basso
Continuo

4
Tba. I
Tba. II III
Timp.
Ob. d'am. I
Ob. dam. II
Tle.
Vl.
Vla.
Cont.

7
Tba. I
Tba. II III
2
Timp.
Ob. d'am. I
Ob. d'am. II
Tle.
Vl.
Vla.
Cont.

10
Tba. I
Tba. II III
Timp.
Ob. d'am. I
Ob. d'am. II
Tle.
Vl.
Vla.
S. e A.
Und
T. e B.
Cont.

14
Ob. d'am. I
Ob. d'am. II
Tle.
Vl.
Vla.
S. e A.
wenn die Welt voll Teu - fel wär,
T. e B.
Cont.

18
Tba. I
2.
Tba. II III
Ob. d'am. I
Ob. d'am. II
Tle.
Vl.
Vla.
Cont.

21
Tba. I
Tba. II III
Timp.
Ob. d'am. I
Ob. d'am. II
Tle.
Vl.
Vla.
S. e A.
und
woll - ten
[wollt uns
T. e B.
Cont.

24
Tba. I
Tba. II III
Timp.
Ob. d'am. I
Ob. d'am. II
Tle.
Vl.
Vla.
S. e A.
uns ver - schlin - gen,
gar]
T. e B.
Cont.

29
Tba. I
Tba. II III
Timp.
Ob. d'am. I
Ob. d'am. II
Tle.
Vl.
Vla.
Cont.

33
Tba. I
Tba. II III
Timp.
Ob. d'am. I
Ob. d'am. II
Tle.
Vl.
Vla.
Cont.

36
Tba. I
Tba. II III
Timp.
Ob. d'am. I
Ob. d'am. II
Tle.
Vl.
Vla.
Cont.
tr

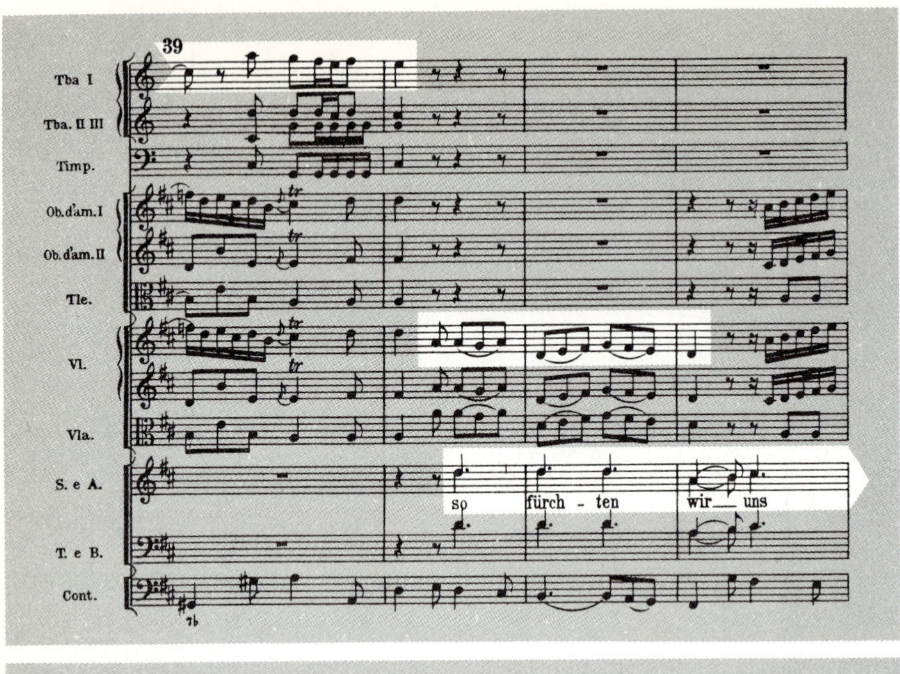
39
Tba I
Tba. II III
Timp.
Ob.d'am. I
Ob.d'am. II
Tle.
Vl.
Vla.
S. e A.
so fürch - ten wir uns
T. e B.
Cont.
7♭

43
Tba. I
Tba. II III
Ob.d'am. I
Ob.d'am. II
Tle.
Vl.
Vla.
S. e A.
nicht so sehr,
T. e B.
Cont.

46
Tba. I
Tba. II III
Ob.d'am.I
Ob.d'am.II
Tle.
Vl.
Vla.
Cont.
tr

49
Tba.I
Tba. II III
Timp.
Ob.d'am.I
Ob.d'am.II
Tle.
Vl.
Vla.
S. e A.
es soll uns doch ge - lin - -
T. e B.
Cont.

53
Tba. I
Tba. II III
2.
Timp.
Ob. d'am. I
Ob. d'am. II
Tle.
Vl.
Vla.
S. e A.
gen.
T. e B.
Cont.
57
Tba. I
Tba. II III
Timp.
Ob. d'am. I
Ob. d'am. II
Tle.
Vl.
Vla.
Cont.

60
Tba. I
2.
Tba. II III
zu 2
Timp.
Ob. d'am. I
Ob. d'am. II
Tle.
Vl.
Vla.
Cont.

63
Tba. I
tr
Tba. II III
Timp.
Ob. d'am. I
tr
Ob. d'am. II
Tle.
Vl.
tr
Vla.
S. e A.
Der
Fürst
die -
T. e B.
Cont.

67
Tba. I
Tba. II III
Timp.
Ob.d'am. I
Ob.d'am. II
Tle.
Vl.
Vla.
S. e A.
- - ser Welt,
T. e B.
Cont.
70
Tba. I
Tba. II III
Timp.
Ob.d'am. I
Ob.d'am. II
Tle.
Vl.
Vla.
Cont.

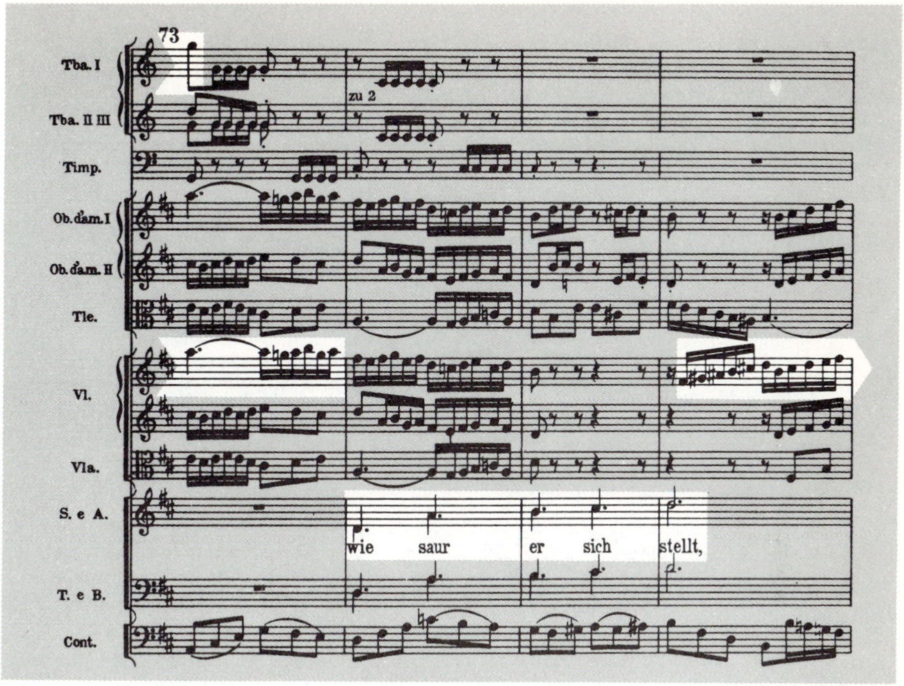

73
Tba. I
Tba. II III
zu 2
Timp.
Ob. d'am. I
Ob. d'am. II
Tle.
Vl.
Vla.
S. e A.
wie saur er sich stellt,
T. e B.
Cont.

77
Tba. I
Tba. II III
2.
Timp.
Ob. d'am. I
Ob. d'am. II
Tle.
Vl.
Vla.
Cont.

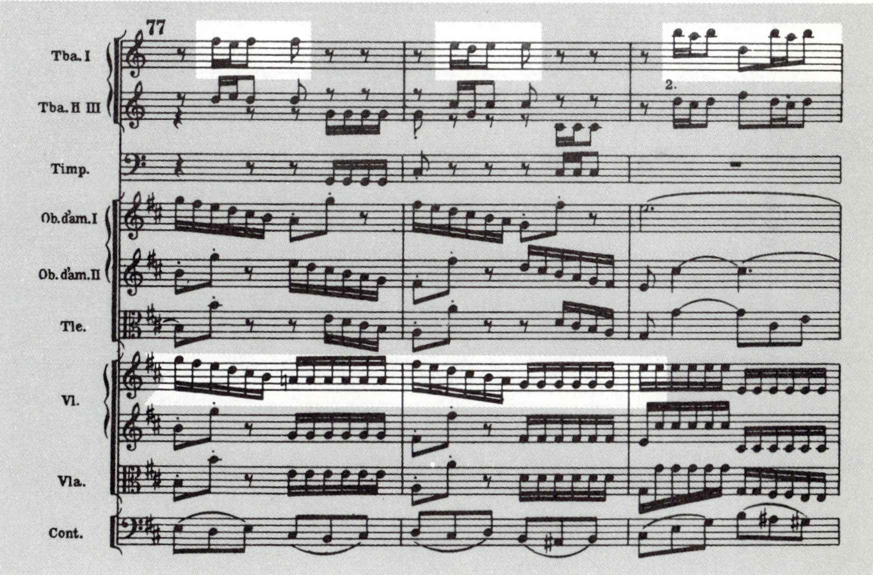

80
tr
Tba. I
2.
zu 2
Tba. II III
Ob. d'am. I
Ob. d'am. II
Tle.
Vl.
Vla.
S. e A.
tut
T. e B.
Cont.
83
Tba. I
Tba. II III
Ob. d'am. I
Ob. d'am. II
Tle.
Vl.
Vla.
S. e A.
er uns doch nicht,
T. e B.
Cont.

87
Tba. I
Ob.d'am.I
Ob.d'am.II
Tle.
Vl.
Vla.
Cont.

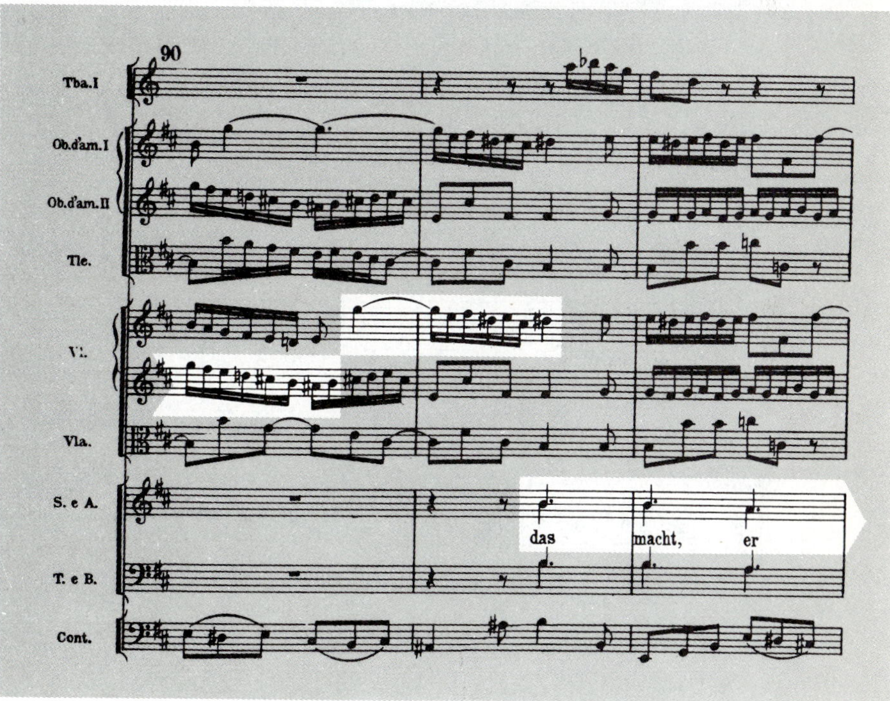
90
Tba.I
Ob.d'am.I
Ob.d'am.II
Tle.
Vl.
Vla.
S. e A.
das
macht,
er
T. e B.
Cont.

93
Tba. I
Ob. d'am. I
Ob. d'am. II
Tle.
Vl.
Vla.
S. e A.
ist ge - richt't;
T. e B.
Cont.

96
Tba. I
Tba. II III
Timp.
Ob. d'am. I
Ob. d'am. II
Tle.
Vl.
Vla.
Cont.

99
Ob.d'am.I
Ob.d'am.II
Tle.
Vl.
Vla.
S.e A.
T.e B.
Cont.
ein Wört - lein

103
Tba.I
Tba.II III
zu 2
Timp.
Ob.d'am.I
Ob.d'am.II
Tle.
Vl.
Vla.
S.e A.
T.e B.
Cont.
kann ihn fäl - - - len.

106
Tba. I
Tba. II III
Timp.
Ob.d'am.I
Ob.d'am.II
Tle.
Vl.
Vla.
S.e A.
T.e B.
Cont.
110
Tba. I
Tba. II III
Timp.
Ob.d'am.I
Ob.d'am.II
Tle.
Vl.
Vla.
Cont.

113
Tba. I
Tba. II III
Timp.
Ob.d'am.I
Ob.d'am.II
Tle.
Vl.
Vla.
Cont.

116
Tba. I
Tba. II III
Timp.
Ob.d'am.I
Ob.d'am.II
Tle.
Vl.
Vla.
Cont.

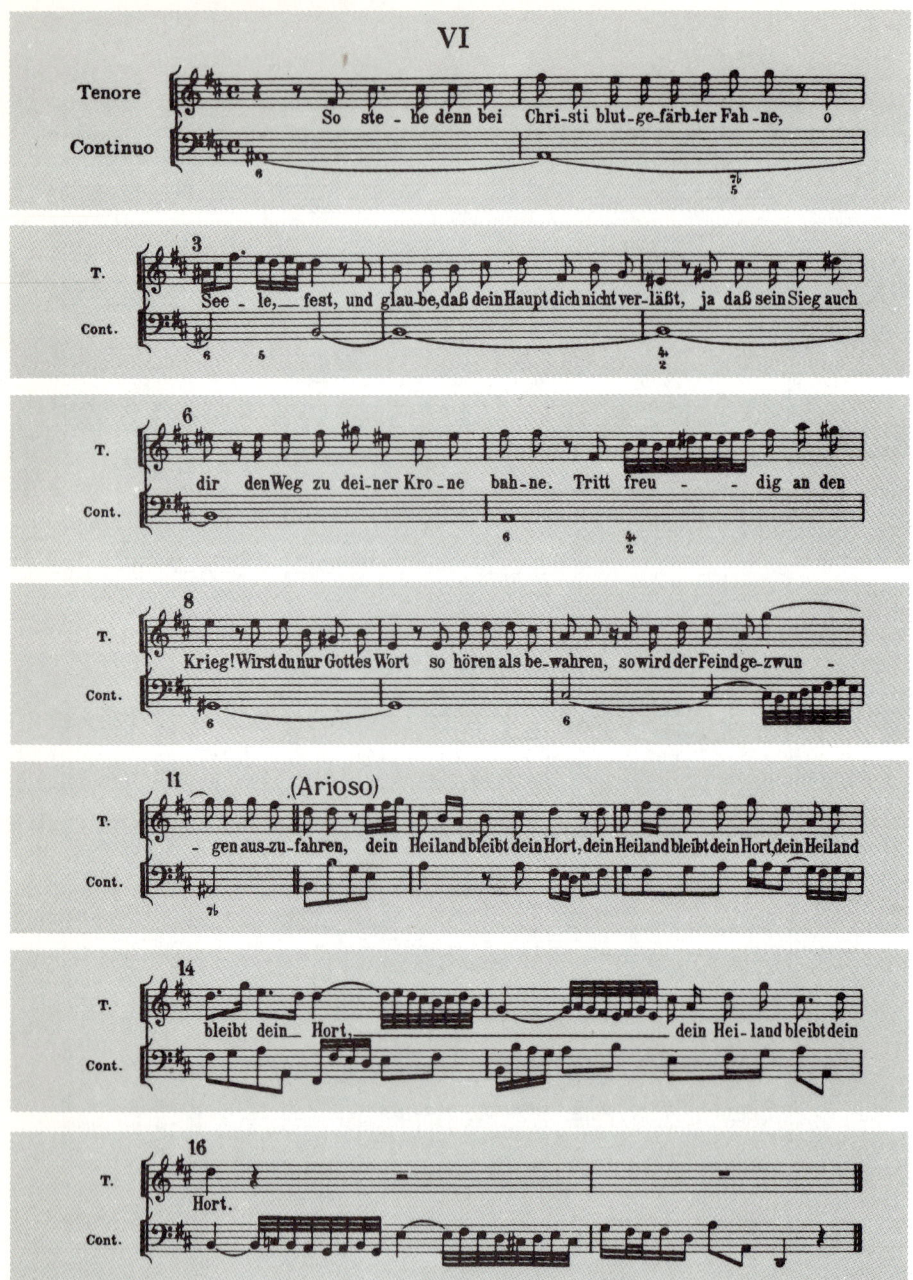
VI
Tenore
Continuo
So ste - he denn bei Chri-sti blut-ge-färb-ter Fah-ne, o
T.
Cont.
See - le, fest, und glau-be, daß dein Haupt dich nicht ver-läßt, ja daß sein Sieg auch
dir den Weg zu dei-ner Kro-ne bah-ne. Tritt freu - dig an den
Krieg! Wirst du nur Gottes Wort so hören als be-wahren, so wird der Feind ge-zwun -
(Arioso)
- gen aus-zu-fahren, dein Heiland bleibt dein Hort, dein Heiland bleibt dein Hort, dein Heiland
bleibt dein Hort, dein Hei-land bleibt dein
Hort.

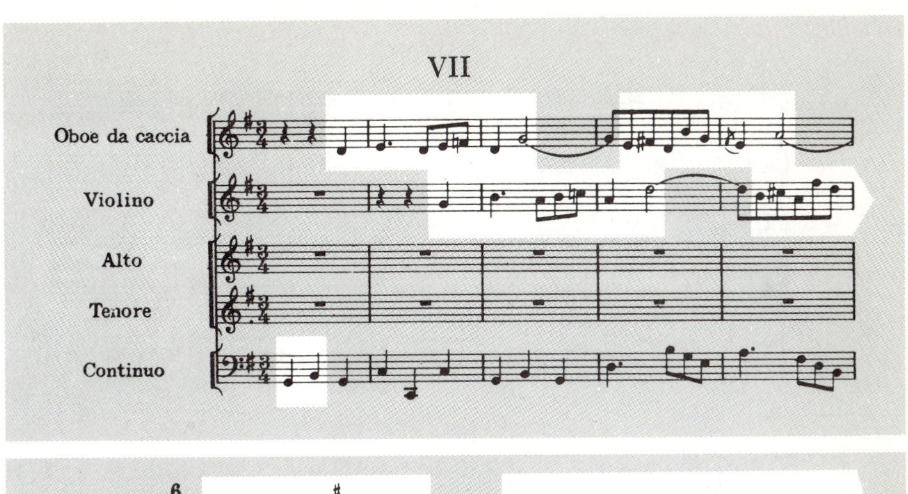
VII
Oboe da caccia
Violino
Alto
Tenore
Continuo

6
Ob.d.c.
Vl.
Cont.
tr

9
Ob.d.c.
Vl.
Cont.

13
Ob.d.c.
Vl.
Cont.
tr

17
Ob.d.c.
Vl.
A.
Wie se - lig sind doch die,
wie se - lig sind doch
T.
Wie se - lig sind doch die,
wie
Cont.

23
Ob.d.c.
Vl.
A.
die, die Gott im Mun - de tra - - - - -
T.
se - lig sind doch die, die Gott im Mun - de
Cont.

26
Ob.d.c.
Vl.
A.
T.
tra -
Cont.

29
Ob. d. c.
Vl.
A.
T.
Cont.

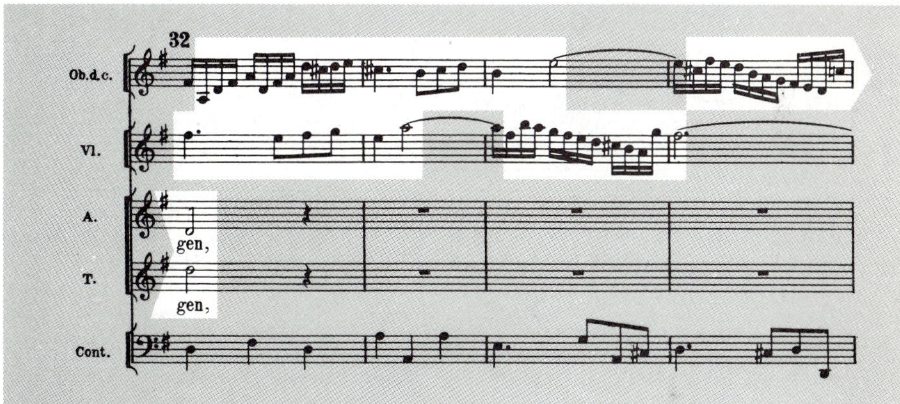
32
Ob. d. c.
Vl.
A.
gen,
T.
gen,
Cont.

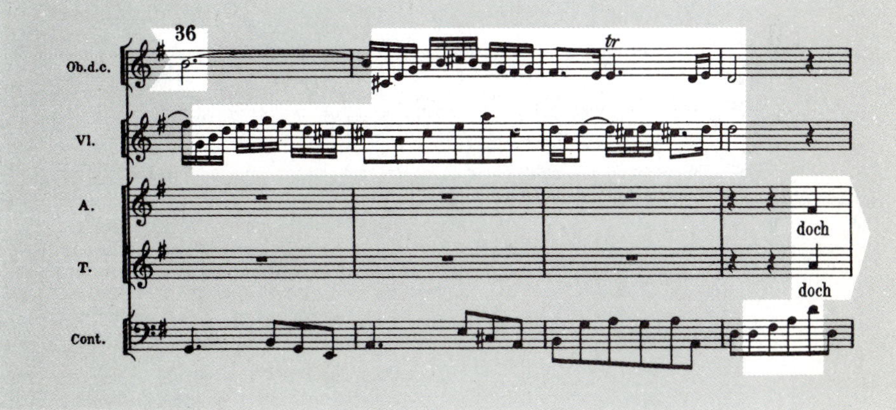
36
Ob. d. c.
tr
Vl.
A.
doch
T.
doch
Cont.

40
Ob. d. c.
Vl.
A.
sel' - ger ist das Herz,
T.
sel' - ger ist das Herz,
doch sel' - ger ist das
Cont.

45
Vl.
A.
doch sel' - ger ist das Herz, das ihn im Glau - - -
T.
Herz, das ihn im Glau - - - - - - - ben
Cont.

49
Ob. d. c.
Vl.
A.
- - - ben trägt, im Glau - ben trägt,
T.
trägt, doch sel' - ger ist das Herz, das ihn im
Cont.

53
Ob. d. c.
Vl.
A.
T.
Cont.
das ihn im Glau - ben trägt, das ihn im Glau - ben
Glau - - ben trägt, das ihn im Glau - ben trägt, im Glau - ben

57
Ob. d. c.
Vl.
A.
T.
Cont.
trägt.
trägt.

62
Ob. d. c.
Vl.
A.
Cont.
tr
Es

65
Ob. d. c.
Vl.
A.
blei- - - - - - - -
T.
Es blei-bet un-be-siegt und kann die Fein-de schla - - -
Cont.

68
Ob. d. c.
Vl.
A.
- bet, es blei-bet un-be-siegt und kann die Fein-de
T.
- gen, es blei- - - - - - - -
Cont.

71
Ob. d. c.
Vl.
A.
schla - - - gen,
T.
- - - - bet,
Cont.

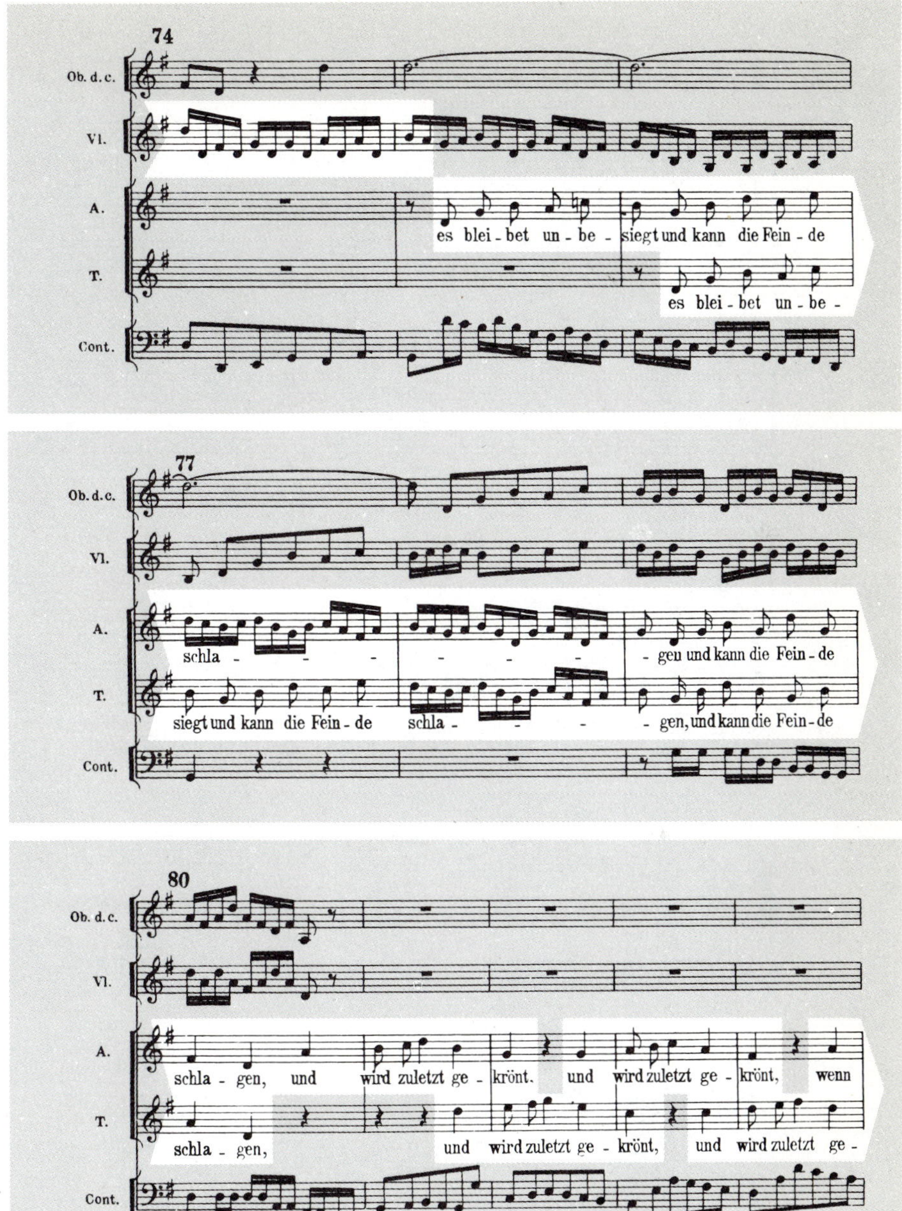
74
Ob. d. c.
Vl.
A.
es blei - bet un - be - siegt und kann die Fein - de
T.
es blei - bet un - be -
Cont.
77
Ob. d. c.
Vl.
A.
schla - - - - - - - gen und kann die Fein - de
T.
siegt und kann die Fein - de schla - - - - gen, und kann die Fein - de
Cont.
80
Ob. d. c.
Vl.
A.
schla - gen, und wird zuletzt ge - krönt. und wird zuletzt ge - krönt, wenn
T.
schla - gen, und wird zuletzt ge - krönt, und wird zuletzt ge -
Cont.

85
Ob. d. c.
A.
es den Tod er legt, den Tod er - legt, wenn es den Tod, den Tod er - legt.
T.
krönt, wenn es den Tod er-legt, den Tod er - legt, den Tod er-legt.
Cont.
91
Ob. d. c.
Vl.
Cont.
96
Ob. d. c.
tr
Vl.
Cont.
99
Ob. d. c.
Vl.
Cont.
103
Ob. d. c.
Vl.
tr
Cont.

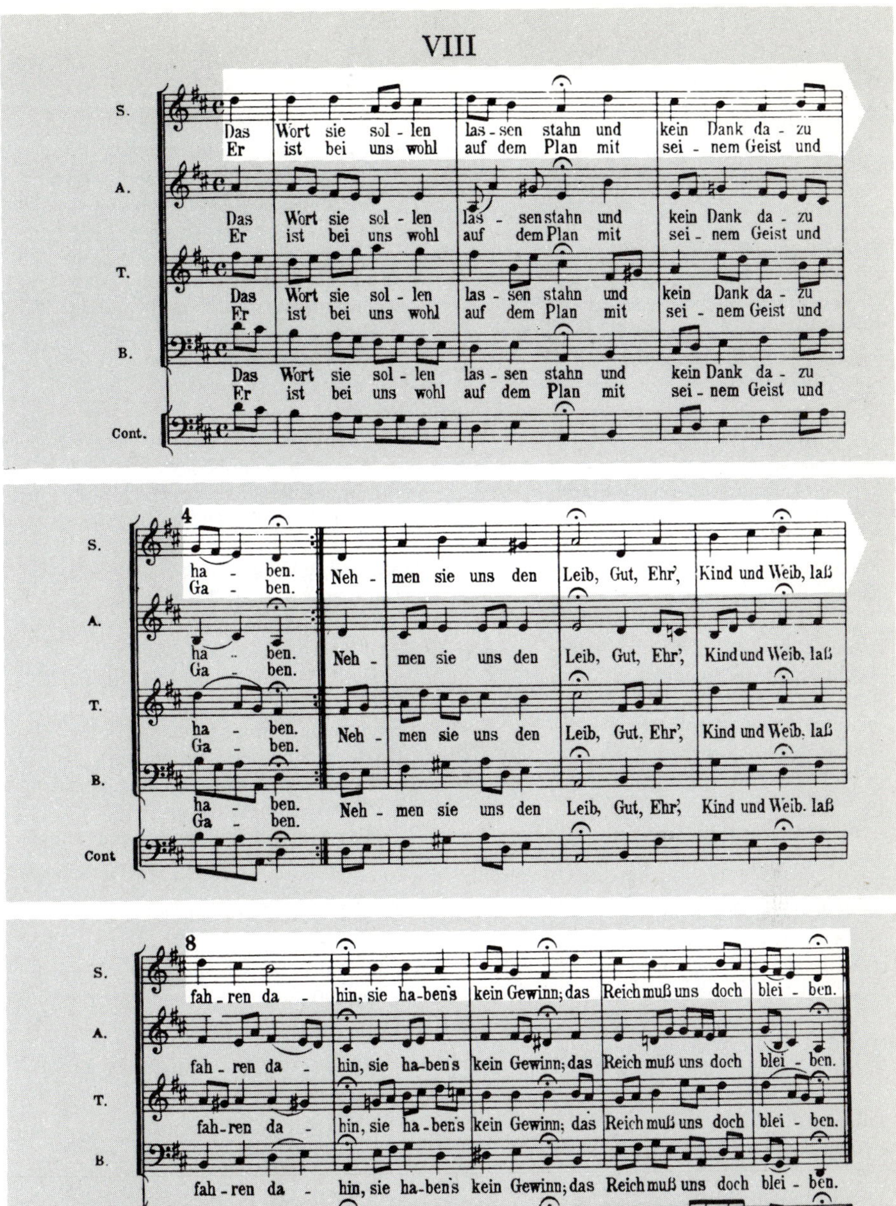
VIII
S.
Das Wort sie sol - len las - sen stahn und kein Dank da - zu
Er ist bei uns wohl auf dem Plan mit sei - nem Geist und
A.
Das Wort sie sol - len las - sen stahn und kein Dank da - zu
Er ist bei uns wohl auf dem Plan mit sei - nem Geist und
T.
Das Wort sie sol - len las - sen stahn und kein Dank da - zu
Er ist bei uns wohl auf dem Plan mit sei - nem Geist und
B.
Das Wort sie sol - len las - sen stahn und kein Dank da - zu
Er ist bei uns wohl auf dem Plan mit sei - nem Geist und
Cont.
4
S.
ha - ben. Neh - men sie uns den Leib, Gut, Ehr', Kind und Weib, laß
Ga - ben.
A.
ha - ben. Neh - men sie uns den Leib, Gut, Ehr', Kind und Weib, laß
Ga - ben.
T.
ha - ben. Neh - men sie uns den Leib, Gut, Ehr', Kind und Weib, laß
Ga - ben.
B.
ha - ben. Neh - men sie uns den Leib, Gut, Ehr', Kind und Weib. laß
Ga - ben.
Cont
8
S.
fah - ren da - hin, sie ha - ben's kein Gewinn; das Reich muß uns doch blei - ben.
A.
fah - ren da - hin, sie ha - ben's kein Gewinn; das Reich muß uns doch blei - ben.
T.
fah - ren da - hin, sie ha - ben's kein Gewinn; das Reich muß uns doch blei - ben.
B.
fah - ren da - hin, sie ha - ben's kein Gewinn; das Reich muß uns doch blei - ben.
Cont.

Translation

	I
	CHORUS
Ein fest Burg ist unser Gott, ein' gute Wehr und Waffen; er hilft uns frei aus aller Not, die uns jetzt hat betroffen.	A mighty fortress is our God, A good defense and weapon; He helps free us from all the troubles That have now befallen us.
Der alte böse Feind, mit Ernst er's jetzt meint, gross Macht und viel List sein grausam Rüstung ist, auf Erd' ist nicht seinsgleichen.	Our ever evil foe; In earnest plots against us, With great strength and cunning He prepares his dreadful plans. Earth holds none like him.
	II
	SOPRANO
Mit unsrer Macht ist nichts getan, wir sind gar bald verloren. Es streit't für uns der rechte Mann, den Gott selbst hat erkoren.	With our own strength nothing is achieved, We would soon be lost. But in our behalf strives the Mighty One, whom God himself has chosen.
Fragst du, wer er ist? Er heisst Jesus Christ, der Herre Zebaoth, und ist kein andrer Gott, das Feld muss er behalten.	Ask you, who is he? He is called Jesus Christ, Lord of Hosts, And there is no other God, He must remain master of the field.
	BASS
Alles was von Gott geboren, ist zum Siegen auserkoren, Wer bei Christi Blutpanier in der Taufe Treu' geschworen, siegt im Geiste für und für.	Everything born of God has been chosen for victory. He who holds to Christ's banner, Truly sworn in baptism, His spirit will conquer for ever and ever.
	III
	BASS
Erwäge doch, Kind Gottes, die so grosse Liebe, da Jesus sich mit seinem Blute dir verschriebe,	Consider, child of God, the great love That Jesus with his sacrifice showed you,
womit er dich zum Kriege wider Satan's Heer, und wider Welt und Sünde geworben hat. Gib nicht in deiner Seele dem Satan und den Lastern statt!	Whereby he enlisted you in the fight against Satan's horde and the sinful world. Yield no place in your soul to Satan and wickedness!
Lass nicht dein Herz, den Himmel Gottes auf der Erden, zur Wuste werden, bereue deine Schuld mit Schmerz,	Do not let your heart, God's heaven on earth, Become a wasteland, repent of your sin with tears,

ARIOSO

dass Christi Geist
mit dir sich fest verbinde.

So that Christ's spirit
may be firmly united with you.

IV

SOPRANO

Komm in mein Herzenshaus,
Herr Jesu, mein Verlangen.
Treib Welt und Satan aus,
und lass dein Bild in mir
erneuert prangen.
Weg, schnöder Sündengraus!

Come dwell within my heart,
Lord Jesus of my desiring.
Drive out the evil of the world,
and let Thine image shine before me
in renewed splendor.
Begone, base shape of sin.

V

CHORUS

Und wenn die Welt voll Teufel wär
und wollten uns verschlingen,
so fürchten wir uns nicht so sehr,
es soll uns doch gelingen.

Though the world were full of devils
eager to devour us,
We need have no fear,
as we will still prevail.

Der Fürst dieser Welt
wie saur er sich stellt,
tut er uns doch nichts,
das macht, er ist gericht't,
ein Wörtlein kann ihm fällen.

The Arch-fiend of this world,
No matter how bitter his stand,
cannot harm us,
Indeed he faces judgment,
One Word from God will bring him low.

VI

TENOR

So stehe denn bei Christi
blutgefärbter Fahne, O Seele, fest
und glaube dass dein Haupt
dich nicht verlässt,
ja, dass sein Sieg auch dir
den Weg zu deiner Krone bahne.

So take your stand firmly
by Christ's bloodstained banner, O my soul,
And believe that God
will not forsake you.
Yea, that His victory will lead you too
On the path to salvation.

Tritt freudig an den Krieg!
Wirst du nur Gottes Wort
so hören als bewahren,
so wird der Feind gezwungen auszufahren,
dein Heiland bleibt dein Heil,
dein Heiland bleibt dein Hort.

Go forth joyfully to do battle!
If you but hear God's word
and obey it,
The Foe will be forced to yield.
Your Savior remains your salvation,
Your Savior remains your refuge.

VII

ALTO AND TENOR

Wie selig sind doch die,

doch selger ist das Herz,
das ihn im Glauben trägt.
Es bleibet unbesiegt
und kann die Feinde schlagen
und wird zuletzt gekrönt,
wenn es den Tod erlegt.

How blessed are they
whose words praise God,
Yet more blessed is he
who bears Him in his heart.
He remains unvanquished
and can defeat his foes,
And is finally crowned
when Death comes to fetch him.

VIII

CHORUS

Das Wort, sie sollen lassen stahn und kein Dank dazu haben. Er ist bei uns wohl auf dem Plan mit seinem Geist und Gaben.	Now let the Word of God abide without further thought. He is firmly on our side with His spirit and strength.
Nehmen sie uns den Leib, Gut, Ehr, Kind und Weib, lass fahren dahin, sie habens kein Gewinn; das Reich muss uns doch bleiben.	Though they deprive us of life, Wealth, honor, child and wife, we will not complain, It will avail them nothing; For God's kingdom must prevail.

MOVEMENTS I, II, V, AND VIII BY MARTIN LUTHER
MOVEMENTS III, IV, VI, AND VII BY SALOMO FRANCK

27. Domenico Scarlatti (1685–1757),

Sonata in D major, K. 491  S1B/5 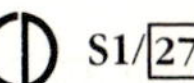 S1/27

Allegro

L

26
29
32
35
38
41

45
50
54
57
62
66

69
72
75
78
81
84

28. Johann Joachim Quantz (1697–1773),

Flute Concerto in G major,
First movement

 S1B/6 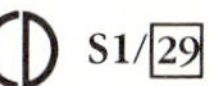

8
(A)
Fl.
I Vl. II
Vla.
Vc. Cb.
Cont.

12
Fl.
I Vl. II
Vla.
Vc. Cb.
Cont.

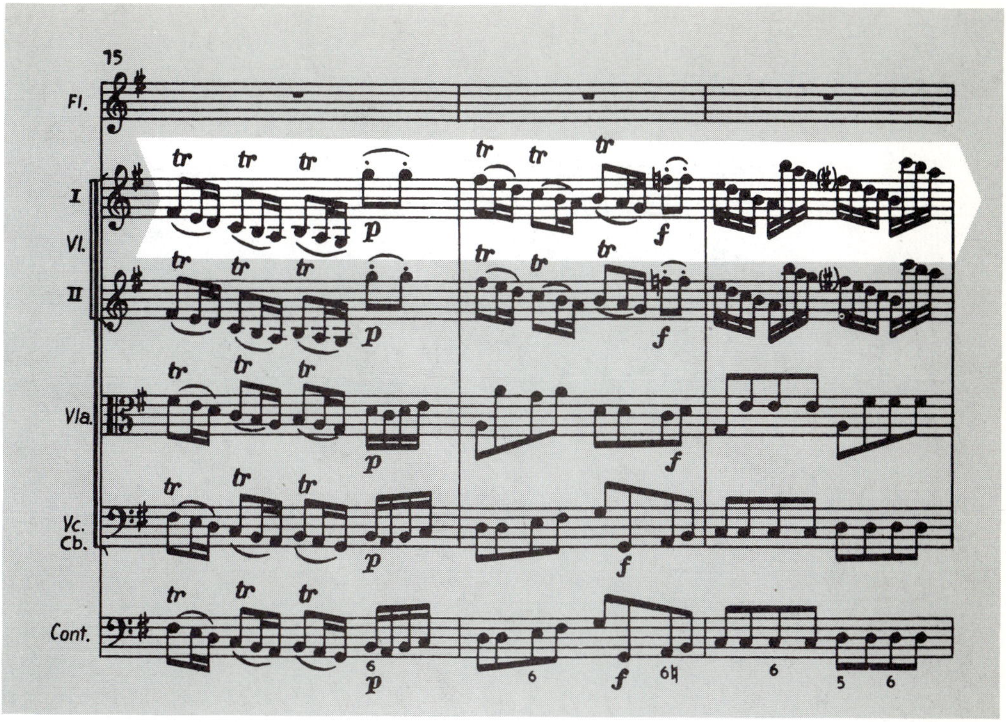
15
Fl.
I
Vl.
II
Vla.
Vc.
Cb.
Cont.

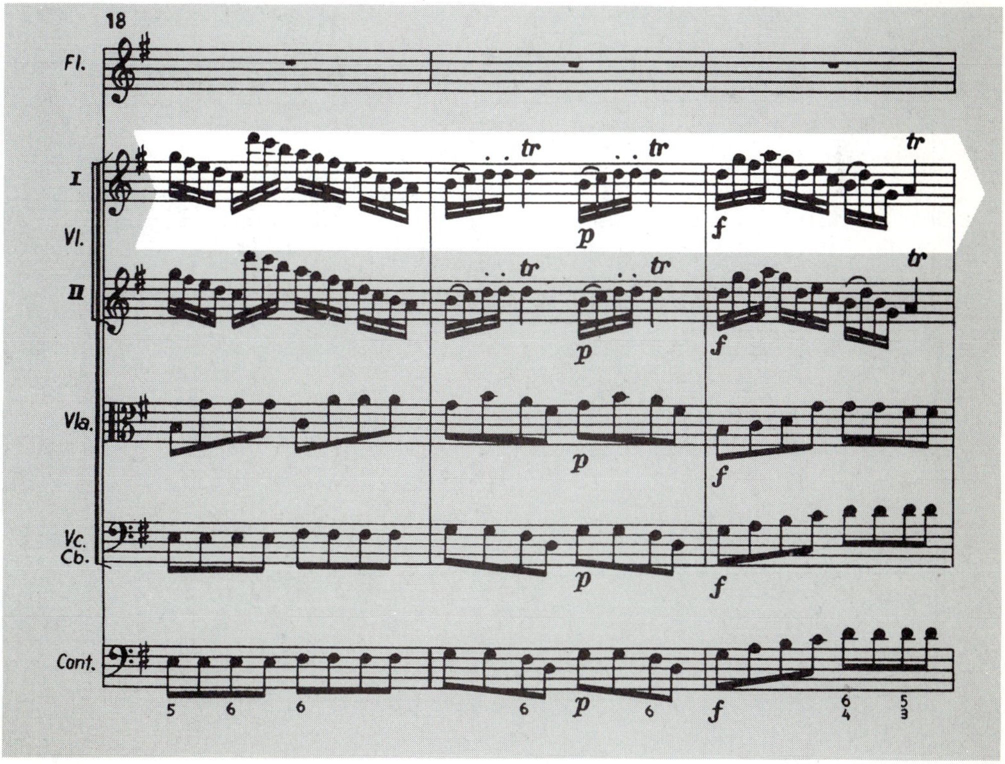
18
Fl.
I
Vl.
II
Vla.
Vc.
Cb.
Cont.

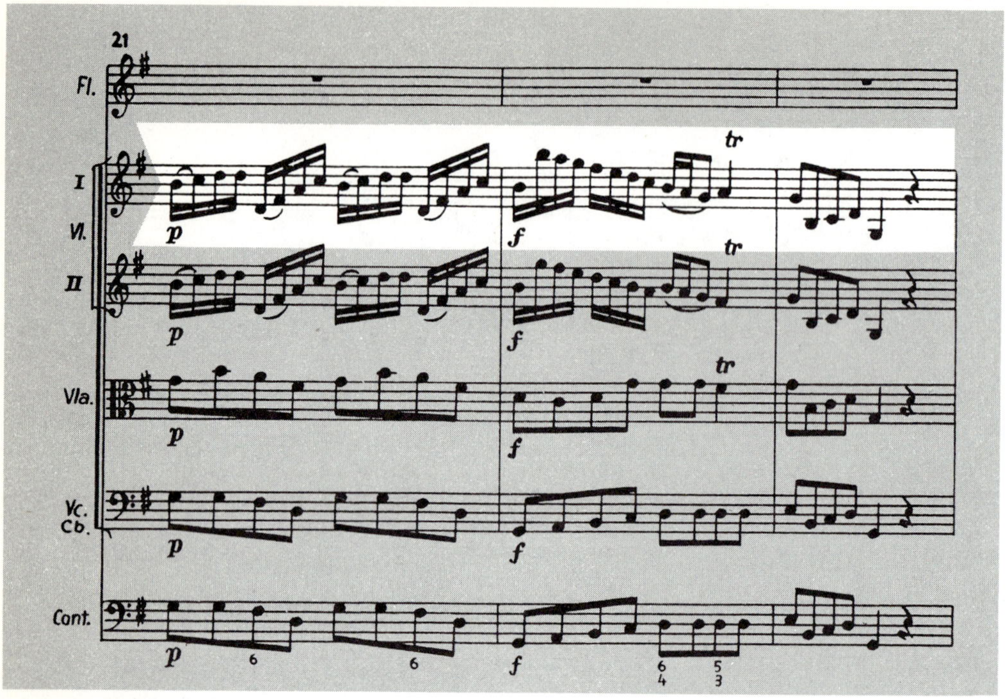

21

Fl.

I VI. II

Vla.

Vc. Cb.

Cont.

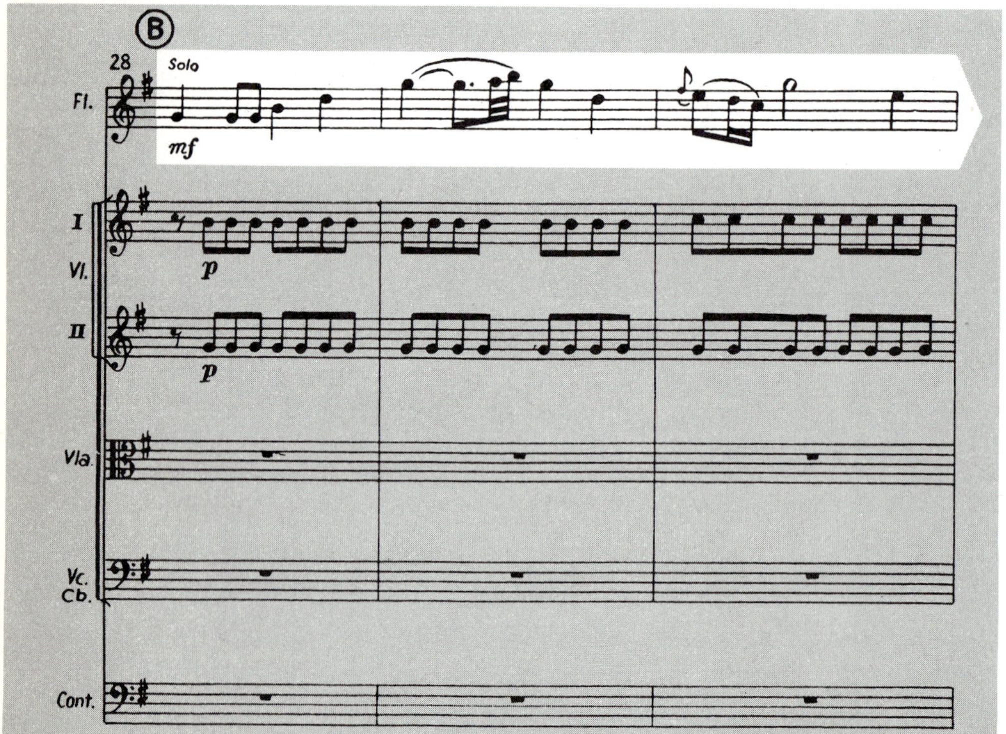

p f tr

B

28 Solo

mf p

27
tr
Fl.
p
f
I
Vl.
II
mf
Vla.
p
Vc.
Cb.
Cont.

31
Fl.
p
I
Vl.
f
p
II
Vla.
Vc.
Cb.
Cont.

C
35
Fl.
f
p
I
Vl.
II
Vla.
Vc.
Cb.
p
Cont.
p
♯
6
4
38
Fl.
f
I
Vl.
II
Vla.
p
Vc.
Cb.
Cont.
7
♯

41

Fl.

p *f*

I
Vl.
II

Vla.

[ein Vc.]

Vc.
Cb.

senza Cb *p*

Cont.

p

44

Fl.

p *f*

I
Vl.
II

[*mf*]

[*mf*]

Vla.

Vc.
Cb.

[*mf*]

Cont.

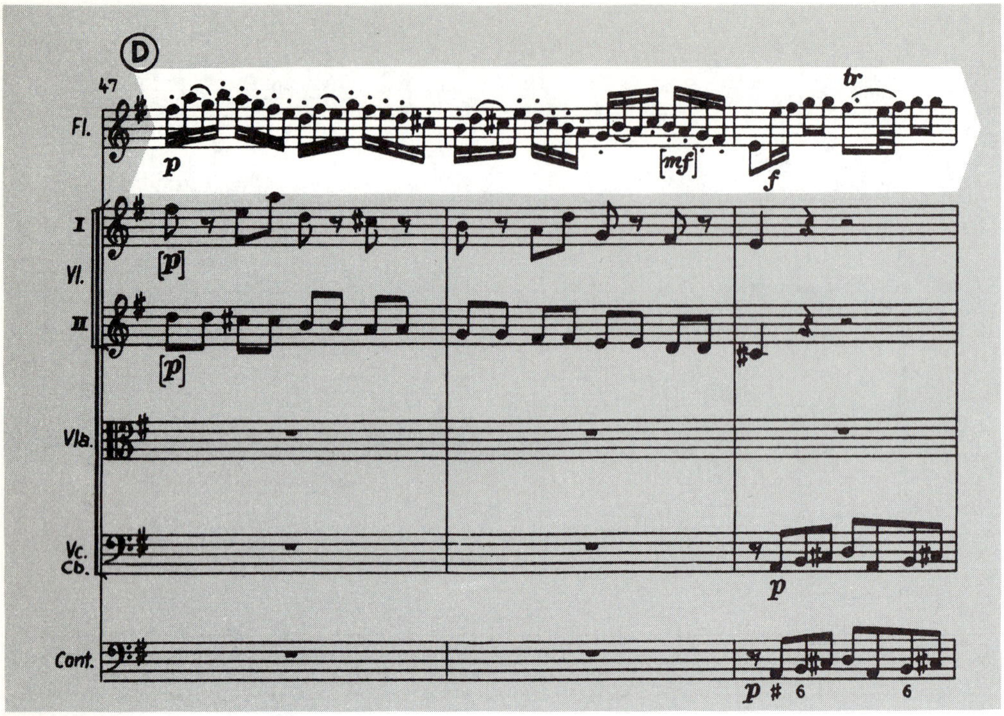

D

47

Fl.

I Vl. II

Vla.

Vc. Cb.

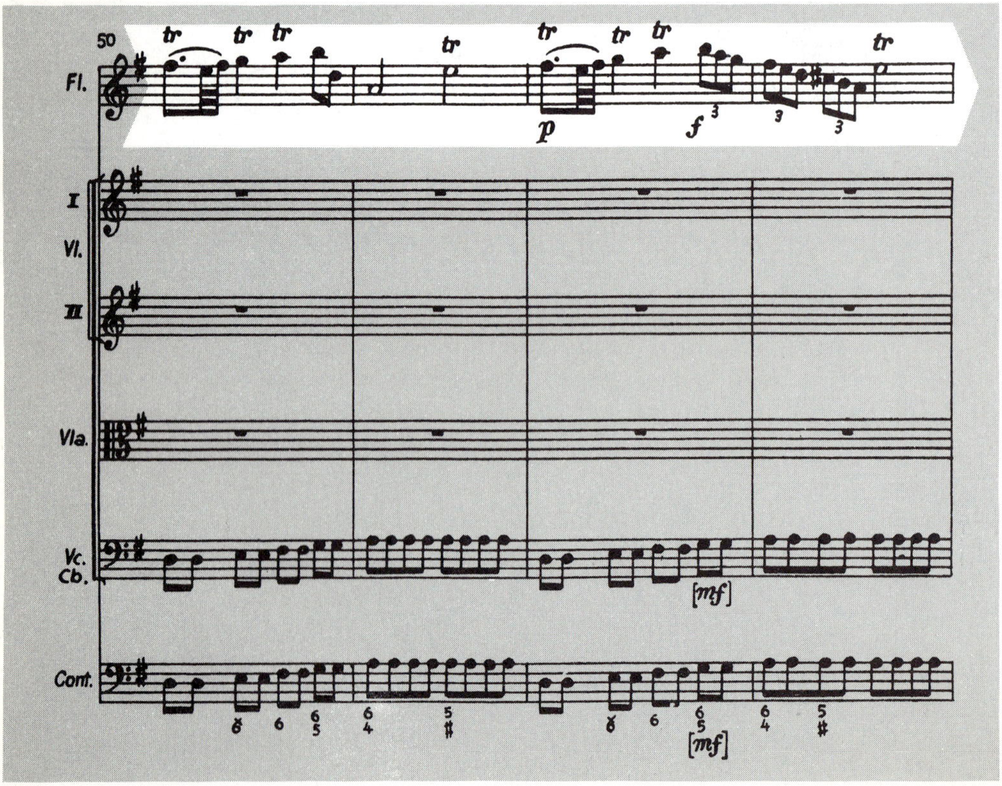

Cont.

50

Fl.

I Vl. II

Vla.

Vc. Cb.

Cont.

E
54
Tutti
Fl.
I
Vl.
II
Vla.
Vc.Cb.
Vc. Cb.
Tutti
Cont.
58
Fl.
I
Vl.
II
Vla.
Vc. Cb.
Cont.

62
F
Solo
Fl.
mf
tr
I
Vl.
II
f
p
Vla.
Vc.
Cb.
Cont.
6
7
4
66

69
Fl.
tr
tr
tr
p
I
Vl.
II
f
p
Vla.
Vc.
Cb.
Cont.
73
Fl.
tr
tr
tr
f
I
Vl.
II
p
Vla.
Vc.
Cb.
Cont.

76
G
Fl.
I
Vl.
II
Vla.
Vc.
Cb.
Cont.
f
p
[ein Vc.]
p senza Cb.

79
Fl.
p
I
Vl.
II
Vla.
Vc.
Cb.
Cont.

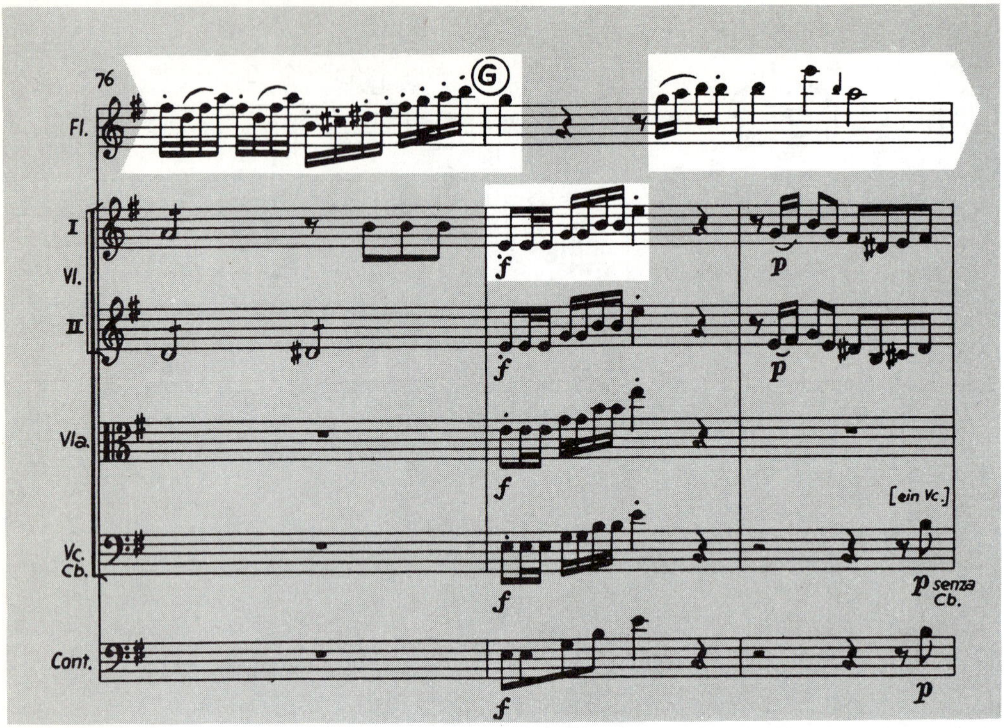

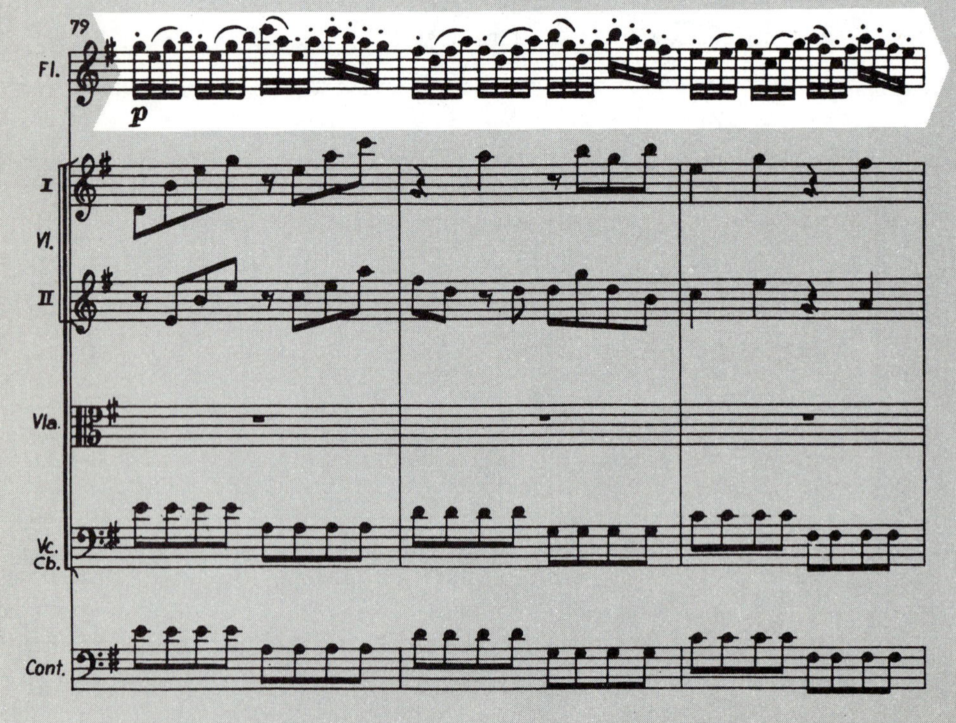

82
Fl.
f
p
I
Vl.
II
Vla.
Vc.
Cb.
Cont.

85
Fl.
tr
H
Tutti
I
Vl.
II
f
Vla.
f
[Vc.Cb.]
Vc.
Cb.
f
Tutti
Cont.
f

88
Fl.
Vl. I
Vl. II
Vla.
Vc. Cb.
Cont.
tr
p
f

91
Fl.
Solo
Vl. I
Vl. II
Vla.
Vc. Cb.
Cont.
Solo
tr
p
f

J
94
Fl.
tr
tr
I
Vl.
tr
tr
II
f
Vla.
Vc.
Cb.
Cont.

97
Fl.
[p]
[f]
I
Vl.
II
Vla.
[ein Vc.]
Vc.
Cb.
senza Cb. p
Cont.
p
6

100
Fl.
p
tr tr
I
Vl.
p
tr tr
II
p
tr tr
Vla.
p
Vc.
Cb.
Cont.

103
Fl.
f
[p]
[mf]
I
Vl.
II
Vla
Vc.
Cb.
p
Cont.
p

106

Fl.

p

I

Vl.

II

Vla.

Vc.
Cb.

Cont.

6 6

(K)

109

Tutti

Fl.

I

Vl.

II

f [p] [f]

Vla.

f [p] [f]

Vc.Cb.

Vc.
Cb.

f [p] [f]

Tutti

Cont.

f 6 4 [p] 5 3 [f]

112
Fl.
tr
I
Vl.
II
Vla.
Vc.
Cb.
Cont.
[p]
[f]
4
2
6
5
6

115
Fl.
L
Solo
[mf]
I
Vl.
II
p
Vla.
Vc.
Cb.
senza Cb.
Cont.
Solo

119
Fl.
tr
tr tr
I
Vl.
II
Vla.
p
Vc.
Cb.
Cont.

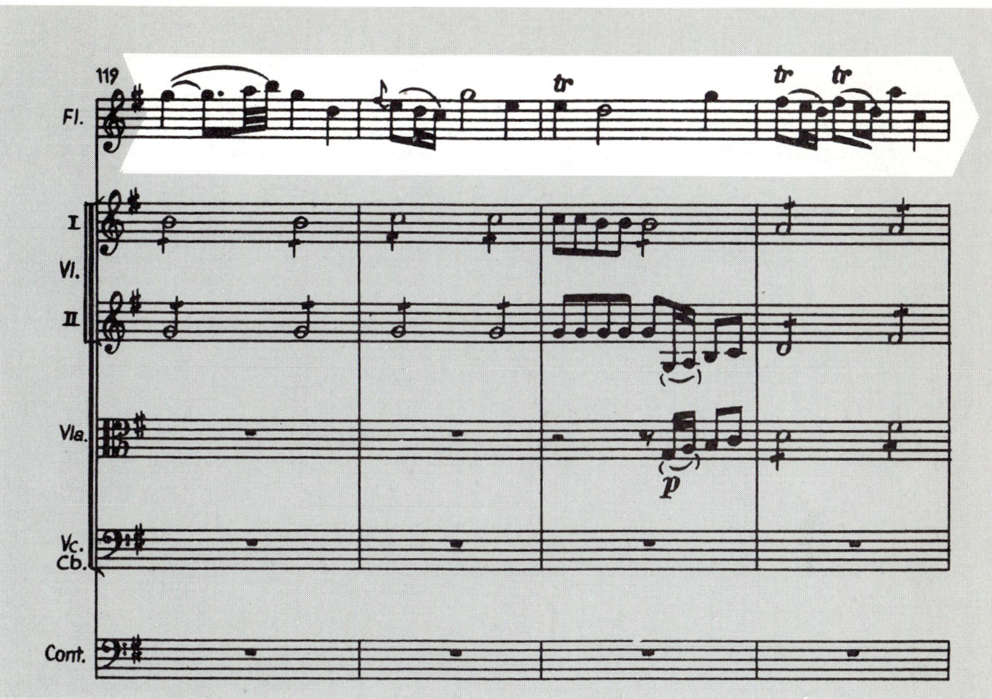

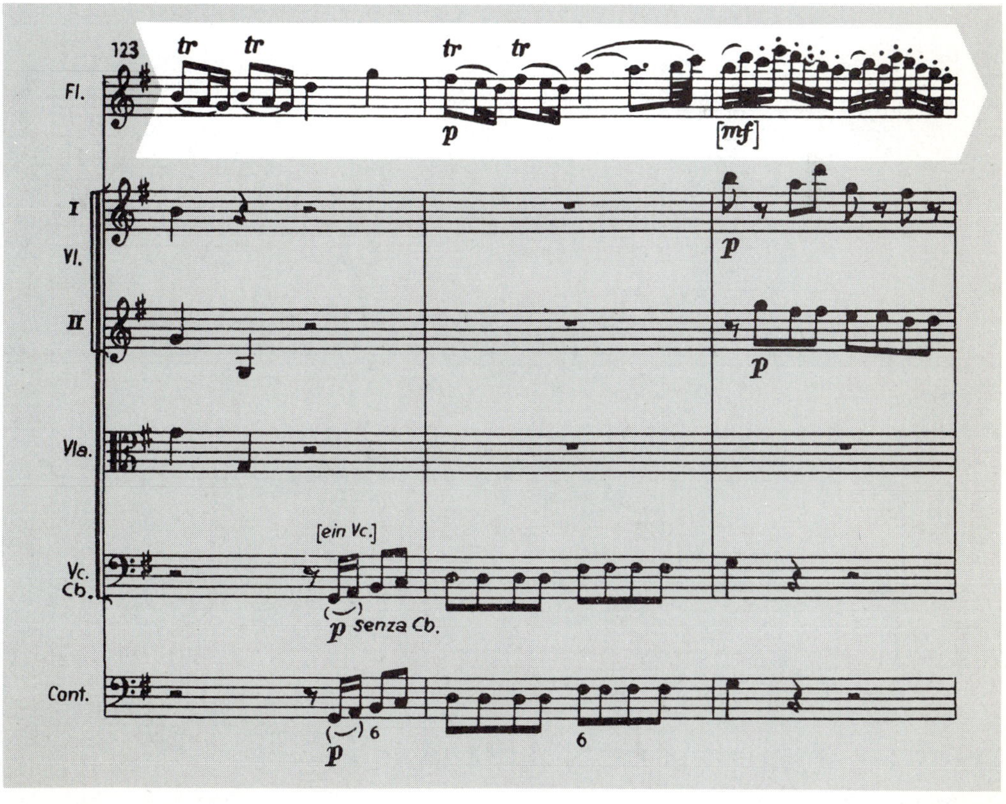

123
tr tr
tr tr
Fl.
p
[mf]
I
Vl.
p
II
p
Vla.
[ein Vc.]
Vc.
Cb.
p senza Cb.
Cont.
6
p
6

126

Fl.

tr tr tr tr

Vl. I

Vl. II

Vla.

Vc. Cb.

p

Cont.

p 6 6 7 6 6 5

129

Fl.

tr

M Tutti

Solo

[mf]

Vl. I

f p

Vl. II

f p

Vla.

f p

Vc. Cb.

Vc. Cb.

f p

Cont.

6 4 5 3

Tutti

f p

132

Fl.

I Vl. II

Vla.

Vc. Cb.

p Cb.

Cont.

135

Fl.

I Vl. II

Vla.

[ein Vc.]

Vc. Cb.

p senza Cb.

Cont.

138
Fl.
p
f
p
f
I
Vl.
II
Vla.
Vc.
Cb.
[mf]
[p]
[mf]
Cont.

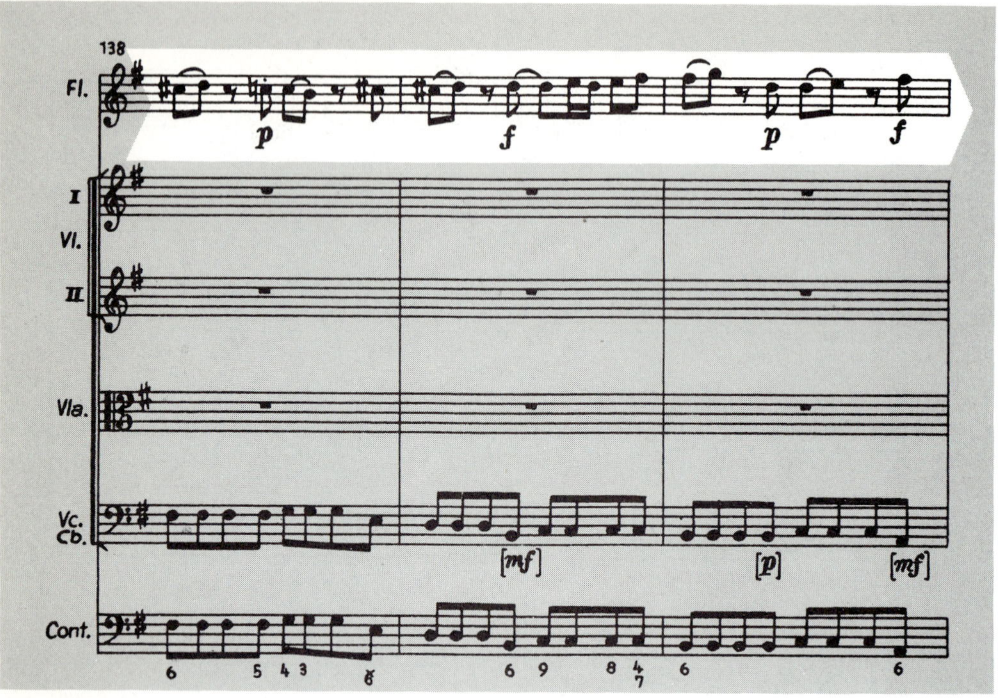

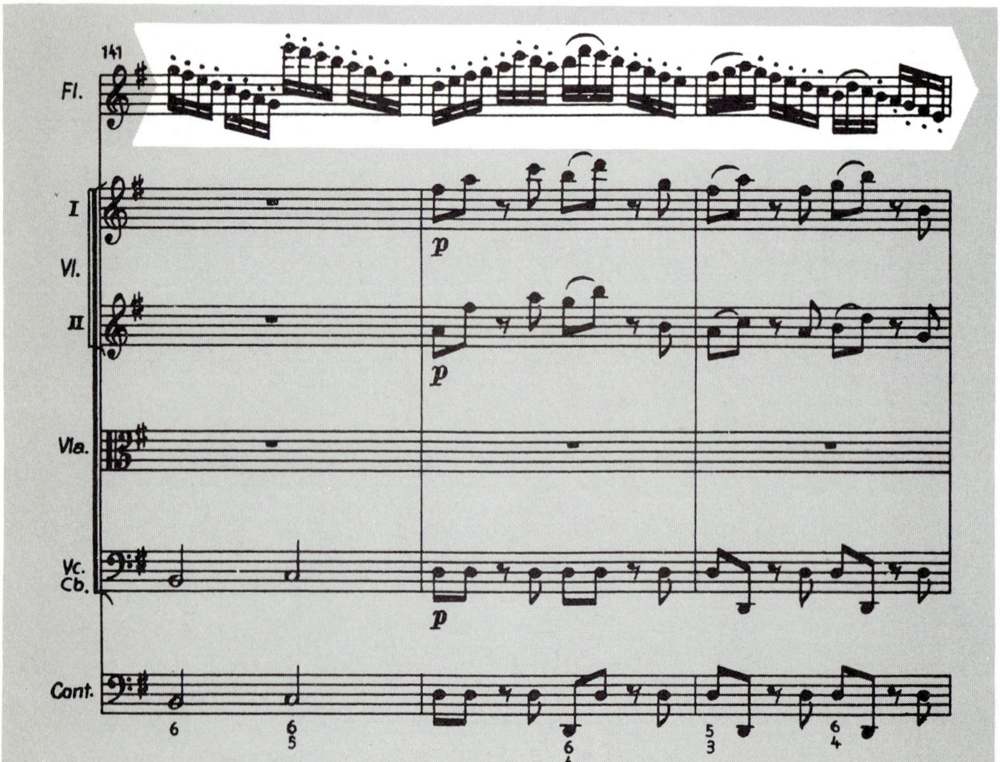

141
Fl.
I
Vl.
II
p
p
Vla.
Vc.
Cb.
p
Cont.

N

144

Fl.

Tutti

Kad.

I VI. II

Vla.

[ein Vc.]

[ein Vc.] [Vc. Cb.]

Vc. Cb.

Cont.

Tutti

7 5   6 4   5 3

148

Fl.

I VI. II

Vla.

Vc. Cb.

Cont.

6   6   6 ♮   6   5 6

151

Fl.

I Vl. II

Vla.

Vc. Cb.

Cont.

154

Fl.

I Vl. II

Vla.

Vc. Cb.

Cont.

29. Christoph Willibald Gluck (1714–1787),

Orphée et Euridice, "J'ai perdu mon Euridice" (1762, revised 1774)

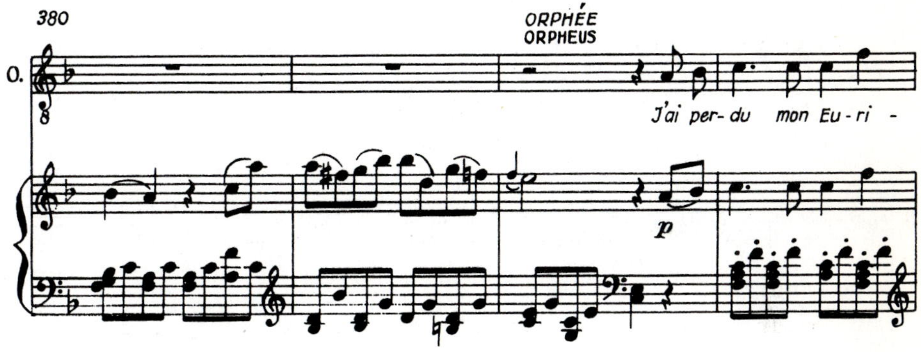

388
O.
- gueur! Rien n'é - ga - le_ mon mal - heur, je suc - com-be à ma dou -
sf
f
392
O.
- leur. Eu-ri - di - ce! Eu-ri - di - ce! Ré -
p
p
simile
p
396
O.
- ponds... quel sup-pli - ce! Ré - ponds
p
cresc.
f
400
Adagio
O.
moi! C'est ton é - poux, ton é - poux fi - dè - le. En - tends ma voix qui t'ap-
p
sf
p

404

Premier mouvement

O. - pel - le, ma voix qui t'ap - pel - le. J'ai per- du mon Eu - ri - di - ce, rien n'é -

simile

408

O. - ga - le mon mal - heur. Sort cru - el___, quel- le ri - gueur! Rien n'é -

412

Moderato

O. - ga - le mon mal - heur, je suc - com - be à ma dou - leur. Eu - ri -

416

Adagio

O. - di - ce! Eu - ri - di - ce! Mor - tel si -

419
O.
- len - ce, vai - ne es- pé - ran - ce! Quel - le souf- fran - ce! Quel tour-
f
p
422
Premier mouvement
- ment__ dé - chi - re mon cœur! J'ai per- du mon Eu - ri -
p
426
- di - ce, rien n'é - ga - le mon mal - heur. Sort cru - el__, quel - le ri -
sf
p
sf
simile
430
- gueur, rien n'é - ga - le__ mon mal - heur. Sort cru - el__, quel - le ri -
sf
rinf.
cresc.

434
O.
-gueur, je_ suc-com-be à ma dou-leur, à_ ma dou-leur
sf
p cresc.
f
ff
438
O.
—, à_ ma dou-leur.
442
O.
447
ORPHÉE
ORPHEUS
Ah! puis-se ma dou-leur fi-nir a-vec ma vi-e. Je ne sur-vi-vrai
Fagotti,
Archi
f Archi

(Orphée tire son épée pour se tuer, et l'Amour qui paraît tout à coup retient son bras.)

463
O.
Tu ne me se-ras plus ra - vi - e, et la mort pour ja-mais va m'u-nir a-vec toi.
Archi (coll'arco)

Translation

J'ai perdu mon Euridice, rien n'égale mon malheur. Sort cruel, quelle rigueur! Rien n'égale mon malheur, Je succombe à ma douleur.	I have lost my Euridice Nothing can equal my misery Cruel fate, how severe! Nothing can equal my misery. I succumb to my pain.
Euridice! Euridice! Réponds . . . quel supplice! Réponds moi. C'est ton époux, ton époux fidèle. Entends ma voix qui t'appelle.	Euridice, Euridice. Speak, I beg you! Speak to me. It is your faithful husband. Hear my voice calling you.
J'ai perdu mon Euridice, rien n'égale mon malheur. Sort cruel, quelle rigueur! Rien n'égale mon malheur, Je succombe à ma douleur.	I have lost my Euridice Nothing can equal my misery Cruel fate, how severe! Nothing can equal my misery. I succumb to my pain.
Euridice! Euridice! Mortel silence, vaine espérance! Quelle souffrance! Quel tourment déchire mon coeur!	Euridice, Euridice. Deathly silence. Hope unfulfilled! What suffering, what torment lacerates my heart.
J'ai perdu mon Euridice rien n'égale mon malheur. Sort cruel, quelle rigueur! Rien n'égale mon malheur, Je succombe à ma douleur.	I have lost my Euridice Nothing can equal my misery Cruel fate, how severe! Nothing can equal my misery. I succumb to my pain.
Ah! puisse ma douleur finir avec ma vie. Je ne survivrai point à ce dernier revers. Je touche encor aux portes des enfers: J'aurai bientôt rejoint mon épouse chérie.	Ah! must I finish my life in pain? I will not survive this latest blow. Once again, I draw near to the gates of Hell So that I may be forever with my beloved wife.

Oui, je te suis, tendre objet de ma foi!	Yes, I follow you, beloved one.
Je te suis, attends moi, attends moi!	I follow you. Wait for me. Wait for me.
Tu ne me seras plus ravie,	You will not be carried away from me,
et la mort pour jamais va m'unir avec toi.	for death will unite me with you forever.

30. Franz Joseph Haydn (1732–1809),

Symphony No. 104 in D major,
(London) (1795)

 3A/1 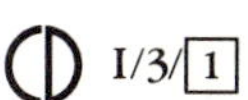 I/3/1

I

Adagio

2 Flauti

2 Oboi

2 Clarinetti in A

2 Fagotti

2 Corni in D

2 Trombe in D

Timpani in D-A

Violino I

Violino II

Viola

Violoncello e Contrabasso

Fl.
Ob.
Fg.
Vl.
Vla.
Vc. e Cb.
zu 2
10
1.
ff
p
Vc.

Fl.
Ob.
Cl.
Fg.
Cor. (D)
Tbe. (D)
Timp.
Vl.
Vla.
Vc. e Cb.
1.
zu 2
Bassi
p
pp
ff

Allegro
1.
Fg.
Vl.
Vla.
Vc. e Cb.
10
Vl.
Vla.
Vc. e Cb.
zu 2
20
Fl.
Ob.
Cl.
zu 2
Fg.
Cor. (D)
Tbe. (D)
Timp.
Vl.
Vla.
Vc. e Cb.

Fl.
Ob.
Cl.
zu 2
Fg.
Cor. (D)
Tbe. (D)
Timp.
Vl.
Vla.
Vc. e Cb.

30
8va
zu 2
Fl.
Ob.
Cl.
Fg.
Cor. (D)
Tbe. (D)
Timp.
Vl.
Vla.
Vc. e Cb.

40
zu 2
zu 2
zu 2
zu 2
zu 2
Fl.
Ob.
Cl.
Fg.
Cor. (D)
Tbe. (D)
Vl.
Vla.
Vc. e Cb.

Fl.
Ob.
Fg.
Vl.
Vla.
Vc.
e Cb.
1.
50
p

Fl.
Ob.
Vl.
Vla.
Vc.
e Cb.
60
1.
Vc.
p
f
f Bassi

Vl.
Vla.
Vc.
e Cb.

70
zu 2
Fl.
Ob.
Cl.
Fg.
Cor. (D)
Tbe. (D)
Timp.
Vl.
Vla.
Vc. e Cb.
f
tr
80
sf
Fl.
Ob.
Cl.
Fg.
Cor. (D)
Tbe. (D)
Vl.
Vla.
Vc. e Cb.

Ob.
1.
p
90
Fg.
Vl.
Vla.
Vc.
e Cb.
p

zu 2
Fl.
Ob.
Cl.
Fg.
Cor. (D)
Tbe. (D)
Timp.
Vl.
Vla.
Vc. e Cb.
100

Fl.
Ob.
Cl.
Fg.
Cor. (D)
Tbe. (D)
Timp.
Vl.
Vla.
Vc. e Cb.

120
zu 2
Fl.
Ob.
Cl.
Fg.
Cor. (D)
Tbe. (D)
Vl.
Vla.
Vc. e Cb.

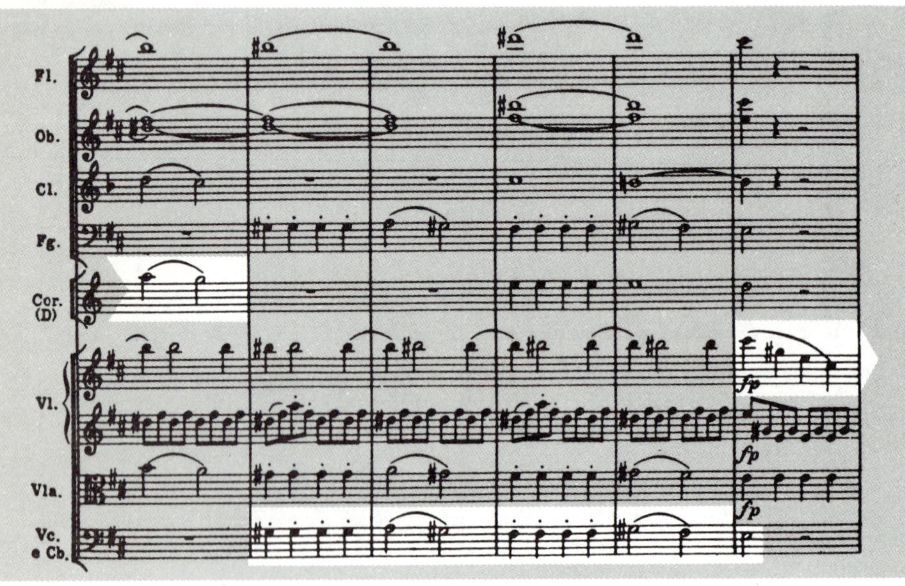
Fl.
Ob.
Cl.
Fg.
Cor. (D)
Vl.
Vla.
Vc. e Cb.

130
Vl.
Vla.
1.
Fg.
p
Vl.
Vla.
140
zu 2
Fl.
f
Ob.
Cl.
zu 2
Fg.
zu 2
Cor. (D)
zu 2
Tbe. (D)
Vl.
Vla.
Vc. e Cb.

Fl.
Ob.
zu 2
Fg.
Cor. (D)
Vl.
Vla.
Vc. e Cb.

150
Fl.
Ob.
Cl.
Fg.
Cor. (D)
Vl.
Vla.
Vc. e Cb.

160
Fl.
Ob.
Cl.
Fg.
Cor. (D)
Tbe. (D)
Timp.
Vl.
Vla.
Vc. e Cb.

Fl.
Ob.
zu 2
Cl.
Fg.
Cor. (D)
zu 2
Tbe. (D)
zu 2
Vl.
Vla.
Vc. e Cb.

170
Fl.
Ob.
Cl.
Fg.
Cor. (D)
zu 2
Tbe. (D)
Timp.
Vl.
Vla.
Vc. e Cb.

180
Fg.
p
Vl.
p
p
Vla.
p
Vc. e Cb.
p

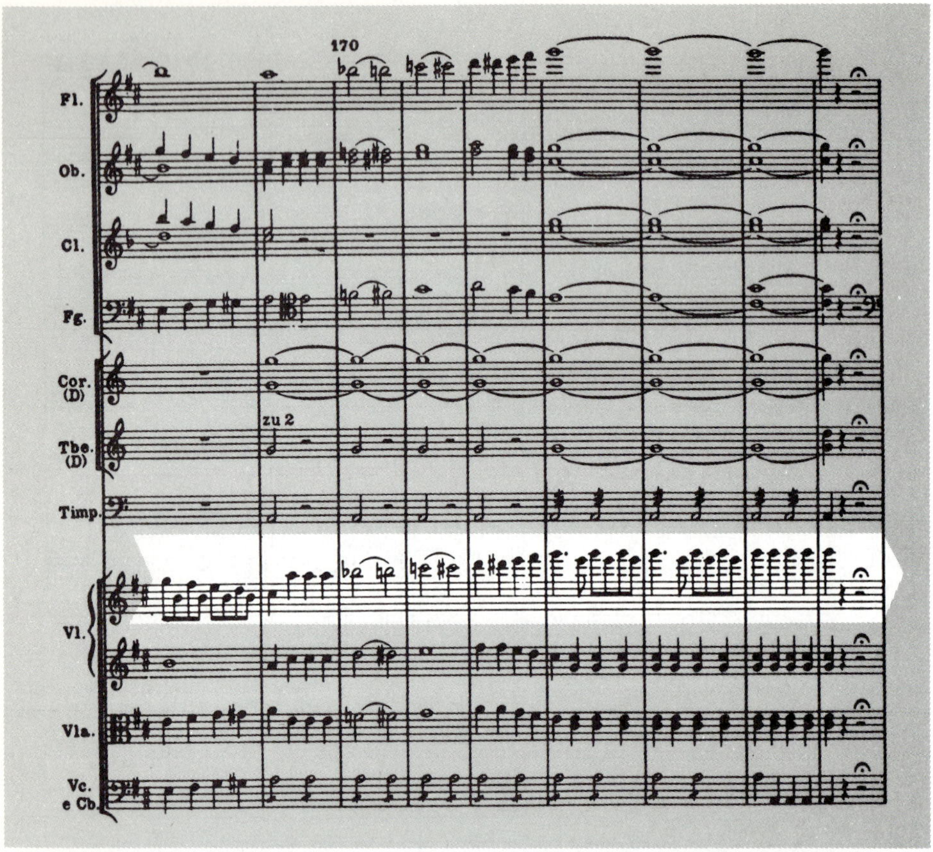

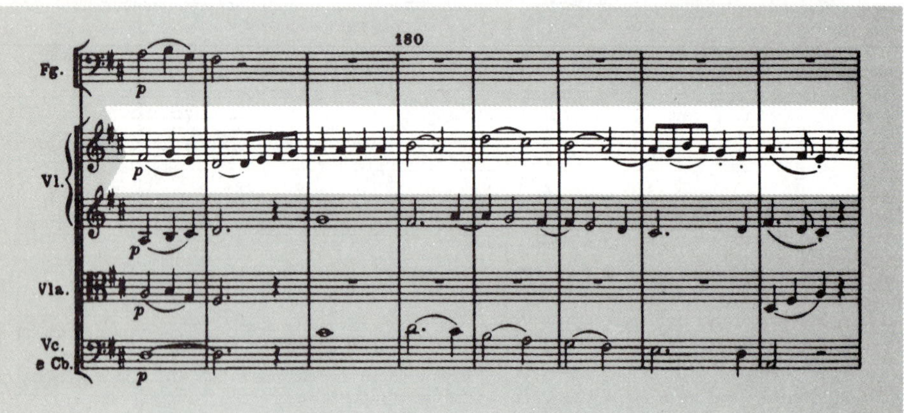

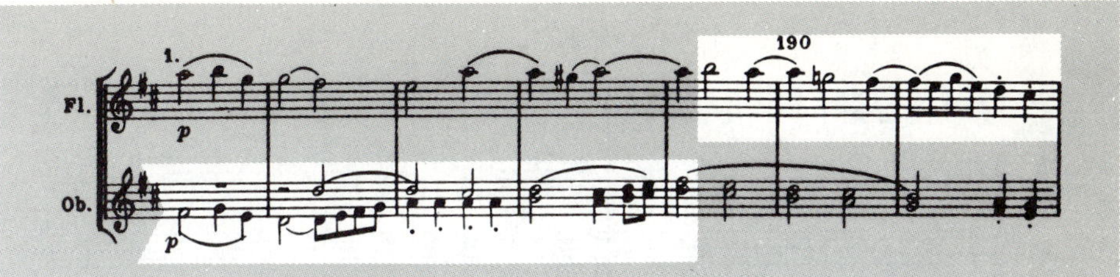

zu 2

Fl.

f

Ob.

f

Cl.

f

zu 2

Fg.

f

Cor. (D)

f

Tbe. (D)

f

Timp.

f

Vl.

f

f

Vla.

f

Vc. e Cb.

f

200
Fl.
Ob.
Cl.
Fg.
Cor. (D)
Tbe. (D)
Timp.
Vl.
Vla.
Vc. e Cb.
zu 2
zu 2

210
Fl.
Ob.
Cl.
Fg.
Vl.
Vla.
Vc.
e Cb.

Fl.
Ob.
Cl.
zu 2
Fg.
Cor.
(D)
Tbe.
(D)
Timp.
Vl.
Vla.
Vc.
e Cb.

220
Fl.
Ob.
Cl.
Fg.
Cor. (D)
Tbe. (D)
Timp.
Vl.
p
Vla.
Vc. e Cb.

230
Ob.
p
Vl.
Vla.
pizz.
Vc. e Cb.

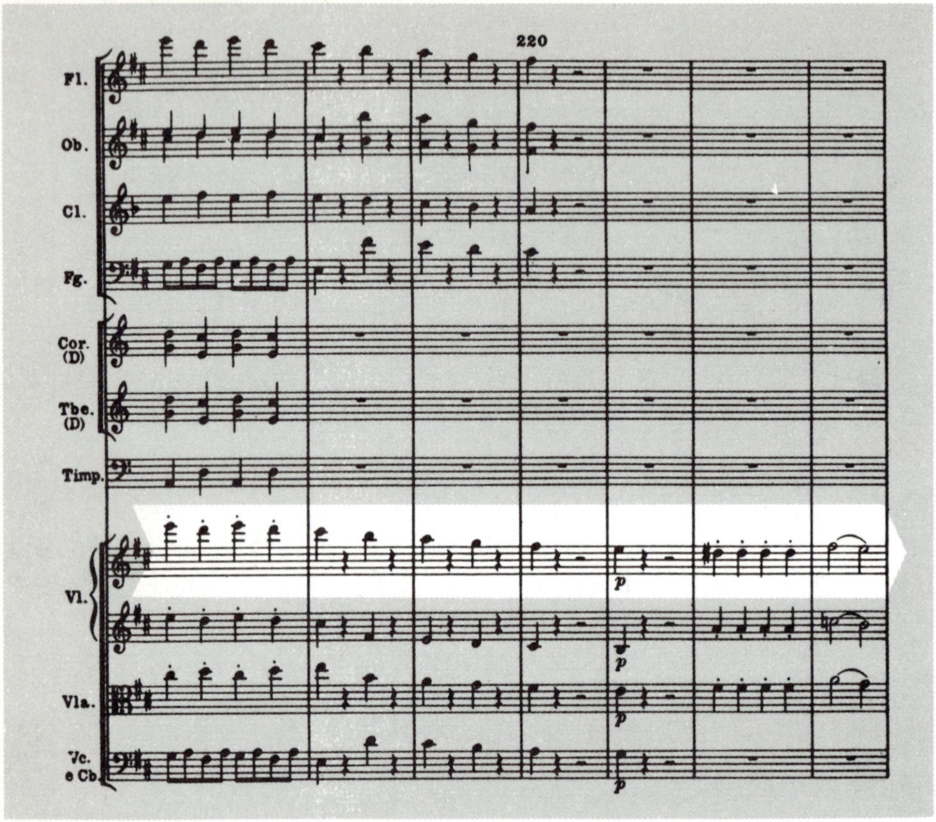

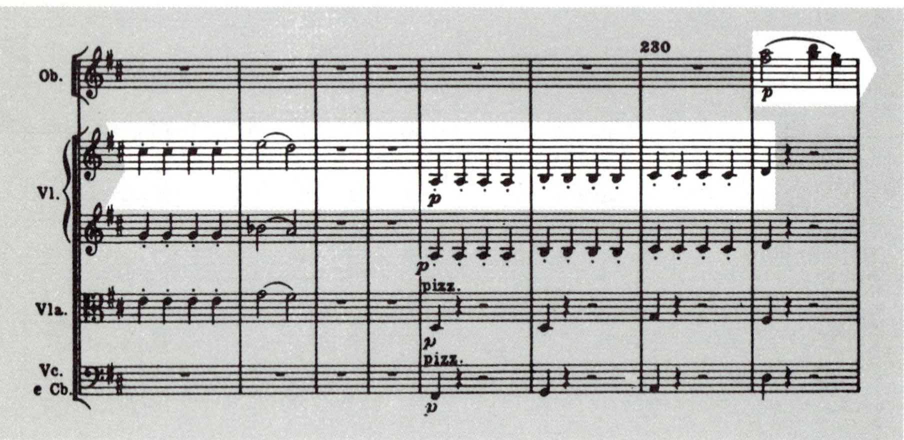

240
zu 2
Fl.
Ob.
Cl.
Fg.
Cor. (D)
Tbe. (D)
Timp.
Vl.
Vla.
Vc. e Cb.
arco
p
f

Fl.
Ob.
Cl.
Fg.
Cor. (D)
Tbe. (D)
Timp.
Vl.
Vla.
Vc. e Cb.
250
1.
p
Vc.

Fl.
Ob.
Cl.
Fg.
Cor. (D)
Tbe. (D)
Timp.
Vl.
Vla.
Vc. e Cb.
Vc.
1.
p
260
zu 2
zu 2
f
Bassi

Fl.
Ob.
Cl.
Fg.
Cor. (D)
Tbe. (D)
Timp.
Vl.
Vla.
Vc. e Cb.

270
Fl.
Ob.
zu 2
Cl.
zu 2
Fg.
Cor. (D)
Tbe. (D)
Timp.
Vl.
Vla.
Vc. e Cb.

Fl.
Ob.
Cl.
Fg.
Cor. (D)
Tbe. (D)
Timp.
Vl.
Vla.
Vc. e Cb.

II

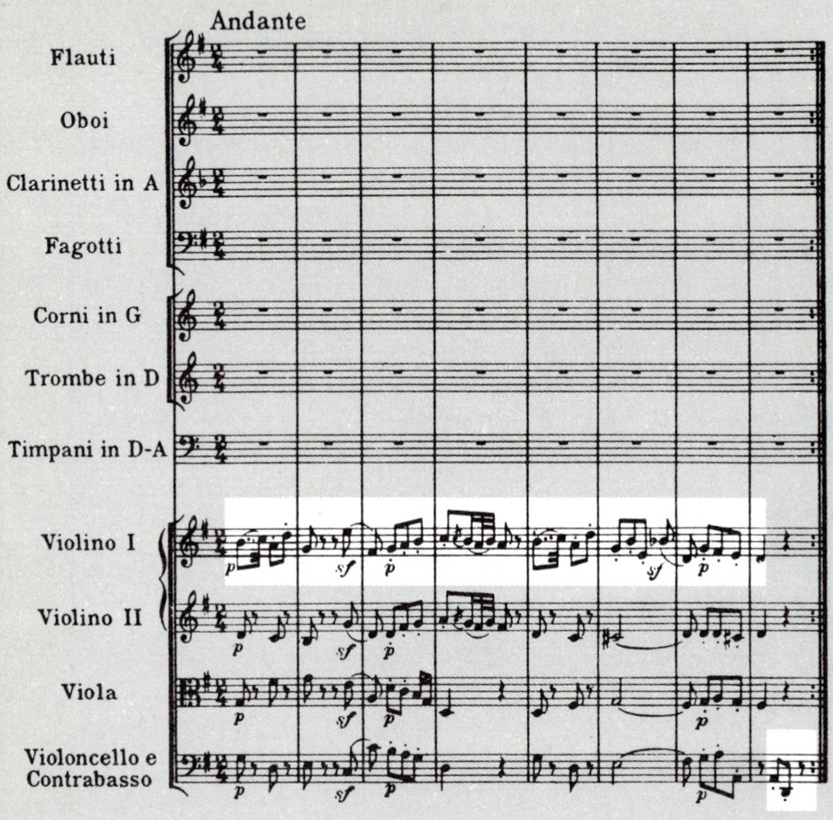

Andante
Flauti
Oboi
Clarinetti in A
Fagotti
Corni in G
Trombe in D
Timpani in D-A
Violino I
Violino II
Viola
Violoncello e Contrabasso
p
sf
p

10
Vl.
Vla.
Vc. e Cb.
Vc.
sf
Bassi

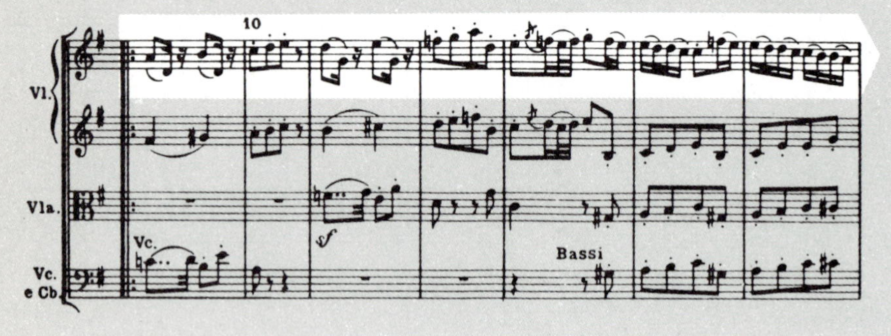

1.
20
Fg.
Vl.
Vla.
Vc. e Cb.
p
sf

30
Fg.
Vl.
Vla.
Vc. e Cb.
sf
p
f

1.
Fg.
Vl.
Vla.
Vc. e Cb.
p

40
1.
zu 2
Fl.
Ob.
Cl.
Fg.
Cor. (G)
Tbe. (D)
Timp.
Vl.
Vla.
Vc. e Cb.

Fl.
Ob.
Cl.
Fg.
zu 2
Cor. (G)
Tbe. (D)
Timp.
Vl.
sf
sf
sf
Vla.
Vc. e Cb.

50
Fl.
Ob.
Fg.
Vl.
Vla.
Vc. e Cb.

Fl.
Ob.
zu 2
Fg.
Vl.
Vla.
Vc. e Cb.

Fl.
Ob.
Fg.
Vl.
Vla.
Vc.
e Cb.
p
sf
p

60
zu 2
Fl.
Ob.
Fg.
Cor.
(G)
Tbe.
(D)
Timp.
Vl.
Vla.
Vc.
Cb.
f
sf

70

Fl.

Ob.

Cl.

Fg.

Cor. (G)

Tbe. (D)

Timp.

Vl.

Vla.

Bassi

Vc. e Cb.

zu 2

80
Fl.
Vl.
Vla.
Vc.
e Cb.
p
sf

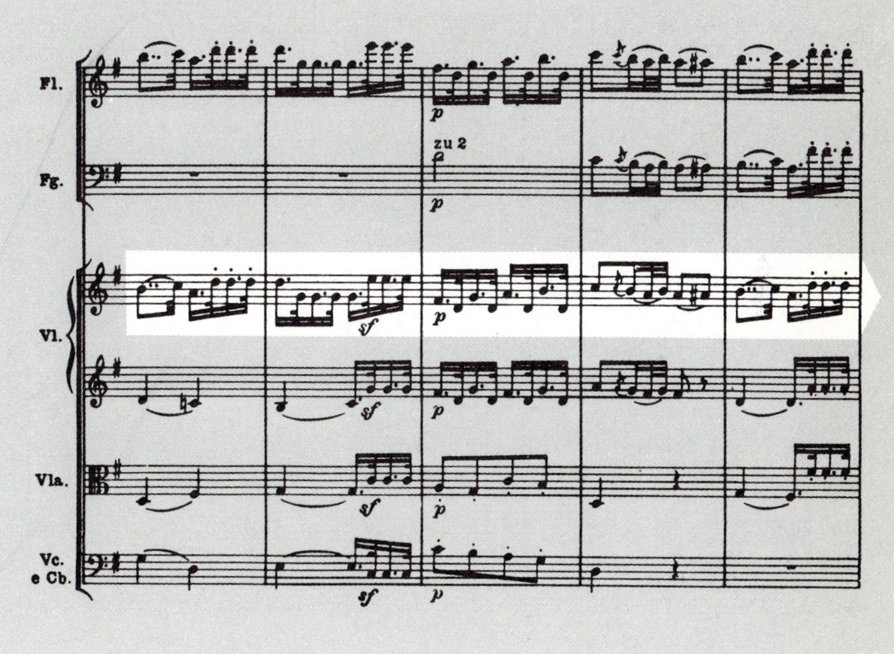
Fl.
Fg.
zu 2
Vl.
Vla.
Vc.
e Cb.
p
sf

zu 2
90
Fl.
Ob.
Cl.
Fg.
Cor. (G)
Tbe. (D)
Timp.
Vl.
Vla.
Vc. e Cb.
ff
p
Vc.

Fl.
Vl.
Vla.
Vc.
e Cb.
1.
100
110
p
rf
cresc.
f

più largo
a tempo
più largo
a tempo
120
1.
Fl.
Ob.
Fg.
Vl.
Vla.
Vc.
e Cb.

zu 2
Fl.
Ob.
Fg.
Cor.
(G)
Timp.
Vl.
Vla.
Vc.
e Cb.

Fl.
Ob.
Fg.
Cor. (G)
zu 2
Vl.
Vla.
Vc. e Cb.

130
Fl.
Ob.
Fg.
Cor. (G)
Vl.
Vla.
Vc. e Cb.

140
Fl.
Ob.
Vl.
Vla.
Vc.
e Cb.

Fl.
Ob.
1.
p
Fg.
Cor. (G)
p
Vl.
Vla.
Vc. e Cb.

150
Fl.
pp
Ob.
pp
Fg.
zu 2
pp
Cor. (G)
pp
Vl.
pp
pp
Vla.
pp
Vc. e Cb.
pp

III
Menuetto Allegro
Flauti
Oboi
Clarinetti in A
Fagotti
Corni in D
Trombe in D
Timpani in D-A
Violino I
Violino II
Viola
Violoncello e Contrabasso
10
Fl.
Ob.
Cor. (D)
Vl.
Vla.
Vc. e Cb.

20
Fl.
Ob.
Cl.
Fg.
Cor. (D)
Tbe. (D)
Timp.
Vl.
Vla.
Vc. e Cb.
Vc.
Passi
Fl.
Ob.
Cl.
Fg.
Cor. (D)
Tbe. (D)
Vl.
Vla.
Vc. e Cb.

30
Fl.
Ob.
Fg.
Cor. (D)
Timp.
pp
cresc.
Vl.
Vla.
Vc. e Cb.
zu 2
40
Cl.
Tbe. (D)

50
Fl.
Ob.
Cl.
Fg.
zu 2
Cor. (D)
Tbe. (D)
Timp.
Vl.
Vla.
Vc. e Cb.

Trio
Ob.
Fg.
Vl.
pizz.
Vla.
Vc. e Cb.

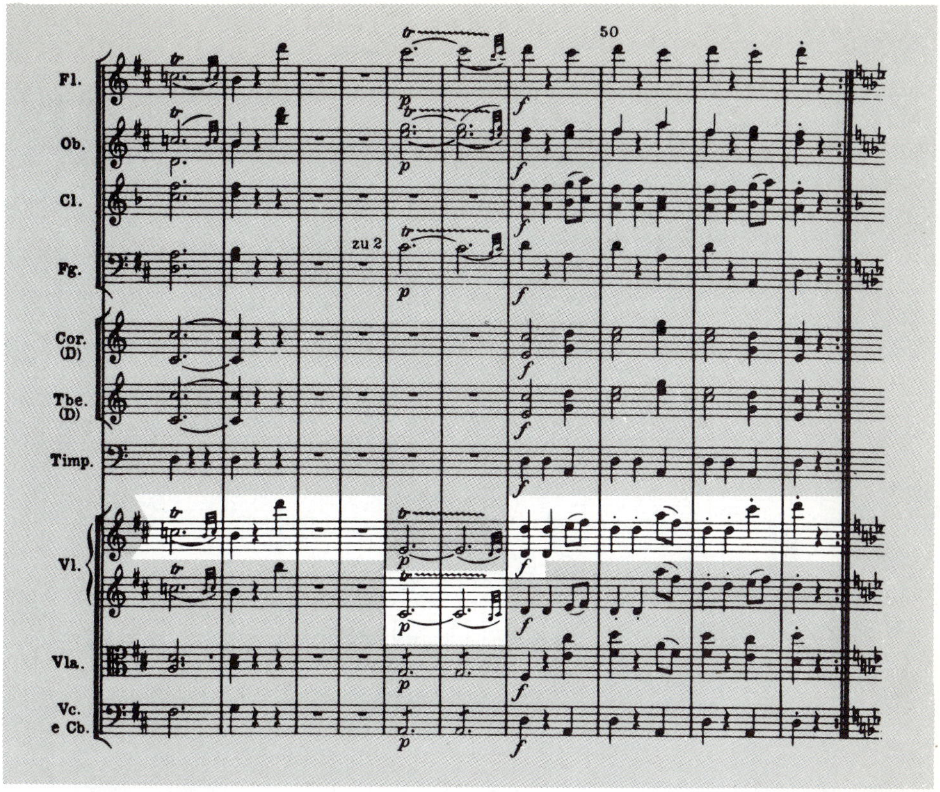

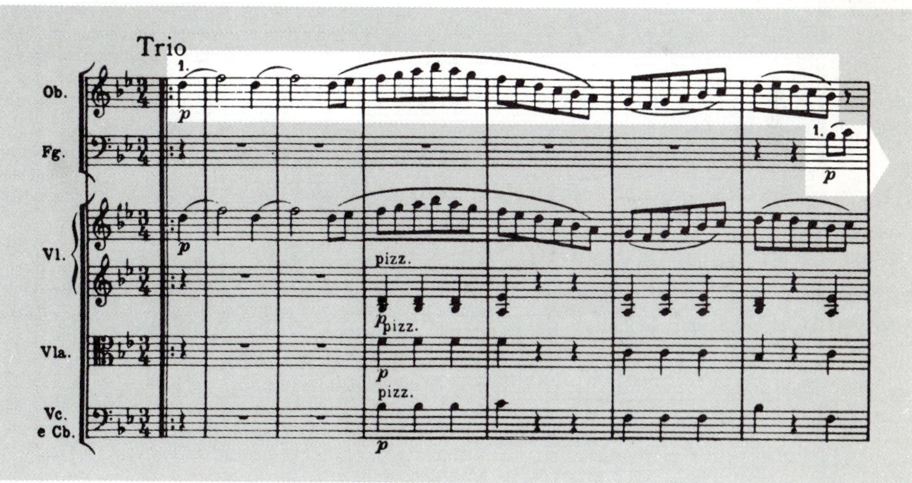

60
Fg.
Vl.
Vla.
Vc. e Cb.
70
Fl.
Ob.
Fg.
Vl.
1.
p
2
arco
Fl.
Ob.
Fg.
Vl.
Vla.
Vc. e Cb.
arco
arco

80
Fl.
Ob.
Fg.
Vl.
Vla.
Vc. e Cb.
p
pizz.
1.
90
arco
100
zu 2
Men. D.C.

IV
Finale: Spiritoso
Flauti
Oboi
Clarinetti in A
Fagotti
Corni in D
Trombe in D
Timpani in D-A
Violino I
Violino II
Viola
Violoncello
Contrabasso
p
10
Ob.
Fg.
Cor. (D)
Vl.
Vla.
Vc.
Cb.
p zu 2

zu 2
20
Fl.
Ob.
Cl.
Fg.
zu 2
Cor. (D)
Tbe. (D)
Timp.
Vl.
Vla.
Bassi
Vc. e Cb.

30
Fl.
Ob.
Cl.
Fg.
Cor. (D)
Tbe. (D)
Timp.
Vl.
Vla.
Vc. e Cb.

Fl.
Ob.
Cl.
Fg.
Cor. (D)
Tbe. (D)
Timp.
Vl.
Vla.
Vc. e Cb.

40
Fl.
Ob.
Cl.
Fg.
Cor. (D)
Tbe. (D)
Timp.
Vl.
Vla.
Vc. e Cb.
zu 2
zu 2
f
sf
sf
sf
sf
sf
sf
sf
sf
sf
sf
sf

50
Fl.
Ob.
Cl.
Fg.
Cor. (D)
Vl.
Vla.
Vc. e Cb.
zu 2
zu 2
sf
p
p
sf

60
Fl.
Ob.
Cl.
Fg.
Cor. (D)
Tbe. (D)
Timp.
Vl.
Vla.
Vc. e Cb.

Fl.
sf
Ob.
sf
Cl.
Fg.
sf
Cor. (D)
Tbe. (D)
Timp.
Vl.
sf
p
sf
p
Vla.
sf
p
Vc. e Cb.

Fl. zu 2 f
Ob. f
Cl. f
Fg. f
Cor. (D) zu 2 f
Tbe. (D) zu 2 f
Timp.
Vl.
Vla. f
Vc. f
Cb. f

80
Fl.
Ob.
Cl.
Fg.
Cor. (D)
Tbe. (D)
Timp.
Vl.
Vla.
Vc.
Cb.
1.
90
Fg.
Vl.
Vla.
Vc. e Cb.
Bassi

zu 2

Fl.

f

Ob.

f sf sf

Cl.

f

Fg.

f sf sf

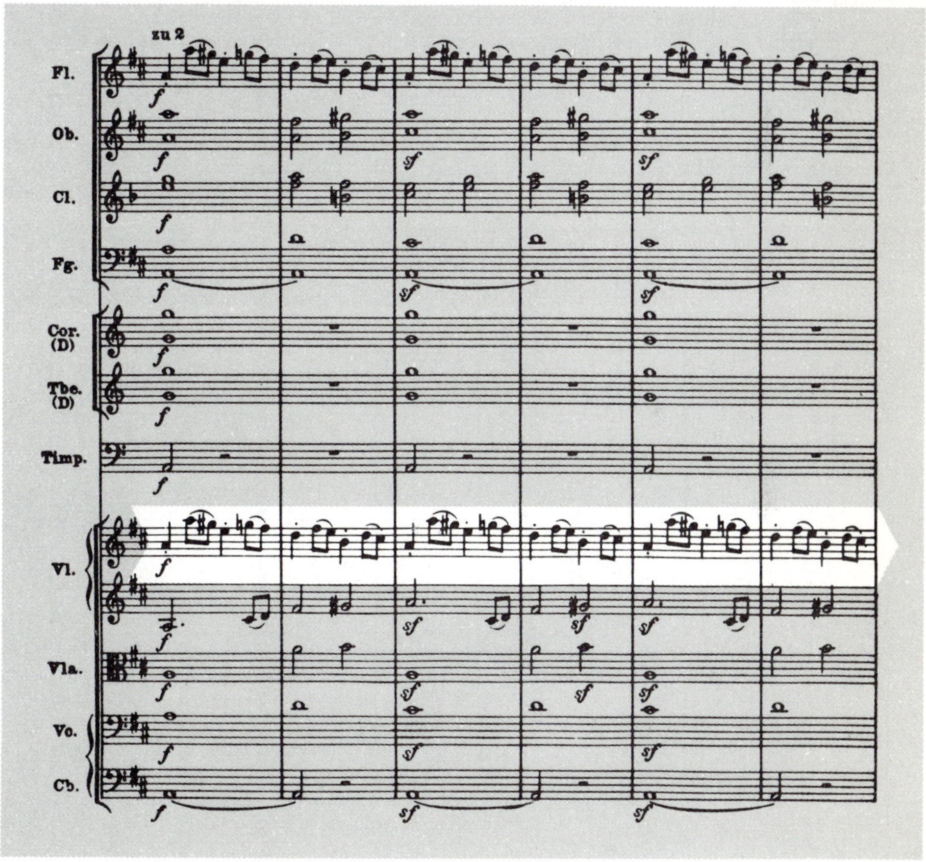

Cor. (D)

f

Tbe. (D)

f

Timp.

f

Vl.

f

f sf sf sf

Vla.

f sf sf sf

Vc.

f sf sf

Cb.

f sf sf

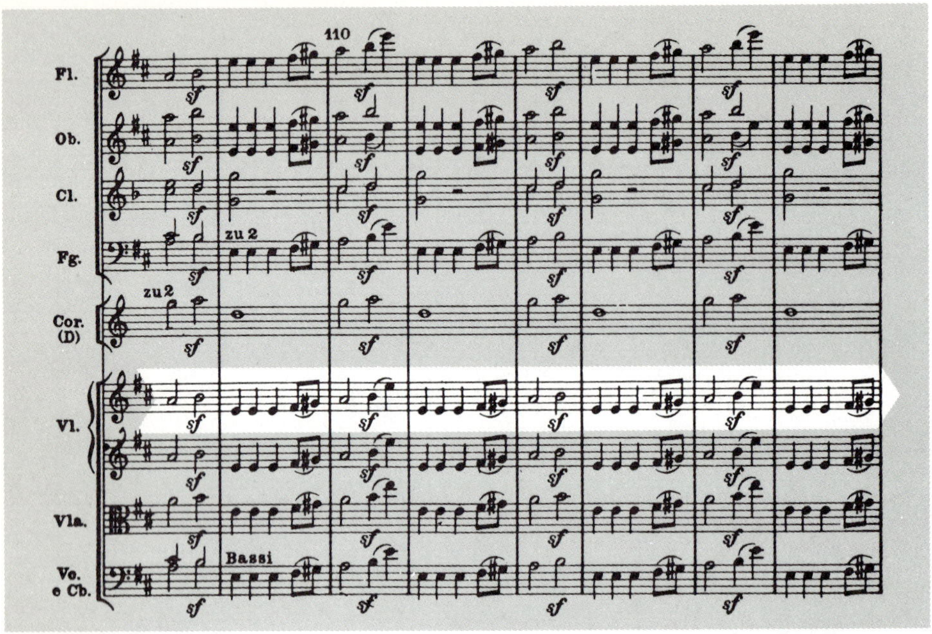

1.
1.
2.
Fl.
Ob.
Cl.
Fg.
Cor. (D)
Vl.
Vla.
Vc. e Cb.
p
Vc.

120
zu 2
zu 2
Fl.
Ob.
Cl.
Fg.
Cor. (D)
Tbe. (D)
Timp.
Vl.
Vla.
Vo. e Cb.

130
Fl.
Ob.
Cl.
Fg.
Cor. (D)
Tbe. (D)
Vl.
Vla.
Vo. e Cb.

140
Fl.
Ob.
Cl.
Fg.
zu 2
Cor. (D)
Tbe. (D)
Vl.
Vla.
Vc. e Cb.
f
Fl.
zu 2
Ob.
Cl.
Fg.
Cor. (D)
zu 2
Tbe. (D)
Vl.
Vla.
Vc.
Cb.

450
Fl.
Ob.
Cl.
Fg.
Cor. (D)
Tbe. (D)
Vl.
Vla.
Vc.
Cb.
Fl.
Ob.
zu 2
Cl.
Fg.
Cor. (D)
Tbe. (D)
Vl.
Vla.
Vc. e Cb.
Bassi
sf

160
Fl.
Ob.
Cl.
Fg.
Cor. (D)
Tbe. (D)
Vl.
Vla.
Vc.
Cb.

170
180
Fl.
Ob.
Fg.
Vl.
Vla.
Vc.
Cb.

190
Fl.
Fg.
Cor. (D)
Vl.
Vla.
Vc. e Cb.
Bassi
sf
p
pp
1.

200
Fl.
Ob.
Fg.
Cor. (D)
Vl.
Vla.
Vc.
Cb.
p

Fl.
Ob.
Cl.
Fg.
zu 2
Cor. (D)
Tbe. (D)
Timp.
Vl.
Vla.
Bassi
Vc. e Cb.
f

210
Fl.
Ob.
Cl.
Fg.
zu 2
Cor. (D)
zu 2
Tbe. (D)
Timp.
Vl.
Vla.
Vc. e Cb.

220
Fl.
Ob.
Cl.
Fg.
Cor.
(D)
Tbe.
(D)
Timp.
Vl.
Vla.
Vc.
e Cb.
zu 2
sf

230
Fl.
Ob.
zu 2
Cl.
Fg.
sf
sf
Cor. (D)
sf
sf
Tbe. (D)
Timp.
Vl.
Vla.
sf
sf
Vc. e Cb.
sf
sf

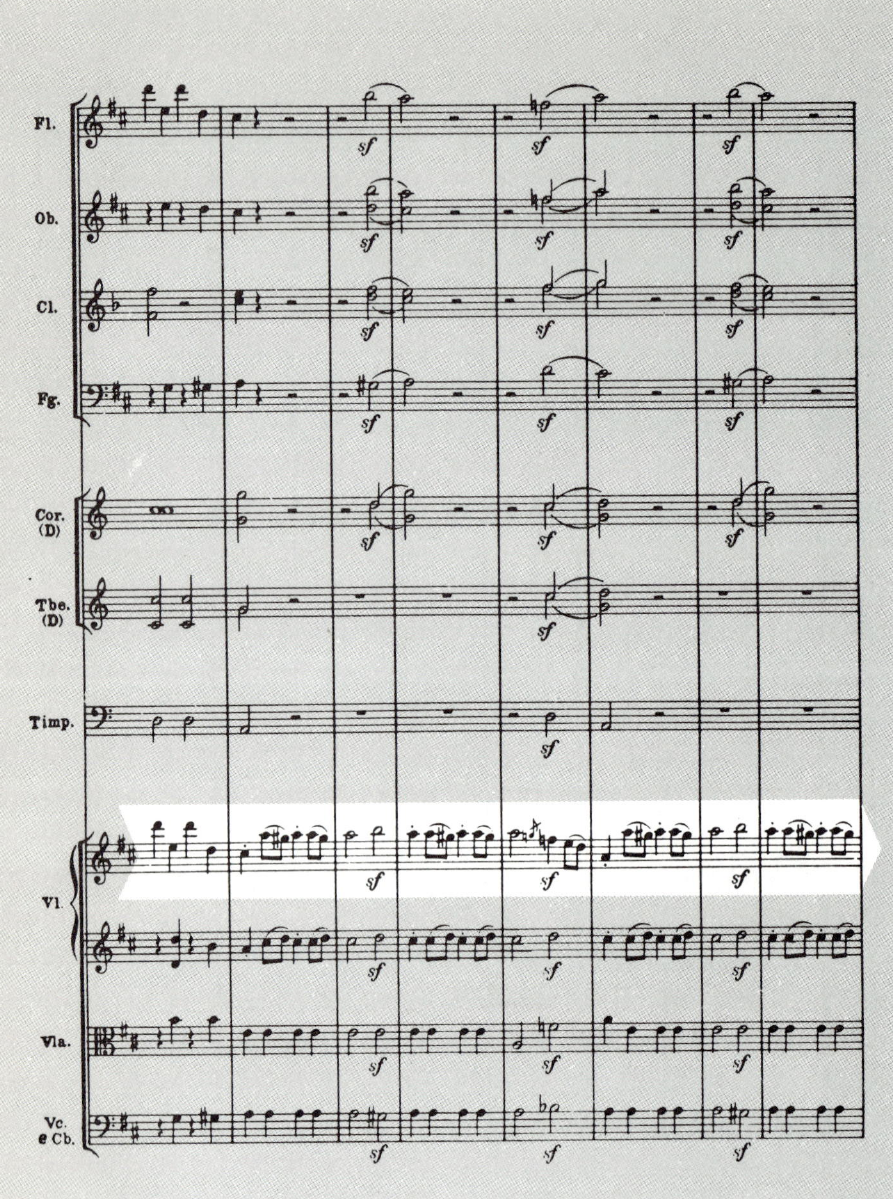
Fl.
Ob.
Cl.
Fg.
Cor. (D)
Tbe. (D)
Timp.
Vl.
Vla.
Vc. e Cb.
sf

240
Fl.
Ob.
Cl.
Fg.
Cor. (D)
Tbe. (D)
Timp.
Vl.
Vla.
Vc. e Cb.

250
Fl.
1.
p
Vl.
p
p
sf
sf
Vla.
p
sf
Vc. e Cb.
p
sf

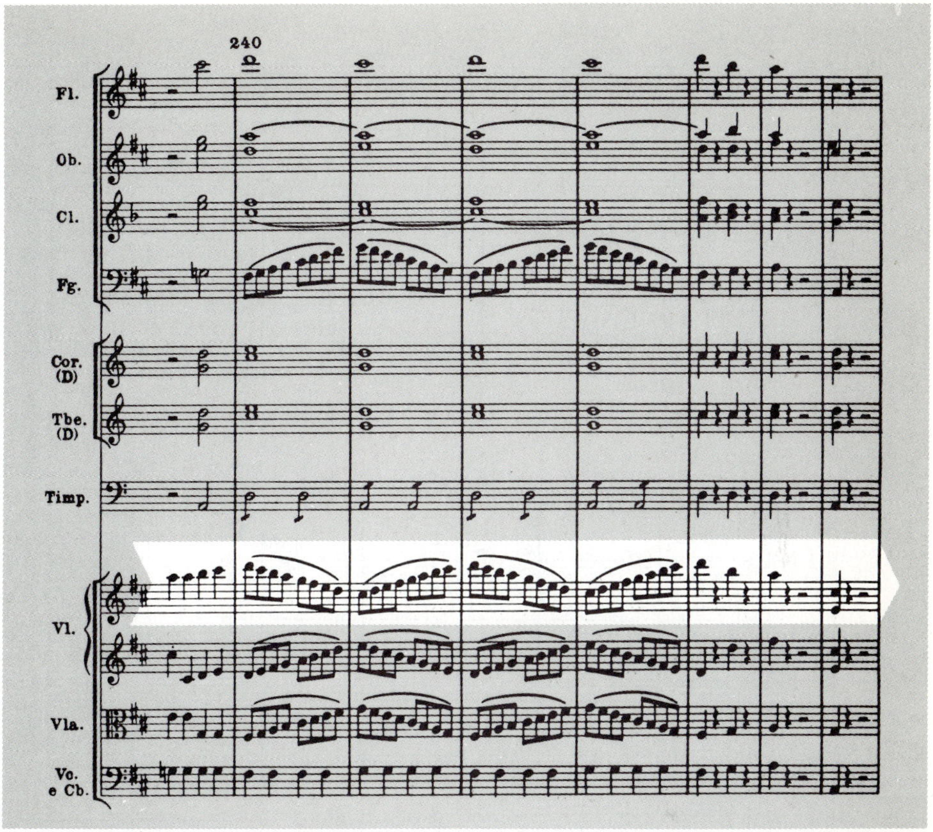

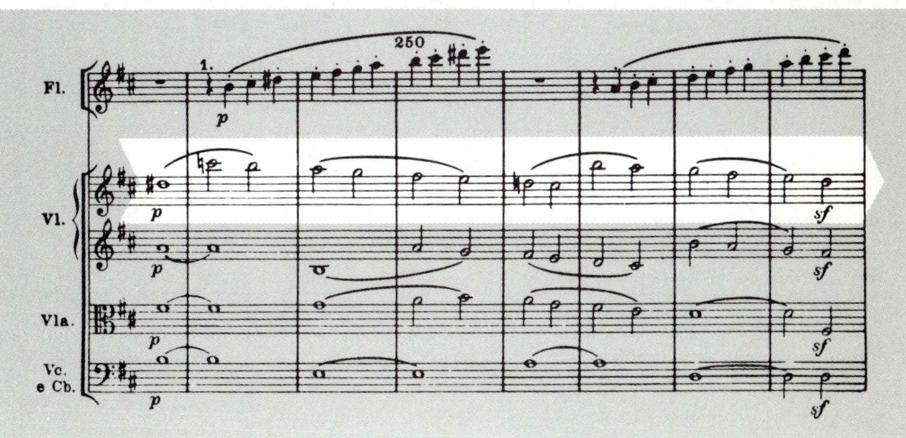

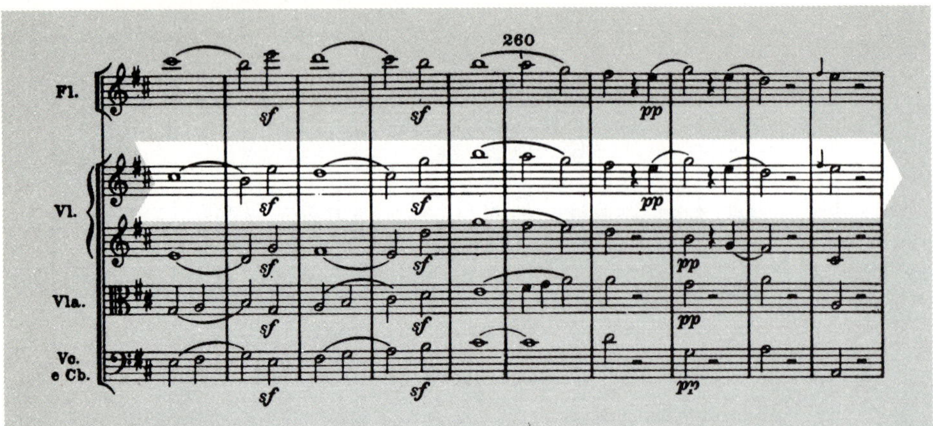
260
Fl.
sf
sf
pp
Vl.
sf
sf
pp
sf
sf
pp
Vla.
sf
sf
pp
Vc.
e Cb.
sf
sf
pp

zu 2
270
Fl.
f
sf
sf
sf
sf
Ob.
f
sf
sf
sf
sf
Cl.
f
zu 2
Fg.
f
Cor.
(D)
f
Tbe.
(D)
f
Timp.
f
Vl.
f
sf
sf
sf
sf
f
Vla.
f
Vc.
e Cb.
f

1.

Fl.
Ob.
Cl.
Fg.
Cor. (D)
Tbe. (D)
Timp.
Vl.
Vla.
Vc. e Cb.

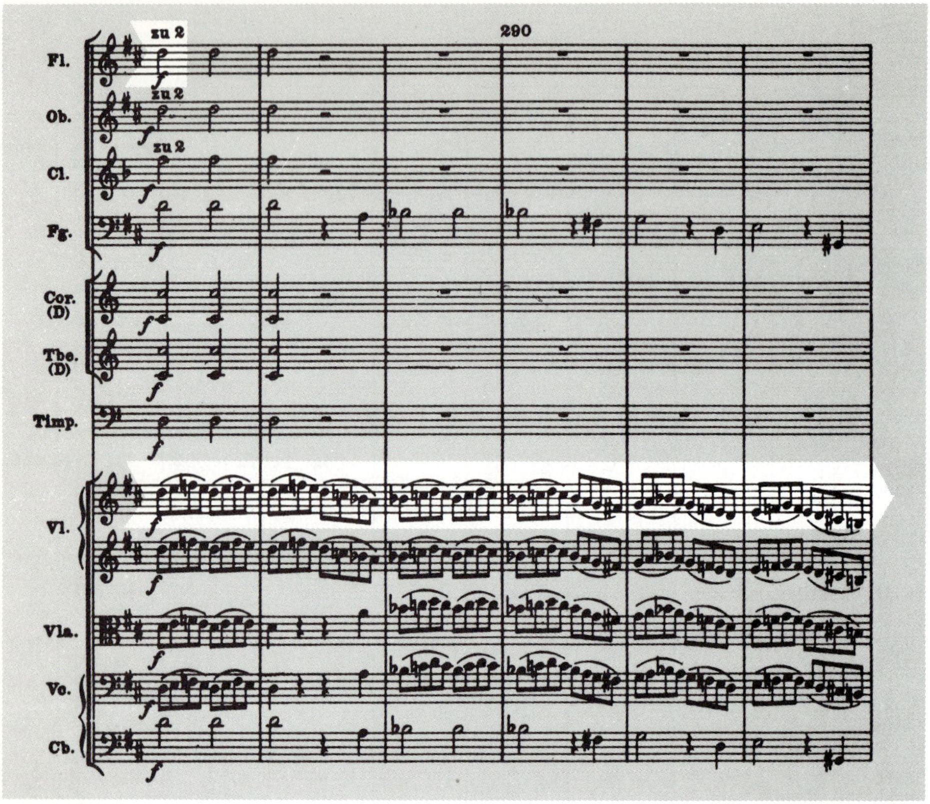

zu 2
290
Fl.
zu 2
Ob.
zu 2
Cl.
Fg.
Cor. (D)
Tbe. (D)
Timp.
Vl.
Vla.
Vc.
Cb.

Fl.
sempre f
Ob.
sempre f
Cl.
sempre f
Fg.
sempre f
Cor. (D)
sempre f
Tbe. (D)
sempre f
Timp.
sempre f
Vl.
sempre f
sempre f
Vla.
sempre f
Vc. e Cb.
sempre f

310

Fl.

Ob.

zu 2

Cl.

Fg.

Cor. (D)

Tbe. (D)

Timp.

Vl.

Vla.

Vc.

Vc. e Cb.

Cb.

820
Fl.
Ob.
zu 2
Cl.
Fg.
zu 2
Cor. (D)
Tbe. (D)
Timp.
Vl.
Vla.
Vc. e Cb.
Bassi
sf
p

330
Fl.
Ob.
Cl.
Fg.
Cor. (D)
Tbe. (D)
Timp.
Vl.
Vla.
Vc. e Cb.

31. Haydn

String Quartet in C major, Op. 76, No. 3, *(Emperor)*, Second movement (1797)

S2A/1 S2/1

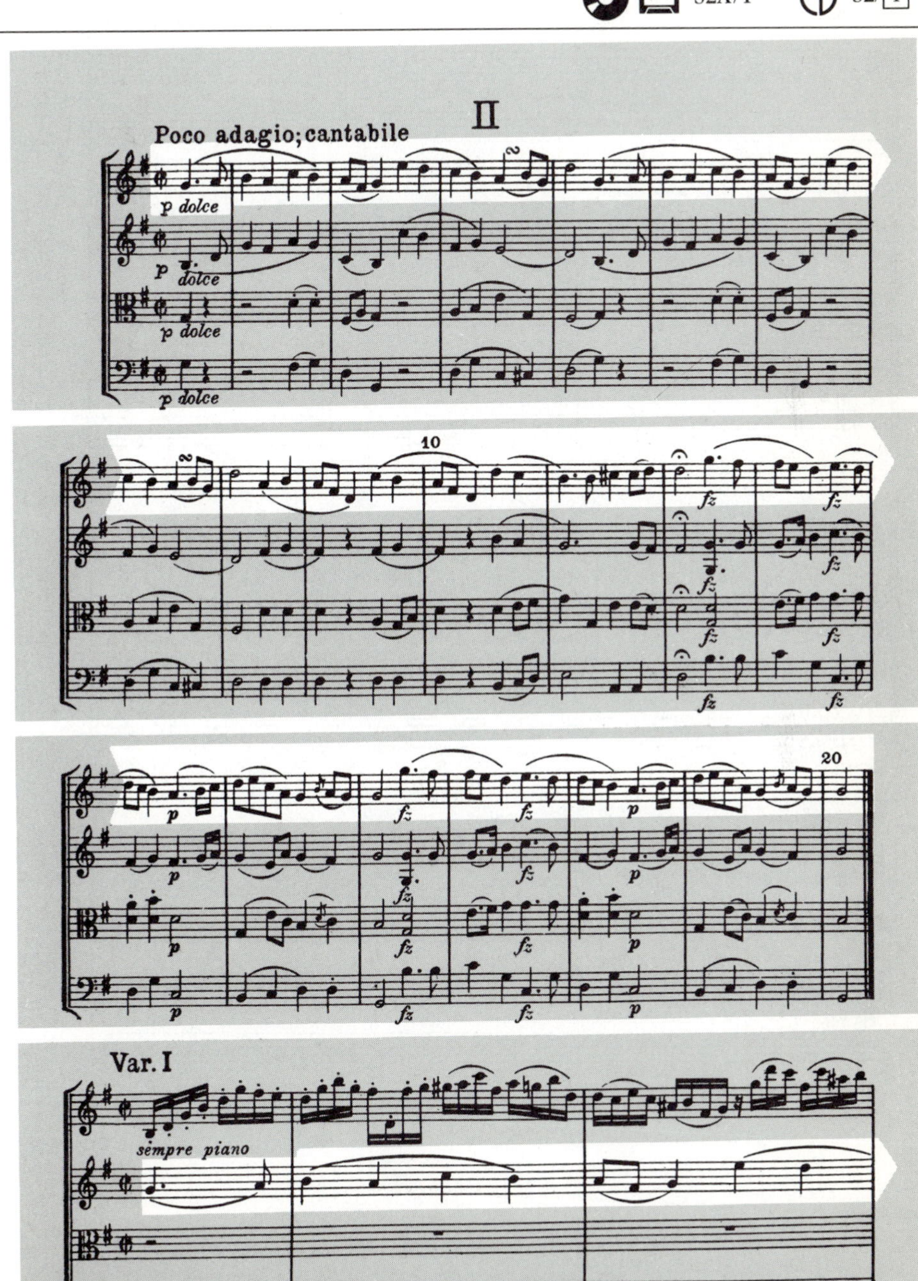

fz
fz
p
p

fz
fz
p
p
40
Var. II
p
p
p
p

50
fz
fz
fz
fz
60

Var. III
p
p
p
70
p

80
Var. IV
p
p
p
p
p
p
p
p
90

100
pp
pp
pp
pp

32. Haydn

Mass in D minor, *(Lord Nelson)*, (1798)

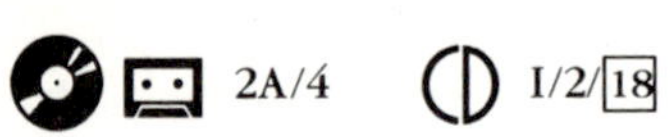

Credo

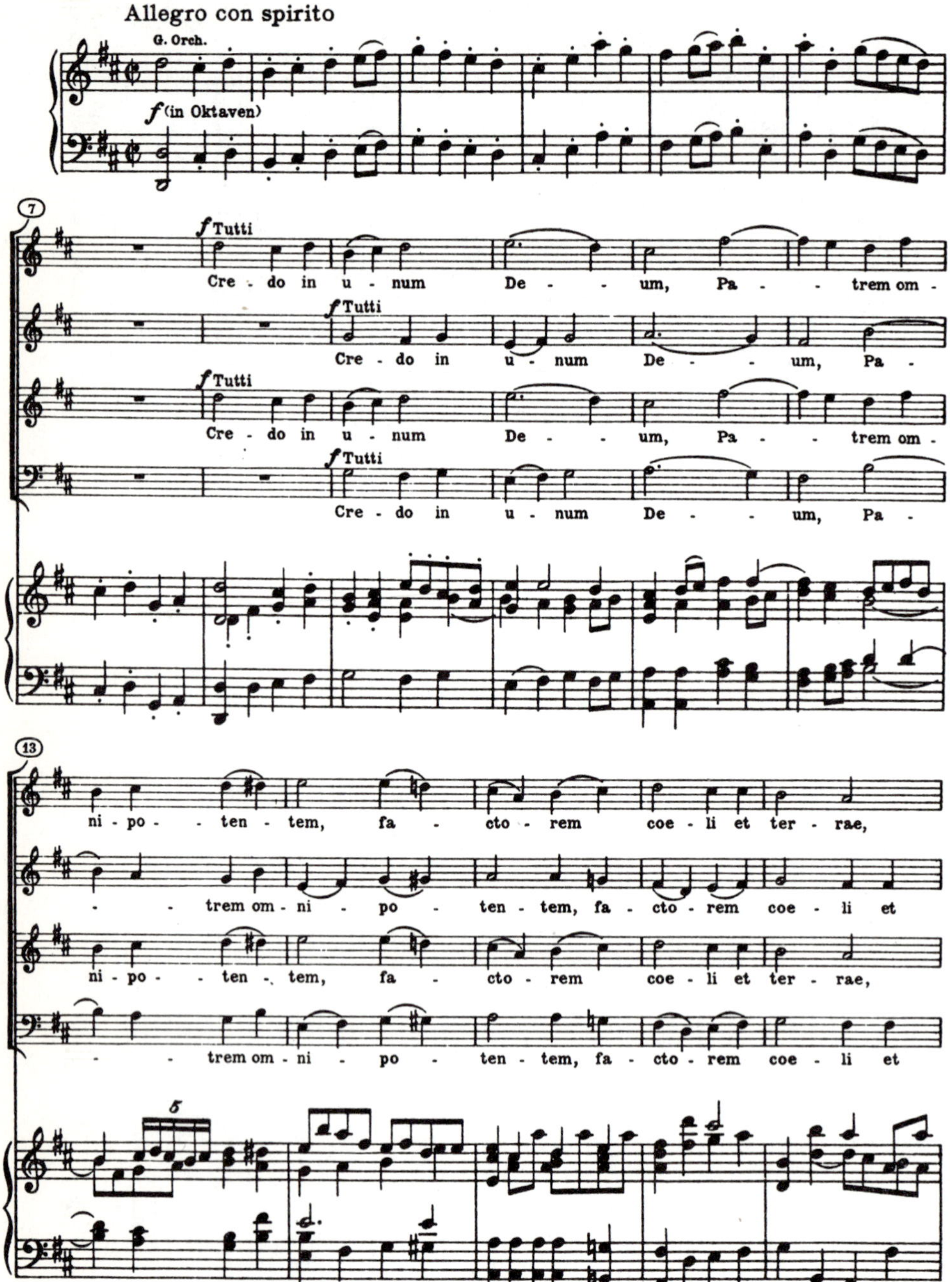

Allegro con spirito

G. Orch.

f (in Oktaven)

7

f Tutti

Cre - do in u - num De - - um, Pa - - trem om -

Cre - do in u - num De - - um, Pa -

Cre - do in u - num De - - um, Pa - - trem om -

Cre - do in u - num De - - um, Pa -

13

ni - po - ten - tem, fa - cto - rem coe - li et ter - rae,

- - trem om - ni - po - ten - tem, fa - cto - rem coe - li et

ni - po - - ten -. tem, fa - cto - rem coe - li et ter - rae,

- - trem om - ni - po - ten - tem, fa - cto - rem coe - li et

18
A
vi - si - bi - li - um om - ni - um, et in - vi - si -
ter - rae, vi - si - bi - li - um om - ni - um, et in -
vi - si - bi - li - um om - ni - um, et in - vi - si -
ter - rae, vi - si - bi - li - um om - ni - um, et in -
A
24
bi - li - um om - ni - um,
vi - si - bi - li - um om - ni - um,
bi - li - um om - ni - um,
vi - si - bi - li - um om - ni - um,
30
B
et ex Pa - tre na - tum an - te
et ex Pa - tre na - tum
et ex Pa - tre na - tum an - te
et ex Pa - tre na - tum
B

36
om - ni - a sae - - - cu - la: De - - um de De - o,
an - te om - - ni - a sae - - cu - la: De - um de
om - ni - a sae - - - cu - la: De - - um de De - o,
an - - te om - - ni - a sae - - cu - la: De - um de
41
lu - - men de lu - mi - ne, De - - um ve - - rum de De - - o
De - - o, lu - - men de lu - mi - ne, De - um ve - rum de
lu - - men de lu - mi - ne, De - - um ve - rum de De - - o
De - - o, lu - - men de lu - - mi - ne, De - um ve - rum de
46
ve - ro; ge -
De - o ve - ro;
ve - ro; ge -
De - o ve - ro;

51
C
- ni - tum, non fa - ctum, con - sub - stan - ti - a - - lem Pa - tri, —
ge - - - - ni - tum, non fa - - ctum, con - sub - stan - ti - a - lem
- ni - tum, non fa - ctum, con - sub - stan - ti - a - lem Pa - tri, —
ge - - - - ni - tum, non fa - - ctum, con - sub - stan - ti - a - lem
C
56
per — quem om - ni - a fa - cta sunt. Qui prop - ter nos
Pa - - tri, — per — quem om - ni - a fa - cta sunt. Qui
per — quem om - ni - a fa - cta sunt. Qui prop - ter nos
Pa - - tri, — per — quem om - ni - a fa - cta sunt. Qui
61
ho - mi - nes et prop - ter no - stram sa - lu - tem de - scen - dit de
prop - ter nos ho - mi - nes et prop - ter no - stram sa - lu - tem de -
ho - mi - nes et prop - ter no - stram sa - lu - tem de - scen - dit de
prop - ter nos ho - mi - nes et prop - ter no - stram sa - lu - tem de -

66
coe - lis, de - scen - dit de coe - lis, de coe - lis, de
scen - dit de coe - lis, de - scen - dit de coe - lis, de coe - lis,
coe - lis, de - scen - dit de coe - lis, de coe - lis, de
scen - dit de coe - lis, de - scen - dit de coe - lis, de coe - lis,
fz
fz
71
coe - lis, de coe - lis, de - scen - dit de coe - - -
de coe - lis, de coe - lis, de - scen - dit de
coe - lis, de coe - lis, de - scen - dit de coe - - -
de coe - lis, de coe - lis, de - scen - dit de
fz
fz
fz
76
- - - - - lis, de - scen - dit de coe - lis, de coe - - lis, de coe - lis.
coe - - - lis, de - scen - dit de coe - lis, de coe - - lis, de coe - lis.
- - - - - lis, de - scen - dit de coe - lis, de coe - - lis, de coe - lis.
coe - - - lis, de - scen - dit de coe - lis, de coe - - lis, de coe - lis.

Et Incarnatus

16
A
et ho - mo fa - ctus est, et ho - mo fa - ctus est.
Sopran
Tutti (mf espress.)
Et in - - car -
Alt
Tutti (mf espress.)
Et in - - car -
Tenor
Tutti (mf espress.)
Et in - - car -
Baß
Tutti (mf espress.)
Et in - - car -
cresc.
f p
f Ob. Fg. Str.
20
na-tus est de Spi - - ri - tu san - cto ex Ma - ri - a, Ma - ri - a
na-tus est de Spi - - ri - tu san - cto ex Ma - ri - a, Ma - ri - a
na-tus est de Spi - - ri - tu san - cto ex Ma - ri - a, Ma - ri - a
na-tus est de Spi - - ri - tu san - cto ex Ma - ri - a, Ma - ri - a

24
vir - gi-ne, et ho-mo fa - ctus est, et ho-mo fa - ctus
vir - gi-ne, et ho-mo fa - ctus est, et ho-mo fa - ctus
vir - gi-ne, et ho - mo fa - ctus est, et ho - mo fa - ctus
vir - gi-ne, et ho-mo fa - ctus est, et ho-mo fa - ctus
28
est. Cru-ci - fi - xus,cru-ci - fi - xus e - ti - am pro no - bis, sub Pon - ti - o Pi -
est. Cru-ci - fi - xus,cru-ci - fi - xus e - ti - am pro no - bis, sub Pon - ti - o Pi -
est. Cru-ci - fi - xus,cru-ci - fi - xus e - ti - am pro no - bis, sub Pon - ti - o Pi -
est. Cru-ci - fi - xus,cru-ci - fi xus e - ti - am pro no - bis, sub Pon - ti - o Pi -
fp Str. cresc.
fz
fp Trp. I II Pk. p
33
B
la - to, sub Pon - ti-o Pi - la - to,
Solo
la - to, sub Pon - ti - o Pi - la - to, pro no - bis, pro
Solo
la - to, sub Pon - ti - o Pi - la - to, Cru - ci - fi - xus, pas-sus,
Solo
la - to, sub Pon - ti - o Pi - la - to, sub Pon-ti - o Pi -
B
Vl. I
Vl. II

38
Tutti
Solo
cru-ci - fi - xus, pas-sus, pas-sus et se-pul - tus
no-bis, pro no - bis, cru-ci - fi - xus,pas-sus, pas-sus et se-pul - tus
pas - sus et se - pul-tus est, se - pul - tus, se - pul - tus, et se - pul - tus
la - to, sub Pi - la - to cru-ci - fi - xus, pas-sus, pas-sus
f Ob.Fg.Str.
Vl.I.II Va.
p
Fg.Vc.
43
Tutti pp
est, et se - pul - tus est, cru-ci-
est, et se - pul - tus est, cru-ci-
est, et se - pul - tus est, cru-ci-
et se - pul - tus est, sub Pon - ti-o Pi-
pp Ob.Fg.Str.
Fg.Vc.
Ob.Va.
Kh
49
fi - xus pro no - bis, pas-sus, pas - sus et se - pul - tus est.
fi - xus pro no - bis, pas-sus, pas - sus et se - pul - tus est.
fi - xus pro no - bis, pas-sus, pas - sus et se - pul - tus est.
la - to, sub Pon - ti-o Pi - la - to pas - sus et se - pul - tus est.

Et resurrexit

10
glo - ri - a, ju - di - ca - re vi - vos,
glo - ri - a, ju - di - ca - re vi - vos,
glo - ri - a, ju - di - ca - re vi - vos,
glo - ri - a, ju - di - ca - re vi - vos,
G.Orch.
13
vi - vos et, et, et mor - tu - os, et vi - vos et mor - tu -
vi - vos et, et, et mor - tu - os, et vi - vos et mor - tu -
vi - vos et, et, et mor - tu - os, et vi - vos et mor - tu -
vi - vos et, et, et mor - tu - os, et vi - vos et mor - tu -
Str. Hbl.
Str.
G.Orch.
Str.
19
A
os, cu - jus re - gni non e - rit, non e - rit
os, et cu - jus re - gni non
os, cu - jus re - gni non e - rit, non e - rit fi - nis, non e - rit
os, cu - jus re - gni non
A
Trp.
Trp.
G.Orch.
Pk.
Pk.

22
fi - nis, non e - rit fi - nis, non e - rit, non e - rit, non, non,
e - rit, non e - rit fi - nis, non e - rit, non e - rit, non, non,
fi - nis, non e - rit fi - nis, non e - rit, non e - rit, non, non,
e - rit, non e - rit fi - nis, non e - rit, non e - rit, non, non,
25
non, non, non e - rit fi - - nis. Et,
non, non, non e - rit fi - - nis. Et,
non, non, non e - rit fi - - nis. Et,
non, non, non e - rit fi - - nis. Et,
Str. Trp.
Str. Hbl.
Pk.
29
et in Spi - ri-tum san - ctum, Do - mi-num, et vi - vi - fi - can - tem; qui cum
et in Spi - ri-tum san - ctum, Do - mi-num, et vi - vi - fi - can - tem; qui cum
et in Spi - ri-tum san - ctum, Do - mi-num, et vi - vi - fi - can - tem; qui cum
et in Spi - ri-tum san - ctum, Do - mi-num, et vi - vi - fi - can - tem; qui cum

33
B
Pa - - tre et Fi - li - o si - - mul a - - do -
Pa - - tre et Fi - li - o si - - mul a - - do -
Pa - - tre et Fi - li - o si - - mul a - - do -
Pa - - tre et Fi - li - o si - - mul a - - do -
B
G.Orch.
37
ra - tur et con-glo-ri-fi - ca - tur, qui lo - - cu - tus est per Pro -
ra - tur et con-glo-ri-fi - ca - tur, qui lo - - cu - tus est per Pro -
ra - tur et con-glo-ri-fi - ca - tur, qui lo - - cu - tus est per Pro -
ra - tur et con-glo-ri-fi - ca - tur, qui lo - - cu - tus est per Pro -
Str. Hbl.
40
phe - - - - - - - - tas.
phe - - - - - - - - tas.
phe - - - - - - - - tas.
phe - - - - - - - - tas.

43
Str.
47
Et, et u - nam san - - ctam Ca -
Et, et u - nam san - - ctam Ca -
Et, et u - nam san - - ctam Ca -
Et, et u - nam san - - ctam Ca -
Str. Hbl.
50
tho-li-cam et A - - po-sto-li-cam ec - cle-si-am.
tho-li-cam et A - - po-sto-li-cam ec - cle-si-am.
tho-li-cam et A - - po-sto-li-cam ec - cle-si-am.
tho-li-cam et A - - po-sto-li-cam ec - cle-si-am.
Str.

53
C
Con - fi - te - or u - num bap - tis - ma in re - mis - si -
Con - fi - te - or u - num bap - tis - ma in re - mis - si -
Con - fi - te - or u - num bap - tis - ma in re - mis - si -
Con - fi - te - or u - num bap - tis - ma in re - mis - si -
C
(>)
56
o - nem pec - - - ca - to - - rum et ex -
o - nem pec - ca - to - - rum et ex -
o - nem pec - - - ca - to - - rum et ex -
o - nem pec - ca - to - - rum et ex -
Trp.
Pk.
59
pe - cto re - sur - re - cti - o - nem mor - - - - - tu -
pe - cto re - sur - re - cti - o - nem mor - - - - - tu -
pe - cto re - sur - re - cti - o - nem mor - - - - - tu -
pe - cto re - sur - re - cti - o - nem mor - - - - - tu -
Trp.
Trp.
Trp.
Fk.
Pk.
Pk.

62
D
Solo
o - rum.
Et,
et
o - rum.
Et,
o - rum.
Et,
o - rum.
Et,
D
Ob.
Trp.
Trp.
Trp. p
Vl.I.II
Pk.
Pk.
Pk.
Vc.
66
vi - tam
ven - tu - ri
sae - cu-li.
A
Ob.
71

76
E
Tutti
men.
Et
vi - - tam
Tutti
Et,
et
vi - - tam
Tutti
Et,
vi - - - tam
et
Tutti
Et,
et
vi - - tam
E
Str. Trp. Pk.
79
ven - tu - ri
sae - - cu - li,
a - - - - -
ven - tu - ri
sae - - cu - li,
a - - - men,
vi - - tam
ven - tu - ri
sae - - - - - cu - li,
ven - tu - ri
sae - - cu - li,
a - - - - - - - - -
82
- - - - - - - - - - men, a - - - men,
a - - - - - - - - - men, a - - - men,
a - - - - - - - - - men, a - - - men,
- - - - - - - - - - men, a - - - men,
G. Orch.

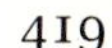

(85)

a - - - men, a - men, a - - - - - - -

a - - men, a - men, a - - - - -

a - - - men, a - men, a - - - men,

a - - - men, a - men, a - - - men,

(88)

men, a - - - - - - - - - - - - - - - - - -

men, a - - - - - - - - - - - - men, a - -

a - - - - - - - - - - - men, a - - - - - - - - - -

a - - - - - - - - - - - - - - - - - - men, a - - - -

Str.

(93)

F

men, a - - - men, a - men,

men, a - - - men, a - men,

men, a - - - men, a - men,

men, a - - - men, a - men,

F

G.Orch.

96
a - - - - - - - - men,
a - - - - - - - -
a - - - - - - - men,
a - - - - - - -
a - - - men, a - - - - - - - - - - - - - men, a -
a - - - men, a - - - - - - - - - - - - -
Str.
100
- - - - - - - - - - - - men,
- - - - - - - men, a - - men,
- - - - - - - - - - - - men,
- - - - - - - - - - - - men,
fz
f Str. Trp. Pk.
104
(ff)
a - - - men, a - - - men, a - - - men.
(ff)
a - - - men, a - - - men, a - - - men.
(ff)
a - - - - - - - - - - men, a - - - - men.
(ff)
a - - - - - - - - - - - - men, a - - - men.
ff G. Orch.

TRANSLATION

I "Credo in unum Deum"
Credo in unum Deum,
Patrem omnipontem,
factorem coeli et terrae,
visibilium omnium et invisibilium omnium,
et ex Patre natum omnia saecula.

I believe in one God,
the Father almighty,
maker of heaven and earth,
and of all things visible and invisible.

And in one Lord Jesus Christ,
the only begotten son of God,
born of the Father before all ages;

Deum de Deo,
lumen de lumine,
Deum verum de Deo vero,
genitum, non factum,
consubstantialem Patri,
per quem omnia facta sunt:
Qui propter nos homines
et propter nostram salutem
descendit de coelis.

God of God,
Light of Light,
true son of God;
begotten, not made
of one being with the Father,
by whom all things were made.
Who for us men,
and for our salvation,
came down from heaven.

II "Et incarnatus est"
Et incarnatus est de Spiritu
sancto ex Maria virgine, et
homo factus est. Crucifixus
etiam pro nobis sub Pontio
Pilato, passus et sepultus est.

And was incarnate by the Holy
Ghost, of the Virgin Mary; and
was made man. He was
crucified for us, suffered under
Pontius Pilate, and was buried.

III "Et resurrexit"
Et resurrexit tertia die

secundum Scripturas, et
ascendit in coelum, sedet ad
dexteram Patris. Et iteram
venturus est cum gloria
judicare vives et mortuos;
Cuius regni non erit finis.
Et in Spiritum Sanctum,
Dominum et vivicantem,
Qui cum Patre et Filio
simul adoratur et conglorificatur,
qui locutus est per Prophetas,
et unam sanctum catholicam et
apostolicam Ecclesiam.
Confiteor unum baptisma in
remissionem peccatorum. Et
expecto resurrectionem
mortuorum, et vitam venturi
saeculi. Amen.

And on the third day He rose
again from the dead according
to the Scriptures; and he
ascended into heaven. He
sitteth at the right hand of the
Father; and he shall come again
to judge the living and the dead;
and his kingdom shall have no end.
And in the Holy Spirit,
the Lord and Giver of life,
who with the Fathr and Son
is worshipped and glorified;
who spoke by the prophets.
And in one holy, catholic, and
apostolic church. I
acknowledge one Baptism for
the remission of sins, and I look
for the resurrection of the
dead, and the life of the world
to come. Amen.

33. Wolfgang Amadeus Mozart (1756-1791),

Violin Sonata in E-flat major,
K. 302, Second movement (1778)

 S2A/2 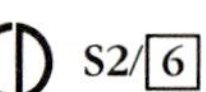 S2/6

Andante grazioso

9

16

25

34

42

80
89
96
105
113

118
124
130
136
142

*) In autogr. and 1st edition based thereon, 7th and 10th sixteenth-notes (semiquavers): f^1 (error in notation?).

**) According to autogr.; first ed.: dotted quarter-notes (crotchets) as in treble of piano part. Likewise b. 171.

34. Mozart

Piano Concerto in C major, K. 467
(1785)

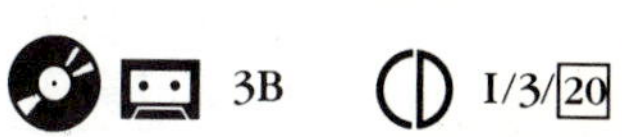

TUTTI

Flauto.

2 Oboi.

2 Fagotti.

2 Corni in C.

2 Trombe in C.

Timpani in C-G.

Klavier.

Violino I.

Violino II.

Viola.

Violoncello e
Contrabasso.

10
Fl.
Ob.
Fag.
Cor. (C)
Trb. (C)
Timp.
Vl.
Vla.
Vlc. e Cb.
p
tr
f
zu 2
3

20
Fl.
Ob.
Fag.
Cor. (C)
zu 2
Trb. (C)
zu 2
Timp.
Vl.
Vla.
Vlc. e Cb.

Fl.
Ob.
Fag.
Cor. (C)
Trb. (C)
Timp.
Vl.
Vla.
Vlc. e Cb.

30
Fl.
Ob.
Fag.
Cor. (C)
Trb. (C)
Timp.
Vl.
Vla.
Vlc. e Cb.

Fl.
Ob.
Fag.
Cor. (C)
Trb. (C)
Vl. I.
Vla.
Vlc. e Cb.

40
zu 2
Ob.
Fag.
Cor.
(C)
Vl.
Vla.
Vlc. e
Cb.

Fl.
Ob.
Fag.
Cor.
(C)
Trb.
(C)
Timp.
Vl.
Vla.
Vlc. e
Cb.

50
Fl.
Ob.
Fag.
zu 2
Cor. (C)
Trb. (C)
zu 2
Timp.
Vl.
Vla.
Vlc. e Cb.
Fl.
p
Ob.
p
Fag.
p
Cor. (C)
Trb. (C)
Timp.
Vl.
p
p
Vla.
p
Vlc. e Cb.
p

60
Fl.
Ob.
Fag.
Vl.
Vla.
Vlc. e Cb.

Fl.
Ob.
zu 2
Fag.
zu 2
Cor. (C)
Trb. (C)
Timp.
Vl.
Vla.
Vlc. e Cb.

70
Fl.
Ob.
zu 2
Fag.
Cor. (C)
Trb. (C)
Timp.
Vl.
Vla.
Vlc. e Cb.
1.
p
[p]
3
SOLO
Klav.

Fl.
Ob.
Fag.
Cor. (C)
Trb. (C)
Klav.

80
tr
Klav.
Vl.
Vla.
Vlc. e Cb.
p

90

Fl.
Ob.
Fag.
Cor. (C)
Trb. (C)
Timp.
Klav.
Vl.
Vla.
Vlc. e Cb.

Klav.
Vl.
Vla.
Vlc. e Cb.

Klav.
Vl.
Vla.
Vlc. e Cb.

100
Klav.
Vl.
Vla.

Klav.
Vl.
Vla.
Vlc. e Cb.

TUTTI.
SOLO.
Fl.
zu 2
Ob.
Fag.
zu 2
Cor. (C)
Trb. (C)
Timp.
Klav.
Vl.
Vla.
Vlc. e Cb.

110
Klav.
p
p
120
Klav.
Klav.
Vl.
Vla.
Vlc.
Vlc.
p
p
p
p
Klav.
Vl.
Vla.
Vlc.

Klav.
130
Klav.
Vl.
[p]
Vla.
Bassi.
Vlc. e Cb.
Fl.
Ob.
1.
Fag.
Klav.
Vlc. e Cb.

140
Fl.
Ob.
Fag.
Klav.
Vlc. e Cb.
Fl.
Klav.
Klav.
Vl.
[p]
[p]
Vla.
[p]
Vlc. e Cb.
[p]

Fl.
Ob.
Fag.
[p]
[p]
p
Klav.
Vl.
Vla.
Vlc. e Cb.

150
Fl.
Ob.
Klav.
Vl
Vla.
Vlc. e Cb.

Fl.
Ob.
Klav.
Vl.
Vla.
Vlc. e Cb.

Klav.
Vl.
Vla.
Vlc. e Cb.

160
Klav.
Vl.
Vla.
Vlc. e Cb.

Fl.
Ob.
Fag.
Cor. (C)
Klav.

Klav.

Klav.
Vl.
Vla.
Vlc. e Cb.
170
Klav.
Klav.
Klav.
Vl.
Vla.
Vlc. e Cb.

180
Klav.
Vl.
Vla.
Vlc. e Cb.
Klav.
Vl.
Vla.
Vlc. e Cb.
Ob.
Klav.
Vl.
Vla.
Vlc. e Cb.

Fl.
Ob.
Fag.
Klav.
Vl.
Vla.
Vlc. e Cb.
Vlc.

190
Fl.
Ob.
Fag.
1.
Klav.
Vl.
Vla.
Vlc.
Vlc.

Fl.
Ob.
Fag.
tr
Klav.
Vl.
Vla.
Vlc. e Cb.
Bassi
TUTTI
Fl.
Ob.
zu 2
Fag.
zu 2
Cor. (C)
zu 2
Trb. (C)
Timp.
Klav.
Vl.
Vla.
Vlc. e Cb.

200
Fl.
Ob.
Fag.
Cor. (C)
Trb. (C)
Timp.
Vl.
Vla.
Vlc. e Cb.

Fl.
Ob.
Fag.
zu 2
Cor. (C)
Trb. (C)
Timp.
Vl.
Vla.
Vlc. e Cb.
p

210
Fl.
Ob.
Fag.
Vl.
Vla.
Vlc. e Cb.
220
p
p

SOLO.
Fl.
Ob.
Klav.
Vl.
Vla.
Vlc. e Cb.
230
Fag.

Fl.
Ob.
1.
Fag.
Klav.
Vl.
Vla.
Vlc. e
Cb.

Fl.
Ob.
Fag.
1.
Klav.
Vl.
Vla.
Vlc. e
Cb.

240
Ob.
Fag.
Klav.
Vl.
Vla.
Vlc. e Cb.

Fl.
Ob.
Fag.
Klav.
Vl.
Vla.
Vlc. e Cb.

Fl.
1.
Ob.
1.
Fag.
Klav.
Vl.
Vla.
Vlc. e
Cb.

250
Fl.
1.
Ob.
1.
Fag.
Klav.
Vl.
Vla.
Vlc. e
Cb.

Fl.
Ob.
Fag.
Klav.
Vl.
Vla.
Vlc. e Cb.

Fl.
Ob.
1.
Klav.
Vl.
Vla.
Vlc. e Cb.

Fl.
Ob.
1.
Klav.
Vl.
Vla.
Vlc. e Cb.

260
Fl.
Klav.
Vl.
Vla.
Vlc. e Cb.

Fl.
Klav.
Vl.
Vla.
Vlc. e Cb.

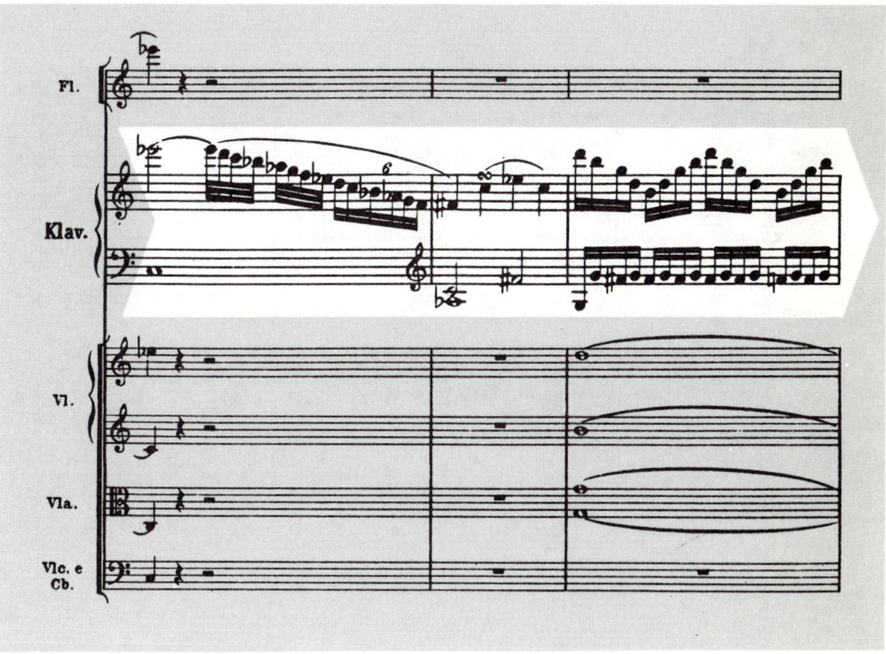
Fl.
Klav.
Vl.
Vla.
Vlc. e Cb.

Fl.
Ob.
Fag.
Cor. (C)
Klav.
Vl.
Vla.
270
Fl.
Ob.
1.
Fag.
Cor. (C)
Trb. (C)
p
Timp.
p
Klav.
Vl.
Vla.
Vlc. e Cb.

TUTTI

Fl.

Ob.

Fag.

Cor. (C)

Trb. (C)

Timp.

Klav.

Vl.

Vla.

Vlc. e Cb.

p

280
Fl.
Ob.
Fag.
Cor. (C)
Trb. (C)
Timp.
Vl.
Vla.
Vlc. e Cb.

Fl.
Ob.
Fag.
zu 2
Cor. (C)
Trb. (C)
Timp.
Vl.
Vla.
Vlc. e Cb.

290
Fl.
Ob.
Fag.
Cor. (C)
Trb. (C)
Timp.
Vl.
Vla.
Vlc. e Cb.

Fl.
Ob.
Fag.
Cor. (C)
Trb. (C)
Timp.
Vl.
Vla.
Vlc. e Cb.

SOLO.
Fl.
Klav.
Vl.
p
300
Ob.
Vla.
Vlc.
[*p*]

Ob.
Fag.
Cor. (C)
Klav.
Vl.
Vla.
Vlc.
2.
p
p
p

310
Fl.
Ob.
Fag.
Cor. (C)
Klav.
[p]

Fl.
Ob.
Fag.
Cor. (C)
Klav.
Vl.
[p]
[p]
Vla.
[p]
Bassi.
Vlc. e Cb.
[p]

320
Fl.
Ob.
Fag.
[p]
Klav.
Vlc. e Cb.
1.
330
Vl.
[p]

Fl.
Ob.
Fag.
Klav.
Vl.
Vla.
Vlc. e Cb.
[p]
1.
2.
3

Fl.
Ob.
Fag.
1.
2.
3
Klav.
Vl.
Vla.
Vlc. e Cb.

Fl.
Ob.
Fag.
1.
3
Klav.
Vl.
Vla.
Vlc. e Cb.

340
Klav.
Vl.
Vla.
Vlc. e
Cb.
Klav.
Vl.
Vla.
Vlc. e
Cb.
Klav.
Vl.
Vla.
Vlc. e
Cb.

350
Fl.
Ob.
Fag.
Cor. (C)
Klav.
Vl.
Vla.
Vlc. e Cb.
TUTTI.
SOLO.
Fl.
Ob.
Fag.
Cor. (C)
Trb. (C)
Klav.
Vl.
Vla.
Vlc. e Cb.

360
Ob.
Fag.
Trb. (C)
Klav.
Vla.
Vlc. e Cb.
Klav.
Klav.
Vl.
Vla.
Vlc. e Cb.
[p]
[p]
[p]
[p]

Ob.
Fag.
[p]
[p]
Klav.
Vl.
Vla.
Vlc. e
Cb.

370
Ob.
Fag.
Klav.
Vl.
Vla.
Vlc. e
Cb.

Fl.
Ob.
Fag.
Klav.
Vl.
Vla.
Vlc. e Cb.
2.
2.
Fl.
Ob.
Fag.
Cor. (C)
Trb. (C)
Timp.
Klav.
Vl.
Vla.
Vlc. e Cb.
1.
1.
p
p
p

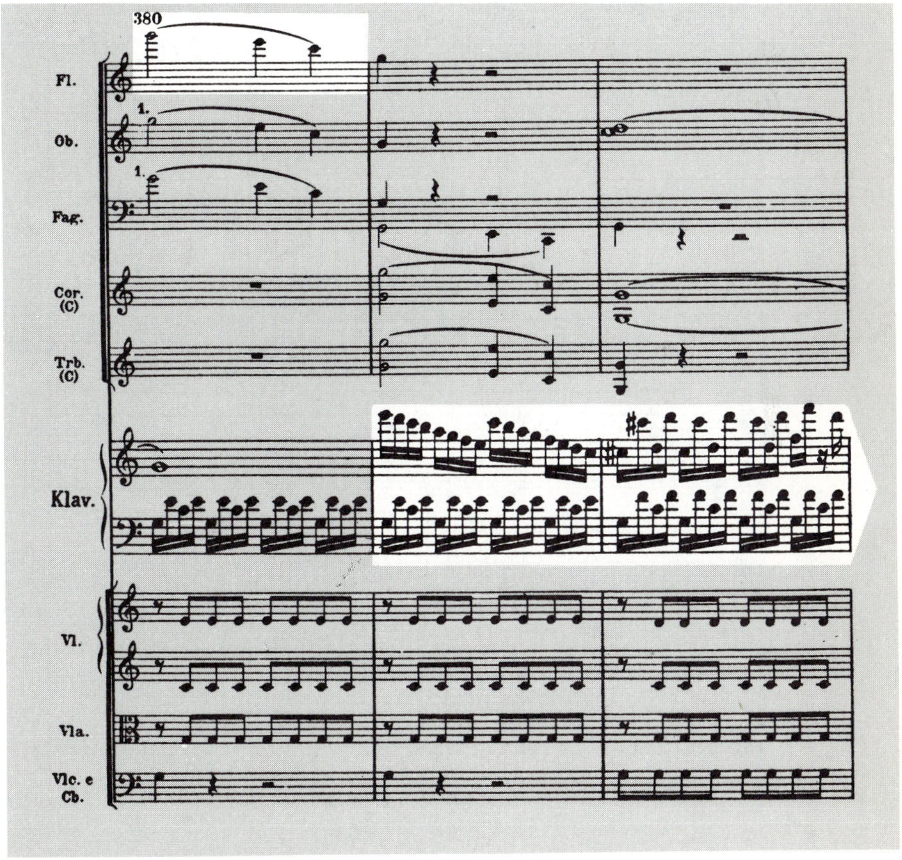

380
Fl.
1.
Ob.
1.
Fag.
Cor.
(C)
Trb.
(C)
Klav.
Vl.
Vla.
Vlc. e
Cb.

TUTTI
Fl.
Ob.
Fag.
zu 2
Cor. (C)
Trb. (C)
Timp.
Klav.
Vl.
Vla.
Vlc. e Cb.
390

* Mozart did not leave written-out cadenzas for this concerto. Modern pianists supply their own or choose from among various published cadenzas.

Fl.
Ob.
Fag.
Cor. (C)
Trb. (C)
Timp.
Vl.
Vla.
Vlc. e Cb.

Fl.
Ob.
Fag.
Cor. (C)
Trb. (C)
Timp.
Vl.
Vla.
Vlc. e Cb.
zu 2
f
p

410
Fl.
Ob.
zu 2
Fag.
Cor. (C)
Trb. (C)
Timp.
Vl.
Vla.
Vlc. e Cb.
Fl.
Ob.
Fag.
zu 2
Cor. (C)
1.
Trb. (C)
Timp.
Vl.
Vla.
Vlc. e Cb.

II.
Andante.
TUTTI
Flauto.
2 Oboi.
2 Fagotti.
2 Corni in F.
Klavier.
Con Sordino
Violino I.
Violino II.
Con Sordino
Con Sordino
Viola.
Violoncello e Contrabasso.
p Pizzicato
Fl.
Ob.
Fag.
Cor. (F)
Vl.
Vla.
Vlc. e Cb.

10
Fl.
Ob.
Fag.
Cor. (F)
Vl.
Vla.
Vlc. e Cb.

Fl.
Ob.
Fag.
Cor. (F)
Vl.
Vla.
Vlc. e Cb.

20
SOLO
Fl.
Ob.
Fag.
Cor. (F)
Klav.
pizz.
Vl.
Vla.
Vlc. e Cb.

Klav.
Vl.
Vla.
Vlc. e Cb.

Klav.
Vl.
Vla.
Vlc. e Cb.

30
Fl.
Ob.
Fag.
Cor. (F)
p
Klav.
Vl.
Vla.
Vlc. e Cb.

Fl.
Ob.
Fag.
Cor. (F)
Klav.
Vl.
Vla.
Vlc. e
arco
Fl.
Ob.
Fag.
Cor. (F)
Klav.
Vl.
arco
Vla.
arco
Vlc. e Cb.
arco

40
tr
Klav.
Vl.
Vla.
pizz.
Vlc. e
Cb.

Fl.
[p]
Ob.
[p]
Fag.
[p]
Klav.
Vl.
Vla.
Vlc. e
Cb.

50
Fl.
Ob.
Fag.
Klav.
Vl.
Vla.
Vlc. e Cb.

TUTTI
Fl.
Ob.
Fag.
Klav.
Vl.
Vla.
Vlc. e Cb.

tr
SOLO
Fl.
Ob.
Fag.
1.
Klav.
Vl.
Vla.
Vlc. e
Cb.
60
Fl.
Ob.
Fag.
Cor.
(F)
tr
Klav.
Vl.
Vla.
Vlc. e
Cb.
f
p
pizz.
[arco]
arco

Fl.
Ob.
Fag.
Klav.
Vl.
Vla.
Vlc. e Cb.
sfp
tr.
f
p
pizz.
70
arco

Fl.
Ob.
Fag.
Klav.
Vl.
Vla.
Vlc. e Cb.
pizz.

Ob.
Fag.
Klav.
Vl.
Vla.
Vlc. e Cb.

80
Ob.
Fag.
Klav.
Vl.
Vla.
Vlc. e Cb.

Fl.
Ob.
Fag.
Cor. (F)
Klav.
arco
arco
arco
Vl.
Vla.
Vlc. e Cb.

Fl.
Ob.
Fag.
Cor. (F)
Klav.
Vl.
Vla.
Vlc. e Cb.
90
1.
pizz.

Fl.
Ob.
1.
Fag.
1.
cresc.
Cor. (F)
cresc.
p
Klav.
Vl.
Vla.
Vlc. e Cb.
Fl.
p
cresc.
Ob.
f
cresc.
Fag.
cresc.
Cor. (F)
Klav.
Vl.
Vla.
Vlc. e Cb.

100
Fl.
Ob.
Fag.
Cor. (F)
Klav.
Vl.
Vla.
Vlc. e Cb.

Fl.
Ob.
Fag.
Cor. (F)
pp
Klav.
Vl.
Vla.
Vlc. e Cb.

III.
Allegro vivace assai.
TUTTI
Flauto.
2 Oboi.
2 Fagotti.
2 Corni in C.
2 Trombe in C.
Timpani in C-G.
Klavier.
Violino I.
Violino II.
Viola.
Violoncello e Contrabasso.

10
Fl.
Ob.
Fag.
Cor. (C)
Trb. (C)
Vl.
Vla.
Vlc. e Cb.
zu 2
zu 2
20
SOLO
Timp.
Klav.

TUTTI
30
Fl.
Ob.
Fag.
Cor. (C)
Trb. (C)
Timp.
Klav.
Vl.
Vla.
Vlc. e Cb.
40
zu 2
1.

Fl.
Ob.
Fag.
Cor. (C)
Trb. (C)
Timp.
Vl.
Vla.
Vlc. e Cb.
50
zu 2

SOLO
60
Cor. (C)
p
Klav.
Cor. (C)
Klav.
70
TUTTI
Klav.
Vl.
p
p
80
1.
SOLO
Ob.
p
1.
Fag.
p
Klav.
Vl.
Vla.
p
Vlc. e Cb.
p

90
Klav.
Vl.
Vla.
Vlc. e Cb.

Klav.
Vl.
Vla.
Vlc. e Cb.

100
Klav.
Vl.
Vla.
Vlc. e Cb.
Vlc.

110
TUTTI
Ob.
Fag.
Cor. (C)
Klav.
Vl.
Vla.
Vlc.
1.
[p]

Fl.
Ob.
Fag.
Cor. (C)
zu 2
Vl.
Vla.
Vlc. e Cb.
Bassi [p]

120
SOLO
Fl.
Ob.
Fag.
Cor.
(C)
tr
tr
Klav.
Vl.
Vla.
Vlc. e
Cb.

130
Fl.
Ob.
1.
Fag.
Klav.
Vl.
Vla.
Vlc. e
Cb.

Fl.
Ob.
Fag.
Klav.
Vl.
Vla.
Vlc. e Cb.

140
Fl.
Ob.
Fag.
Klav.
Vl.
Vla.
Vlc. e Cb.

150
Klav.
Vl.
Vla.
Vlc. e
Cb.
Klav.
Vl.
Vla.
Vlc. e
Cb.
160
Fl.
Ob.
Fag.
Klav.

170
Fl.
Ob.
Fag.
Klav.
Vl.
Vla.
Vlc. e
Cb.
p

Klav.
Vl.
Vla.
Vlc. e
Cb.

180
Klav.
Vl.
Vla.
Vlc. e Cb.

TUTTI
190
Fl.
Ob.
Fag.
Cor. (C)
Trb. (C)
Timp.
Vl.
Vla.
Vlc. e Cb.

SOLO
200
Klav.
Vl.
Vla.
Vlc. e Cb.
Klav.
Vl.
Fl.
Ob.
Fag.
Cor. (C)
210
Klav.

TUTTI
220
Fl.
Ob.
zu 2
Fag.
Cor. (C)
Trb. (C)
Timp.
Klav.
Vl.
Vla.
Vlc. e Cb.

230
Fl.
Ob.
zu 2
Fag.
Vl.
Vla.
Vlc. e Cb.

Ob.
Fag.
SOLO
240
Klav.
Vl.
Vla.
Vlc. e Cb.
Klav.
TUTTI
250
SOLO
Fl.
Ob.
Fag.
Klav.
Vl.
Vlc. e Cb.

260
Klav.
TUTTI
SOLO
TUTTI
SOLO
Fl.
[p]
Ob.
[p]
Fag.
[p]
Klav.
Vl.
[p]
[p]
Vla.
[p]
Vlc. e
Cb.
[p]
270
Klav.
Vl.
Vla.
Vlc. e
Cb.

280
zu 2
Ob.
Fag.
Klav.
zu 2
Ob.
Fag.
Klav.
zu 2
290
Ob.
Fag.
Klav.
Fl.
Ob.
Fag.
Klav.

300
Fl.
Ob.
Fag.
Klav.
Vl.
Vla.
Vlc. e Cb.
p
TUTTI
310
zu 2

SOLO
320
Ob.
Fag.
Klav.
Vl.
Vla.
Vlc. e Cb.
330
TUTTI
Fl.
Ob.
zu 2
Fag.
Cor. (C)
Trb. (C)
Timp.
Klav.
Vl.
Vla.
Vlc. e Cb.

tr
SOLO
Fl.
Ob.
Fag.
Cor. (C)
p
zu 2
Trb. (C)
Timp.
Klav.
Vla.
Vlc. e Cb.

340
Fag.
[p]
Klav.
Vl.
p
Vla.
Vlc. e
p

350
Fag.
Klav.
Klav.
Vl.
Vla.
Vlc.
Vlc.
360
SOLO
Fl.
Ob.
Fag.
Cor. (C)
[p]
Klav.
Vl.
Vla.
Bassi
Vlc. e Cb.

370
Ob.
Fag.
Cor. (C)
Klav.
Vl.
Vla.
Vlc. e Cb.

Fl.
Ob.
Fag.
Cor. (C)
Klav.

380
Ob.
Fag.
[p]
Klav.
Vl.
Vla.
Vlc. e
Cb.
Fl.
Ob.
Fag.
Klav.
Vl.
Vla.
Vlc. e
Cb.

390
Fl.
Ob.
Fag.
Klav.
Vl.
Vla.
Vlc. e
Cb.

Klav.
Vl.
Vla.
Vlc. e
Cb.

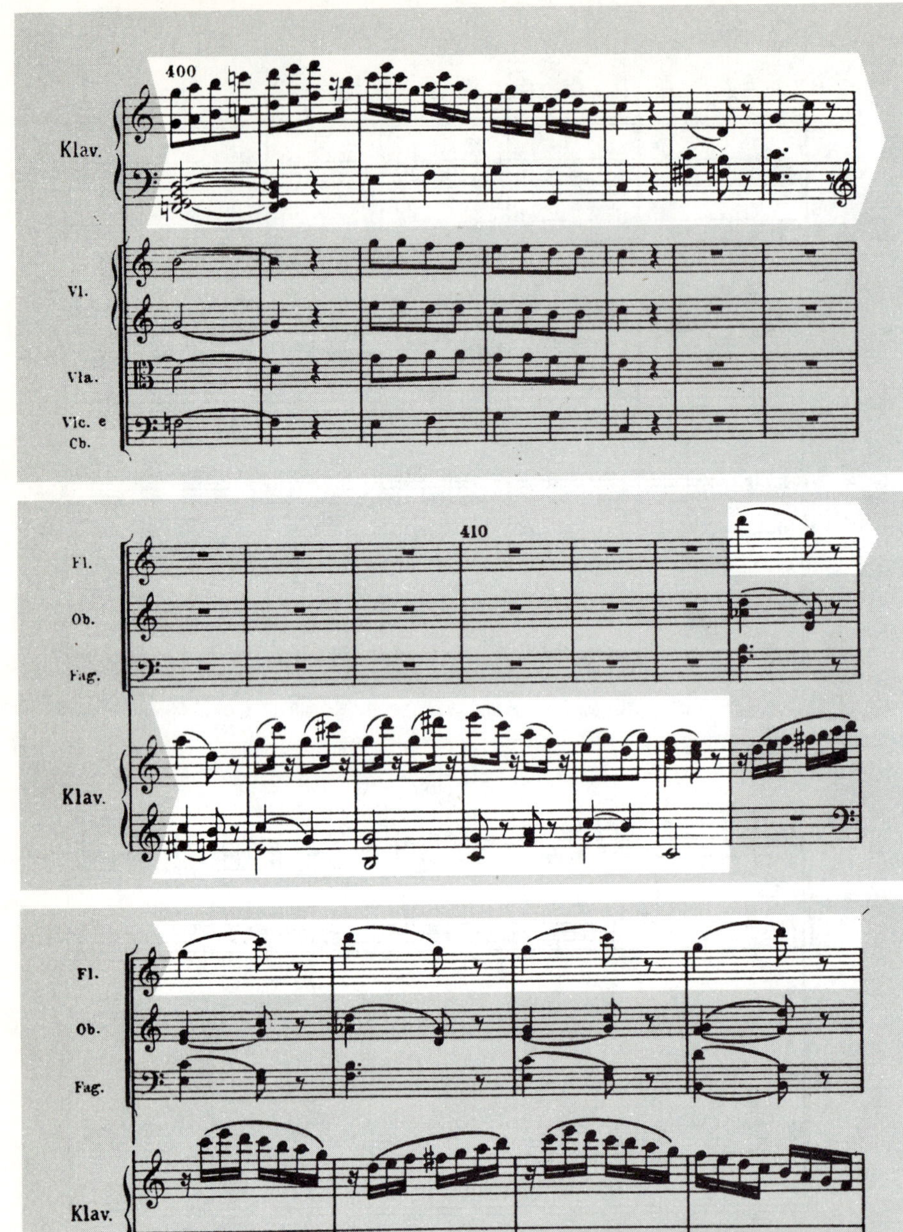
400
Klav.
Vl.
Vla.
Vlc. e
Cb.
410
Fl.
Ob.
Fag.
Klav.
Fl.
Ob.
Fag.
Klav.

TUTTI
420
Fl.
Ob.
zu 2
Fag.
Cor. (C)
Trb. (C)
Timp.
Cadenz*
tr
Klav.
Vl.
Vla.
Vlc. e Cb.

* See note on p. 475.

Fl.
Ob.
Fag.
Cor. (C)
Trb. (C)
Timp.
Klav.
Vl.
Vla.
Vlc. e
Cb.

440
Fl.
Ob.
Fag.
Cor. (C)
Trb. (C)
Timp.
Klav.
Vl.
Vla.
Vlc. e Cb.

Fl.
Ob.
Fag.
zu 2
Cor. (C)
Trb. (C)
Timp.
Klav.
Vl.
Vla.
Vlc. e Cb.

35. Mozart

Le Nozze di Figaro, K. 492, Scene from Act I (1786)

No. 6: Non so più cosa son, cosa Faccio

Allegro vivace

Cherubino

Non so più co - sa son, co - sa fac - cio, or di
I can't give you a good ex - pla - na - tion for this

fo - co, o-ra so - no di ghiac - cio, o - gni don - na can-giar di co -
new and con-fus - ing sen - sa - tion. Ev-'ry la - dy I see makes me

lo - re, o - gni don - na mi fa pal - pi - tar, o - gni
trem - ble, makes me trem - ble with plea - sure and pain, makes me

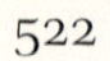

don - na mi fa pal - pi - tar, o - gni don - na mi
trem - ble with plea - sure and pain, makes me trem-ble with

fa pal - pi - tar. So - lo ai no - mi d'a-mor, di di -
plea - sure and pain. When of love there is mere - ly a

let - to, mi si tur - ba, mi s'al - te-ra il pet - to,
men - tion, I am spell-bound and rapt with at - ten - tion.

e a par - la - re mi sfor - za d'a - mo - re
I weave ro - manc - es and day-dreams to - geth - er,

un de - si - o, un de - si - o ch'io non
filled with long-ing, filled with long - ing I
pos - so spie - gar, un de - si - o, un de -
can - not ex - plain, filled with long - ing, filled with
si - o ch'io non pos - so spie - gar.
long - ing I can - not ex - plain.
Non so
If I
più co - sa son, co - sa fac - cio, or di fo - co, o - ra so - no di
knew what it is I'd con - fess it, but I am at a loss to ex -
p
f
p

ghiac - cio, o - gni don - na can-giar di co - lo - re, o - gni
press it, yet I know that it al - ways ex - cites me, that it
f
p
don - na mi fa pal - pi - tar, o - gni don - na mi_
thrills me a - gain and a - gain, that it thrills me a -
mf
p
fa pal - pi - tar, o - gni don - na mi fa pal - pi -
gain and a - gain, that it thrills me a - gain and a -
mf
p
tar. Par - lo d'a-mor ve -
gain. Love is my in - spi -

glian - do, par - lo d'a - mor so -
ra - tion, on - ly con - sid - er -
gnan - do, all' ac - qua, all'om - bra, ai mon - ti, ai fio - ri, all'er - be, ai
a - tion. In riv - ers, woods, and flow - ers, I feel its mag - ic
fp
fon - ti, all' e - co, all' a - ria, ai ven - ti, che il suon de' va - ni ac -
stream - ing, a - wake, a - sleep, and dream - ing. In gen - tle winds and
fp
f
p
cen - ti, por - ta - no via con se, por - ta - no
show - ers, I hear its mel - low tone, I hear its
cresc.
f
colla voce
p

via con se. Par - lo d'a-mor ve - glian - do,
mel - low tone. Love is my con - ver - sa - tion,
par - lo d'a-mor so - gnan - do, all' ac - qua, all' om - bra,
themewith-out var - i - a - tion, I tell my love - song
ai mon - ti, ai fio - ri, all' er - be, ai fon - ti, all'
to glens and moun-tains, to riv - ers and foun-tains, to
e-co, all' a - ria, ai ven - ti, che il suon de' va - ni ac - cen - ti,
moon and stars in heav - en. The gen - tle breez - es ech - o
cresc.
f
p
cresc.

por - ta - no via con se, por - ta - no via con
my ev - 'ry word and tone, my ev - 'ry word and
f
colla voce
p
Adagio
se. E se non ho chi m'o - da, e
tone. And if no one will lis - ten... and
se non ho chi m'o - da,
if no one will lis - ten,
Tempo I
par - lo d'a - mor con
then I will talk a -
cresc.
me, con me, par - lo d'a - mor con me.
lone of love, talk to my - self a - lone.
p
f

Recitative

(As Cherubino is leaving, he sees the Count in the distance, turns around in fright, and hides himself behind the arm-chair.)
Cherubino
Susanna (trying to screen Cherubino)
Ah, son per-du - to! Che ti - mor! il Con - te! mi - se - ra
Wait, I hear foot-steps! It's the Count! Hide quick - ly or you are
Count (entering)
Susanna
me! Su - san - na, tu mi sem-bri a - gi - ta - ta e con-fu - sa. Si -
lost! Su - san - na, you seem ner-vous, so con - fused and ex- cit - ed. My
gnor, io chie-do scu - sa, ma, se ma - i, qui sor - pre - sa, par ca-ri - tà, par -
lord, you must ex-cuse me, but, if some-one should come in now — I beg of you, don't
Count (Seats himself in the arm-chair, and takes Susanna's hand.)
Susanna (pulling her hand back)
Count
ti - te. Un mo-men - to, e ti la - scio. O - di. Non o - do nul - la. Due pa -
stay here. It will take but a min - ute. Lis - ten: I will not lis - ten. Just two
ro - le: tu sai che am - ba - scia - to - re a Lon - dra il Re mi di - chia -
words: you know the King has ap-point - ed me am - bas - sa - dor to

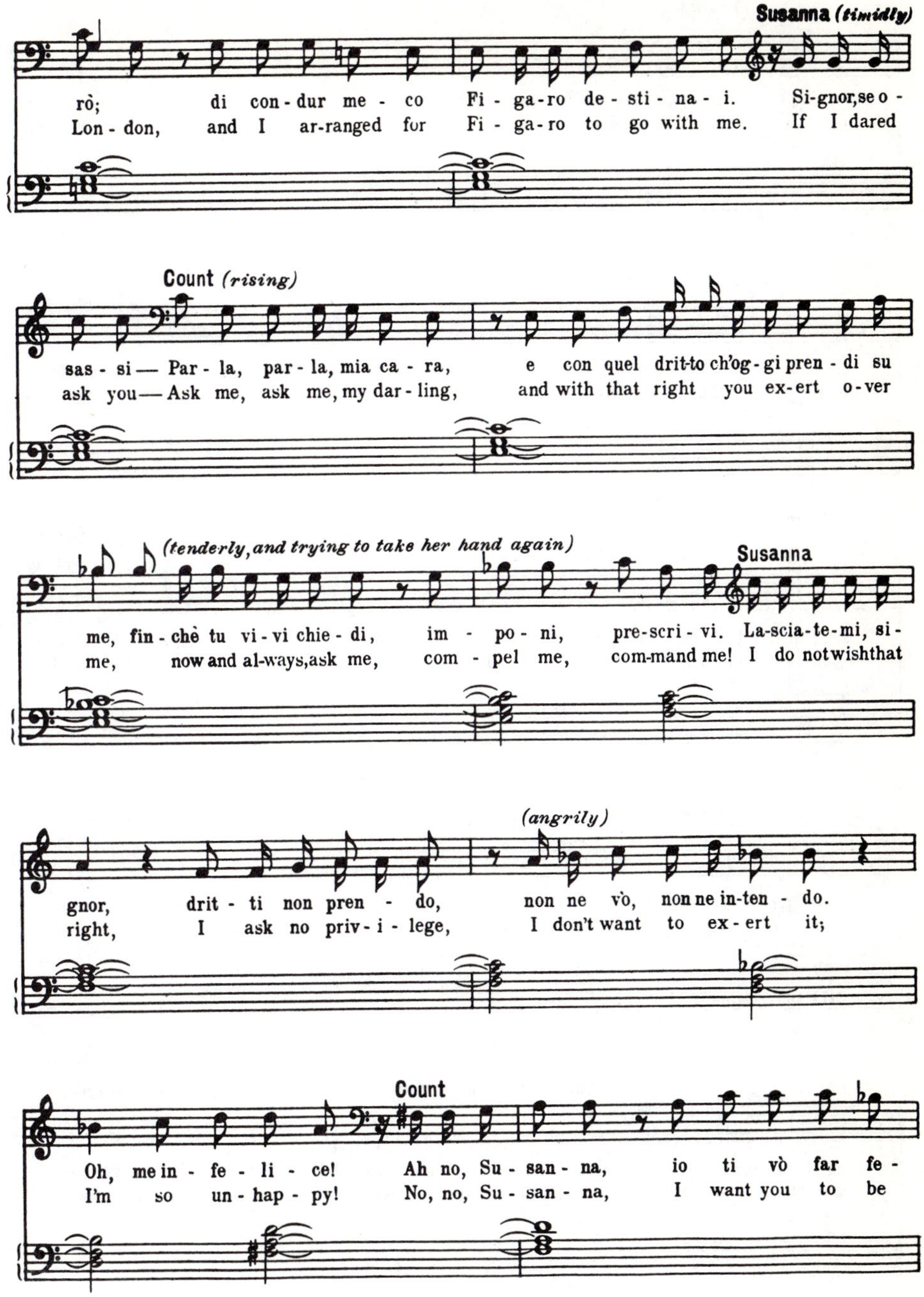

Susanna *(timidly)*

rò; di con-dur me-co Fi-ga-ro de-sti-na-i. Si-gnor, se o-
Lon-don, and I ar-ranged for Fi-ga-ro to go with me. If I dared

Count *(rising)*

sas-si— Par-la, par-la, mia ca-ra, e con quel drit-to ch'og-gi pren-di su
ask you—Ask me, ask me, my dar-ling, and with that right you ex-ert o-ver

(tenderly, and trying to take her hand again)

Susanna

me, fin-chè tu vi-vi chie-di, im-po-ni, pre-scri-vi. La-scia-te-mi, si-
me, now and al-ways, ask me, com-pel me, com-mand me! I do not wish that

(angrily)

gnor, drit-ti non pren-do, non ne vò, non ne in-ten-do.
right, I ask no priv-i-lege, I don't want to ex-ert it;

Count

Oh, me in-fe-li-ce! Ah no, Su-san-na, io ti vò far fe-
I'm so un-hap-py! No, no, Su-san-na, I want you to be

(as above)
li - ce! Tu ben sai quan-to io t'a - mo; a te Ba-si - lio tut - to già
hap-py! You must know how much I love you; I'm sure Ba-si - lio told you al-
dis - se. Or sen - ti, se per po - chi mo - men - ti me - co in giar -
read - y! Now lis - ten, if you on - ly con - sent to meet me to -
Basilio
(offstage)
din sull' im-bru-nir del gior - no, ah per que - sto fa - vo-re io pa-ghe-rei. E u -
night in the gar-den of the cas - tle, I will am - ply re-pay you for this fa-vor. He
Count
Susanna
Count
sci - to po - co fa. Chi par - la? O De - i! E - sci,
left not long a - go. Ba - si - lio! Good Heav - ens! Hur - ry,
Susanna (very agitated)
Basilio (still offstage)
ed al-cun non en - tri. Ch'io vi la - sci quì so - lo? Da ma-da - ma sa - rà,
don't let him en - ter. I should leave you a - lone here? He can't be ver - y far, per-

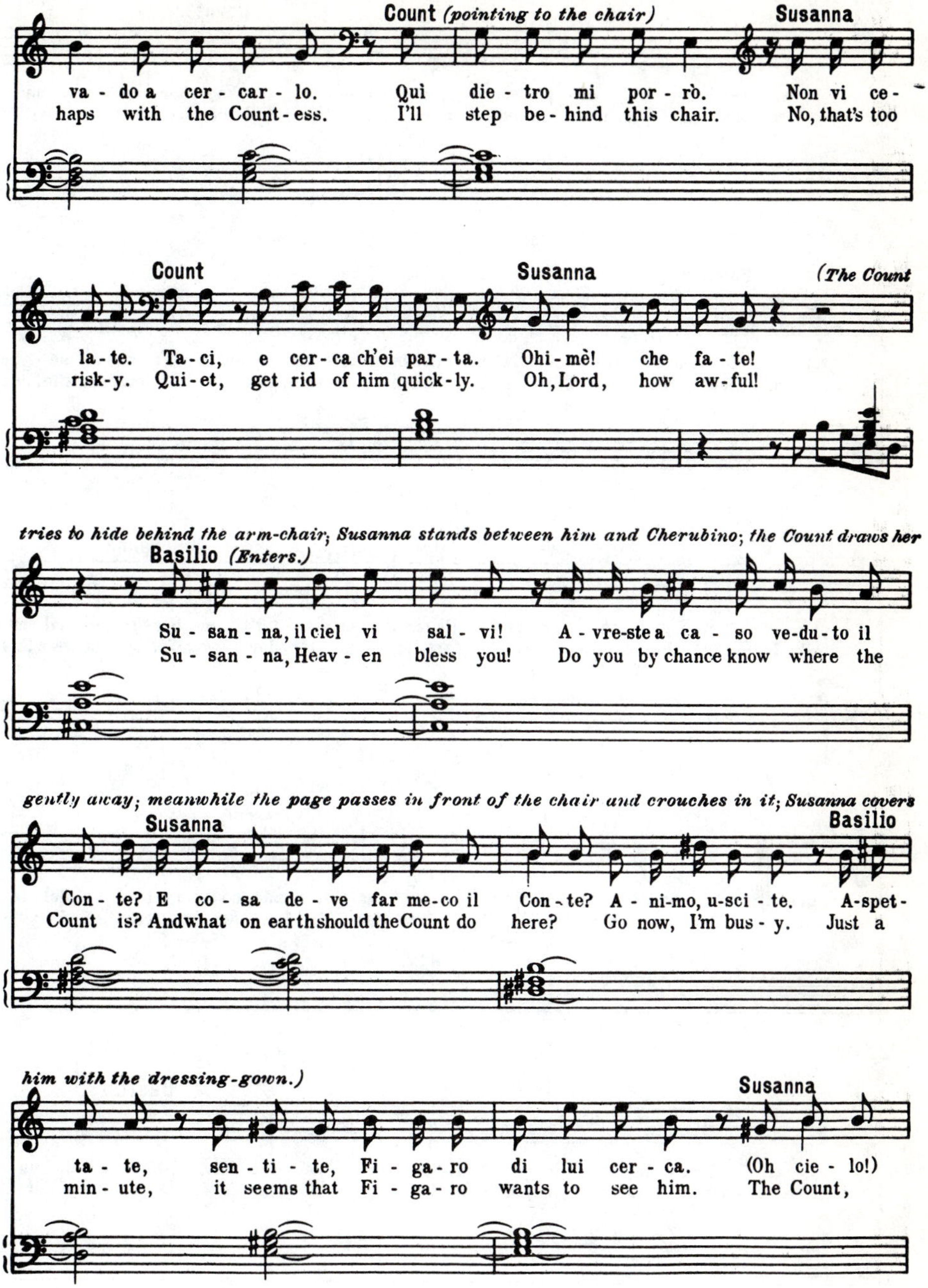

Count *(pointing to the chair)* **Susanna**

va - do a cer - car - lo. Qui die - tro mi por - rò. Non vi ce -
haps with the Count - ess. I'll step be - hind this chair. No, that's too

Count **Susanna** *(The Count*

la - te. Ta - ci, e cer - ca ch'ei par - ta. Ohi - mè! che fa - te!
risk - y. Qui - et, get rid of him quick - ly. Oh, Lord, how aw - ful!

tries to hide behind the arm-chair; Susanna stands between him and Cherubino; the Count draws her

Basilio *(Enters.)*

Su - san - na, il ciel vi sal - vi! A - vre - ste a ca - so ve - du - to il
Su - san - na, Heav - en bless you! Do you by chance know where the

gently away; meanwhile the page passes in front of the chair and crouches in it; Susanna covers

Susanna **Basilio**

Con - te? E co - sa de - ve far me - co il Con - te? A - ni - mo, u - sci - te. A - spet -
Count is? And what on earth should the Count do here? Go now, I'm bus - y. Just a

him with the dressing-gown.)

Susanna

ta - te, sen - ti - te, Fi - ga - ro di lui cer - ca. (Oh cie - lo!)
min - ute, it seems that Fi - ga - ro wants to see him. The Count,

Count
ei cer - ca chi, do - po voi, più l'o - dia. (Ve - diam co - me mi
the one man who hates him more than you do? (Let's see how he will
Basilio
ser - ve.) Io non ho mai nel - la mo - ral sen - ti - to ch'u - no ch'a - ma la mo - glie o -
serve me.) That is not so. There is no such con - clu - sion, that if one loves the wife, one
Susanna
di il ma - ri - to, per dir che il Con - te v'a - ma. Sor - ti - te, vil mi -
must hate the hus - band. In fact, my mas - ter loves you. Get out of here this
(resentfully)
ni - stro dell' al - trui sfre - na - tez - za: io non ho d'uo - po del - la
min - ute with your hints and sug - ges - tions. I have no in - t'rest in your
Basilio
vo - stra mo - ra - le, del Con - te, del suo a - mor. Non c'è al - cun
lec - tures on mor - als, in your mas - ter, in his love. Don't take it

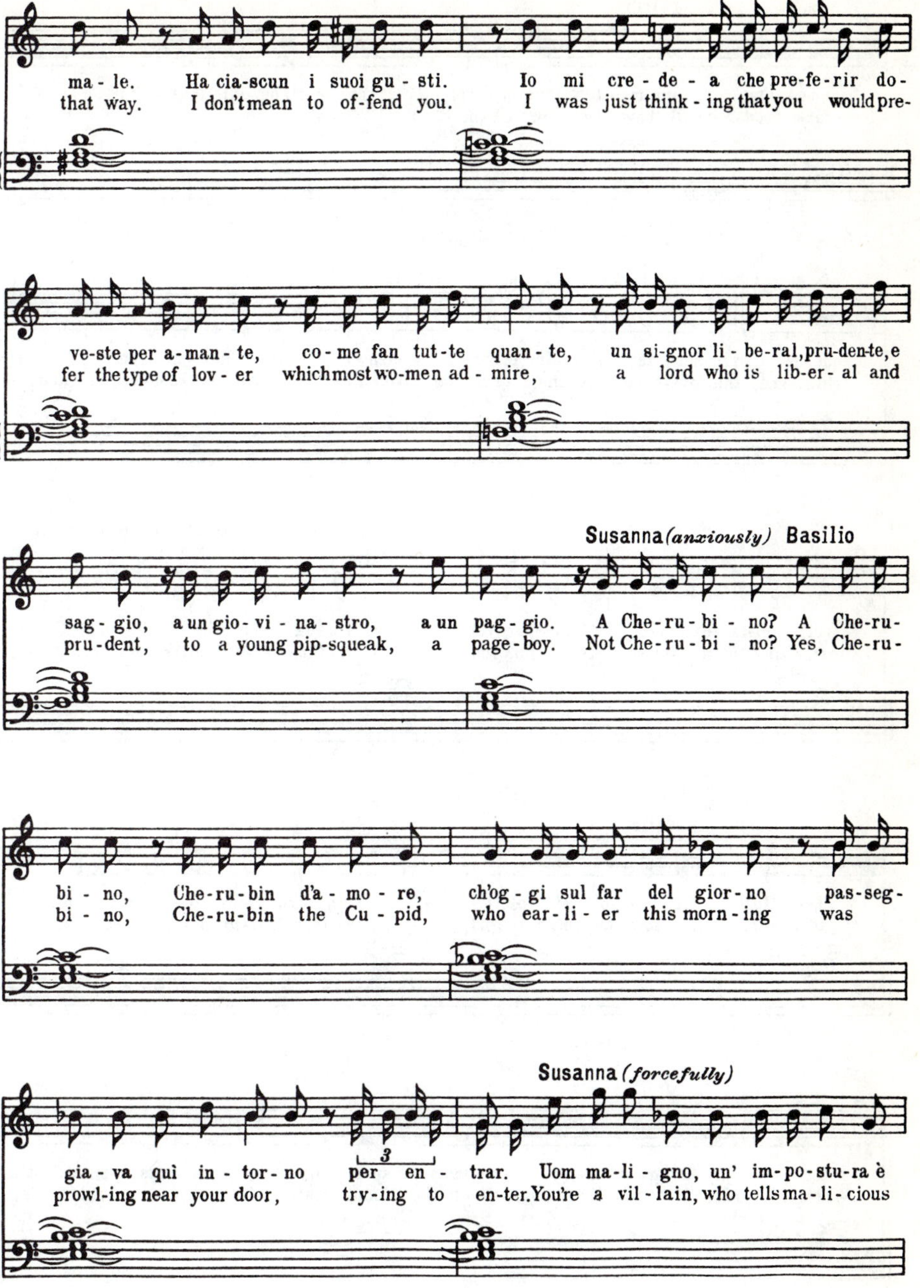
ma - le. Ha cia-scun i suoi gu - sti. Io mi cre - de - a che pre-fe-rir do-
that way. I don't mean to of-fend you. I was just think - ing that you would pre-
ve-ste per a-man - te, co - me fan tut-te quan - te, un si-gnor li - be-ral, pru-den-te, e
fer the type of lov - er which most wo-men ad - mire, a lord who is lib-er - al and
Susanna (anxiously) Basilio
sag - gio, a un gio - vi - na - stro, a un pag - gio. A Che - ru - bi - no? A Che-ru-
pru - dent, to a young pip-squeak, a page - boy. Not Che - ru - bi - no? Yes, Che-ru-
bi - no, Che - ru - bin d'a - mo - re, ch'og - gi sul far del gior - no pas - seg-
bi - no, Che - ru - bin the Cu - pid, who ear - li - er this morn - ing was
Susanna (forcefully)
gia - va quì in - tor - no per en - trar. Uom ma - li - gno, un' im - po - stu - ra è
prowl-ing near your door, try - ing to en - ter. You're a vil - lain, who tells ma - li - cious
3

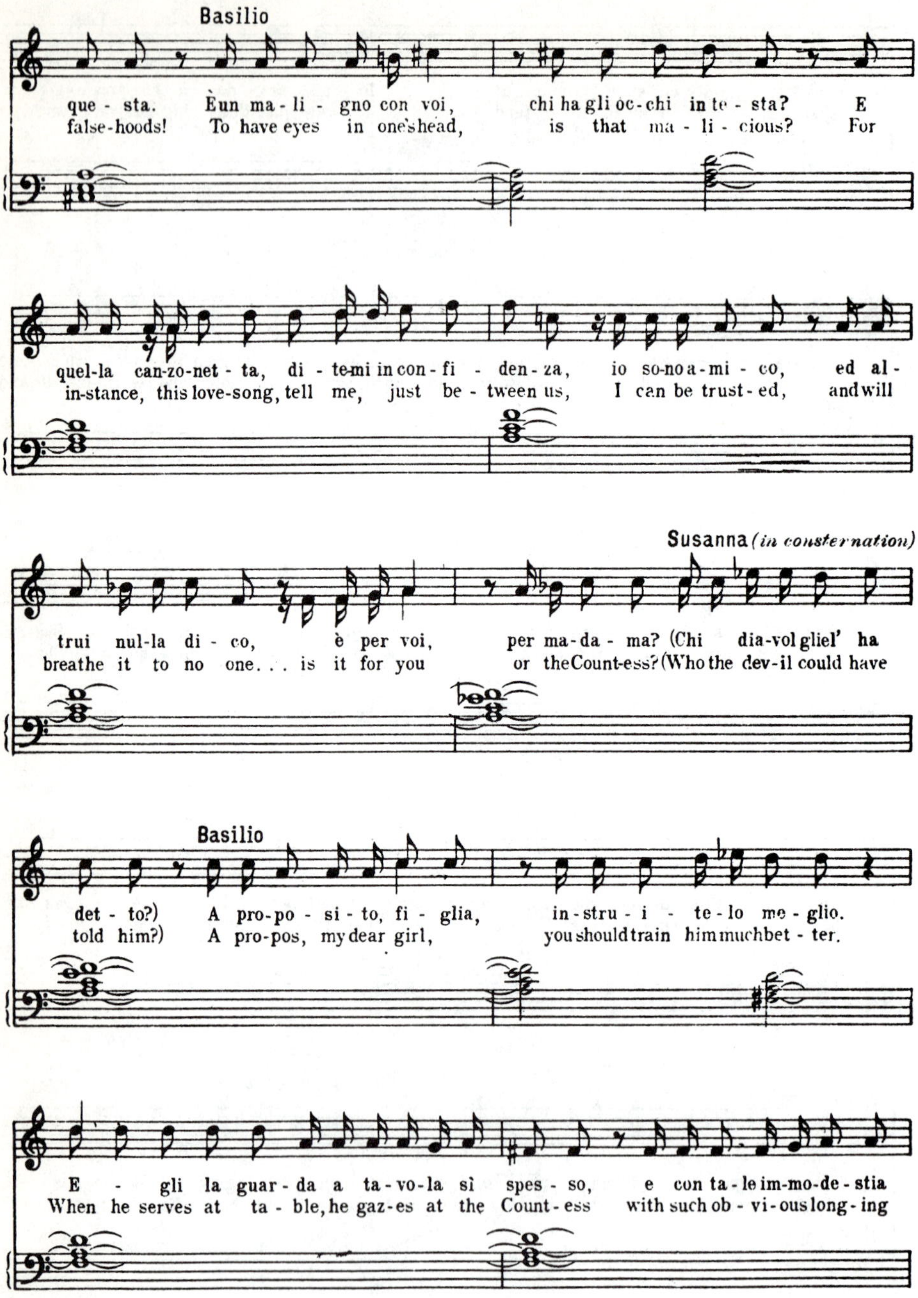

Basilio

que - sta. Èun ma - li - gno con voi, chi ha gli oc - chi in te - sta? E
false-hoods! To have eyes in one's head, is that ma - li - cious? For

quel-la can-zo-net - ta, di - te-mi in con - fi - den - za, io so-no a - mi - co, ed al -
in-stance, this love-song, tell me, just be - tween us, I can be trust - ed, and will

Susanna *(in consternation)*

trui nul-la di - co, è per voi, per ma - da - ma? (Chi dia-vol gliel' ha
breathe it to no one. . . is it for you or the Count-ess? (Who the dev - il could have

Basilio

det - to?) A pro-po - si - to, fi - glia, in - stru - i - te - lo me - glio.
told him?) A pro-pos, my dear girl, you should train him much bet - ter.

E - gli la guar - da a ta - vo - la sì spes - so, e con ta - le im - mo - de - stia
When he serves at ta - ble, he gaz - es at the Count - ess with such ob - vi - ous long - ing

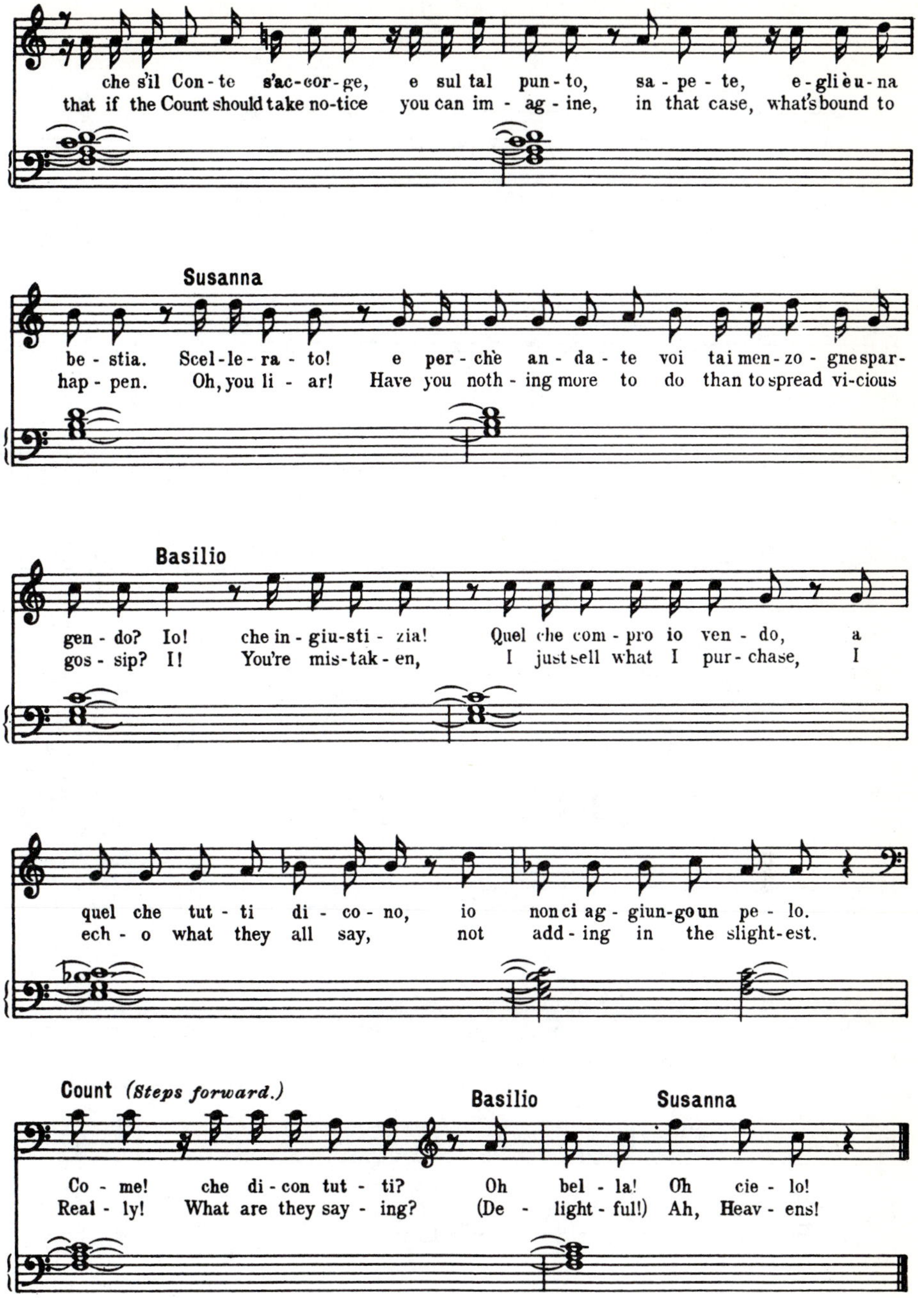

che s'il Con - te s'ac-cor-ge, e sul tal pun - to, sa - pe - te, e - gli è u - na
that if the Count should take no-tice you can im - ag - ine, in that case, what's bound to

Susanna

be - stia. Scel-le-ra - to! e per - chè an - da - te voi tai men - zo - gne spar-
hap - pen. Oh, you li - ar! Have you noth - ing more to do than to spread vi-cious

Basilio

gen - do? Io! che in - giu-sti - zia! Quel che com - pro io ven - do, a
gos - sip? I! You're mis-tak - en, I just sell what I pur - chase, I

quel che tut - ti di - co - no, io non ci ag - giun-go un pe - lo.
ech - o what they all say, not add - ing in the slight-est.

Count (Steps forward.)
Basilio
Susanna
Co - me! che di - con tut - ti? Oh bel - la! Oh cie - lo!
Real - ly! What are they say - ing? (De - light - ful!) Ah, Heav - ens!

No. 7: Cosa sento! Tosto andate

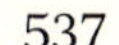

son qui giun - to; per - do - na - te, o mio si -
was my sto - ry, just a ru - mor, with - out a

Susanna
gnor. Che ru - i - na! me me - schi - na! son' op - pres - sa dal do -
doubt. We'll be ru - ined by the scan - dal if this gos - sip gets a -

lor!
bout!
Basilio
In mal pun - to
How ill - cho - sen
Count
To - sto an - da - te, an - da - te,
Don't de - lay an - y long - er,

Che ru - i - na!
This is aw - ful!
son qui giun - to, per - do - na - te, o
was my sto - ry, just a ru - mor, with -
e scac - cia - te il se - dut - tor.
go and throw the scoun - drel out.
f
Me me - schi - na! me me - schi - na! Son' op -
What will hap - pen! Heav - en help us! I am
(half fainting)
mio si - gnor.
out a doubt.
sf
p
pres - sa dal do - lor, son' op - pres - sa dal do -
feel - ing ver - y faint, I am feel - ing ver - y

lor.
faint.
Basilio (supporting her)
Ah! già svien la po - ve - ri - na!
Ah! poor girl, her strength is fail - ing!
Count (supporting her)
Ah! già svien la po - ve - ri - na!
Ah! poor girl, her strength is fail - ing!
Co - me, oh Di - o! le bat - te il
We must help her, re - vive her
Co - me, oh Di - o! le bat - te il
We must help her, re - vive her
cor, co - me, oh Di - o! le bat - te il
fast, or, good Lord, she might not
cor, co - me, oh Di - o! le bat - te il
fast, or, good Lord, she might not
cresc.
p

cor, co - me, oh Di - o! le bat - te il cor.
last, or, good Lord,_ she_ might not last.
cor, co - me, oh Di - o! le bat - te il cor.
last, or, good Lord,_ she_ might not last.
cresc.
p.
Basilio
(approaching the arm-chair to sit down in it)
Pian, pian - in su que - sto seg - gio.
Let us put her in this arm-chair.
tr
Susanna
(recovering)
(repulsing them both)
Do - ve so - no? Co - sa veg - gio! Che in-so -
Ah, where am I? Am I dream-ing? You in -
tr
cresc.
len - za! an - da - te fuor, an - da - te fuor, an - da - te fuor!
sult me, go a - way, leave me a - lone, leave me a - lone!
f p
cresc.
f

Basilio *(maliciously)*

Sia - mo quì per a - iu - tar - vi, è si -
We are on - ly here to help you, I as -

Count

Sia - mo quì per a - iu - tar - vi, non tur -
We are on - ly here to help you, I as -

p *p*

cu - ro il vo - stro o - nor, è si - cu - ro il
sure you, we meant no harm, I as - sure you, we

bar - ti, o mio te - sor, non tur - bar - ti, o
sure you, we meant no harm, I as - sure you, we

p *cresc.* *cresc.*

vo - stro o - nor, è si - cu - ro il vo - stro o - nor.
meant no harm, I as - sure you, we meant no harm.

mio te - sor, non tur - bar - ti, o mio te - sor.
meant no harm, I as - sure you, we meant no harm.

p *sfp* *cresc.*

Basilio
(to the Count)
Ah, del pag-gio, quel che ho det-to, e-ra so-lo un
What I told you was a ru-mor, mere sus-pi-cion, with
mio so-spet-to.
no foun-da-tion.
Susanna
È un' in-si-dia, u-na per-fi-dia, non cre-
He is vi-cious and ma-li-cious; it's a
p
cresc.
de-te all'im-po-stor, non cre-de-te all' im-po-stor, all' im-po-
lie, it is not true, it's a lie, it is not true, it is not
f
stor, all' im-po-stor!
true, it is not true!
Count
Par-ta, par-ta il da-me-ri-no,
Or-der him to leave the cit-y!
f
p

Susanna
Po - ve - ri - no!
What a pit - y!
Po - ve -
What a
Basilio
Po - ve - ri - no!
What a pit - y!
Po - ve -
What a
par - ta, par-ta il da - me - ri - no!
Or - der him to leave the cit - y!
f
p
ri - no!
pit - y!
ri - no!
pit - y!
(ironically)
Po - ve - ri - no! po - ve - ri - no! ma da
What a pit - y! what a pit - y! I have
Co - me?
Caught him?
Che?
How?
Che?
How?
me sor - pre-so an - cor!
caught him once be - fore!

Co - me? Che?
Real - ly? Where?
Co - me? Co - me? Che!
Did you? Real - ly? Where?
Recit.
Da tua cu - gi - na,
At Bar-ba - ri - na's,
Recit.
p
Count
l'u - scio jer tro-vai rin-chiu-so, pic-chio,
yes-ter-day, I went to see An-to - nio, I knocked,
m'a-pre Bar-ba-ri - na pau - ro - sa fuor dell' u - so,
Bar-ba-ri - na o-pened, and looked ex-treme-ly ner-vous.
io, dal mu-so in-so-spet-ti - to, guar - do, cer-co in o-gni si - to.
I be-gan to grow sus-pi - cious and ex - am-ined ev-'ry cor - ner.
f

a tempo
Ed al - zan - do, pian, pia - ni - no, il tap - pe - to al
When I gent - ly drew the cov - er from the ta - ble I
p a tempo
ta - vo - li - no, ve - do il pag - gio.
found be - neath it Che - ru - bi - no!
(Showing how he found the page, he lifts the dressing-
gown from the chair and discovers Cherubino.)
p
Susanna (agitated)
Ah! cru - de stel - le!
Ah, this is aw - ful!
(astonished)
Ah! co - sa veg - gio!
Ha! What does this mean?
Susanna
Ac - ca -
Noth - ing
Basilio (laughing sardonically)
Ah! me-glio an - co - ra!
Ah, this is price-less!
Count
O - ne - stis - si - ma si - gno - ra!
Now at last my eyes are o - pen!
pp

der non può di peg - gio. Giu - sti
worse than this could hap - pen! This af -
Or ca - pi - sco co - me va!
Now I see how mat - ters stand!
Dei, che mai sa - rà! Giu - sti Dei,
fair is out of hand! This af - fair
Basilio
Co - sì fan tut - te le bel - le, non c'è al -
That's the way all wo - men do it, they will
Or ca - pi - sco
Now I see how
cresc.
che mai sa - rà! ac - ca - der non può di peg - gio, ah,
is out of hand. Noth - ing worse than this could hap - pen, ah,
cu - na no - vi - tà, co - sì
nev - er show their hand. That's the
co - me va, o - ne - stis - si -
mat - ters stand. Now at last my
f
p
cresc.

no! ah, no! giu - sti Dei, che mai sa - rà, che mai sa -
no! ah, no! This af - fair is out of hand; how will this
fan tut - te_ le_ bel - le, non c'è al - cu - na_ no - vi -
way all wo - men do it, they will nev - er_ show their
ma_ si - gno - ra! or ca - pi - sco co - me
eyes_ are o - pen, now I see_ how mat - ters
f

rà! ac - ca - der non può di peg - gio,
end? Noth - ing worse than this could hap - pen,
tà, co - sì fan tut - te le bel - le,
hand. That's the way all wo - men do it,
va, o - ne - stis - si - ma si - gno - ra,
stand. Now at last_ my eyes are o - pen,
p

giu - sti Dei,— che— mai sa - rà!
no one knows how— this will end.
(to the Count, with malice)
non c'è al - cu - na— no - vi - tà. Ah, del pag - gio
they will nev - er— show their hand. What I told you
or ca - pi - sco— co - me va!
now I see— how— mat - ters stand.
cresc.
p

quel che ho det - to, e - ra so - lo un mio so -
was a ru - mor, mere sus - pi - cion with no foun -

Ac - ca-der non può di peg-gio, ah, no, ah, no! giu - sti
Noth - ing worse than this could hap-pen, ah, no, ah, no! No one
spet-to. Co - sì fan tut-te le bel-le,
da - tion. That's the way all wo - men do it,
O - ne - stis - si - ma si - gno - ra,
Now at last my eyes are o - pen,
cresc.
f

Dei, che mai sa - rà, che mai sa - rà! Ac - ca -
knows how this will end, how this will end! Noth - ing
non c'e al - cu - na no - vi - tà, co - sì
they will nev - er show their hand. That's the
or ca - pi - sco co - me va! o - ne -
now I see how mat - ters stand. Now at
p

der non può di peg-gio, giu - sti Dei,_ che_
worse than this could hap-pen, no one knows how_
fan tut-te le bel-le, non c'è al - cu - na_
way all wo - men do it, they will nev - er_
stis - si-ma si - gno-ra, or ca - pi - sco_
last_ my eyes are o-pen, now I see_ how_
cresc.

mai sa - rà, giu - sti Dei,_ che_ mai sa - rà, giu - sti
this will end, no one knows how_ this will end, this af -
no - vi - tà, non c'è al - cu - na_ no - vi - tà, non c'è al -
show their hand, they will nev - er_ show their hand, they will
co - me va, or ca - pi - sco_ co - me va, or ca -
mat - ters stand, now I see_ how_ mat - ters stand, now I
p
sfp
cresc.
p

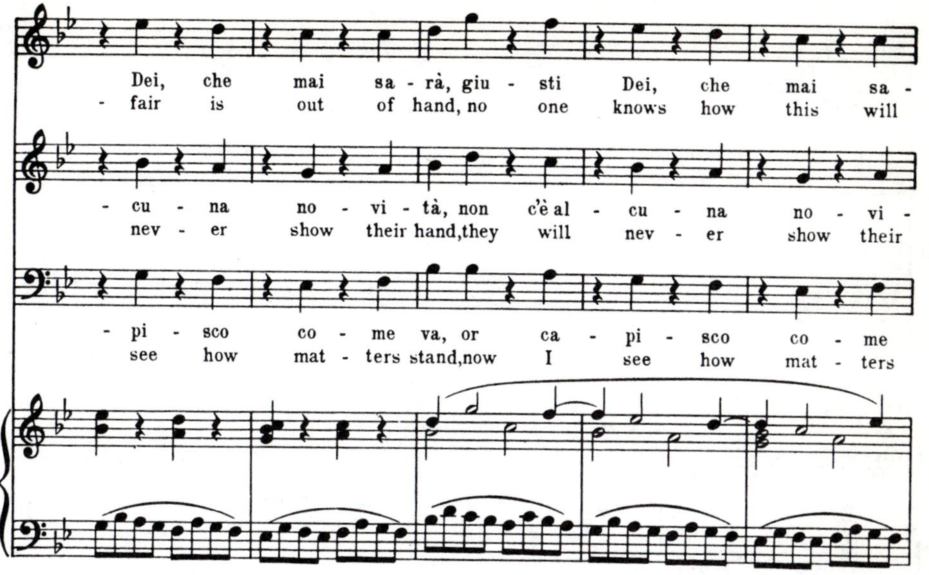
Dei, che mai sa - rà, giu - sti Dei, che mai sa -
- fair is out of hand, no one knows how this will
- cu - na no - vi - tà, non c'è al - cu - na no - vi -
nev - er show their hand, they will nev - er show their
- pi - sco co - me va, or ca - pi - sco co - me
see how mat - ters stand, now I see how mat - ters

rà, giu - sti Dei, che mai sa - rà,
end, this af - fair is out of hand,
tà, co - sì fan tut - te le bel - le, co - sì fan tut - te le bel - le, non c'è al -
hand. That's the way all wo - men do it, that's the way all wo - men do it, they will
va! o - ne - stis - si - ma si - gno - ra, or ca -
stand. Now at last my eyes are o - pen, now I
cresc.
f

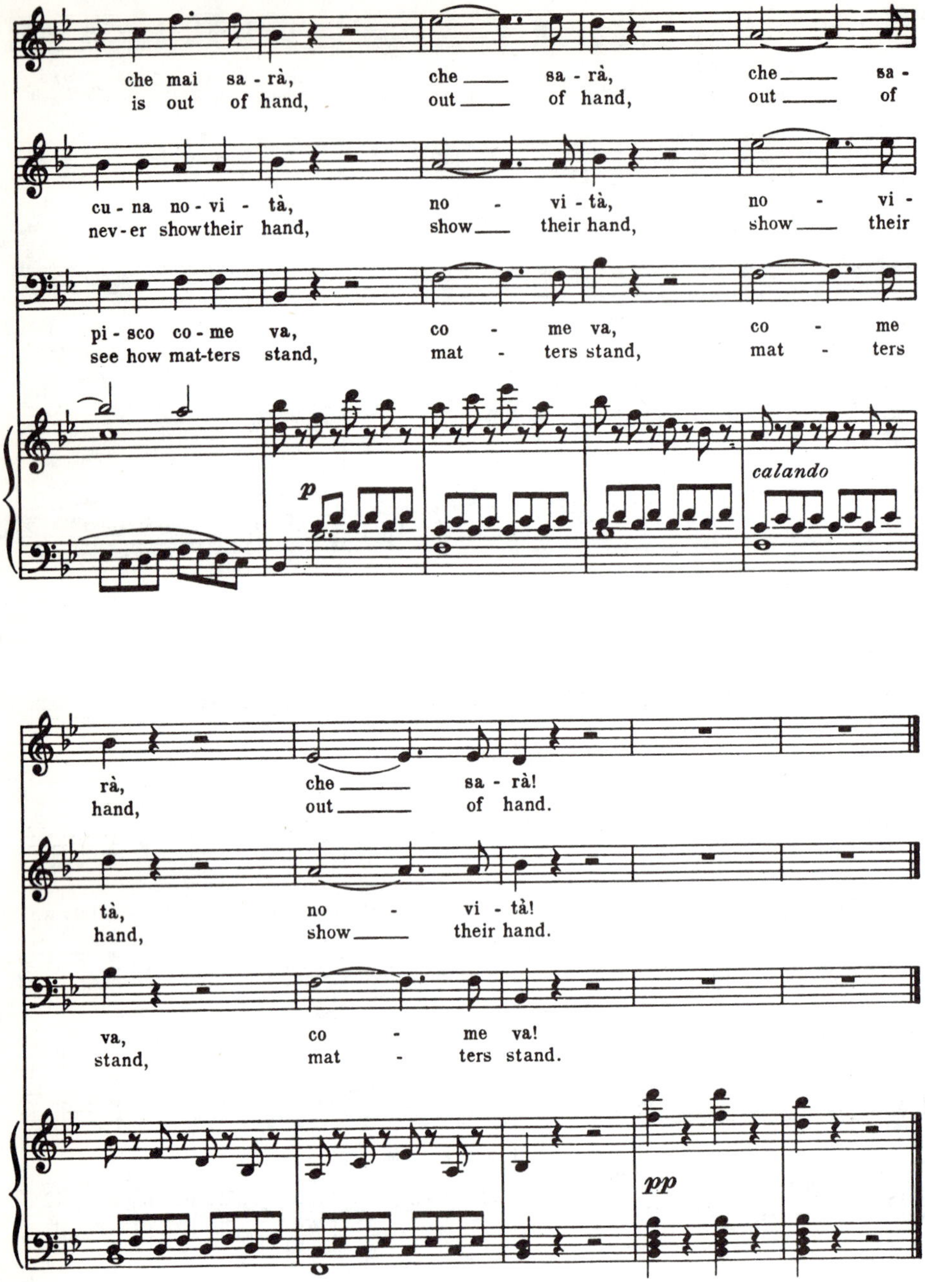

che mai sa - rà, che ___ sa - rà, che ___ sa -
is out of hand, out ___ of hand, out ___ of

cu - na no - vi - tà, no - vi - tà, no - vi -
nev - er show their hand, show ___ their hand, show ___ their

pi - sco co - me va, co - me va, co - me
see how mat-ters stand, mat - ters stand, mat - ters

p

calando

rà, che ___ sa - rà!
hand, out ___ of hand.
tà, no - vi - tà!
hand, show ___ their hand.
va, co - me va!
stand, mat - ters stand.
pp

36. Mozart

Eine kleine Nachtmusik,
K. 525 (1787)

  4A/1  I/4/1

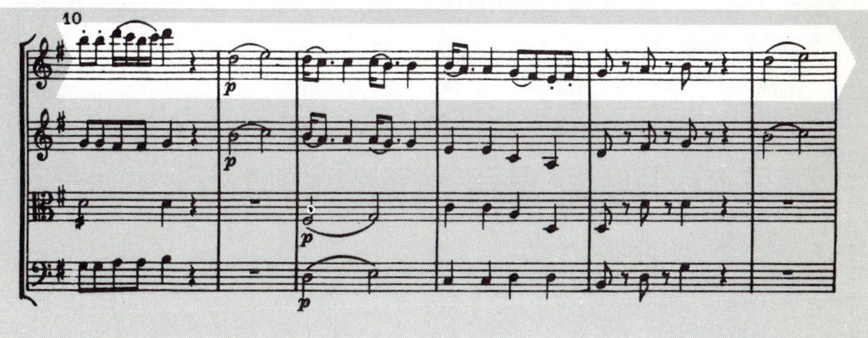

tr
tr
20
sf
p
cresc.
sf
p
cresc.
sf
p
cresc.
sf
p
cresc.
f
f
f
f
30
3
p
p
p
p

40
50

110
tr
f
3
p
120

tr
p
130
f

II
Romanze
Andante
10
cresc.

20
30

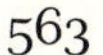

50
p
p
p
f
f

60
cresc.
fp
p
f
70

Menuetto
III
Allegretto
f
p
10
cresc.
TRIO
sotto voce
Fine.
20

30
sotto voce
Menuetto da Capo.
IV
Allegro
1.
2.

80

40

f
f
f
f
p
50
p
p
p
1.
2.
f
f
f
f
p
60
p
p
p

70

80
f
p
fp
90

100
110

f
p
120
f
p
f

CODA
130
140
p
tr

f
f
f
150
160

37. Mozart

Symphony No. 40 in G minor, K. 550,
First movement (1788)

  S2A/3  S2/10

I

Molto Allegro

Flauto

2 Oboi

2 Clarinetti in B

2 Fagotti

I. in B alto
2 Corni
II. in G

Violino I

Violino II

[div.]

Viola

Bassi

p

This edition presents the score of Mozart's second version, with clarinets.

10
Fl.
Cl.
(B)
Fg.
1.
p
Vl.
Vla.
Bi.

20
Fl.
Ob.
Cl.
(B)
Fg.
(B)
Cor.
(G)
f
Vl.
Vla.
Bi.
p

Ob.
Fg.
Vl.
Vla.
Bi.
p
[div.]

30
Fl.
Ob.
Cl. (B)
Fg.
Cor. (B)
Vl.
Vla.
Bi.
zu 2
1.
f

Fl.
Ob.
Cl. (B)
zu 2
Fg.
(B) Cor. (G)
Vl.
Vla.
Bi.
[sf]
zu 2
40
Cor. (B)
1.
Solo
p

50
Fl.
1.
Cl. (B)
1.
Fg.
Solo
[p]
p
Vl.
Vla.
Bi.

Fl.
[p]
Cl. (B)
[p]
p
Fg.
[p]
Vl.
Vla.
Bi.

60
Fl.
Ob.
Cl. (B)
Fg.
(B) Cor. (G)
Vl.
Vla.
Bi.
cre - scen - do
[p]
zu 2
p
cresc.

Fl.
Ob.
Cl. (B)
Fg.
Cor. (B)
Vl.
Vla.
Bi.
zu 2
1.
[div.]
tr
f
sf

70
Fl.
Cl. (B)
Fg.
Vl.
Vla.
Bi.
80
Fl.
Ob.
Cl. (B)
Fg.
(B) Cor. (G)
Vl.
Vla.
Bi.

Fl.
Ob.
Cl. (B)
Fg.
(B) Cor. (G)
Vl.
Vla.
Bi.
1.
zu 2
90

100
Fl.
Ob.
Cl. (B)
zu2
Fg.
(B) Cor. (G)
Vl.
Vla.
Bi.
Fl.
Ob.
Cl. (B)
Fg.
(B) Cor. (G)
Vl.
Vla.
Bi.
p
[div.]

Fl.
Ob.
Cl. (B)
Fg.
zu 2
Cor. (G)
2.
Vl.
Vla.
Bi.

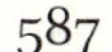

120

Fl.
Ob.
Cl. (B)
zu2
Fg.
(B) Cor. (G)
Vl.
Vla.
Bi.

Fl.
Ob.
Cl. (B)
zu2
Fg.
(B) Cor. (G)
Vl.
Vla.
Bi.

130
Fl.
Ob.
Cl.
(B)
Fg.
zu 2
(B)
Cor.
(G)
Vl.
Vla.
Bi.

Fl.
Ob.
Cl.
(B)
Fg.
zu 2
Cor.
(G)
2.
Vl.
[div.]
p
Vla.
Bi.

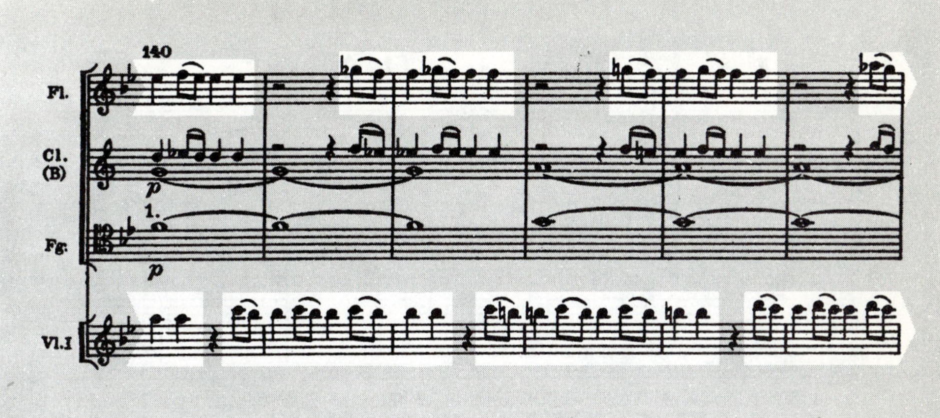
140
Fl.
Cl.
(B)
p
1.
Fg.
p
Vl. I

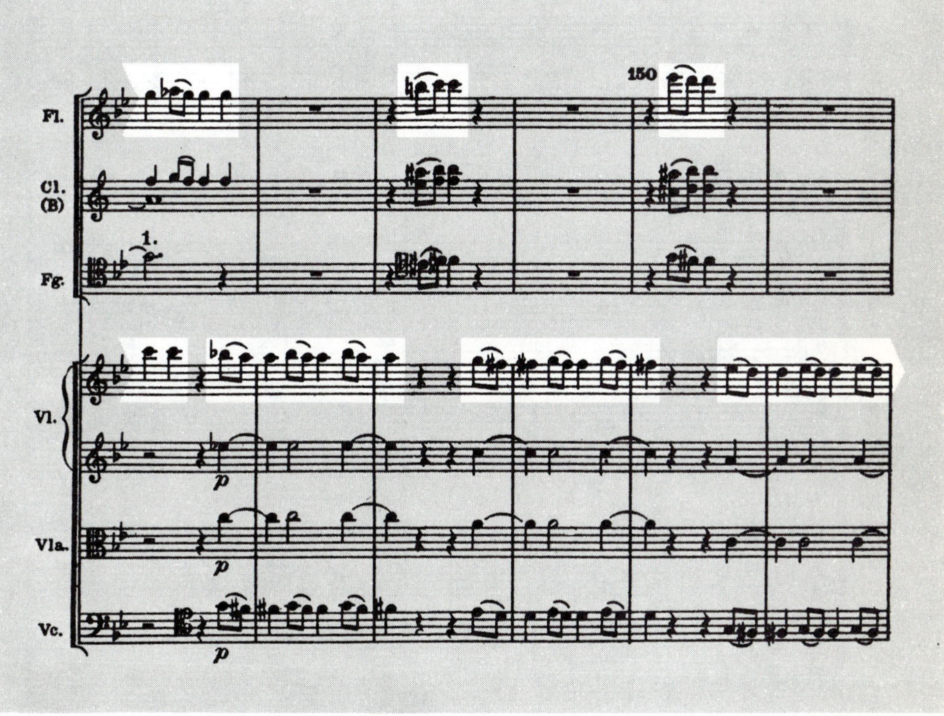
150
Fl.
Cl.
(B)
1.
Fg.
Vl.
p
Vla.
p
Vc.
p

Fl.
Ob.
Cl. (B)
Fg.
(B) Cor. (G)
Vl.
Vla.
Vc.
Cb.
Tutti Bassi
160
Fl.
Ob.
Cl. (B)
Fg.
(B) Cor. (G)
Vl.
Vla.
Bi.

Fl.
Cl. (B)
Fg.
1.
(B) Cor. (G)
Vl.
[div.]
Vla.
Bi.

1.
170
Fg.
Vl.
Vla.
Bi.

Fl.
Ob.
Cl. (B)
Fg.
(B) Cor. (G)
Vl.
Vla.
Bi.
1.
1.
p
f
180
p
[div]

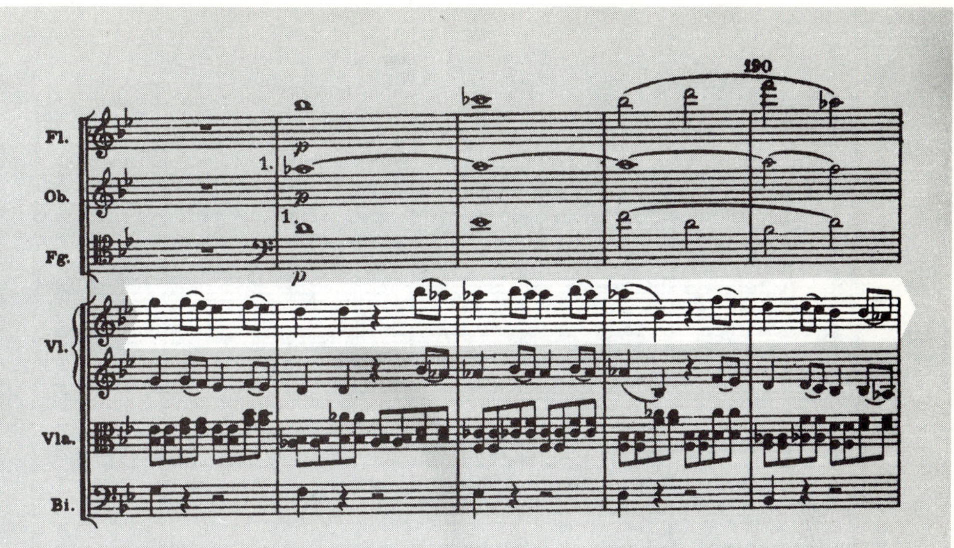
190
Fl.
Ob.
Fg.
Vl.
Vla.
Bi.
1.
p

Fl.
Ob.
Cl.
(B)
zu 2
Fg.
(B)
Cor.
(G)
Vl.
Vla.
Bi.
f

200

Fl.
Ob.
Cl. (B)
zu 2
Fg.
(B) Cor. (G)
Vl.
Vla.
Bi.

Fl.
Ob.
Cl. (B)
zu 2
Fg.
(B) Cor. (G)
Vl.
Vla.
Bi.

210
Fl.
Ob.
Cl. (B)
zu 2
Fg.
(B) Cor. (G)
Vl.
Vla.
Bi.
220
sf
[sf]

Fl.
Ob.
Cl. (B)
zu 2
Fg.
(B) Cor. (G)
Vl.
Vla.
Bi.

230
Fl.
Ob.
1.
Fg.
Vl.
Vla.
Bi.
p

240
Fl.
Ob.
Fg.
Vl.
Vla.
Bi.
1.
1.
p
1.

Fl.
Cl. (B)
Fg.
(B)
Cor.
(G)
Vl.
Vla.
Bi.
p
p
p
cresc.
cresc.
cresc.
cresc.
cresc.
cresc.
cresc.
cresc.
cresc.

250
Fl.
Ob.
Cl. (B)
Fg.
(B) Cor. (G)
Vl.
Vla.
Bi.
tr
f
zu 2
sf

260
Fl.
Ob.
Cl.
(B)
Fg.
zu 2
1.
(B)
Cor.
(G)
Vl.
Vla.
Bi.
p

Fl.
Ob.
Cl.
(B)
Fg.
1.
zu 2
(B)
Cor.
(G)
Vl.
Vla.
Bi.
p
f

270
Fl.
Ob.
Cl. (B)
Fg.
su2
(B) Cor. (G)
Vl.
Vla.
Bi.
1.
p
f

280
Fl.
Ob.
Cl.
(B)
zu2
Fg.
(B)
Cor.
(G)
Vl.
Vla.
Bi.

Fl.
Ob.
zu2
Cl.
(B)
Fg.
(B)
Cor.
(G)
Vl.
Vla.
Bi.
p

290
Fl.
Cl. (B)
Fg.
(B) Cor. (G)
Vl.
Vla.
Bi.
Fl.
Ob.
Cl. (B)
Fg.
(B) Cor. (G)
Vl.
Vla.
Bi.

38. Mozart

Requiem in D minor, K. 626, (1791)   S2A/4  S2/15

Dies irae

Allegro assai.

Soprano. Tutti. *f* Di - es i - rae di - es il - la solvet sae-clum in fa - vil - la, te - ste Da - vid cum Sy - bil - la. Quan - tus

Alto. Tutti. *f* Di - es i - rae di - es il - la solvet sae-clum in fa - vil - la, te-ste Da - vid cum Sy - bil - la. Quan - tus

Tenore. Tutti. *f* Di - es i - rae di - es il - la solvet sae-clum in fa - vil - la, te-ste Da - vid cum Sy - bil - la. Quan - tus,

Basso. Tutti. *f* Di - es i - rae di - es il - la solvet sae-clum in fa - vil - la, te-ste Da - vid cum Sy - bil - la. Quan - tus

Allegro assai.

PIANO. *f* Volles Orch.

0

tre - mor est fu - tu - - - rus, quan - - - - - - do
tre - mor est fu - tu - - - rus, quan - - - - - - do
quan - - - - tus tre - mor est fu - tu - - - - rus,
tre - mor est fu - tu - - - rus, quan - - - - - - do
ju - dex est ven - tu - - - rus, cun - - - cta
ju - dex est ven - tu - - rus, cun - - - cta
quan - - - - do ju - dex est ven - tu - - rus, cun - - - cta
ju - dex est ven - tu - - - rus, cun - - - cta
stri - - - cte dis - cus - su - - rus.
stri - - - - cte dis - cus - su - - - rus.
stri - cte stri - cte dis - cus - su - - - rus.
stri - - - cte dis - cus - su - - - rus.
Streichinstr.

p
Di - - es
Di - - es
Di - - es
Di - - es
p Tutti.
i - rae
di - - es
il - la solvet saeclum in fa-
i - rae
di - - es
il - la solvet saeclum in fa-
i - rae
di - - es
il - la solvet saeclum in fa-
i - rae
di - - es
il - la solvet saeclum in fa-
vil - la te - ste Da - vid cum Sy - bil - la.
vil - la te - ste Da - vid cum Sy - bil - la.
vil - la te - ste Da - vid cum Sy - bil - la.
vil - la te - ste Da - vid cum Sy - bil - la.
tr.

Q
Quan - - - - tus tre - mor est fu - tu - - rus quan - - - - - - do ju - dex est ven - tu - - rus, cun - - - cta stri - - - cte
Quan - - - - tus tre - mor est fu - tu - - rus quan - - - - - - do ju - dex est ven - tu - - rus, cun - - - cta stri - - - cte
Quan - - - - tus tre - mor est fu - tu - - rus quan - - - - - - do ju - dex est ven - tu - - rus, cun - - - cta stri - - - cte
Quan - - - - tus tre - mor est fu - tu - - rus quan - - - - - - do ju - dex est ven - tu - - rus, cun - - - cta stri - - - cte
Q

R

dis - - cus - - su - rus Di - es

dis - - cus - - su - rus Di - es

dis - - cus - - su - rus Di - es

dis - - cus - - su - rus. Quantus tre - mor est fu - tu-rus.

R

sf

i - rae, di - es il - la, di - es

i - rae, di - es il - la, di - es

i - rae, di - es il - la, di - es

quantus tre - mor est fu - tu-rus

sf

S

i - rae, di - es il - la, quan - tus

i - rae, di - es il - la, quan - tus

i - rae, di - es il - la, quan - tus

quantus tre - mor est fu - tu - rus, quan tus

S

sf

tre - mor est fu - tu - rus, quan-do ju - dex est ven -
tre - mor est fu - tu - rus, quan-do ju - dex est ven -
tre - mor est fu - tu - rus, quan-do ju - dex est ven -
tre - mor est fu - tu - rus, quan-do ju - dex est ven -
tu - rus, cuncta stri - cte dis - cus - su - rus.
tu - rus, cuncta stri - cte dis - cus - su - rus.
tu - rus, cuncta stri - cte dis - cus - su - rus.
tu - rus, cuncta stri - cte dis - cus - su - rus.
T
cun - - - cta stri - cte, stri - cte
cun - - cta stri - cte, stri - cte
cun - - cta stri - cte, stri - cte
cun - - cta stri - cte, stri - cte
T

dis - cus - su - - - rus, cun - - - cta stri - cte,
dis - cus - su - - - rus, cun - - - cta stri - cte,
dis - cus - su - - - rus, cun - - - cta
dis - cus - su - - - rus, cun - - - cta
stri - cte dis - cus - su - - - rus.
stri - cte dis - cus - su - - - rus.
stri - cte, stri - cte dis - cus - su - - - rus.
stri - cte, stri - cte dis - cus - su - - - rus.

Tuba mirum

Andante.
Basso Solo.
Piano.
Trombone.
Tu_ba mi_rum spargens so- - - - - -
Trombone.
f
p
-num,
tu- - ba mi_rum spargens so_num per se-
pul_chra re_gi_o_num, co_get om_nes an_te thronum, co_get
Tenore Solo.
a
Mors stu_pe_bit et na_tu_ra, cum re-
om_nes an_te thro- - - -num.
a Streichinstr.
f p
sur- get cre- a_tu_ra, ju_di_can_ti re_spon_su_ra.
f

Li- - ber scrip-tus pro- fe - re - tur, in quo to - tum con - ti-
p Fag.
ne - tur, un- - de mun - dus, mun- - dus
b Alto Solo.
Ju- - dex er - go cum se-
ju- - di ce- - tur.
cresc.
f
p
de - bit, quid- - quid la - tet, ap - pa - re - bit, nil in - ul - tum re - ma-
sf
p
c Soprano Solo.
Quid sum mi - ser, tunc di - ctu - rus? quem pa - tro - num ro - ga-
ne - bit.
c

tu-rus? cum vix ju-stus, ju-stus sit se-
mfp
Sopr. Solo.
d
sotto voce
cu - rus? cum vix ju-stus, ju-stus sit se-
Alto Solo.
sotto voce
cum vix ju-stus, ju-stus sit se-
Ten. Solo.
sotto voce
cum vix ju-stus, ju-stus sit se-
Basso Solo.
sotto voce
cum vix ju-stus, ju-stus sit se-
d Fag., Corni di B.
sfp
sfp
f p cresc. f
cu-rus, cum vix ju-stus, vix ju-stus sit se - cu- - -rus?
f p cresc. f
cu-rus, cum vix ju-stus, vix ju-stus sit se - cu- - -rus?
f p cresc. f
cu-rus, cum vix ju-stus, vix ju-stus sit se - cu- - -rus?
f p cresc. f
cu-rus, cum vix ju-stus, vix ju-stus sit se - cu- - -rus?
f p cresc. f p

Rex tremendae

sta - - - - - - - - tis, rex tre - men - - - - - - - dae ma - je -
- tis, rex tre - men - - - - - - - dae ma - je - sta - - - - - -
gra - tis, qui sal - van - dos sal - - vas gra - -
sal - -vas gra - tis, sal - -vas gra - - - - -
V
sta - tis, rex tre - men - dae ma - je - sta - tis, qui sal -
tis, rex tre - men - dae ma - je - sta - tis,
-tis, rex tre - men - dae ma - je - sta - tis, rex tre - men - - - - -
tis, rex tre - men - dae ma - je - sta - tis, rex tre -
V
van - dos sal - vas gra - tis, rex tre - men - -
qui sal - van - dos sal - -vas gra - tis,
- dae ma - -je - sta - - - - - - tis, rex tre - men - - - - -
men - - - - - - - dae ma - -je - sta - - - - - - - tis, rex tre -

-dae, rex tre-men-dae ma-je-sta-tis, qui sal-van-dos sal-vas
rex tre-men-dae ma-je-sta-tis, qui sal-van-dos sal-vas
-dae, rex tre-men-dae ma-je-sta-tis, qui sal-van-dos sal-vas
men-dae, rex tre-men-dae ma-je-sta-tis, qui sal-van-dos sal-vas
W
gra-tis, sal-va me!
gra-tis, sal-va me!
gra-tis,
gra-tis,
W
sal-va me fons pi-e-ta-tis!
sal-va me fons pi-e-ta-tis!
sal-va me! sal-va me fons pi-e-ta-tis!
sal-va me! sal-va me fons pi-e-ta-tis!

Translation

Dies irae, dies illa Solvet saeculum in favilla, Teste David cum Sibylla.	Day of anger, day of mourning When to ashes all is burning, So spake David and the Sibyl.
Quantus tremor est futurus, Quando judex est venturus, Cuncta stricte discussurus!	Oh, what fear man's bosom rendeth. When from Heaven the Judge descendeth. On whose sentence all dependeth!
Tuba mirum spargens sonum Per sepulchra regionum, Coget omnes ante thronum.	Wondrous sound the trumpet flingeth, Through earth's sepulchres it ringeth, All before the throne it bringeth.
Mors stupebit et natura, Cum resurget creatura, Judicanti responsura.	Death with wonder is enchained, When man from the dust regained, Stands before the Judge arraigned.
Liber scriptus proferetur, In quo totum continetur, Unde mundus judicetur.	Now the record shall be cited, Wherein all things stand indited, Whence the world shall be requited.
Judex ergo cum sedebit, Quidquid latet apparebit, Nil inultum remanebit.	When to judgment all are bidden, Nothing longer shall be hidden, Not a trespass go unsmitten.
Quid sum miser tunc dicturus? Quem patronem rogaturus, Cum vix justus sit securus?	What affliction mine exceeding? Who shall stand forth for me pleading? When the just man aid is needing?
Rex tremendae majestatis! Qui salvandos salvas gratis! Salve me, fons pietatis!	King of might and awe, defend me! Freely Thy salvation send me! Fount of mercy, save, befriend me!

39. Ludwig van Beethoven (1770–1827),

String Quartet in F major, Op. 18,
No. 1, First movement (1799)

Allegro con brio. 𝅗𝅥. = 54

Violino I.

Violino II.

Viola.

Violoncello.

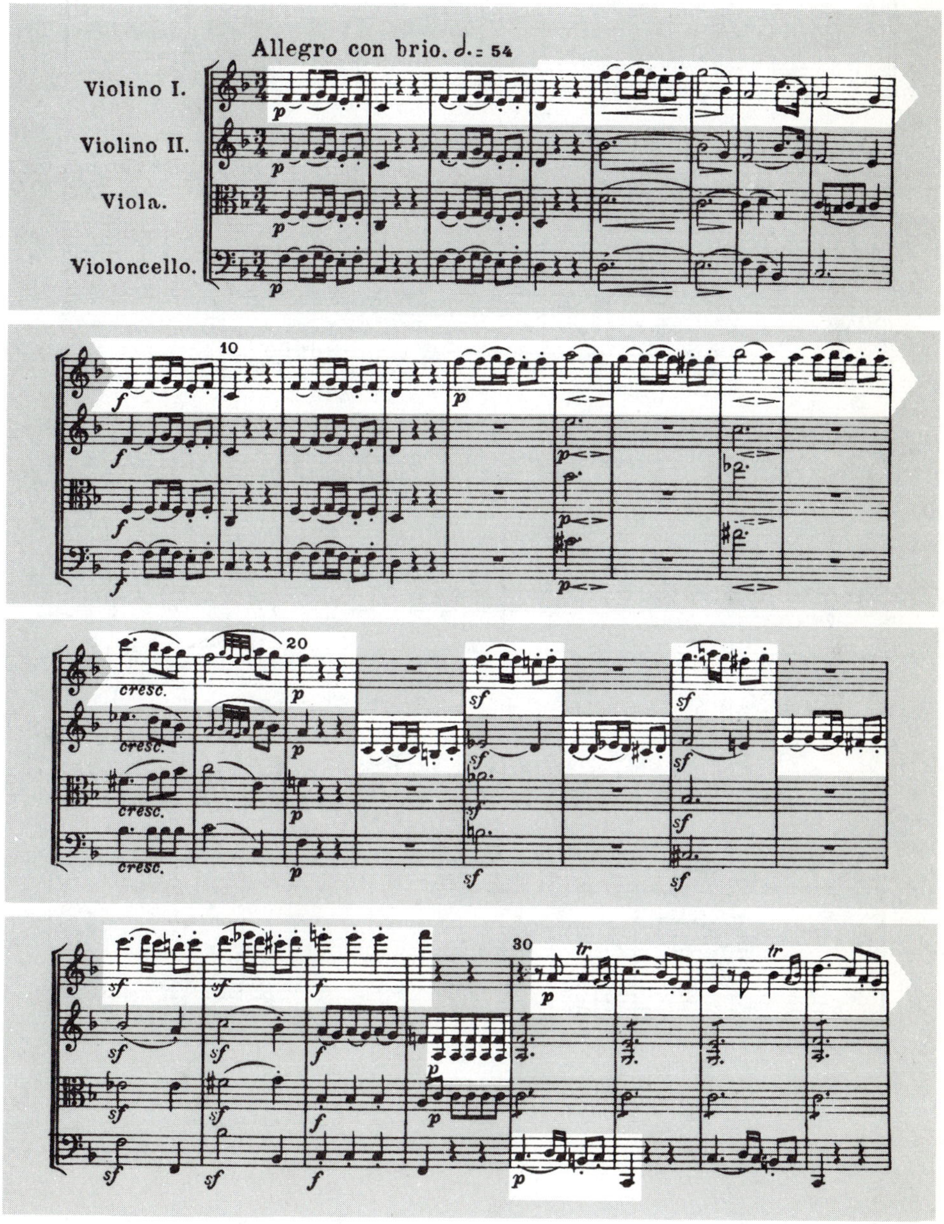

tr
40
pp
pp
pp
pp
cresc.
sf
f
p
50
cresc.
cresc.
cresc.
sf
f
p
cresc.
sf
f
p
cresc.
sf
f
p
p
cresc.
cresc.
ff
cresc.
ff
cresc.
cresc.
ff
cresc.
ff

60
decresc.
p
p
p
p
70
cresc.
cresc.
cresc.
sf
p
p
p
p
cresc.
cresc.
cresc.
cresc.
f
f
f
f
fp
fp
fp

80
cresc.
cresc.
f
cresc.
cresc.
f
cresc.
f
cresc.
f
tr
90
fp
p cresc.
fp
fp
p cresc.
fp
fp
p cresc.
fp
p cresc.
fp
100
fp
sf
sf
sf
sf
ff
fp
sf
sf
sf
sf
ff
fp
sf
sf
sf
sf
ff
sf
sf
sf
sf
ff
tr
p
tr
p
p
p

110
cresc.
cresc.
cresc.
cresc.
cresc.
f
f
f
f
f
f
f
f
120
fp
fp
fp
fp
fp
p
fp
fp
fp
pp
pp
pp
pp
pp

130
f
sf
140
fp

160
fp
fp
fp
fp
fp
fp
fp
fp
fp
fp
fp
sf
sf
sf
sf
170
sf
sf
sf
sf
sf
sf
sf
sf
sf
sf
sf
sf
sf
sf
sf
sf
sf
sf
sf

180
sf
sf
sf
sf
sf
cresc.
cresc.
cresc.
cresc.
ff
ff
ff
ff
p
p
p
p
p
p
190
cresc.
cresc.
cresc.
cresc.
p
200
tr
tr
tr
p
p
p
p

210
cresc.
f
p
cresc.
f
p
cresc.
f
p
cresc.
f
p
cresc.
cresc.
cresc.
cresc.
ff
decresc.
220
ff
ff
ff
ff
p
p
p

230
cresc.
sf
p
cresc.
sf
p
cresc.
sf
p
p
240
cresc.
f
fp
cresc.
cresc.
f
fp
cresc.
f
fp
cresc.
f
fp
tr
f
fp
cresc.
f
fp
cresc.
f
fp
cresc.
f
250
pp
fp
fp
pp
fp
fp
pp
fp
fp
pp
fp

260
tr
p
sf
ff
270
cresc.
280
16-2

290
cresc.
sf
300
pp
f

40. Beethoven

Piano Sonata in C minor, *(Pathétique)*, Op. 13 (1797–98)

4A/5 I/4/16

Allegro di molto e con brio.
p
cresc.
cresc.
p
sf
sf
sf
sf
cresc.
sf
sf
sf
sf
sf
sf
p
sf
sf
sf
sf
sf
sf

sf
decresc.
pp
p
cresc.
f
p
cresc.
f
p
cresc.
f
f
f
f
f
ff
sf
ff

Tempo I.
fp
fp
fp
p
decresc.
pp
attacca subito Allegro molto e con brio.
Allegro molto e con brio.
p
cresc.
f
p
cresc.
f
p
cresc.
p
pp
cresc.

sf
pp
cresc.
sf
sf
sf
fp
p
sf
cresc.
p
sf
cresc.
p
cresc.
p
cresc.
p

decresc.
pp
p
cresc.
f
p

cresc.
f
p
cresc.
f
f
ff
sf
Grave.
p
cresc.
sf
decresc.
pp
Allegro molto e con brio.
p
cresc.
ff
ff

Adagio cantabile.
p
cresc.

cresc.
p
pp
p
pp
cresc.
sf
sf
[sf]
fp
decresc.
pp

cresc.
p
pp
rf
rf
rf
pp

RONDO.
Allegro.
p
f
fp
fp
dolce
p
sf
sf

p
cresc.
sf
p
sf
sf
cresc.
ff
sf
[p]

cresc.
f
p
p
cresc.
f
sf
cresc.
ff
sf
sf
sf

ff
sf
p
p
sf
p dolce
cresc.

p
ca - - - - lan - - - - - - - do.
p

cresc.
p
cresc.
sf
sf
ff
sf
sf
p
cresc.
f
sf
sf
sf
sf
sf
sf
ff
sf
p
decresc.
pp
ff

41. Beethoven

Symphony No. 5 in C minor,
Op. 67 (1808)

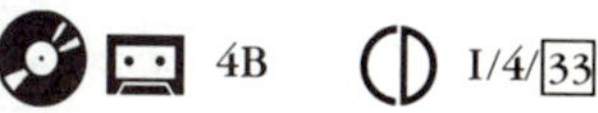

I

Allegro con brio (𝅗𝅥. = 108)

2 Flauti

2 Oboi

2 Clarinetti in B

2 Fagotti

2 Corni in Es

2 Trombe in C

Timpani in C-G

Violino I

Violino II

Viola

Violoncello

Contrabasso

zu 2

ff

zu 2

p

10

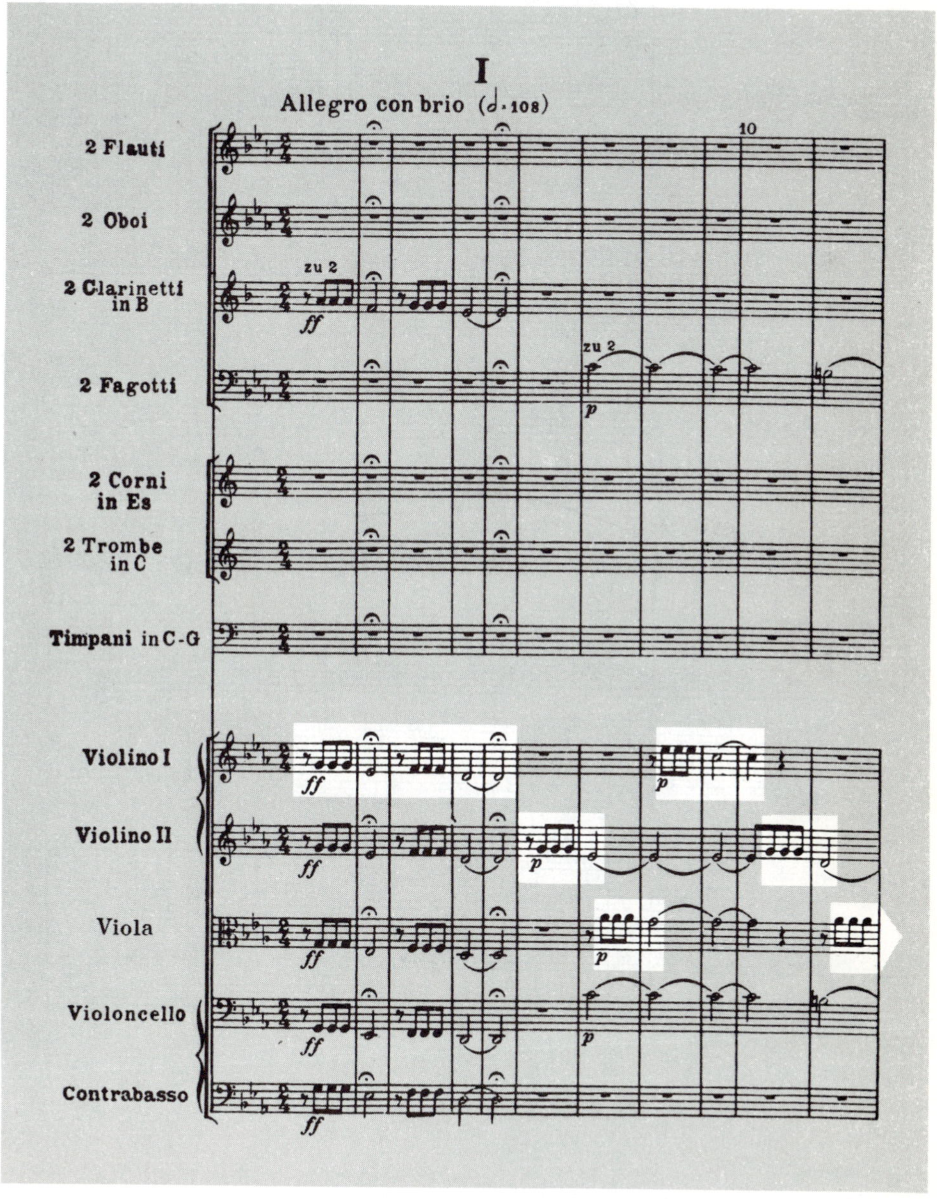

20
Fl.
Ob.
Cl.
Fg.
Cor. (Es)
Tr. (C)
Tp.
Vl.
Vla.
Vc.
Cb.
p cresc.
cresc.
zu 2
f
30
ff
zu 2
1.
p

Fl.
Ob.
Cl.
Fg.
Cor. (Es)
Vl.
Vla.
Vc. Cb.
Tr. (C)
Timp.
1.
40
50
cresc.
sf
f
ff

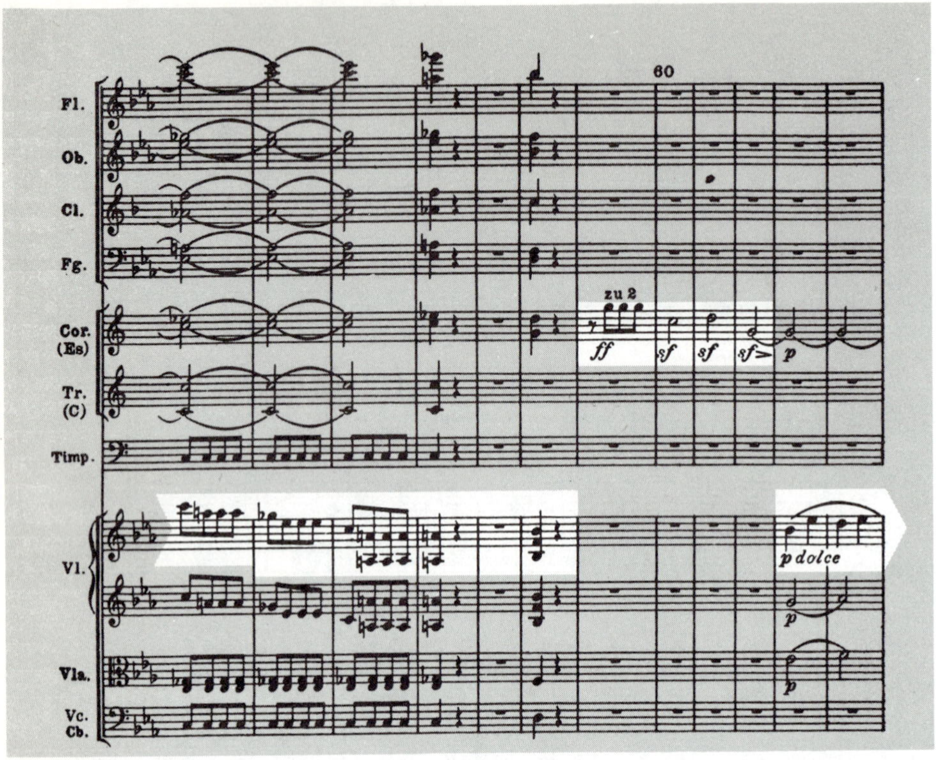

70
Fl.
1.
Cl.
1.
p
Fg.
p
Cor.
(Es)
Vl.
p
Vla.
Vc.
Cb.
p

80
1.
Ob.
Cl.
Fg.
Cor.
(Es)
Vl.
Vla.
Vc.
Cb.
perese.
pcresc.
cresc.
pcresc.
cresc.
cresc.
cresc.
cresc.
cresc.
90
1.
cresc.
Fl.
Ob.
Cl.
Fg.
Cor.
(Es)
Tr.
(C)
zu 2
ff
Vl.
Vla
Vc.
Cb.

100
Fl.
Ob.
Cl.
Fg.
Cor. (Es)
Tr. (C)
Timp.
Vl.
Vla.
Vc. Cb
ff
f
110
zu 2
Fl.
Ob.
Cl.
Fg.
Cor. (Es)
Vl.
Vla.
Vc. Cb.

120
130
Fl.
Ob.
Cl.
Fg.
Cor. (Es)
Vl.
Vla.
Vc.
Cb.
zu 2
ff
p
140

150
Cl.
Fg.
Cor.
(Es)
Vl.
Vla.
Vc.
Cb.
cresc.
p
pizz.
Fl.
Ob
Cl.
Fg.
zu 2
Cor.
(Es)
Tr.
(C)
Timp.
pp
Vl.
Vla.
Vc.
Cb
arco

160
Fl.
Ob.
Cl.
Fg.
Cor. (Es)
Tr. (C)
Timp.
Vl.
Vla.
Vc.
Cb.
cresc.
f

170
180
Fl.
Ob.
Cl.
Fg.
Cor. (Es)
Tr. (C)
Timp.
Vl.
Vla.
Vc.
b.
più f
ff
sf

Fl.
Ob.
Cl.
Fg.
Cor. (Es)
Tr. (C)
Timp.
Vl.
Vla.
Vc.
Cb.
190
zu 2
zu 2
sf

zu 2
200
zu 2
Fl.
Ob.
Cl.
Fg.
Cor. (Es)
zu 2
Tr. (C)
Timp.
Vl.
Vla.
Vc. Cb.
210
220
dimin.
p
sempre più p
pp

Fl.
Ob.
Cl.
Fg.
Cor. (Es)
Tr. (C)
Vl.
Vla.
Vc. Cb.
230
1.
zu 2
ff
pp
240
Vc.
Cb.
f

250
Fl.
Ob.
Cl
Fg.
Cor. (Es)
Tr. (C)
Timp.
ff
ten.
Vl.
Vla.
Vc.
Cb.
1.
p
pizz.
260
zu 2
cresc.
arco

Adagio.
270
Fl.
Ob.
Cl.
Fg.
Cor. (Es)
Tr. (C)
Timp
Vl.
Vla.
Vc. Cb.
cresc.
arco
p
f
ff
280
Timp.

290
Fl.
Ob.
Cl.
Fg.
Cor. (Es)
Tr. (C)
Timp
Vl.
Vla.
Vc. Cb.
300
Fl.
Ob.
Cl.
Fg.
zu 2
Cor. (Es)
zu 2
Tr. (C)
Timp
Vl.
p dolce
Vla.
Vc. Cb.

310
320
330
Fl.
Ob.
Fg.
Cor. (Es)
Timp
Vl.
Vla.
Vc. Cb.
Cl.
Vc.
Cb.
cresc.

340
Fl.
Cl.
Fg.
Cor
(Es)
Vl.
Vla.
Vc.
Cb.
cresc.
cresc
zu 2
cresc.

350
Fl.
Ob.
Cl.
Fg.
Cor.
(Es)
Tr.
(C)
Timp.
Vl.
Vla.
Vc.
Cb.
ff
tr

360
zu 2
Fl.
Ob.
Cl.
Fg.
Cor. (Es)
Tr. (C)
Timp.
Vl.
Vla.
Vc. Cb.
370
sf
f

380
Fl.
Ob.
Cl.
Fg.
(zu 2)
Cor. (Es)
Tr. (C)
Timp
Vl.
sf
ff
Vla.
Vc. Cb.

390
Fl.
Ob.
Cl.
Fg.
Cor. (Es)
Tr. (C)
Timp.
Vl.
Vla.
Vc. Cb.
zu 2
ff
p

400
Fl.
Ob
Cl.
Fg.
Cor. (Es)
Tr. (C)
Timp.
Vl.
Vla.
Vc.
Cb.

1.
410
Fl.
Ob.
zu 2
Cl.
zu 2
Fg.
zu 2.
Cor. (Es)
Tr. (C)
Timp.
Vl.
Vla.
Vc.
Cb.

420
Fl.
Ob.
Cl.
Fg.
Cor. (Es)
Tr. (C)
Timp.
Vl.
Vla.
Vc. Cb.

430
440
zu 2
ff
Fl.
Ob.
Cl.
Fg.
Cor. (Es)
Tr. (C)
Timp.
Vl.
Vla.
Vc. Cb.

450
Fl.
Ob
Cl.
Fg
Cor. (Es)
Tr. (C)
Timp.
Vl.
Vla.
Vc.
Cb.

460
Fl.
Ob.
Cl.
Fg.
Cor.
(Es)
Tr.
(C)
Timp.
Vl.
Vla.
Vc.
Cb.
sf

470
Fl.
Ob.
zu 2
Cl.
Fg.
Cor. (Es)
zu 2
Tr. (C)
Timp.
Vl.
Vla.
Vc. Cb.
ff

480
490
Fl.
Ob.
Cl.
Fg.
Cor (Es)
Tr. (C)
Timp.
Vl.
Vla.
Vc.
Cb.
1.
p
pp
tr

500
Fl.
Ob.
Cl
Fg.
Cor. (Es)
Tr. (C)
Timp.
Vl.
Vla.
Vc.
Cb.
ff

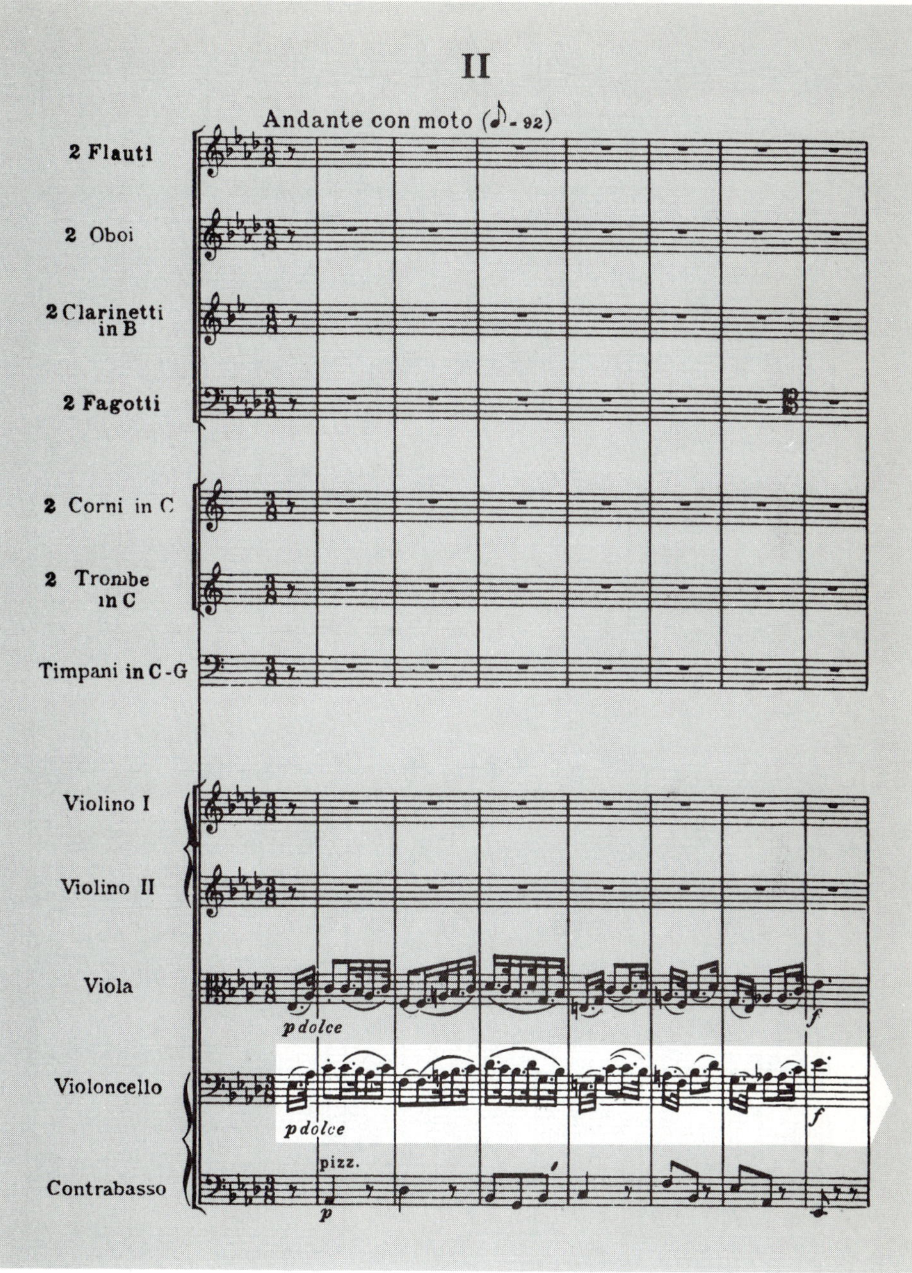
II
Andante con moto (♪ = 92)
2 Flauti
2 Oboi
2 Clarinetti in B
2 Fagotti
2 Corni in C
2 Trombe in C
Timpani in C-G
Violino I
Violino II
Viola
p dolce
f
Violoncello
p dolce
f
Contrabasso
pizz.
p

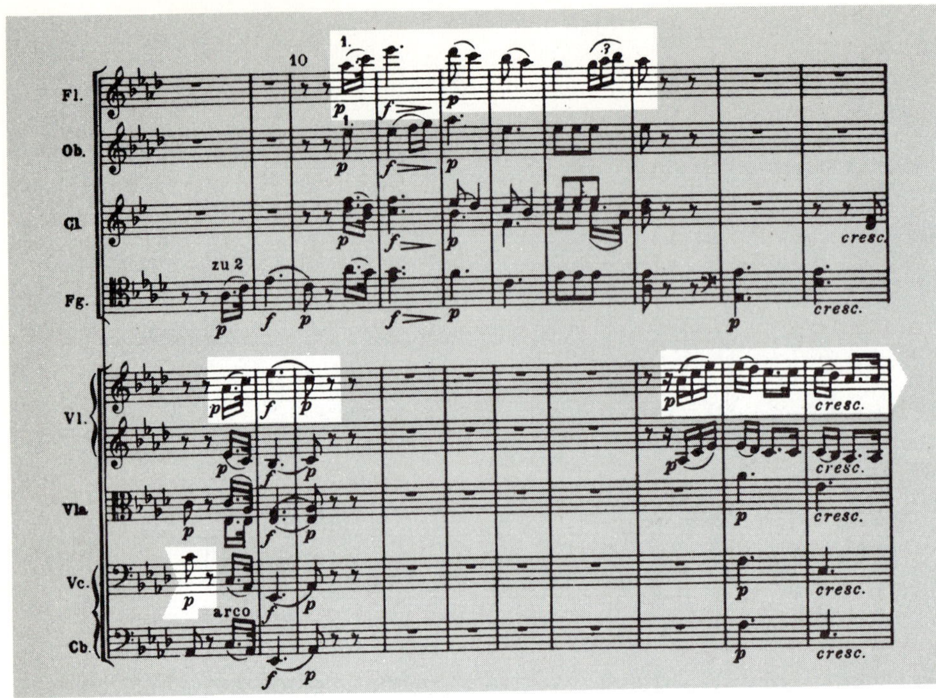
10
Fl.
Ob.
Cl.
Fg.
zu 2
Vl.
Vla.
Vc.
arco
Cb.
cresc.

20
Fl.
Ob.
Cl.
Fg.
dolce
Vl.
pdolce
Vla.
pizz.
Vc.
Cb.

Fl.
Ob.
Cl.
Fg.
Cor. (C)
Tr. (C)
Timp.
Vl.
Vla.
Vc.
Cb.
pp
ff
arco
30
sempre ff
sf
Vc. Cb.

40
Ob.
Cl.
Fg.
Cor. (C)
Tr. (C)
Vl.
Vla.
Vc.
Cb.
p
pp
sempre pp
cresc. f
f
1.
pizz.
50
dolce

60
Fl.
Ob.
Cl.
Fg.
Vl.
Vla.
Vc.
Cb.
cresc.
zu 2
arco
dolce

70
Fl.
Ob.
Cl.
Fg.
Vl.
Vla.
Vc. Cb.
cresc.
dolce
pizz.

Fl.
Ob.
Cl.
Fg.
Vl.
Vla.
Vc.
Cb.
1.
pp
80
Cor. (C)
Tr. (C)
Timp
ff
arco
Vc.
Cb

Ob.
Cor. (C)
Tr. (C)
Timp.
Vl.
Vla.
Vc. Cb.
sf
tr
f
90
Fg.
f dim.
p
pp
sempre pp
Vc.
Cb.

Fl.
Ob.
Cl.
Fg.
Vl.
Vla.
Vc.
Cb.
1.
zu 2
cresc.
ff
f
100
p
pizz.
p dolce

Fl.
Ob.
Fg.
Vl.
Vla
Vc.
Cb.
pp
Fl.
Ob.
Cl.
Fg.
Vl.
Vla.
Vc.
Cb.
1.
p
arco
dolce
sempre pp
pizz.

110
Cl.
Fg.
Vl.
Vla.
Vc.
Cb.
Fl.
Ob.
Cl.
Fg.
Cor.
(C)
zu 2
Tr.
(C)
Timp.
Vl.
Vla.
arco
Vc.
Cb.
arco

120
Fl.
Ob.
Cl.
Fg.
Cor. (C)
Tr. (C)
Timp.
Vl.
Vla.
Vc. Cb.
zu 2
130
1.
dolce
pp
sempre pp
f

Fl.

Ob.

Cl

p

140

Fl.

cresc.

ff

Ob.

cresc.

ff

Cl.

cresc.

Fg.

ff

Cor. (C)

f

ff

Tr. (C)

ff

Timp.

ff

Vl.

p

ff

p

ff

Vla.

p

ff

Vc. Cb.

p

ff

150
Fl.
Ob.
Cl.
Fg.
Cor. (C)
Tr. (C)
Timp.
Vl.
Vla.
Vc. Cb.
ff
dimin.
p
tr
pizz.
160
Vl.
Vla.
Vc.
Cb.
più p
pp
arco

Fl.
Ob.
Cl.
Fg.
Vl.
Vla
Vc.
Cb.
1.
p
pp
pizz.
170
Vc.
Cb.

Fl.
Ob.
Cl.
Fg.
Vl.
Vla.
Vc.
Cb.
cresc.
p dolce
f
sf
180
1.
arco
pp
cresc.

zu 2
Fl.
cresc.
ff
Ob.
cresc.
ff
zu 2
Cl.
cresc.
ff
zu 2
1.
Fg.
cresc.
ff
Cor.
(C)
ff
Tr.
(C)
ff
Timp
ff
Vl.
cresc.
ff
ff
Vla.
ff
Vc.
Cb.
ff

190

Fl.
Ob.
Cl.
Fg.
Cor. (C)
Tr. (C)
Timp.
Vl.
Vla
Vc. Cb.

Fl.
Ob.
Cl.
Fg.
Cor. (C)
Tr. (C)
Timp.
Vl.
Vla.
Vc. Cb.
zu 2
sf
1.
p dolce
200
p
Vla

Più mosso. (♪= 116.)
Fl.
Cl.
dolce
Fg.
pp
Vl.
pp
Vla.
Vc.
Cb.
210
Ob.
p
Cor. (C)
zu 2
cresc.
f

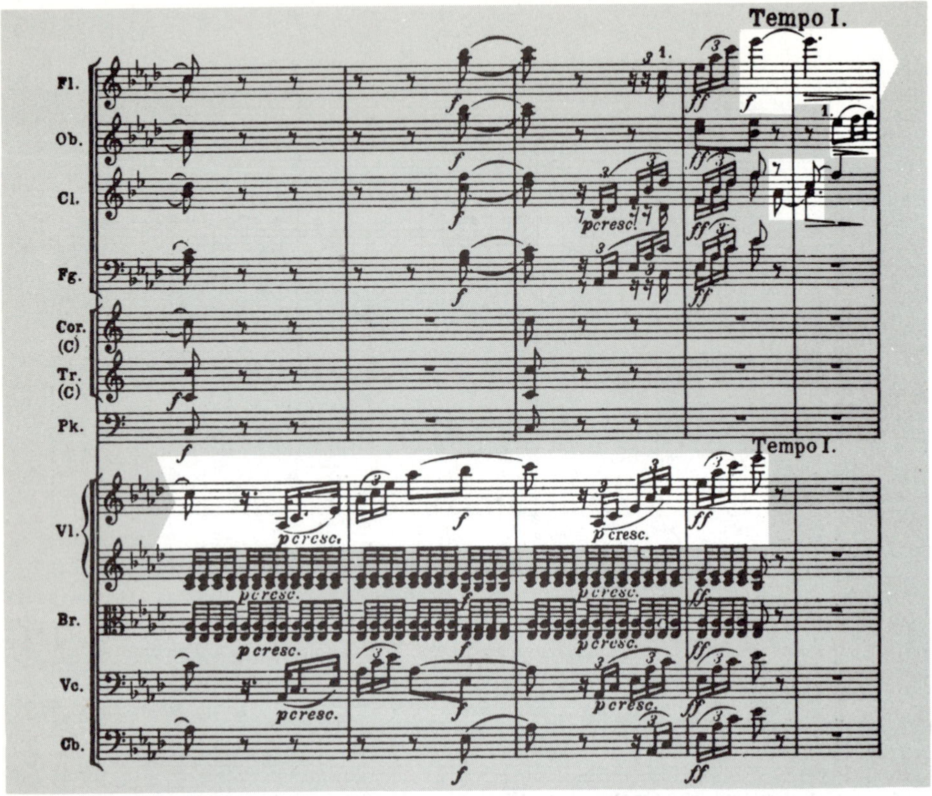

Tempo I.
Fl.
Ob.
Cl.
Fg.
Cor. (C)
Tr. (C)
Pk.
Tempo I.
Vl.
Br.
Vc.
Cb.
p cresc.
f
ff

220
Fl.
Ob.
Cl.
Fg.
Vl.
Vla.
Vc. Cb.
p dolce
cresc.
f
sf
p
pp
dolce

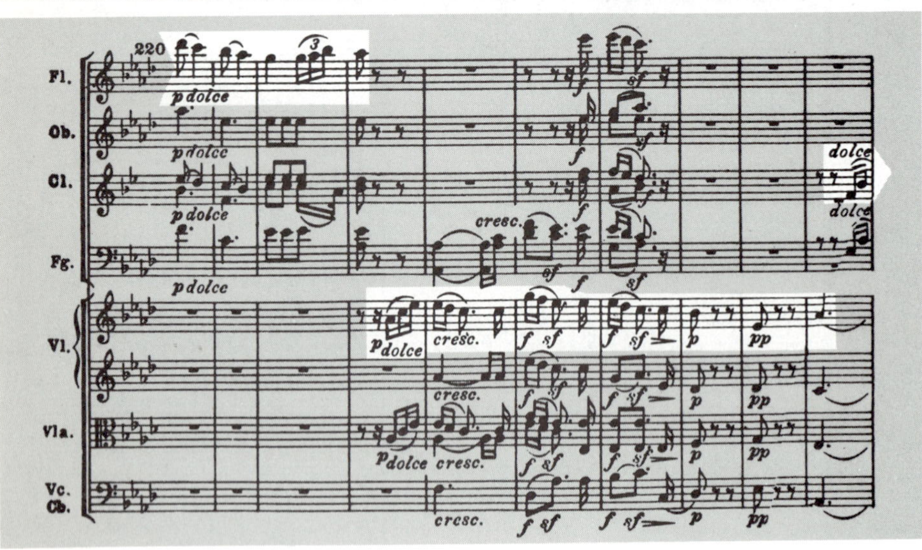

280
Cl.
Fg.
Vl.
Vla.
Vc.
Cb.
cresc.
f

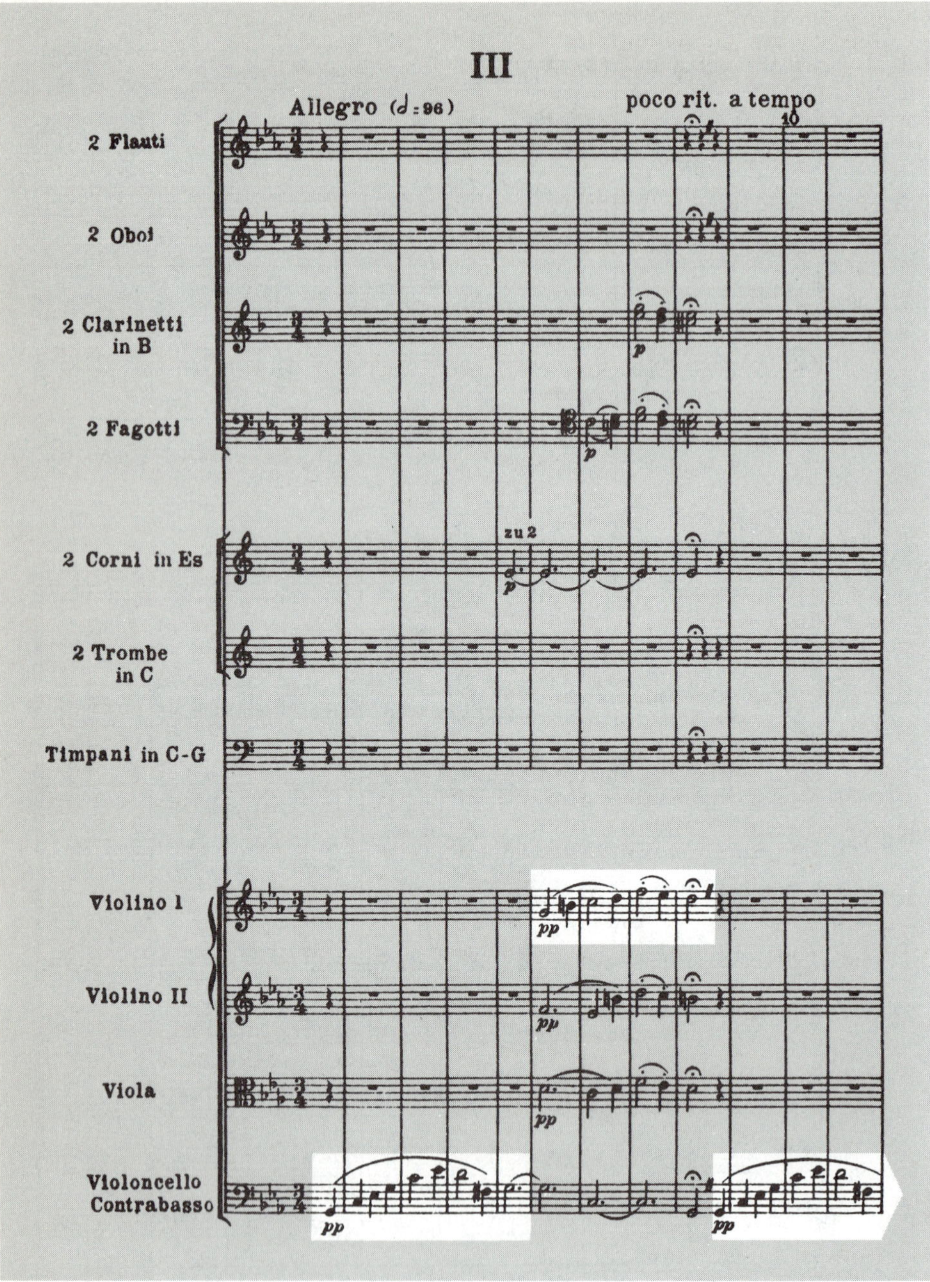
III
Allegro (𝅗𝅥 = 96)
poco rit. a tempo
10
2 Flauti
2 Oboi
2 Clarinetti in B
2 Fagotti
2 Corni in Es
zu 2
2 Trombe in C
Timpani in C-G
Violino I
Violino II
Viola
Violoncello Contrabasso
p
pp

poco rit.
1.
a tempo
20
Fl.
Cl.
Fg.
Cor. (Es)
zu 2
Vl.
Vla
Vc. Cb.
p
pp
ff
f
fp
zu 2
30
Fl.
Ob.
Cl.
Fg.
Cor. (Es)
Vl.
Vla.
Vc. Cb.

40
Fl.
Ob.
Cl.
Fg.
Cor. (Es)
Vl.
Vla
Vc. Cb.
zu 2
sf
dimin. pp
2.
p
pp

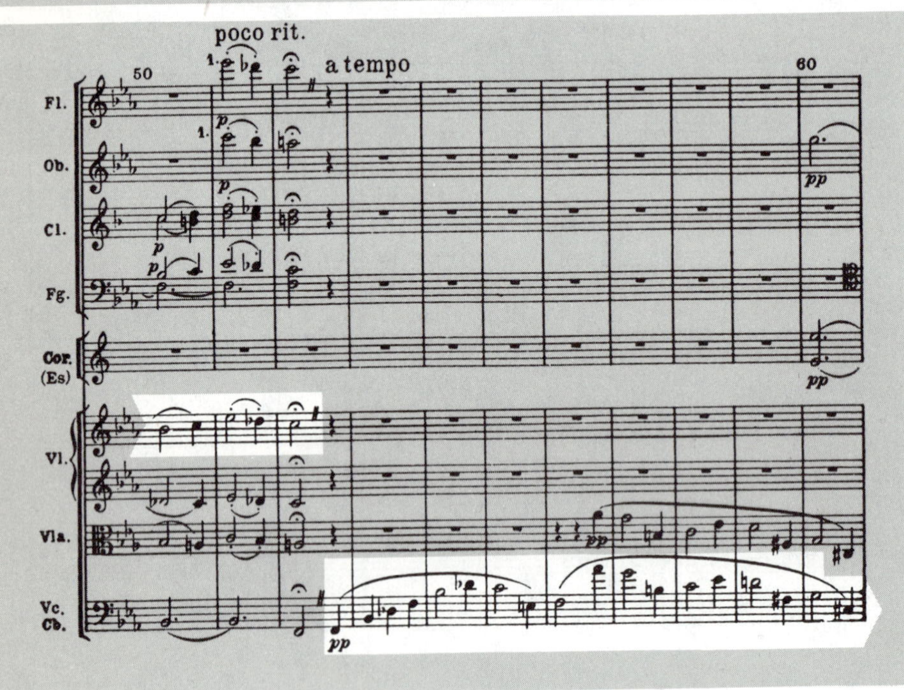
poco rit.
a tempo
50
60
Fl.
Ob.
Cl.
Fg.
Cor. (Es)
Vl.
Vla.
Vc. Cb.
1.
p
pp

70
Ob.
Cl.
Cor. (Es)
Vl.
Vla.
Vc. Cb.
pp
cresc.
1.
zu 2
80
Fl.
Fg.
Tr. (C)
Timp.
f
ff

90
Fl.
Ob.
zu 2
Cl.
Fg.
Cor. (Es)
Tr. (C)
Timp.
Vl.
Vla.
Vc. Cb.
sf
ff

Fl.
Ob.
Cl.
Fg.
Cor. (Es)
Tr. (C)
Timp.
Vl.
Vla.
Vc.
Cb.
100
1.
zu 2
sf
dimin. pp
p
pdimin. pp

Fl.
Ob.
Cl.
Fg.
Cor. (Es)
Timp.
Vl.
Vla.
Vc.
Cb.
110
p
zu 2
arco
pizz.
f>p
120
pp
sempre p
cresc.

Fl.
Ob.
Cl.
Fg.
Cor. (Es)
Tr. (C)
Timp.
Vl.
Vla.
Vc.
Cb.
130
cresc.
arco

140
Fl.
1.
Ob.
zu 2
Cl.
Fg.
Cor (Es)
Tr. (C)
Timp.
Vl.
Vla.
Vc. Cb.
zu 2
Fg.
Vla.
Vc. Cb.

150
Fl.
Ob.
Fg.
Cor.
(Es)
Timp.
Vl.
Vla.
Vc.
Cb.
1.
2.
160
Tr.
(C)
f
ff

170
zu 2
Cl.
Fg.
zu 2
f
f
Vla.
f
Vc.
Cb.

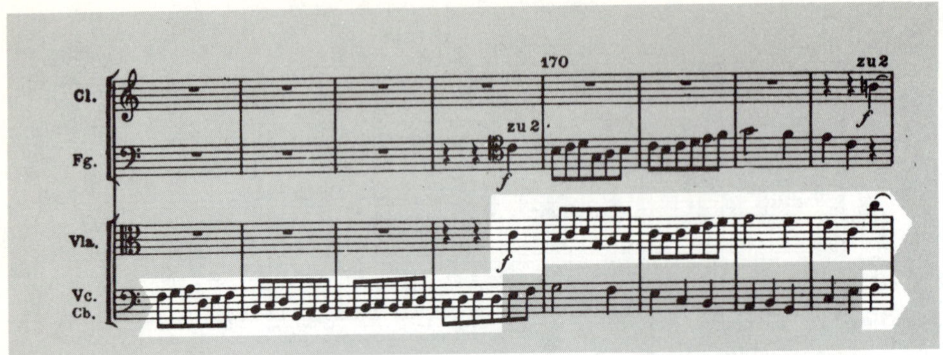

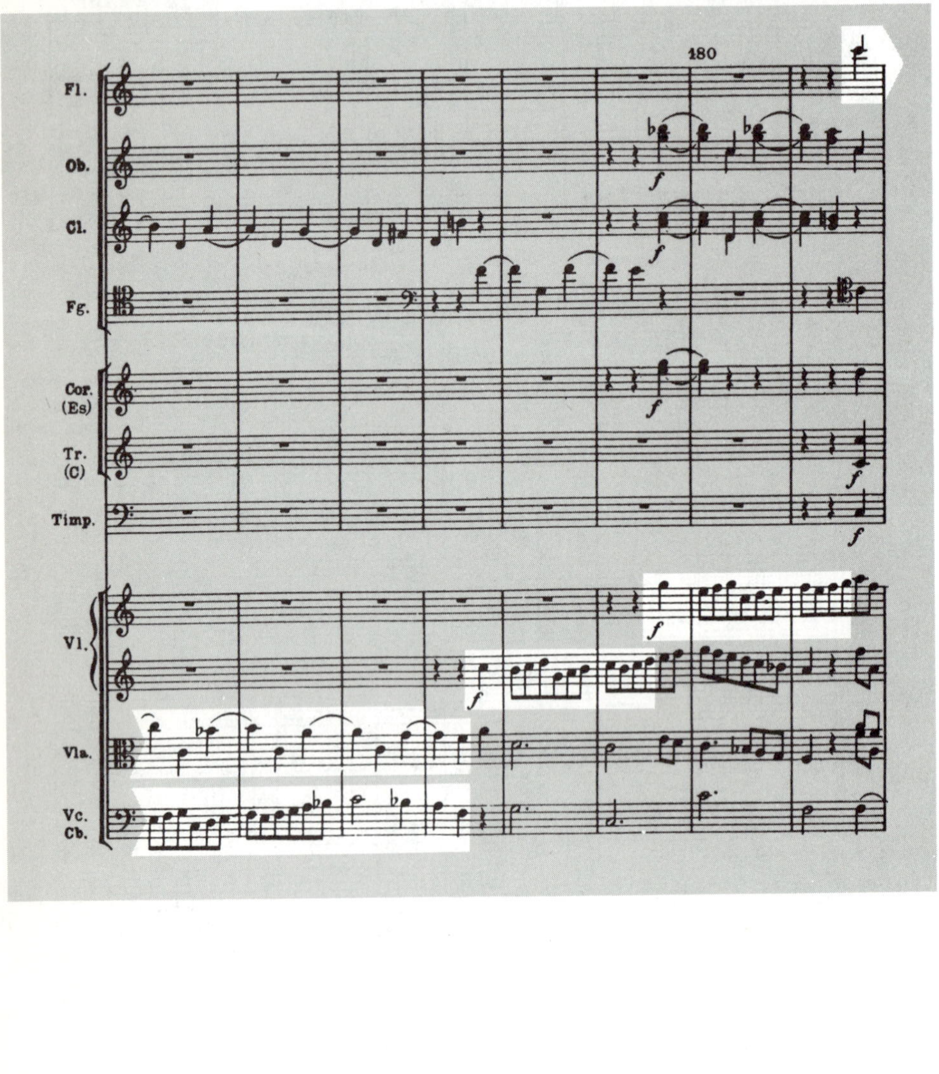

180
Fl.
Ob.
f
Cl.
f
Fg.
Cor.
(Es)
f
Tr.
(C)
f
Timp.
f
Vl.
f
f
Vla.
Vc.
Cb.

Fl.
Ob.
Cl.
Fg.
zu 2
Cor. (Es)
Tr. (C)
Timp.
Vl.
Vla.
Vc.
Cb.
sf

190

zu 2

Fl.

Ob.

Cl.

Fg.

Cor. (Es)

Tr. (C)

Timp.

Vl.

ff

Vla

ff

Vc.

Cb.

Cl.
Vla.
Vc.
Cb.
1.
210
p
sempre più p

Fl.
Ob.
Cl.
Fg.
Vl.
Vla.
Vc.
Cb.
1.
pp
sempre pp
220

Fl.
Ob.
Cl.
Fg.
1.
230
pp

240
Cl.
Fg.
Cor. (Es)
Vc. Cb.
pizz.
p
arco
pp
pp
pp
pp
poco ritard. a tempo
250
zu 2
p
Vl.
Vla.
Vc.
Cb.
pizz.
p
pizz.
p
pizz.
p
pizz.
p
poco ritard. a tempo
260
zu 2
pp
pp
arco
sempre pp
pizz.
pp
arco
pp
sempre pp
pp

270
Ob.
Fg.
Vl.
Vla.
Vc.
1.
pp
pizz.
arco
sempre pp
280
290
Cor. (Es)
p

300
1.
Fg.
Cor. (Es)
p
Vl.
Vla.
Vc.
310
Fg.
Vl.
Vla.
Vc.
320
Fg.
pp
Vl.
pizz.
arco
Vla.
Vc

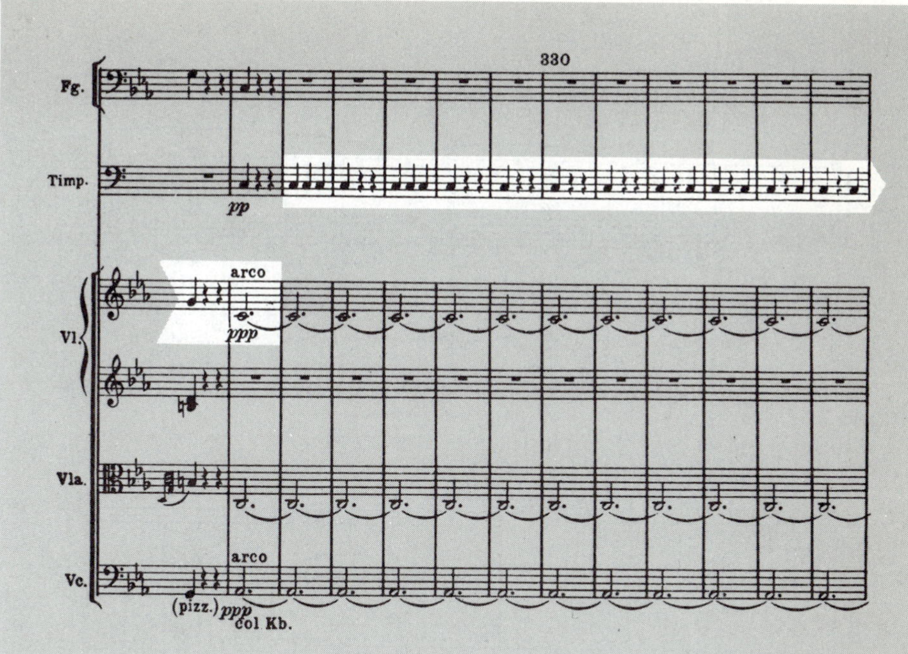
330
Fg.
Timp.
pp
arco
ppp
Vl.
Vla.
arco
Vc.
(pizz.) ppp
col Kb.

340
Timp.
sempre pp
Vl.
sempre pp
arco
sempre pp
Vla.
sempre pp
Vc
Cb.
sempre pp

370
Fl.
p cresc.
Ob.
pp cresc.
Fg.
pp cresc.
in C
Cor. (C)
p cresc.
Tr. (C)
p cresc.
Timp.
cresc.
Vl.
cresc.
cresc.
Vla.
cresc.
Vc.
Cb.
cresc.
Attacca:

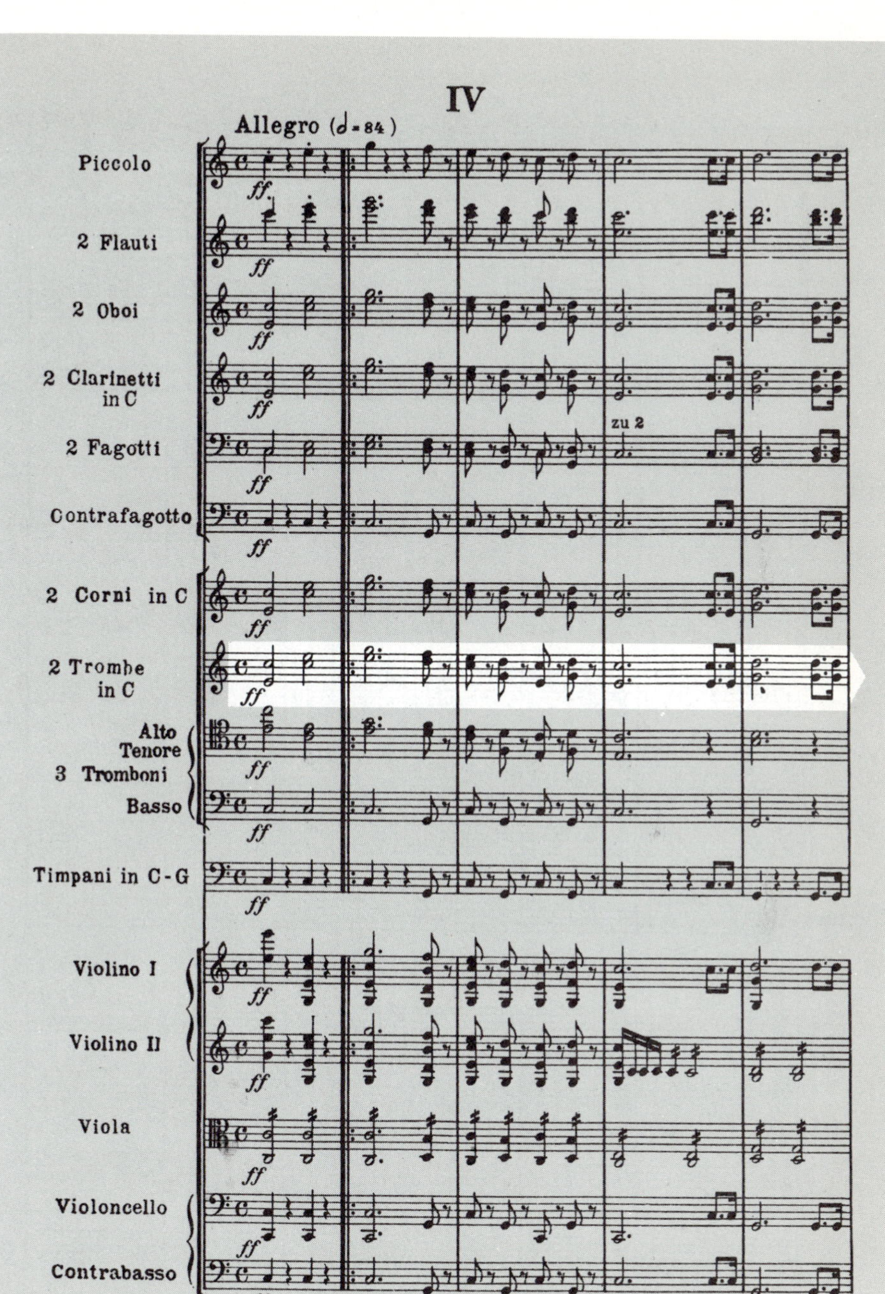
IV
Allegro (𝅗𝅥 = 84)
Piccolo
2 Flauti
2 Oboi
2 Clarinetti in C
2 Fagotti
Contrafagotto
2 Corni in C
2 Trombe in C
Alto
Tenore
3 Tromboni
Basso
Timpani in C-G
Violino I
Violino II
Viola
Violoncello
Contrabasso
zu 2
ff

10
Picc.
Fl.
zu 2
Ob.
zu 2
Cl.
Fg.
Cfg.
Cor. (C)
Tr. (C)
Tbni.
Timp.
Vl.
Vla.
Vc. Cb.

Picc.
Fl.
Ob.
Cl.
Fg.
Cfg.
Cor. (C)
Tr. (C)
Tbni.
Timp.
Vl.
Vla.
Vc. Cb.

20
zu 2
Picc.
Fl.
Ob.
Cl.
Fg.
Cfg.
Cor.
(C)
Tr.
(C)
Tpni.
Timp.
Vl.
Vla.
Vc.
Cb.

Picc.
Fl.
Ob.
Cl.
Fg.
Cfg.
Cor. (C)
Tr. (C)
Tbni.
Timp.
Vl.
Vla.
Vc.
Cb.
zu 2
zu 2
sf

80
Picc.
Fl.
Ob.
Cl.
Fg.
Cfg.
Cor. (C)
Tr. (C)
Tbni
Timp.
Vl.
Vla.
Vc.
Cb.

Fl.
Ob.
Cl.
Fg.
Cfg.
zu 2
Cor.
(C)
zu 2
Tr.
(C)
Tbni.
Timp.
Vl.
Vla.
Vc.
Cb.

40
zu 2
Fl.
Ob.
Cl.
Fg.
Cfg.
Cor. (C)
Tr. (C)
Tbni.
Vl.
Vla.
Vc. Cb.
ff
1.

Picc.
Fl.
Ob.
Cl.
Fg.
Cfg.
Cor. (C)
Tr. (C)
Timp.
Vl.
Vla.
Vc.
Cb.
cresc.
zu 2

50
Picc
Fl.
Ob.
Cl.
Fg.
Cfg.
Cor. (C)
Tr. (C)
Tbni.
Timp.
Vl.
Vla.
Vc.
Cb.

Fl.
Ob.
Cl.
Fg.
Cfg.
Cor. (C)
Tr. (C)
Tbni.
Timp.
Vl.
Vla
Vc.
Cb.
ff
pp
cresc.
f
dolce
zu 2

60
Fl.
Ob.
zu 2
Cl.
Fg.
Cfg.
Cor
(C)
Tr.
(C)
Tbni.
Timp.
Vl.
Vla.
Vc.
Cb.

Fl.
Ob.
Cl.
Fg.
Cfg.
Cor. (C)
Tr. (C)
Tbni.
Timp.
Vl.
Vla
Vc.
Cb.
fp
p
sf

70
Picc.
Fl.
Ob.
Cl.
Fg.
Cfg.
Cor. (C)
Tr. (C)
Tbni.
Timp.
Vl.
Vla.
Vc.
Cb.
1.
p dolce
zu 2
f
p

80
Picc.
Fl.
Ob.
Cl.
Fg.
Cfg.
Cor. (C)
Tr. (C)
Tbni.
Timp.
Vl.
Vla.
Vc. Cb.
zu 2
sf
più f
ff

1.
Picc.
Fl.
Ob.
zu 2
Cl.
Fg.
zu 2
Cfg.
Cor. (C)
Tr. (C)
Tbni.
Timp.
Vl.
Vla.
Vc.
Cb.

2.

Picc.
zu 2
Fl.
zu 2
Ob.
Cl.
zu 2
Fg.
Cfg.
Cor. (C)
Tr. (C)
Tbni.
Timp.
Vl.
Vla.
Vc. Cb.

90
Picc.
Fl.
Ob.
Cl.
Fg.
Cfg.
zu 2
Cor.
(C)
Tr.
(C)
Tbni.
Vl.
p
Vla.
Vc.
Cb.

Fl.
Ob.
Cor.
(C)
Vl.
Vla.
Vc.
1.
p
1.
3
3
dolce
p

Fl.
Ob.
Cl.
Fg.
Cor.
(C)
Vl.
Vla.
Vc.
100
dolce
1.
3
p
zu 2

Fl.
Ob.
Cl.
Fg.
Cfg.
Vl.
Vla.
Vc.
Kb.
110
Vc.
Cb.

Fl.
Ob.
Cl.
Fg.
zu 2
ff
zu 2
C fg.
Cor. (C)
zu 2
f
Tr. (C)
f
Tbni.
zu 2
f
Timp.
tr
f
Vl.
Vla.
Vc.
Cb.

zu 2
120
Fl.
Ob.
Cl.
Fg.
Cfg.
Cor. (C)
Tr. (C)
Trbni
Timp.
Vl.
Vla.
Vc.
Cb.

Fl.
Ob.
Cl.
Fg.
Cfg.
Cor. (C)
Tr. (C)
Tbni.
Timp.
Vl.
Vla.
Vc.
Cb.
più f
zu 2

130
Fl.
Ob.
1.
Cl.
Fg.
Cfg.
zu 2
Cor. (C)
zu 2
Tr. (C)
Tbni.
Timp.
Vl.
Vla.
Vc. Cb.

Picc.
Fl.
Ob.
Cl.
zu 2
Fg.
Cfg.
Cor. (C)
Tr. (C)
Tbni
Timp.
Vl.
Vla.
Vc. Cb.
ff
3

Picc.
Fl.
Ob.
Cl.
Fg.
Cfg.
Cor. (C)
Tr. (C)
Tbni.
Timp.
Vl.
Vla.
Vc.
Cb.

140
Picc.
Fl.
Ob.
Cl.
Fg.
Cfg.
Cor. (C)
Tr. (C)
Tbni.
Timp.
Vl.
Vla.
Vc.
Cb.
sempre ff
sf
tr

Picc.
Fl.
Ob.
Cl.
Fg.
Cfg.
Cor.
(C)
Tr.
(C)
Tbni.
Timp.
Vl.
Vla.
Vc.
Cb.

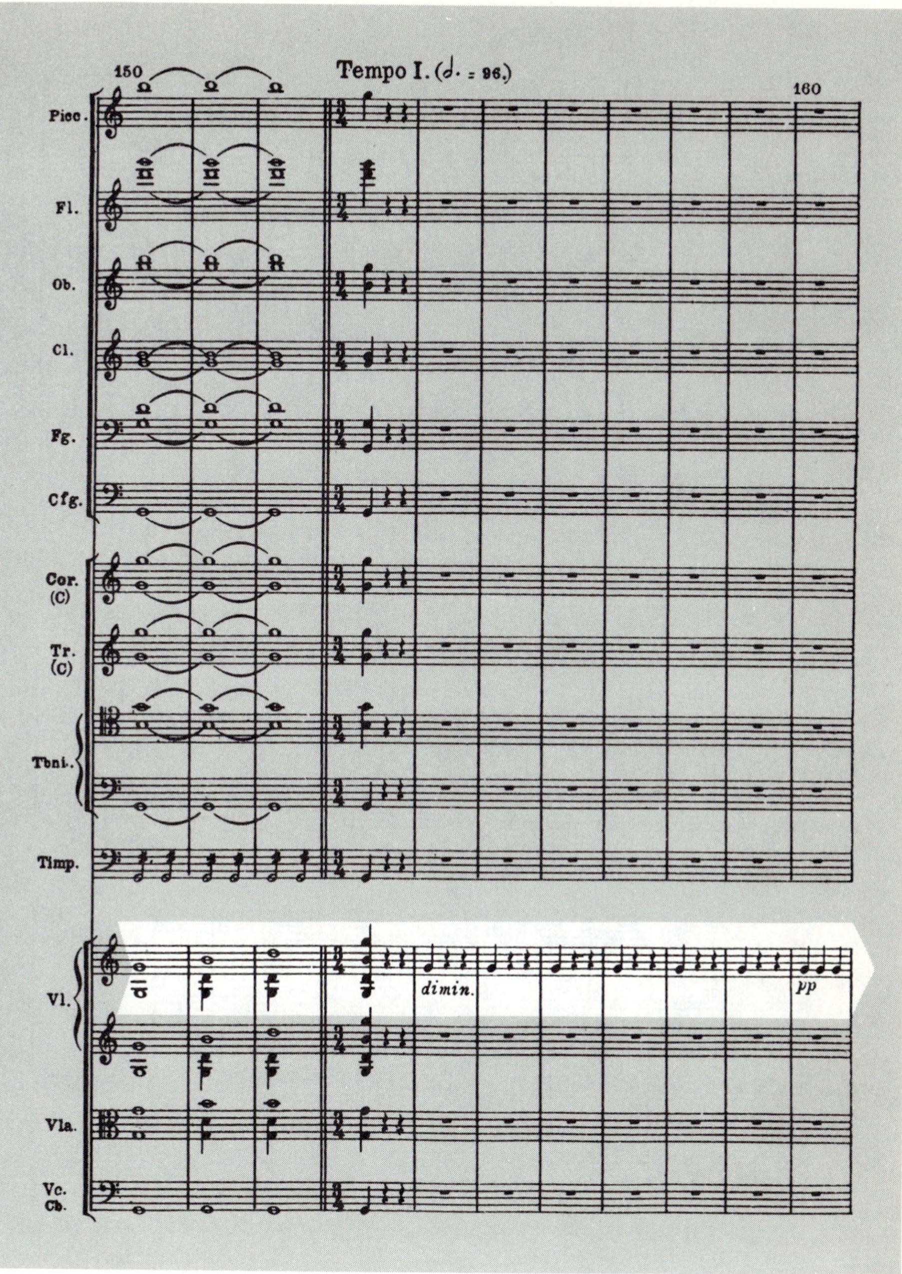
150
Tempo I. (𝅗𝅥. = 96.)
160
Picc.
Fl.
Ob.
Cl.
Fg.
Cfg.
Cor. (C)
Tr. (C)
Tbni.
Timp.
Vl.
dimin.
pp
Vla.
Vc. Cb.

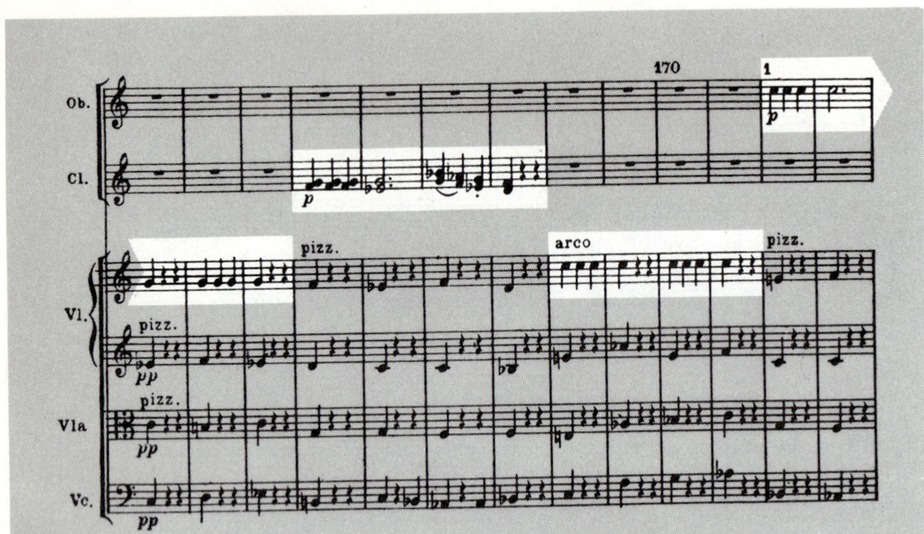
170
1
Ob.
Cl.
p
p
arco
pizz.
pizz.
Vl.
pizz.
pp
pizz.
Vla
pp
Vc.
pp

180
Ob
Cl.
Cor.
(C)
pp
pp
Vl.
arco
Vla.
Vc.

190
1.
Fl.
p dolce
Ob.
Cl.
Fg.
1.
p dolce
Cor
(C)
Vla.

200
Fl.
cresc.
Ob.
cresc.
Cl.
cresc.
Fg.
cresc.
Cor.
(C)
cresc.
Timp.
pp
cresc.
arco
Vl.
cresc.
arco
cresc.
Vla
cresc.
Vc.
Cb.
arco
cresc.

Allegro. (𝅗𝅥 = 84)
210
Picc.
Fl.
zu 2
Ob.
zu 2
Cl.
Fg.
Cfg.
Cor. (C)
Tr. (C)
Tbni.
Timp.
Vl.
Vla.
Vc.
Cb.
ff

Picc.
Fl.
Ob.
Cl.
Fg.
Cfg.
Cor.
(C)
Tr.
(C)
Tbni.
Timp.
Vl.
Vla.
Vc.
Cb.

220
Picc.
Fl.
Ob.
Cl.
Fg.
Cfg.
Cor
(C)
Tr.
(C)
Tbni.
Timp.
Vl.
Vla.
Vc.
Cb.

Picc.
Fl.
zu 2
Ob.
Cl.
Fg.
Cfg.
Cor. (C)
Tr. (C)
Tbni.
Timp.
Vl.
Vla.
Vc.
Cb

230
Picc.
Fl.
Ob.
Cl.
zu 2
Fg.
Cfg.
Cor. (C)
Tr. (C)
Tbni.
Timp.
Vl.
Vla.
Vc.
Cb.

Fl.
Ob.
Cl.
Fg.
Cfg.
Cor. (C)
Tr. (C)
Tbni.
Timp.
Vl.
Vla.
Vc. Cb.

240
Picc.
Fl.
zu 2
Ob.
zu 2
Cl.
Fg.
zu 2
Cfg.
Cor. (C)
Tr. (C)
Tbni.
Timp.
Vl.
Vls.
Vc. Cb.

250
Picc.
Fl.
Ob.
Cl.
zu 2
Fg.
Cfg.
Cor.
(C)
Tr.
(C)
Tbni.
Timp.
Vl.
Vla.
Vc.
Cb.

Fl.
Ob.
Cl.
Fg.
Cfg.
Cor. (C)
Tr. (C)
Tbni.
Timp.
Vl.
Vla.
Vc.
Cb.

260
Picc.
Fl.
Ob.
Cl.
Fg.
Cfg.
Cor. (C)
Tr. (C)
Tbni.
Timp.
Vl.
Vla.
Vc.
Cb.
1.
p dolce
cresc.

Fl.
Ob.
Cl.
Fg.
Cfg.
Cor (C)
Tr. (C)
Tbni.
Timp.
Vl.
Vla.
Vc.
Cb.
1.
pp
cresc.
ff
p dolce
p
f

270
Picc.
Fl.
zu 2
Ob.
zu 2
Cl.
zu 2
Fg.
Cfg.
Cor. (C)
Tr. (C)
Tbni.
Timp.
Vl.
Vla.
Vc. Cb

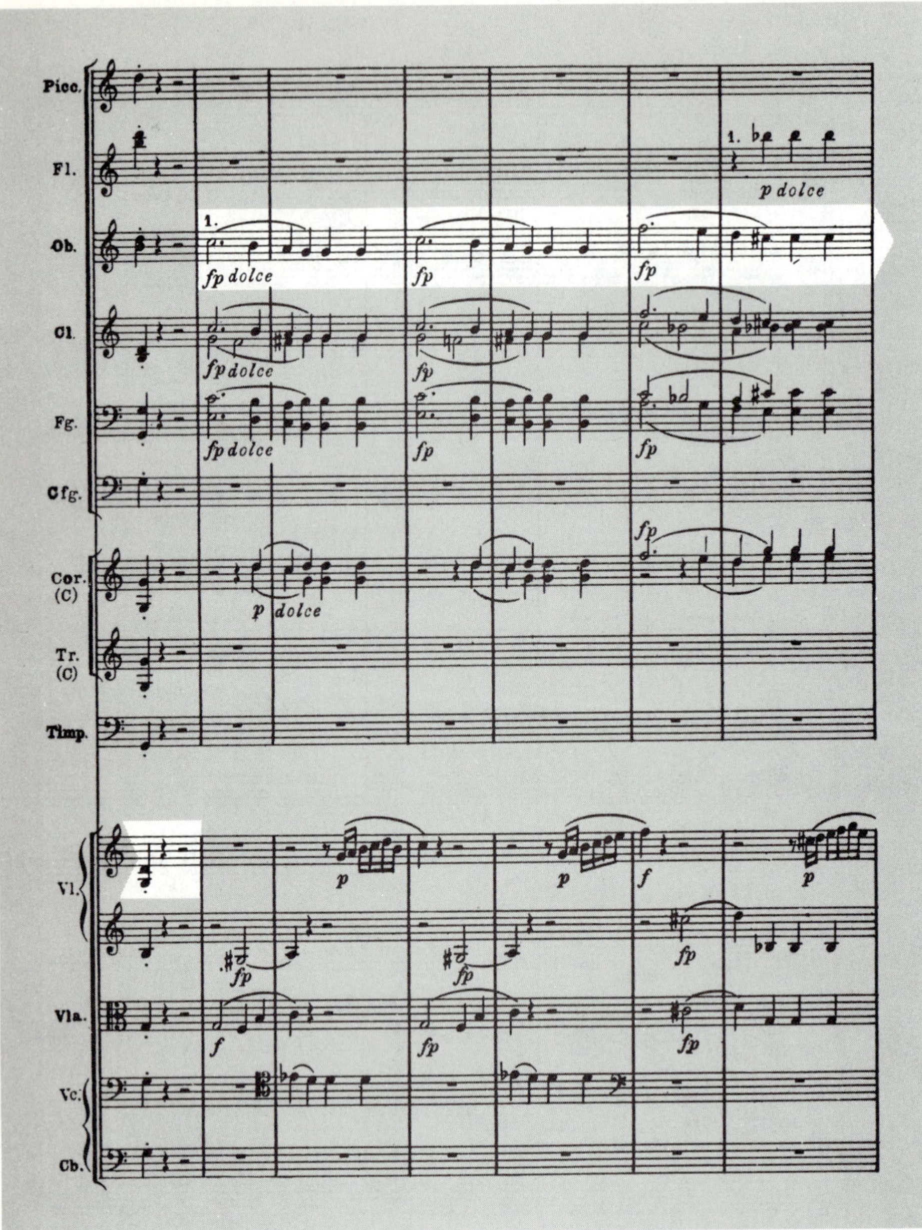
Picc.
Fl.
Ob.
Cl.
Fg.
Cfg.
Cor. (C)
Tr. (C)
Timp.
Vl.
Vla.
Vc.
Cb.
p dolce
fp dolce
fp
p
f

280
zu 2
Fl.
Ob.
Cl.
Fg.
Cfg.
Cor. (C)
Tr. (C)
Tbni.
Timp.
Vl.
Vla.
Vc. Cb.
f
sf

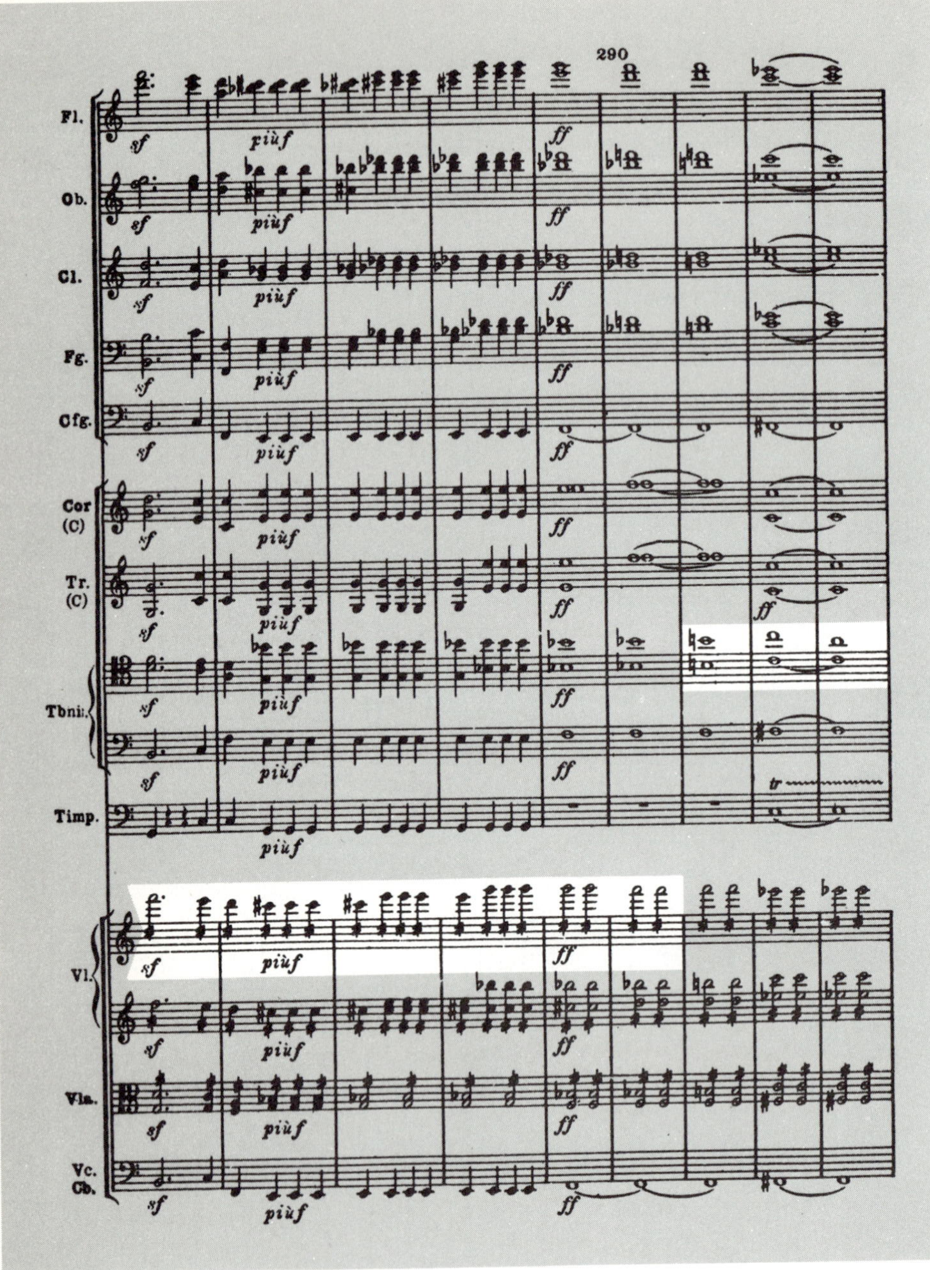
290
Fl.
Ob.
Cl.
Fg.
Cfg.
Cor (C)
Tr. (C)
Tbni.
Timp.
Vl.
Vla.
Vc. Cb.
sf
più f
ff
tr

Fl.
Ob.
Cl.
Fg.
C.fg.
Cor (C)
Tr. (C)
Tbni.
Timp.
Vl.
Vla.
Vc.
Cb.
sf
f
1.

300
1.
Fl.
Ob.
Cl.
Fg.
Cfg.
Cor. (C)
Tr. (C)
Tbni.
Timp
Vl.
Vla.
Vc.
Cb.
sf
più f

Fl.
Ob.
Cl.
zu 2
Fg.
Cfg.
Cor. (C)
Tr. (C)
Tbni.
Timp.
Vl.
Vla.
Vc. Cb.
ff
sf

310
Fl.
Ob.
Cl.
Fg.
C fg.
Cor.
(C)
Tr.
(C)
Tbni.
Timp.
Vl.
Vla.
Vc.
Cb.
sf

320
Fl.
1.
p dolce cresc. poco a poco
Ob.
Cl.
1.
p cresc. poco a poco
Fg.
zu 2
ff
1.
p
cresc.
Cfg.
Cor. (C)
zu 2
p dolce
cresc. poco a poco
Tr. (C)
Tbni.
Timp.
Vl.
p cresc. poco a poco
Vla.
p cresc. poco a poco
Vc. Cb.

Picc.
p cresc.
f
Fl.
f
Ob.
1.
p cresc.
f
Cl.
f
Fg.
f
C-fg.
f
Cor. (C)
f
Tr. (C)
p cresc.
f
Tbni.
f
f
Timp.
tr
p cresc.
f
Vl.
f
p cresc.
f
Vla.
f
Vc.
p cresc. poco a poco
f
Cb.
cresc.
f

330
Picc.
Fl.
Ob.
Cl.
Fg.
Cfg.
Cor. (C)
Tr. (C)
Tbni.
Timp.
Vl.
Vla.
Vc. Cb.

340
Picc.
p dolce
cresc. poco a poco
Fl.
1.
p cresc. poco a poco
p cresc.
Ob.
1.
p dolce
p cresc. poco a poco
Fg.
p cresc.
Cfg.
Cor. (C)
zu 2
p dolce
cresc. poco a poco
Vl.
p cresc. poco a poco
p cresc. poco a poco
Vla.
p cresc. poco a poco
Vc.
p cresc. poco a poco
Cb.
p cresc.

Picc.
Fl.
zu 2
Ob.
Cl.
cresc.
Fg.
Cfg.
Cor. (C)
Tr. (C)
p cresc.
Tbni.
Timp.
p cresc.
Vl.
Vla
Vc.
Cb.

350
Sempre
Picc
Fl.
Ob.
Cl.
Fg.
Cfg.
Cor. (C)
Tr. (C)
Tbni.
Timp.
Vl.
Vla.
Vc. Cb.
1.
zu 2
zu 2
p
cresc. poco a poco

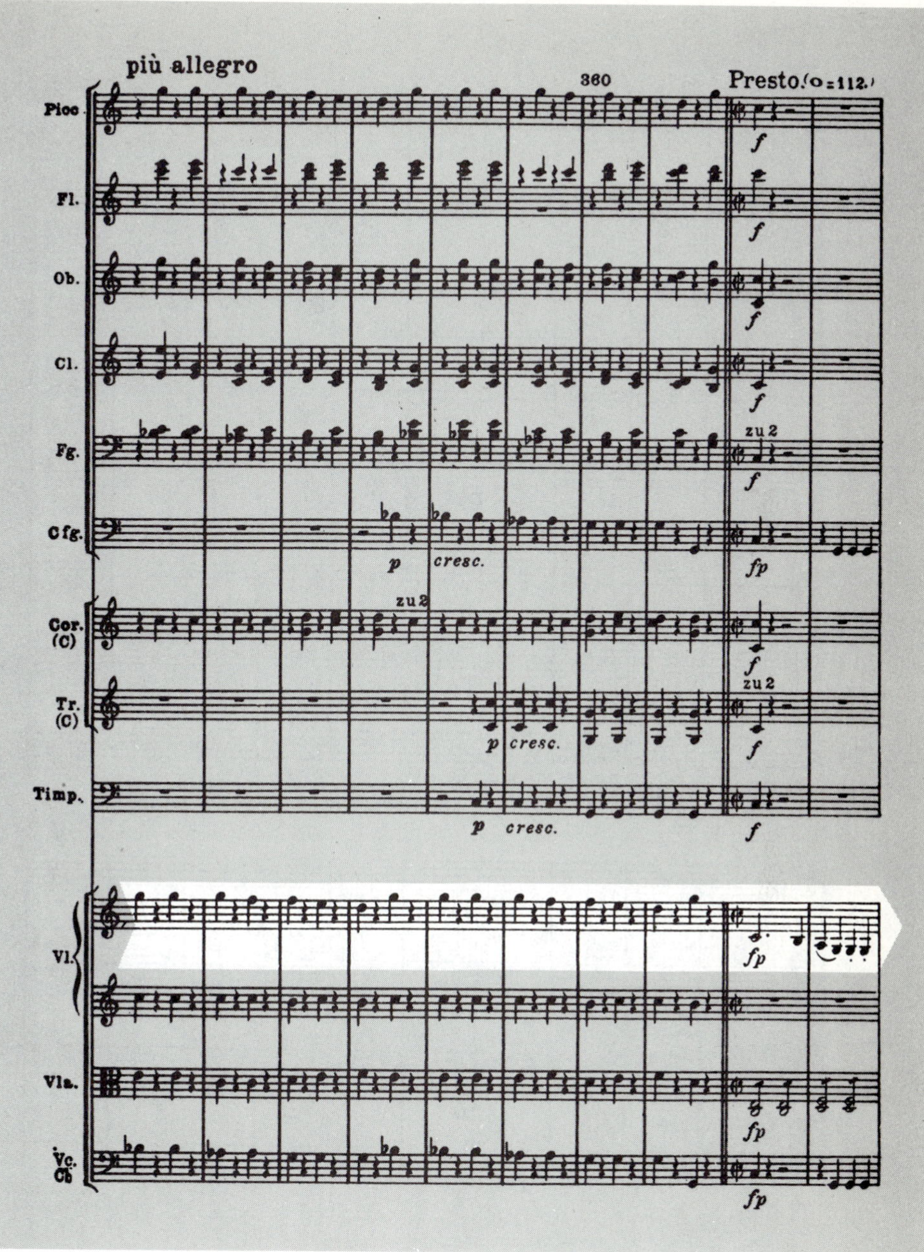
più allegro
360
Presto (𝅝 = 112.)
Picc.
Fl.
Ob.
Cl.
Fg.
Cfg.
Cor. (C)
Tr. (C)
Timp.
Vl.
Vla.
Vc. Cb.
f
fp
p
cresc.
zu 2

370
Fl.
Ob.
Cl.
Fg.
Cfg.
Cor. (C)
Tr. (C)
Timp.
Vl.
Vla
Vc. Cb.

380
Fl.
fp
fp
cresc.
Ob.
fp
fp
cresc.
Cl.
fp
fp
cresc.
Fg.
fp
fp
cresc.
Cfg.
fp
fp
cresc.
Cor. (C)
f
fp
cresc.
Tr. (C)
f
f
p cresc.
Timp.
f
f
p cresc.
Vl.
fp
fp
cresc.
fp
fp
cresc.
Vla.
fp
fp
cresc.
Vc. Cb.
fp
fp
cresc.

390
Picc.
cresc.
f
ff
Fl.
zu 2
Ob.
Cl.
Fg.
Cfg.
Cor. (C)
Tr. (C)
Tbni.
Timp.
Vl.
Vla.
Vc. Cb.

Picc.
Fl.
Ob.
Cl.
Fg.
zu 2
C fg.
Cor. (C)
zu 2
Tr. (C)
zu 2
Timp.
Vl.
Vla.
Vc. Cb.

400
Picc.
Fl.
Ob.
zu 2
Cl.
zu 2
Fg.
Cfg.
Cor (C)
Tr. (C)
tr
Timp.
Vl.
Vla.
Vc. Cb.

410
Picc.
Fl.
Ob.
Cl.
Fg.
C fg.
Cor. (C)
Tr. (C)
Tbni.
Timp.
Vl.
Vla.
Vc. Cb.
sempre ff

420
Picc
Fl.
zu 2
Ob.
zu 2
Cl.
Fg.
zu 2
Cfg.
Cor. (C)
Tr. (C)
zu 2
Tbni.
Timp.
Vl.
Vla.
Vc. Cb.

430
Picc.
Fl.
Ob.
Cl.
Fg.
Cfg.
Cor. (C)
Tr. (C)
Tbni.
Timp.
Vl.
Vla.
Vc. Cb.

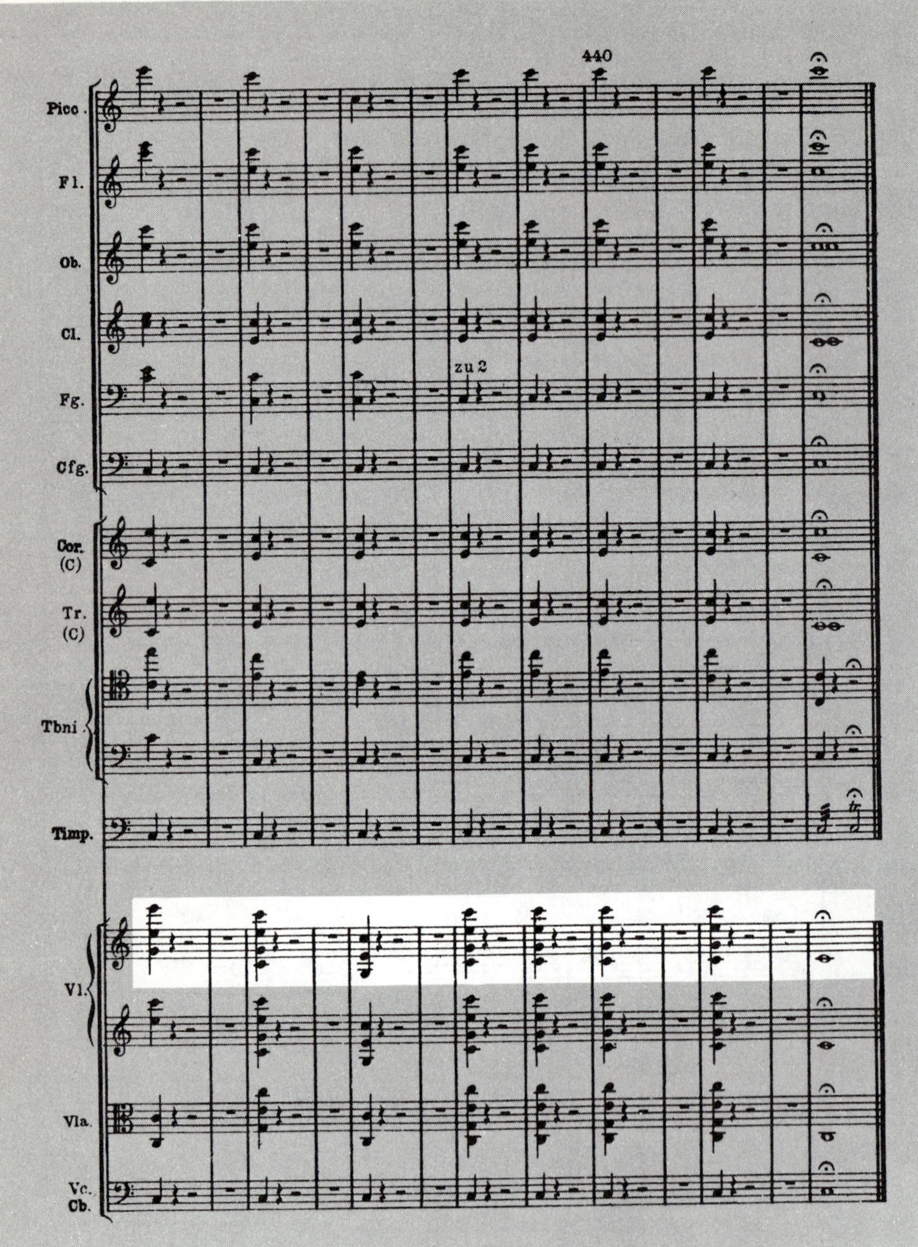
440
Picc.
Fl.
Ob.
Cl.
zu 2
Fg.
Cfg.
Cor. (C)
Tr. (C)
Tbni
Timp.
Vl.
Vla.
Vc. Cb.

42. Beethoven

Piano Concerto No. 5 in E-flat major, *(Emperor)*, First movement (1809)

S2B/1 S2/23

8

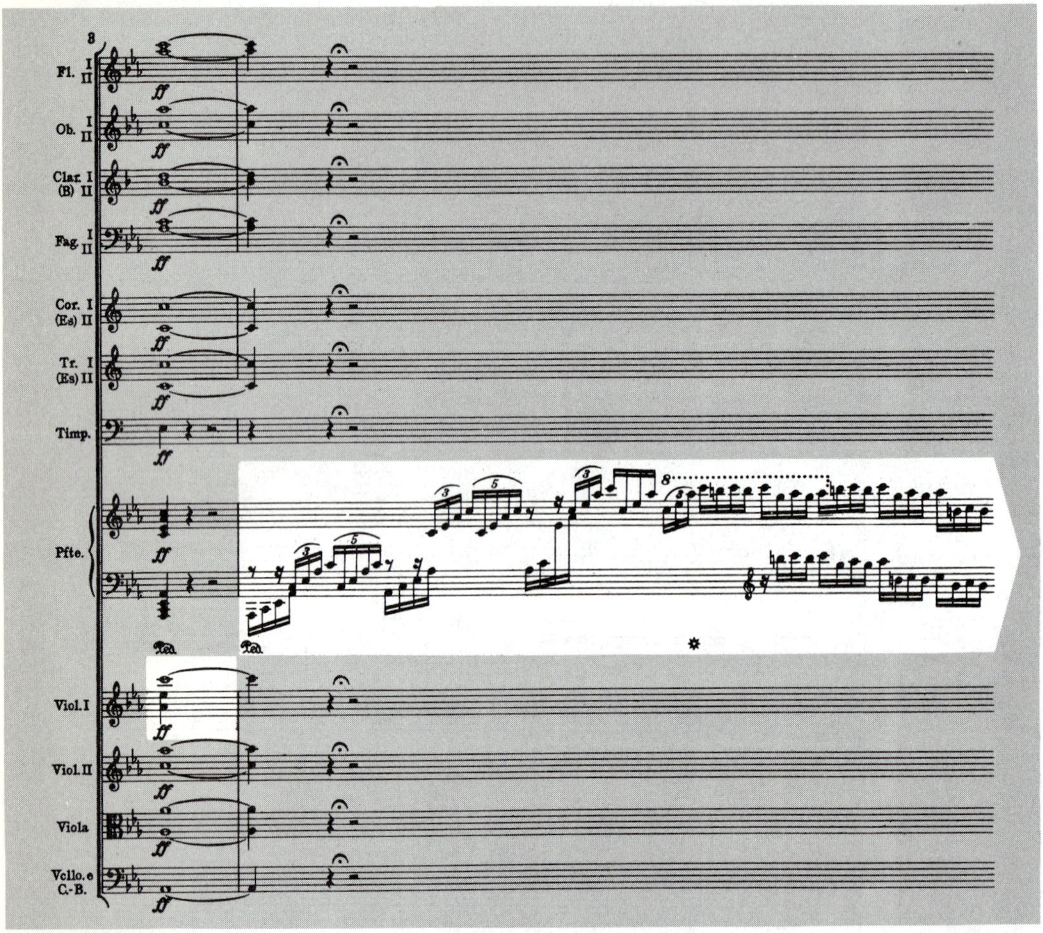

Fl. I II

Ob. I II

Clar. I (B) II

Fag. I II

Cor. I (Es) II

Tr. I (Es) II

Timp.

Pfte.

Viol. I

Viol. II

Viola

Vcllo. e C.-B.

ff

Ped.

5
Fl. I II
Ob. I II
Clar. I (B) II
Fag. I II
Cor. I (Es) II
Tr. I (Es) II
Timp.
Pfte.
Viol. I
Viol. II
Viola
Vcllo. e C.-B.
ff
a tempo
7
a tempo
pizz.
arco
div.

14
Fl. I II
Ob. I II
p dolce
Clar. I (B) II
Fag. I II
Cor. I (Es) II
Tr. I (Es) II
Timp.
Viol. I
Viol. II
Viola
Vello. e C.-B.
18
A
uniss.
div.
unis.

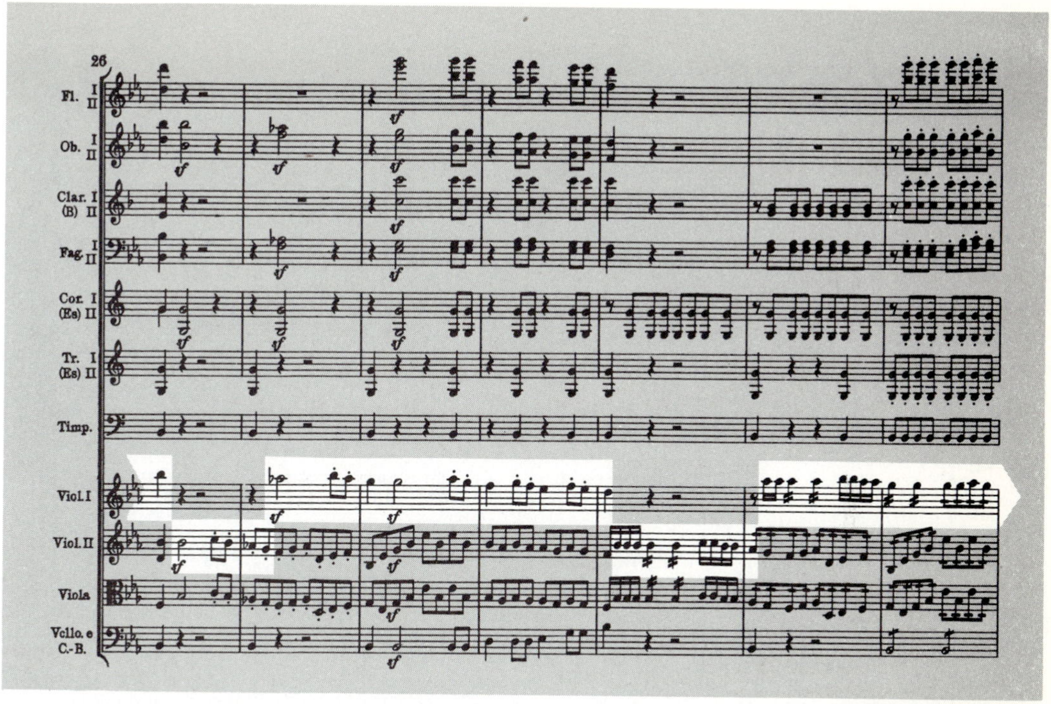

26
Fl. I II
Ob. I II
Clar. I (B) II
Fag. I II
Cor. I (Es) II
Tr. I (Es) II
Timp.
Viol. I
Viol. II
Viola
Vcllo. e C.-B.
sf

33
Fl. I II
Ob. I II
Clar. I (B) II
Fag. I II
Cor. I (Es) II
Tr. I (Es) II
Timp.
Viol. I
Viol. II
Viola
Vcllo. e C.-B.
Vcllo.
sf
dim.
pp

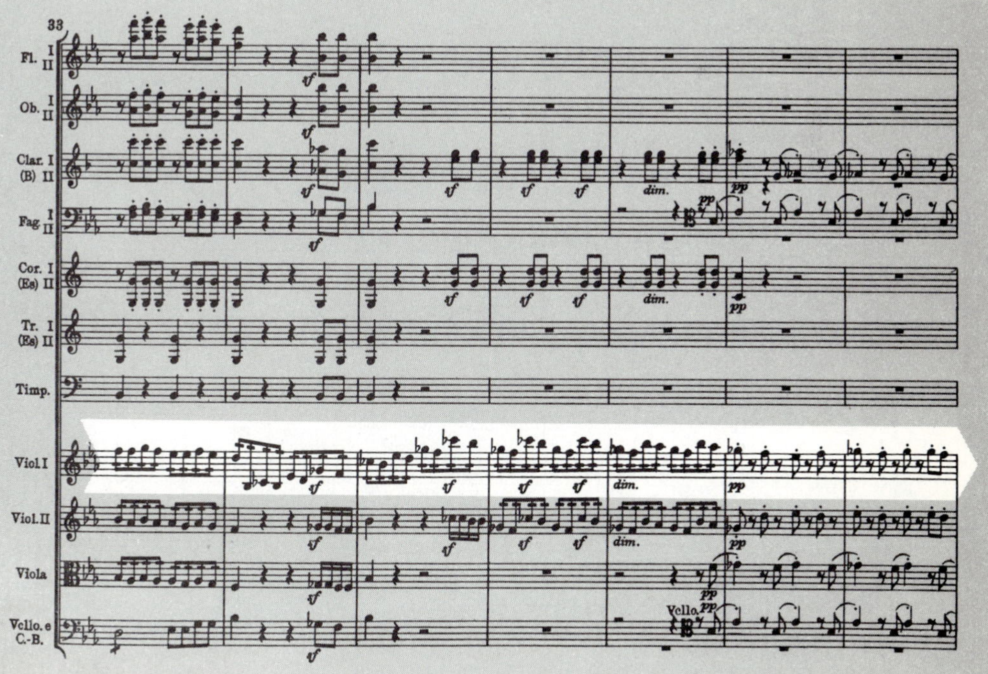

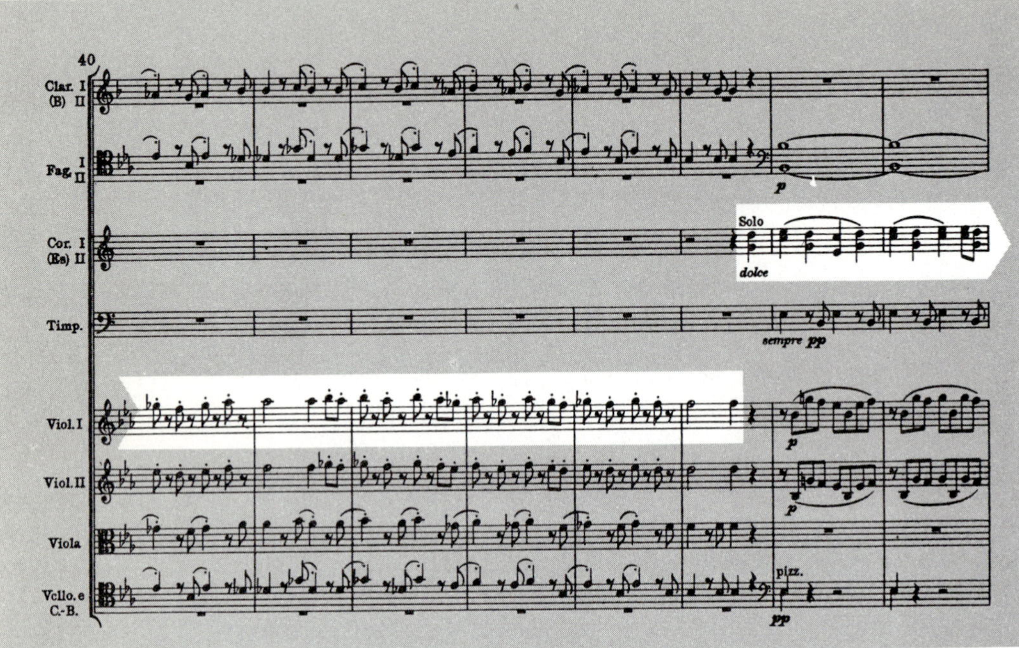
40
Clar. I (B) II
Fag. I II
Cor. I (Es) II
Solo
dolce
Timp.
sempre pp
Viol. I
Viol. II
Viola
Vcllo. e C.-B.
pizz.
pp

48
Fl. I II
Clar. I (B) II
Fag. I II
Cor. I (Es) II
Timp.
Viol. I
Viol. II
Viola
Vcllo. e C.-B.
arco
pp legato

56
Fl. I II
Ob. I II
Clar. I (B) II
Fag. I II
Cor. I (Es) II
Tr. I (Es) II
Timp.
Viol. I
Viol. II
Viola
Vcllo. e C.-B.
cresc.
B
f
62

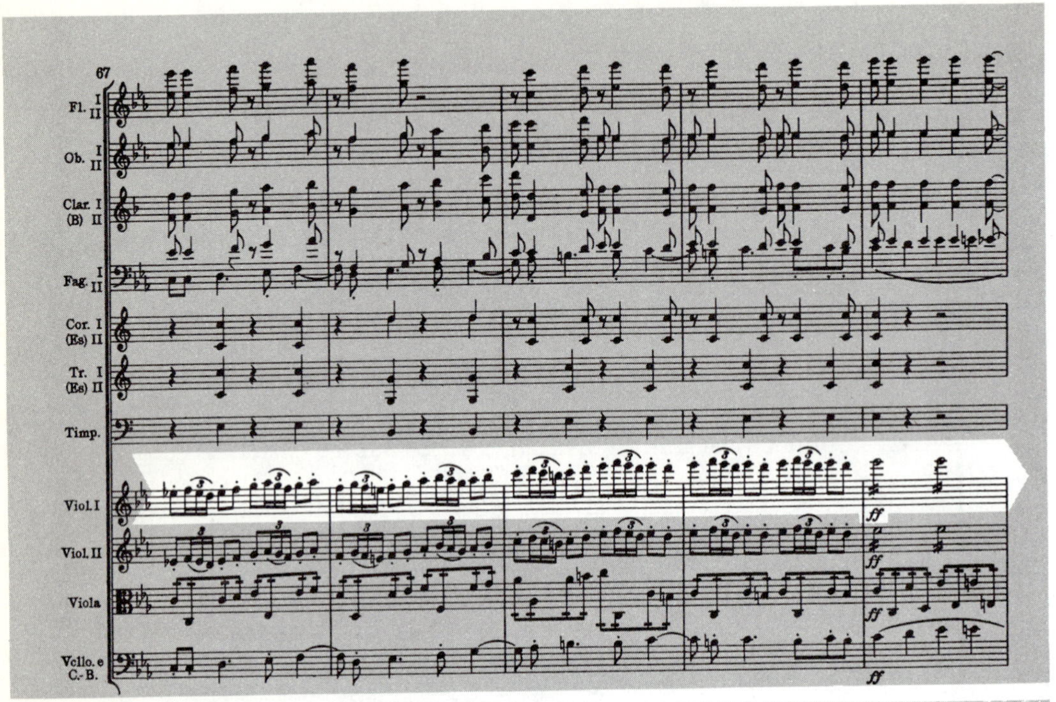

67
Fl. I II
Ob. I II
Clar. I (B) II
Fag. I II
Cor. I (Es) II
Tr. I (Es) II
Timp.
Viol. I
Viol. II
Viola
Vcllo. e C.-B.
ff
ff
ff
ff

72
Fl. I II
Ob. I II
Clar. I (B) II
Fag. I II
Cor. I (Es) II
Tr. I (Es) II
Timp.
Viol. I
Viol. II
Viola
Vcllo. e C.-B.
p dolce
I.
p dolce
I.
p dolce
I.
a 2
p dolce
p dolce
tr
p
p
p
p
p

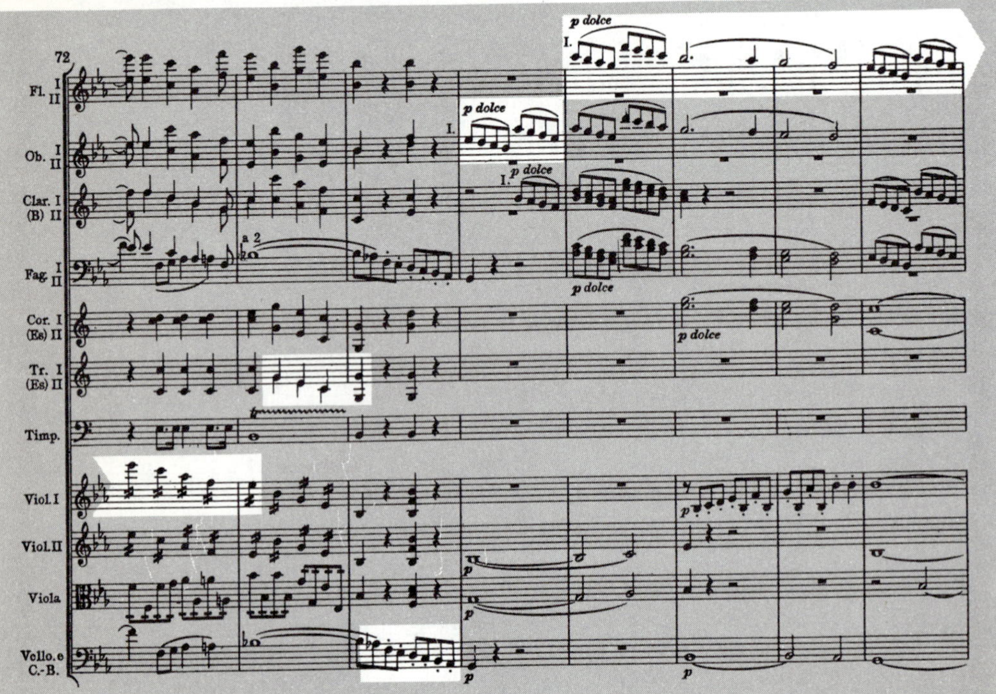

80
Fl. I II
Ob. I II
Clar. I (B) II
Fag. I II
Cor. I (Es) II
Tr. I (Es) II
Timp.
Viol. I
Viol. II
Viola
Vcllo. e C.-B.
p
cresc.
f
87
C
ff
sf
div.

94
Fl. I II
Ob. I II
Clar. I (B) II
Fag. I II
Cor. I (Es) II
Viol. I
Viol. II
Viola
Vcllo.
C.-B.
dim.
pizz.
legato
99
Tr. I (Es) II
Timp.
Pfte.
cresc.
arco
unis.
Vcllo. e C.-B.

105
dim.
p
dim.
pp
Fl. I II
Ob. I II
Clar. I (B) II
Fag. I II
Cor. I (Es) II
Pfte.
dolce
Viol. I
Viol. II
Viola
Vcllo.
C.-B.
arco

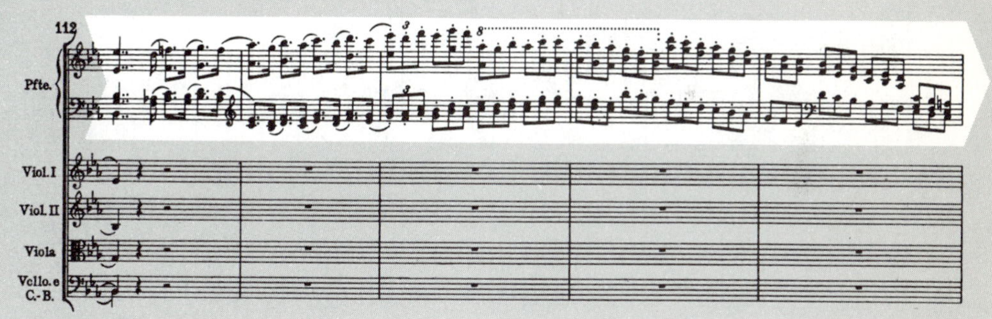
112
Pfte.
Viol. I
Viol. II
Viola
Vcllo. e C.-B.

117
Pfte.
Viol. I
Viol. II
Viola
Vcllo. e C.-B.

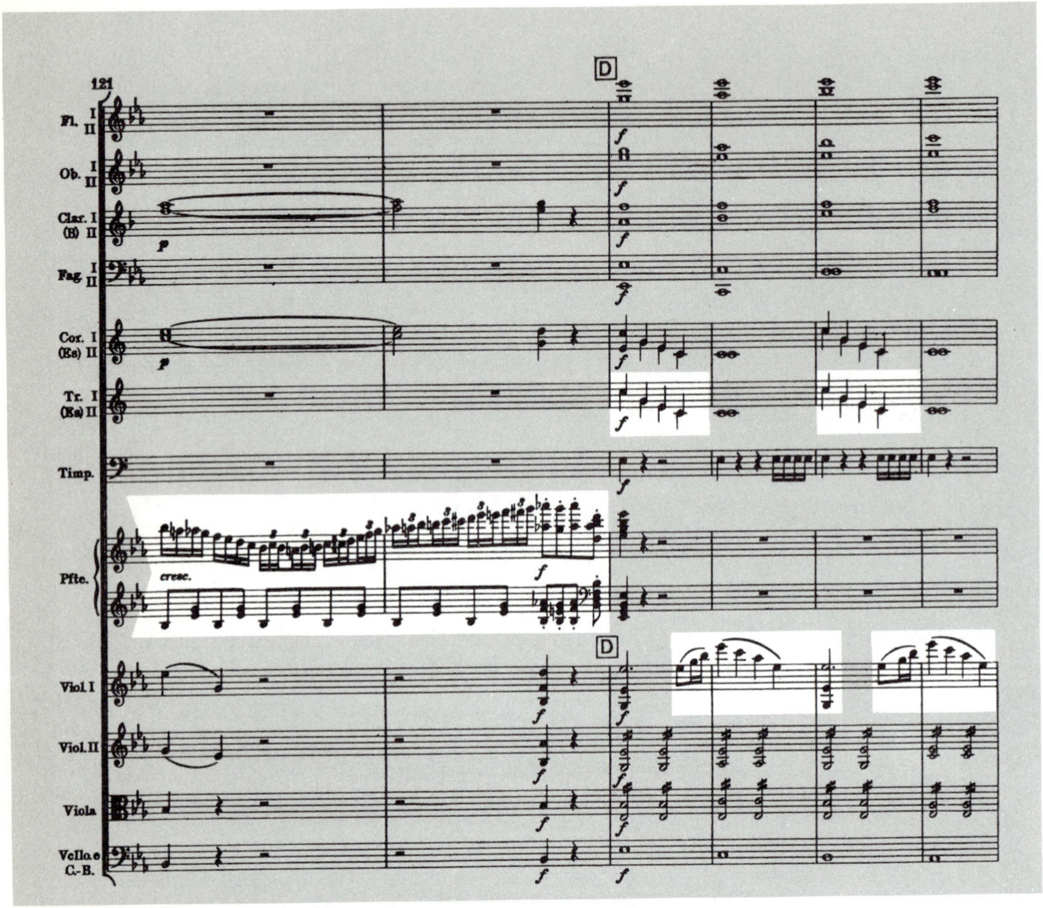

121
D
Fl. I II
Ob. I II
Clar. I (B) II
Fag. I II
Cor. I (Es) II
Tr. I (Es) II
Timp.
Pfte.
cresc.
D
Viol. I
Viol. II
Viola
Vcllo. e C.-B.

127
Fag. I II
Pfte.
cresc.
sfz
Viol. I
Viol. II
Viola
Vcllo. e C.-B.

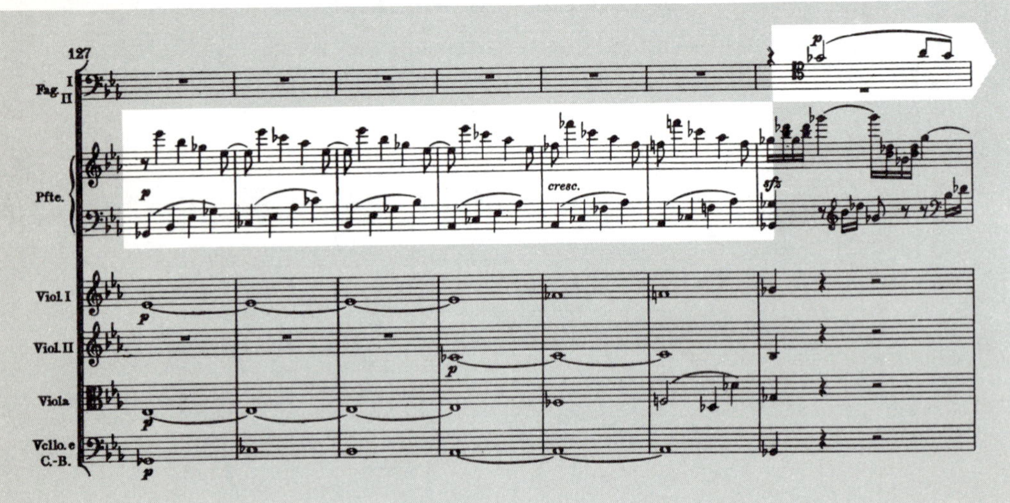

134
Fl. I II
Ob. I II
Fag. I II
Pfte.
Viol. I
Viol. II
Viola
Vcllo. e C.-B.

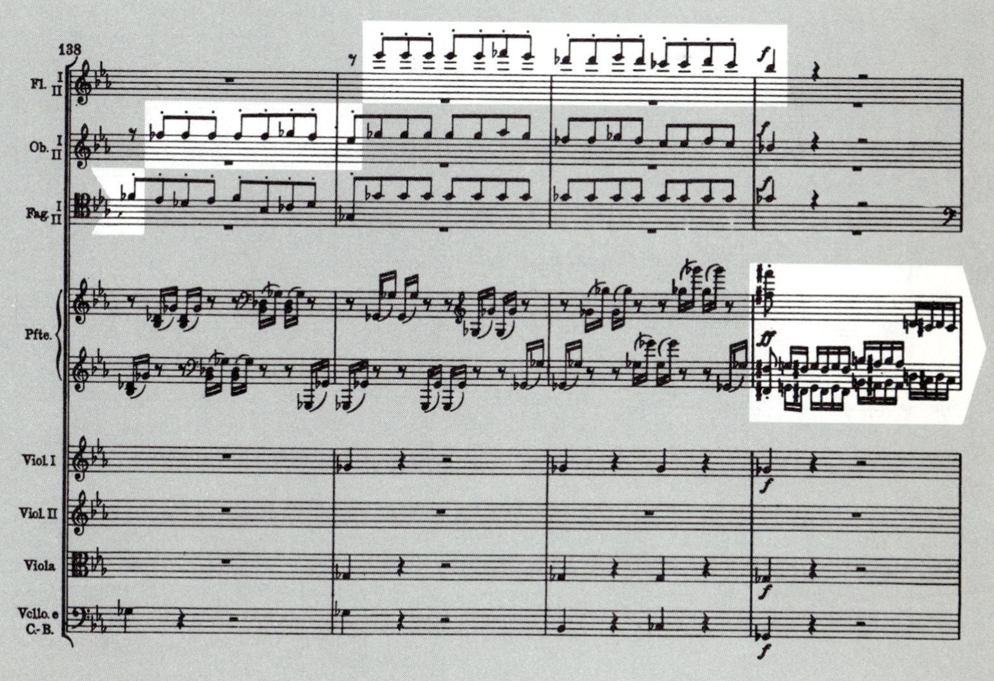
138
Fl. I II
Ob. I II
Fag. I II
Pfte.
Viol. I
Viol. II
Viola
Vcllo. e C.-B.

142
Pfte.
sf
sf
sf
sf
sf

146
Pfte.
sf sf sf sf
dim.
pp leggiermente
pizz.
pp
Viol. I
Viol. II
Viola
Vcllo. e C.-B.

151
Clar. I (B) II
Fag. I II
pp
Pfte.
Viol. I
Viol. II
Viola
Uno Vcllo.
Vcllo.
p
C.-B.

156
Fl. I II
Ob. I II
Clar. I (B) II
Fag. I II
Pfte.
Viol. I
Viol. II
Viola
Vcllo.
C.-B.
cresc.
pizz.
arco
Tutti

164
E
Fl. I II
Ob. I II
Clar. I (B) II
Fag. I II
Cor. I (Es) II
Tr. I (Es) II
Timp.
Viol. I
Viol. II
Viola
Vcllo. e C.-B.
ten.

171
Fl. I II
Ob. I II
Clar. I (B) II
Fag. I II
Cor. I (Es) II
Pfte.
Viol. I
Viol. II
Viola
Vello. e C.-B.
pp
dolce
p
176
pizz.

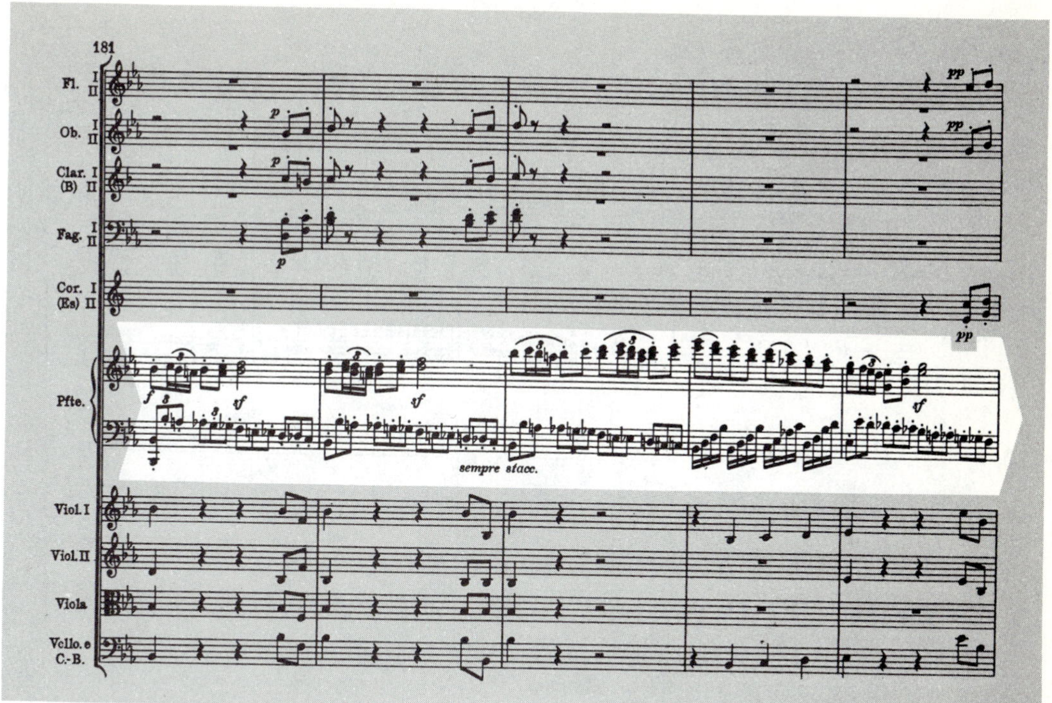

181
Fl. I II
Ob. I II
Clar. I (B) II
Fag. I II
Cor. I (Es) II
Pfte.
Viol. I
Viol. II
Viola
Vcllo. e C.-B.
p
pp
f
sf
sempre stacc.

186
Fl. I II
Ob. I II
Clar. I (B) II
Fag. I II
Cor. I (Es) II
Pfte.
Viol. I
Viol. II
Viola
Vcllo. e C.-B.
sf

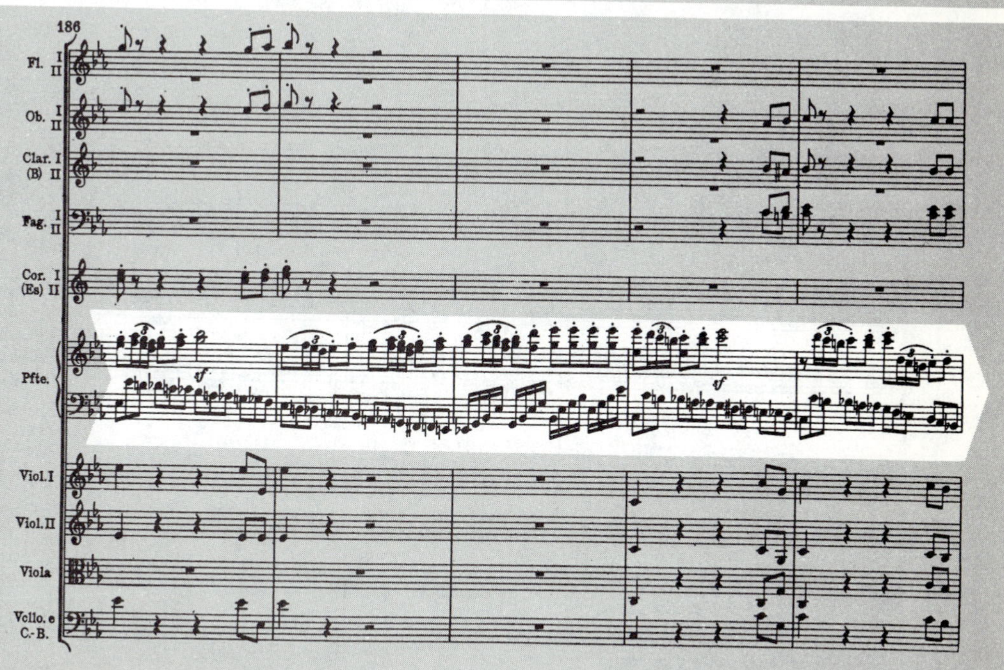

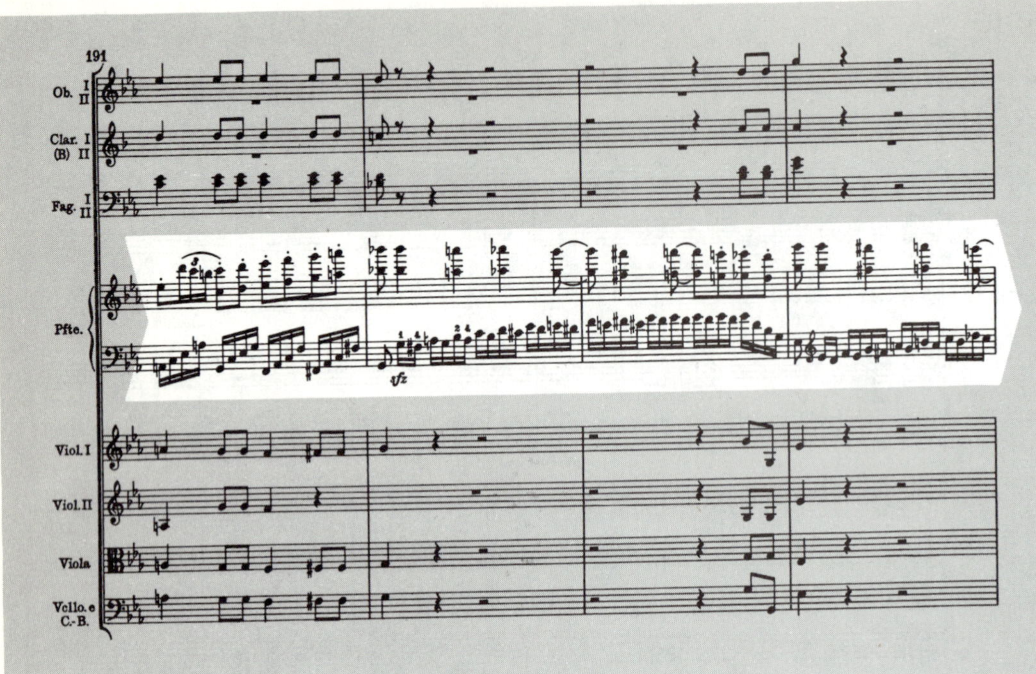
191
Ob. I II
Clar. I (B) II
Fag. I II
Pfte.
sfz
Viol. I
Viol. II
Viola
Vcllo. e C.-B.

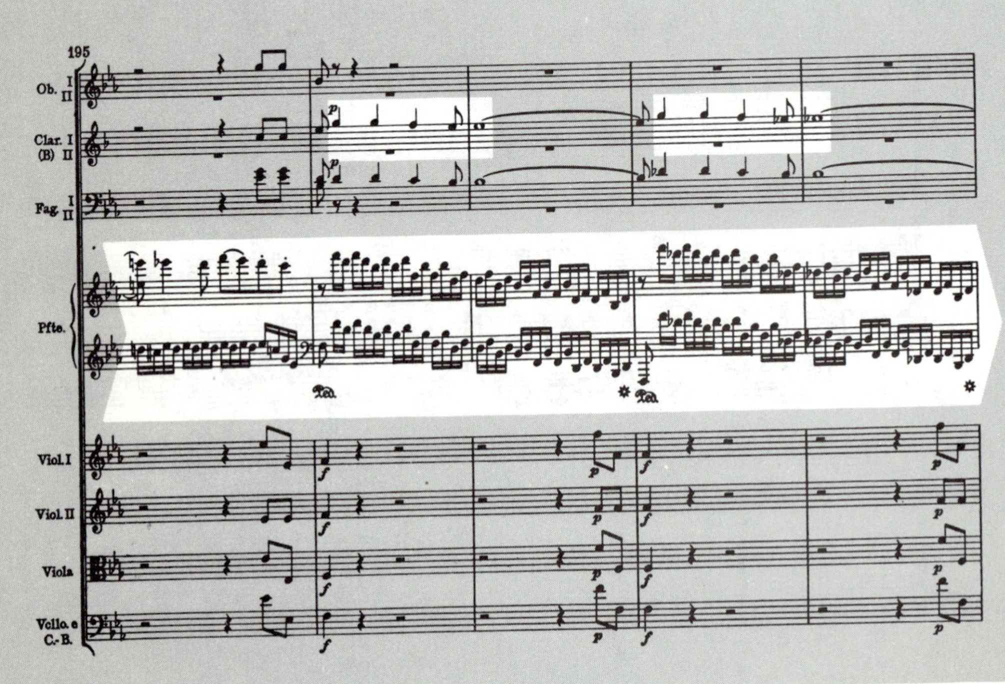
195
Ob. I II
Clar. I (B) II
Fag. I II
p
Pfte.
Ped.
Viol. I
Viol. II
Viola
Vcllo. e C.-B.
f
p

200
Clar. I (B) II
Fag. I II
Pfte.
dim.
pp
Viol. I
arco
pp
Viol. II
Viola
arco
pp
Uno Vello.
arco
pp
Vello.
C.-B.

204
p
F
dolce
Fl. I II
p
Ob. I II
dolce
p dolce
Clar. I (B) II
p dolce
p dolce
Fag. I II
p dolce
Pfte.
Ped.
Ped.
F
Viol. I
Viol. II
arco
pp
Viola
Vello.
C.-B.
pizz.

208
Fl. I II
cresc.
Ob. I II
Clar. I (B) II
Fag. I II
Pfte.
Viol. I
Viol. II
Viola
Vello.
C.-B.
Tutti
arco
214
pp
p leggiermente
pizz.
Vello. e C.-B.

219
Ob. I II
Clar. I (B) II
Fag. I II
Pfte.
Viol. I
Viol. II
Viola
Vcllo. e C.-B.
cresc.
arco
223
Fl. I II
Cor. I (Es) II
Tr. I (Es) II
Timp.
Ped.

228
Fl. I II
Ob. I II
Clar. I (B) II
Fag. I II
Cor. I (Es) II
Tr. I (Es) II
Timp.
Viol. I
Viol. II
Viola
Vcllo. e C.-B.
233
a 2
G
ff
G

246
Fl. I II
f
ff
p
Ob. I II
f
ff
p
Clar. I (B) II
f
ff
Fag. I II
f
ff
p
Cor. I (Es) II
f
ff
Tr. I (Es) II
f
ff
Viol. I
f
ff
p
Viol. II
f
ff
div.
p
Viola
f
ff
unis.
p
Vcllo. e C.-B.
f
ff
legato
p

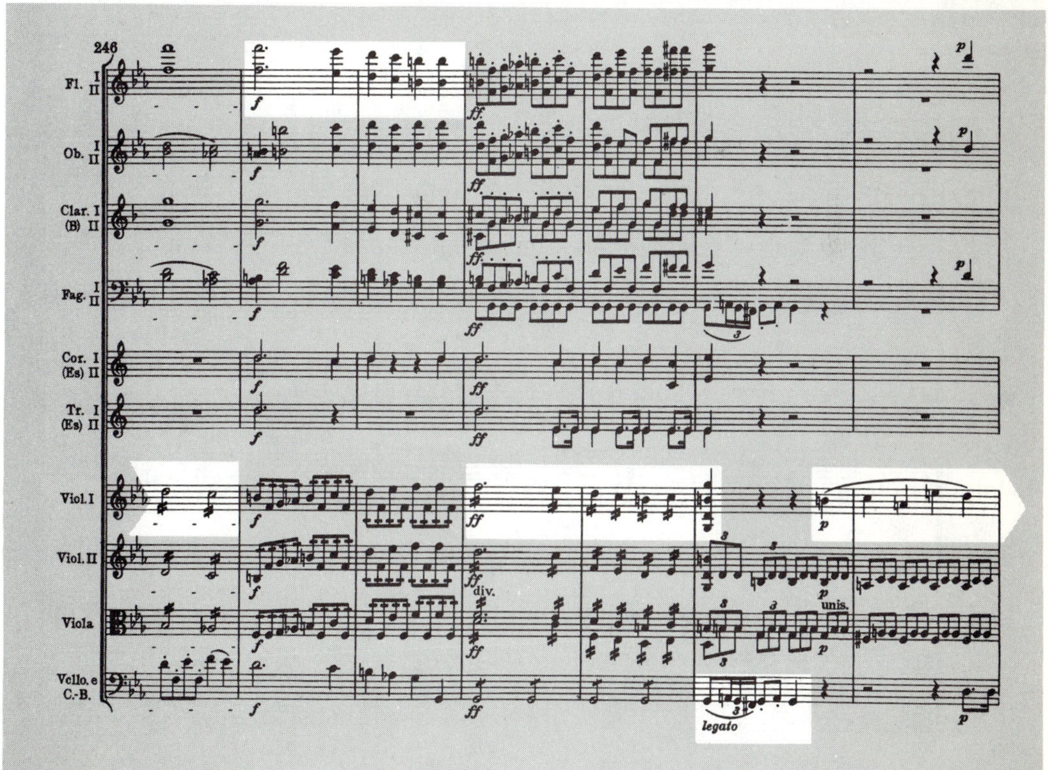

253
Fl. I II
Ob. I II
Clar. I (B) II
Fag. I II
Viol. I
Viol. II
Viola
Vcllo. e C.-B.
f
p
cresc.
3

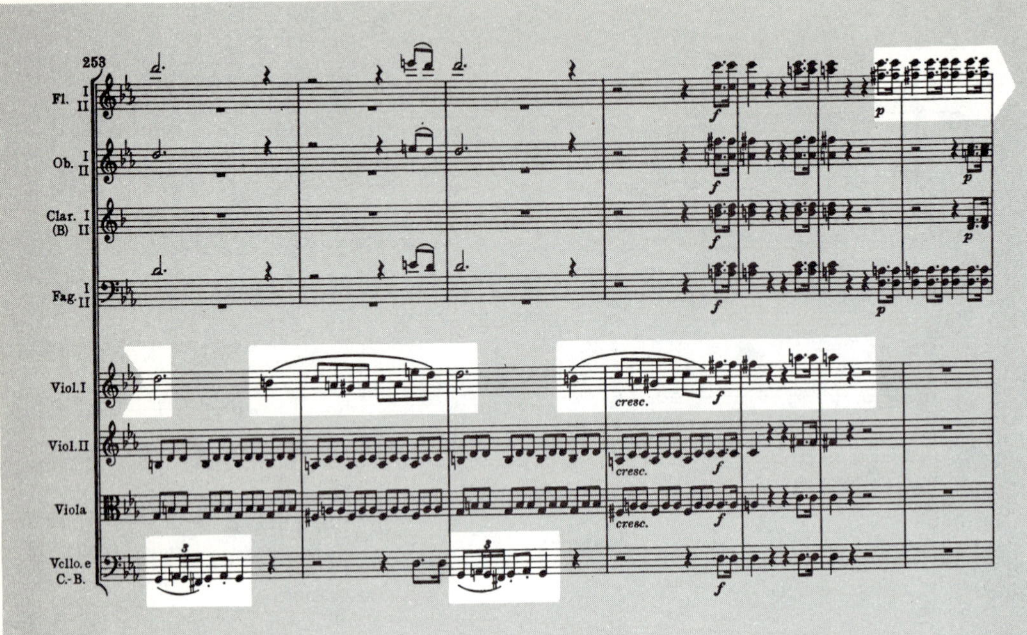

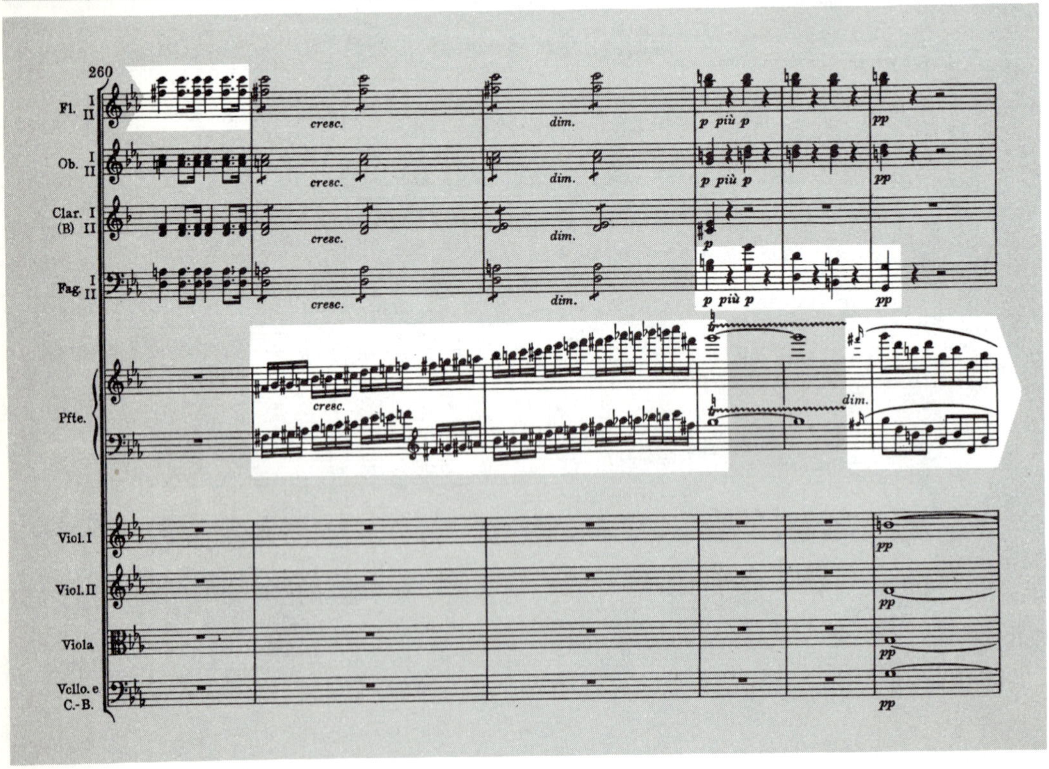

260
Fl. I II
Ob. I II
Clar. I (B) II
Fag. I II
Pfte.
Viol. I
Viol. II
Viola
Vcllo. e C.-B.
cresc.
dim.
p più p
pp
p

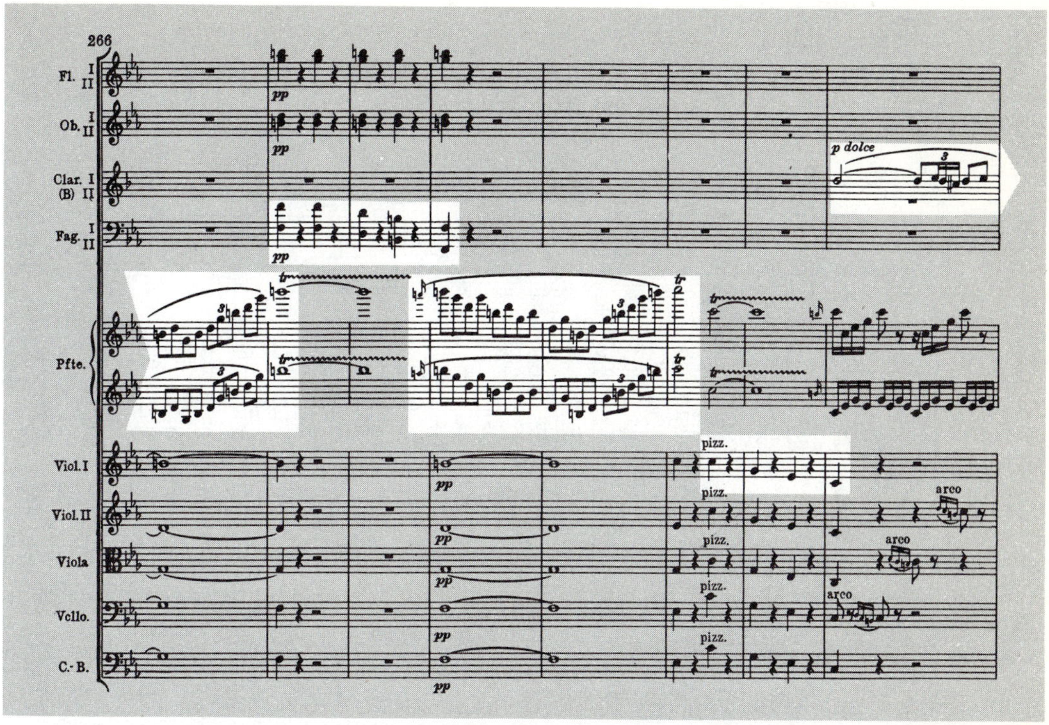

266
Fl. I II
pp
Ob. I II
pp
Clar. I (B) II
p dolce
Fag. I II
pp
Pfte.
Viol. I
pp
pizz.
Viol. II
pp
pizz.
arco
Viola
pp
pizz.
arco
Vcllo.
pp
pizz.
arco
C.-B.
pp
pizz.

278
Fl. I II
Ob. I II
Clar. I (B) II
Fag. I II
Pfte.
leggiermente
p dolce
Viol. I
Viol. II
Viola
Vcllo.
C.-B.
pizz.
arco
pizz.
282
Ob. I II
Clar. I (B) II
Fag. I II
Pfte.
Viol. I
Viol. II
Viola
Vcllo.
C.-B.
pizz.
arco
pizz.

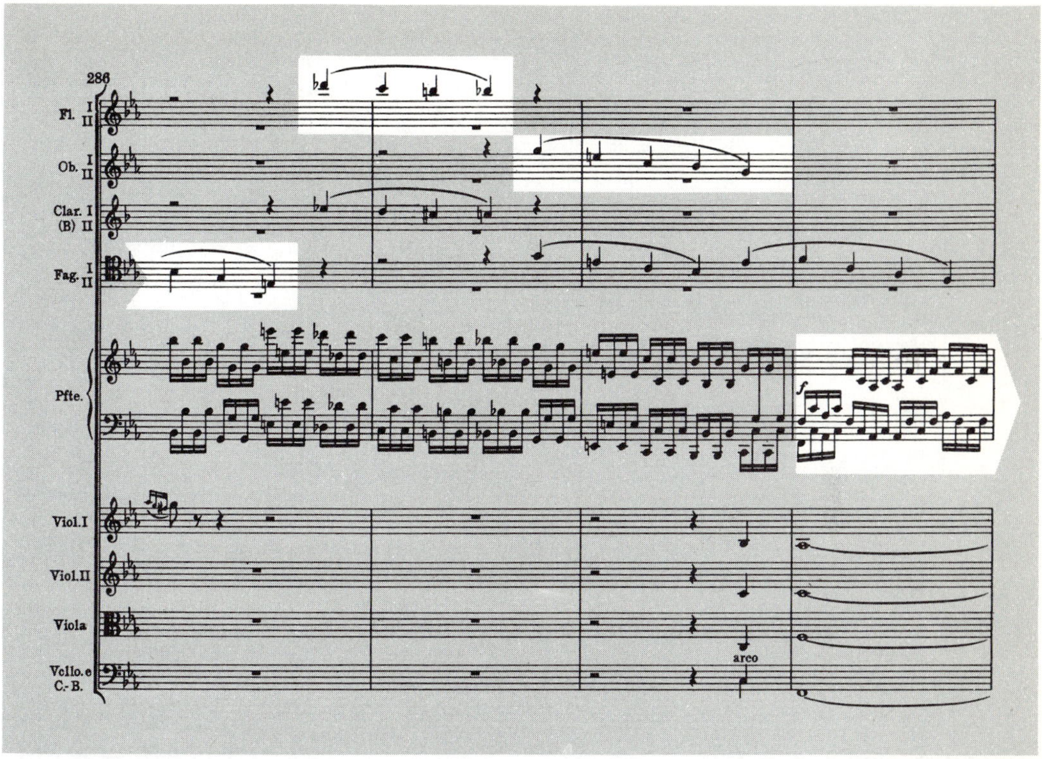

286
Fl. I II
Ob. I II
Clar. I (B) II
Fag. I II
Pfte.
f
Viol. I
Viol. II
Viola
Vcllo. e C.-B.
arco

290
Ob. I II
Clar. I (B) II
Fag. I II
Pfte.
Viol. I
Viol. II
Viola
Vcllo. e C.-B.

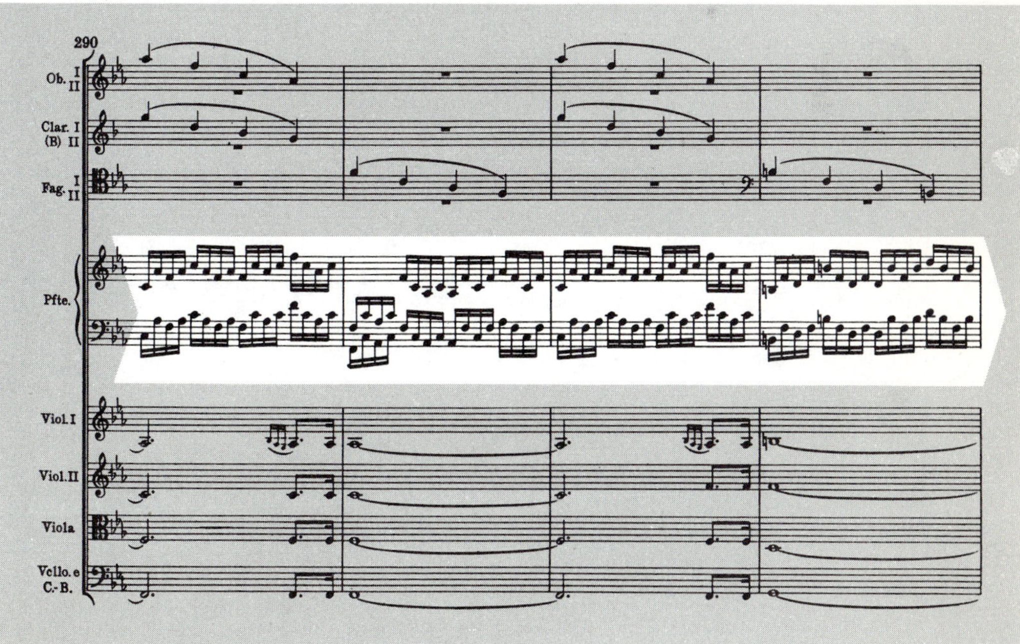

294
Fl. I II
Ob. I II
Clar. I (B) II
Fag. I II
Pfte.
Viol. I
Viol. II
Viola
Vcllo. e C.-B.
298
H
Cor. I (Es) II
Tr. I (Es) II
Timp.
H

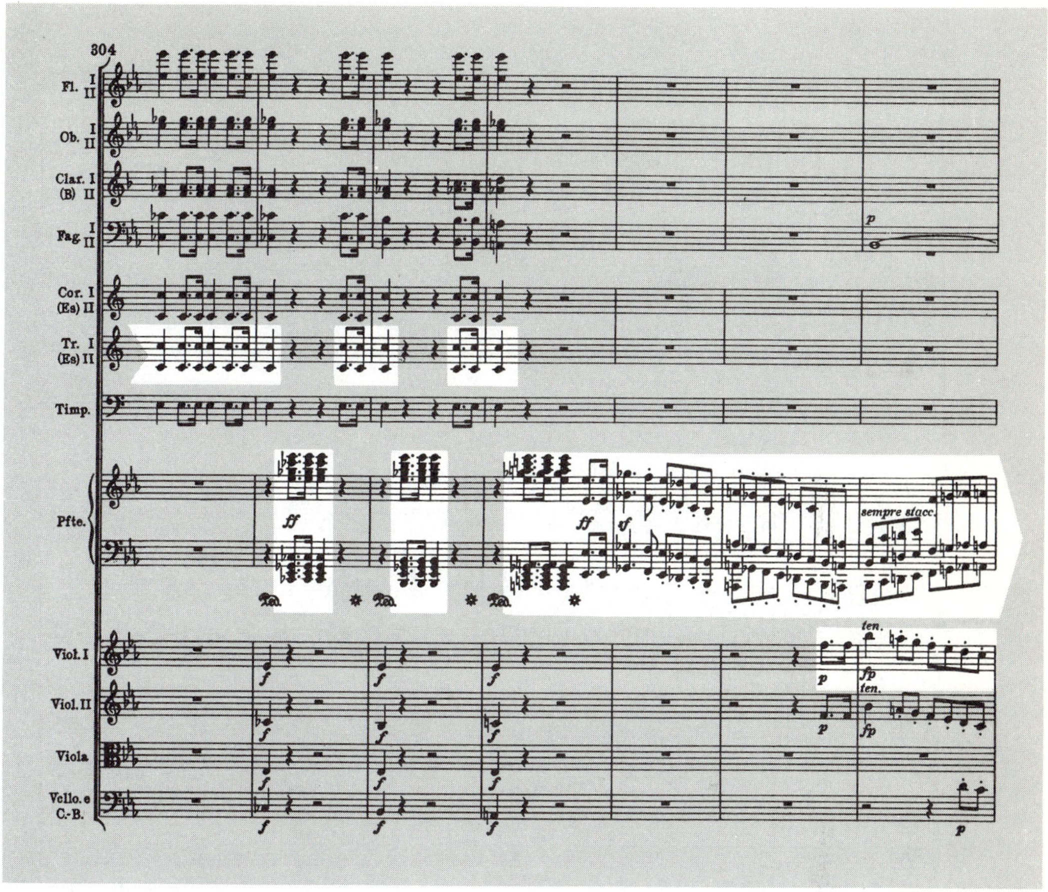

304
Fl. I II
Ob. I II
Clar. I (B) II
Fag. I II
Cor. I (Es) II
Tr. I (Es) II
Timp.
Pfte.
Viol. I
Viol. II
Viola
Vello. e C.-B.
ff
sf
sempre stacc.
ten.
fp
p
f

311
Fag. I II
Pfte.
Viol. I
Viol. II
Viola
Vello. e C.-B.
sf
ten.
fp
p

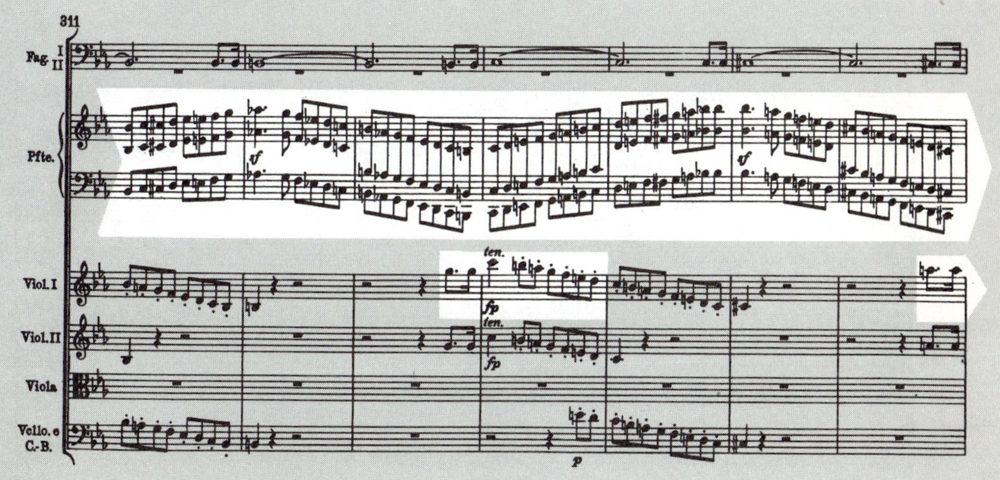

318
Fag. I II
Pfte.
Viol. I
Viol. II
Viola
Vcllo. e C.-B.
ten.
fp
p
dim.
sempre più p
325
espressivo
cresc.
p dim.
pp
dim.
332
Clar. I (B) II
tr
legato
pp legato

338
Ob. I II
Clar. I (B) II
Cor. I (Es) II
Pfte.
Viol. I
Viol. II
Viola
Vcllo. e C.-B.
p cresc.
p
cresc.
tr
pp
344
dim.
349
più p
pp
cresc.

354
Fl. I II
Ob. I II
Clar. I (B) II
Fag. I II
Cor. I (Es) II
Tr. I (Es) II
Timp.
Pfte.
Viol. I
Viol. II
Viola
Vcllo. e C.-B.
cresc.
359
I
ff
p

363
Fl. I II
Ob. I II
Clar. I (B) II
Fag. I II
Cor. I (Es) II
Tr. I (Es) II
Timp.
Pfte.
Viol. I
Viol. II
Viola
Vcllo. e C-B

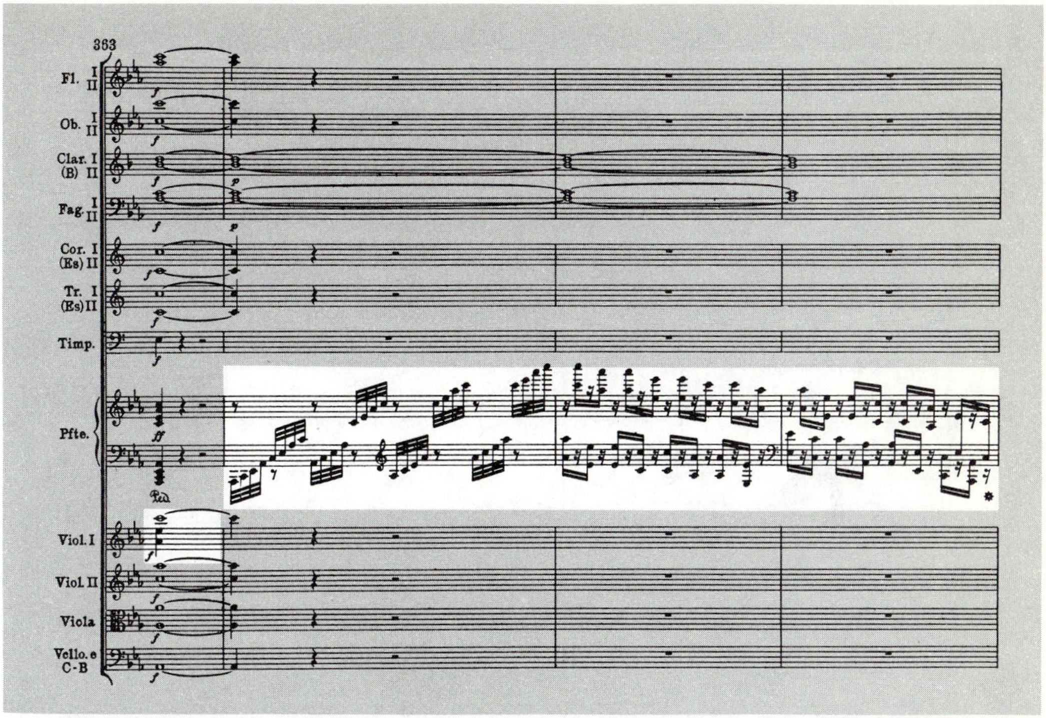

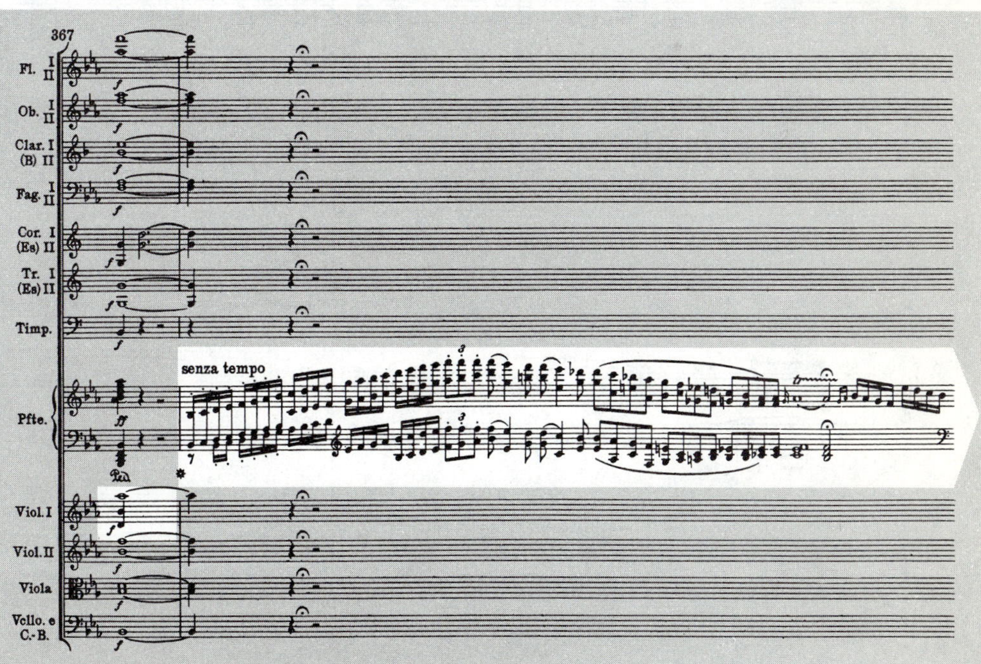

367
Fl. I II
Ob. I II
Clar. I (B) II
Fag. I II
Cor. I (Es) II
Tr. I (Es) II
Timp.
Pfte.
senza tempo
Viol. I
Viol. II
Viola
Vcllo. e C.-B.

Pfte.
369
Fl. I II
Ob. I II
Clar. I (B) II
Fag. I II
Cor. I (Es) II
Tr. I (Es) II
Timp.
Pfte.
Viol. I
Viol. II
Viola
Vcllo. e C.-B.
p dolce
377
cresc.
p cantabile
pp
p

382
Clar. I (B) II
Fag. I II
Pfte.
Viol. I
Viol. II
Viola
Vcllo. e C.-B.
sempre pp
sempre pp
385
389
K
Cor. I (Es) II
sfz

393

Clar. I (B) II

Fag. I II

Cor. I (Es) II

Pfte.

Viol. I

Viol. II

Viola

Vcllo. e C.-B.

397

Clar. I (B) II

f

Fag. I II

Cor. I (Es) II

f

Pfte.

ff

sf

Viol. I

f

Viol. II

f

Viola

f

Vcllo. e C.-B.

f

404
Pfte.
dim.
pp leggiermente
Viol. I
Viol. II
Viola
Vcllo. e C.-B.
pizz.
pp
408
Clar. I (B) II
Fag. I II
Pfte.
Viol. I
Viol. II
Viola
Vcllo.
C.-B.
Uno Vcllo.
p
pp
413
Clar. I (B) II
Fag. I II
Pfte.
Viol. I
Viol. II
Viola
Vcllo.
C.-B.
pizz.

420
L
Fl. I II
Ob. I II
Clar. I (B) II
Fag. I II
Cor. I (Es) II
Tr. I (Es) II
Timp.
Pfte.
Viol. I
Viol. II
Viola
Vcllo. e C.-B.
cresc.
f
ten.
sf
tr
arco
Tutti
427
pp
p

432
Ob. I II
Clar. I (B) II
Fag. I II
Cor. I (Es) II
Pfte.
Viol. I
Viol. II
Viola
Vcllo. e C.-B.
pizz.
p
f
sf

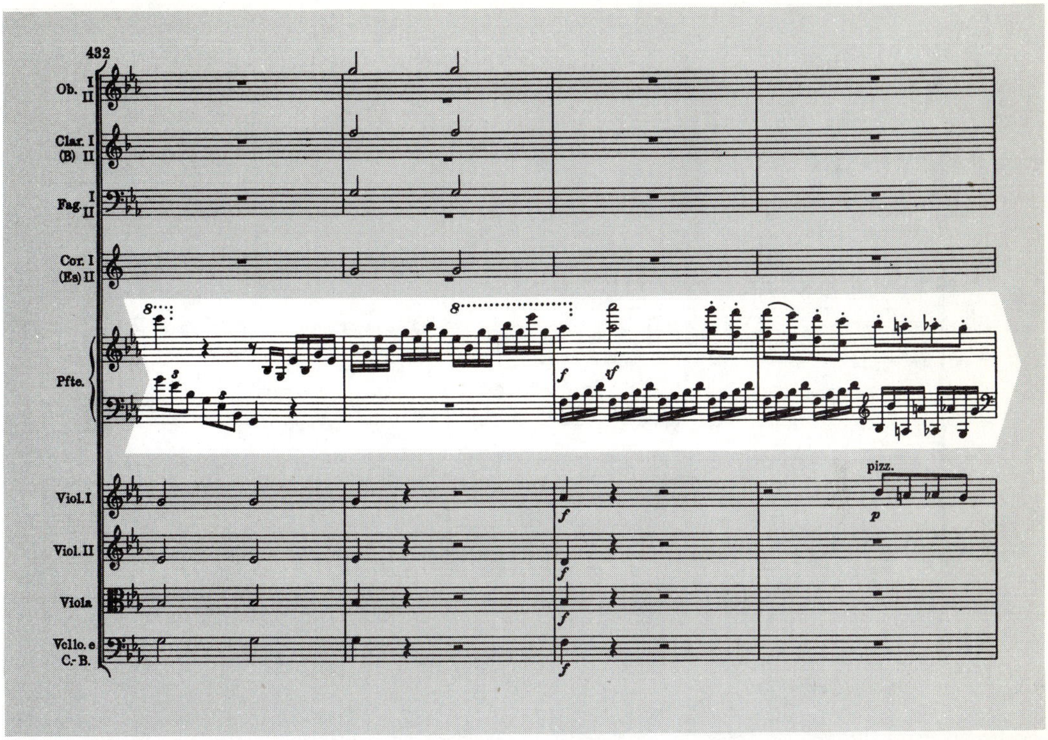

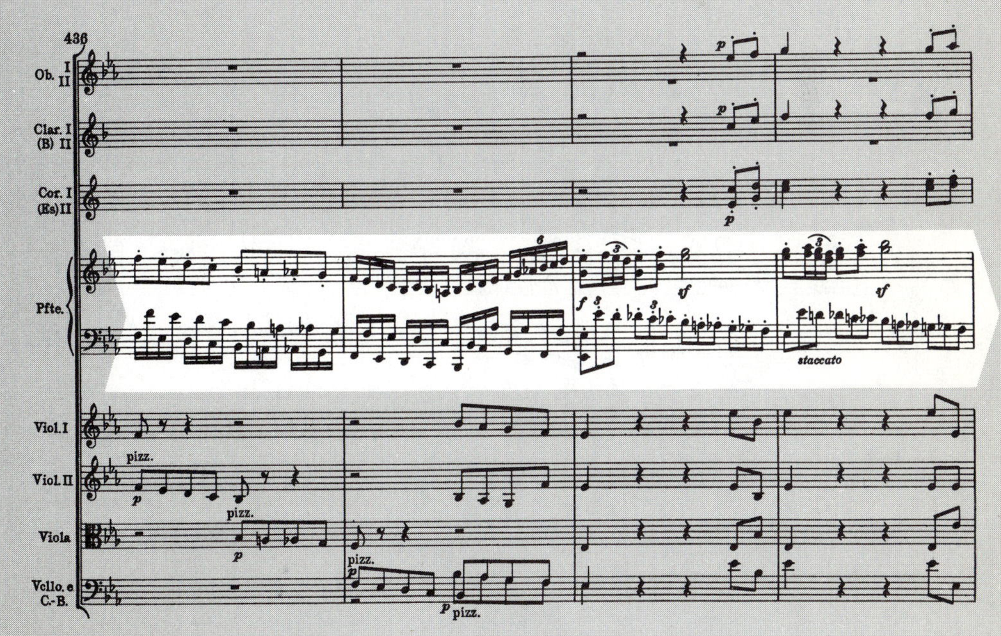

436
Ob. I II
Clar. I (B) II
Cor. I (Es) II
Pfte.
Viol. I
Viol. II
Viola
Vcllo. e C.-B.
staccato
pizz.
p
f
sf

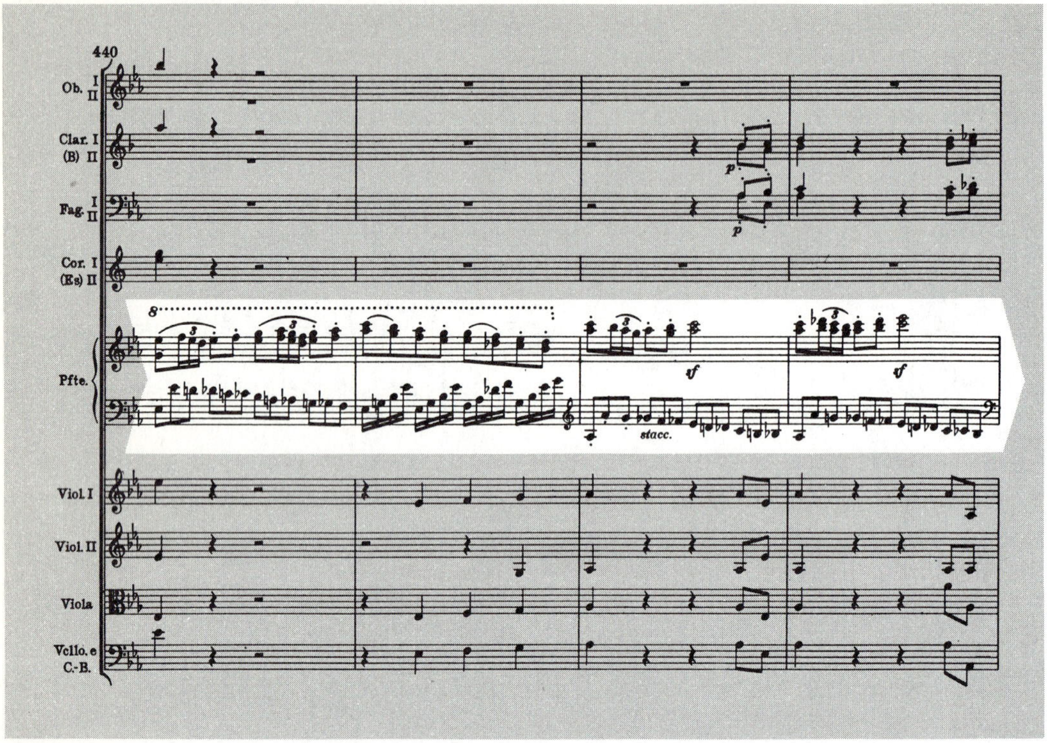

440
Ob. I II
Clar. I (B) II
Fag. I II
Cor. I (Es) II
Pfte.
Viol. I
Viol. II
Viola
Vcllo. e C.-B.
p
p
sf
sf
stacc.

448
Ob. I II
Clar. I (B) II
Fag. I II
Cor I (Es) II
Pfte.
Viol. I
Viol. II
Viola
Vcllo. e C.-B.

452
Ob. I II
Clar. I (B) II
Fag. I II
Cor. I (Es) II
Pfte.
Viol. I
Viol. II
Viola
Vcllo. e C.-B.

456
Ob. I II
Fag. I II
Pfte
dim.
pp
Viol. I
Viol. II
Viola
Vcllo.
C.-B.
p
arco
pp
Uno Vcllo.
arco
pp

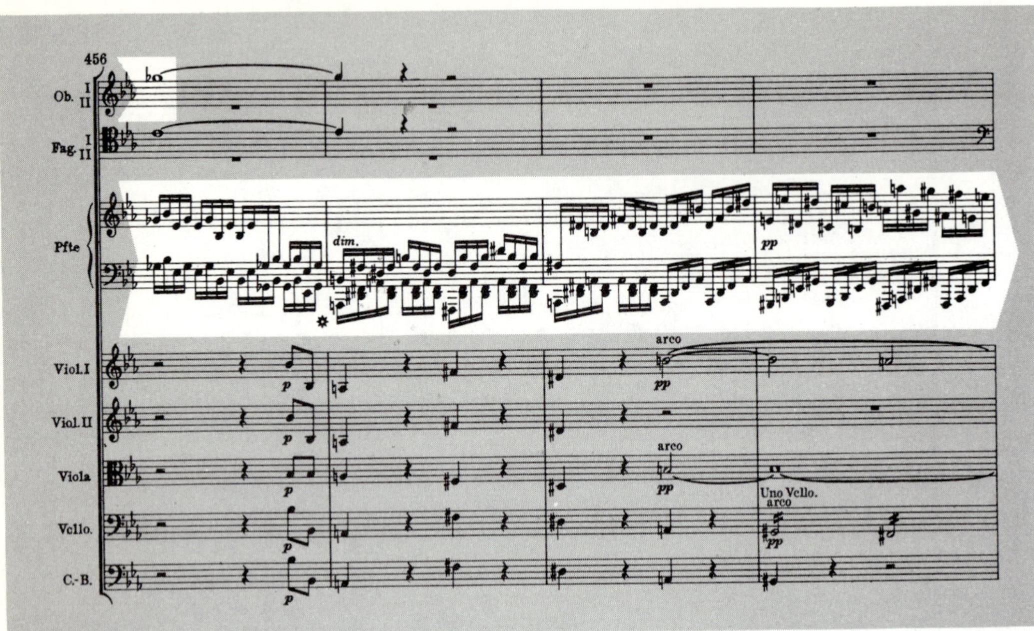

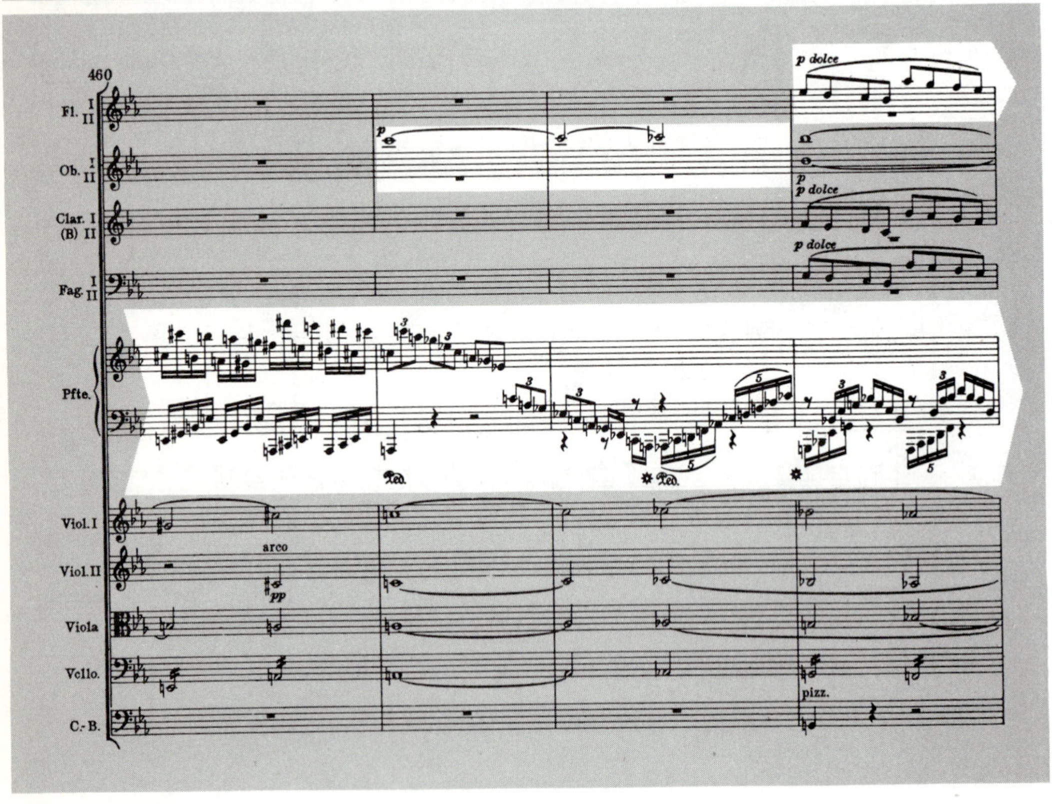

460
Fl. I II
Ob. I II
Clar. I (B) II
Fag. I II
Pfte.
p dolce
p
p dolce
p dolce
Ped.
3
5
Viol. I
Viol. II
Viola
Vcllo.
C.-B.
arco
pp
pizz.

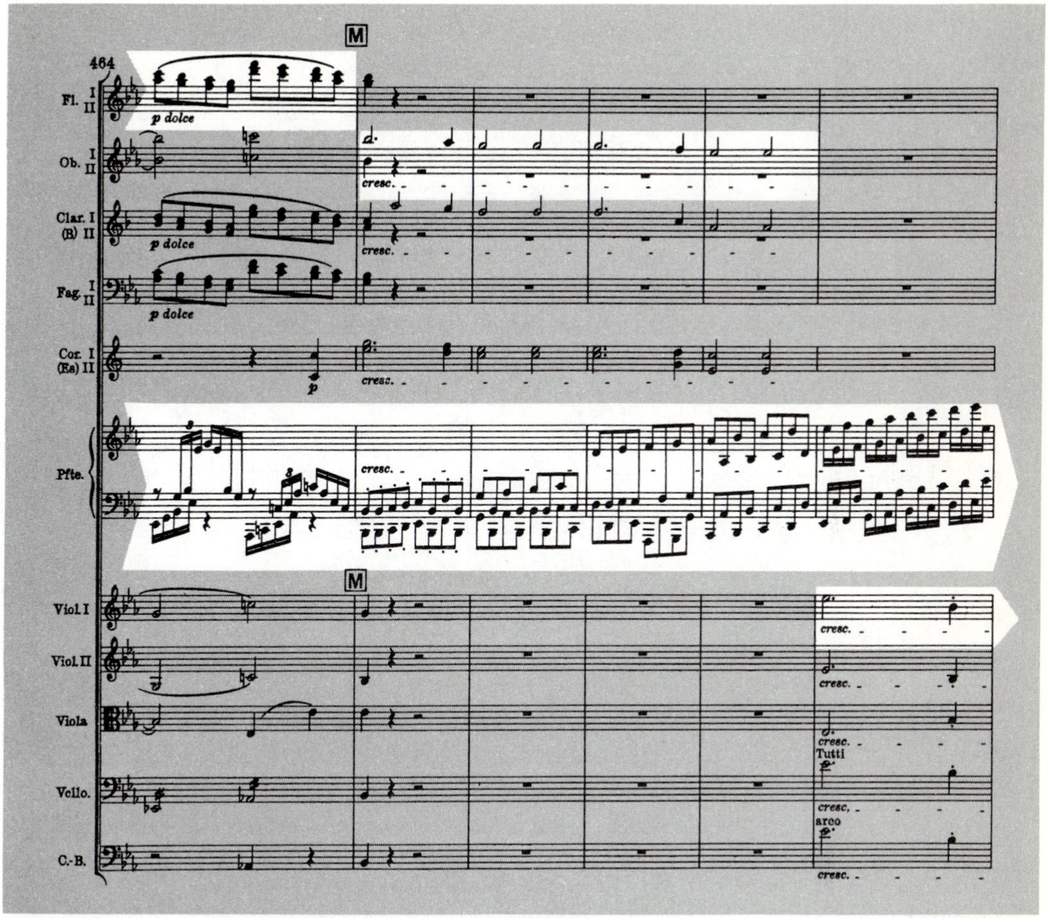

M
464
Fl. I II
p dolce
Ob. I II
cresc.
Clar. I (B) II
p dolce
cresc.
Fag. I II
p dolce
Cor. I (Es) II
p
cresc.
Pfte.
cresc.
M
Viol. I
cresc.
Viol. II
cresc.
Viola
cresc.
Tutti
Vcllo.
cresc.
arco
C.-B.
cresc.

470
Pfte.
p leggiermente
Viol. I
pizz.
p
Viol. II
pizz.
p
Viola
pizz.
p
Vcllo. e C.-B.
pizz.
p

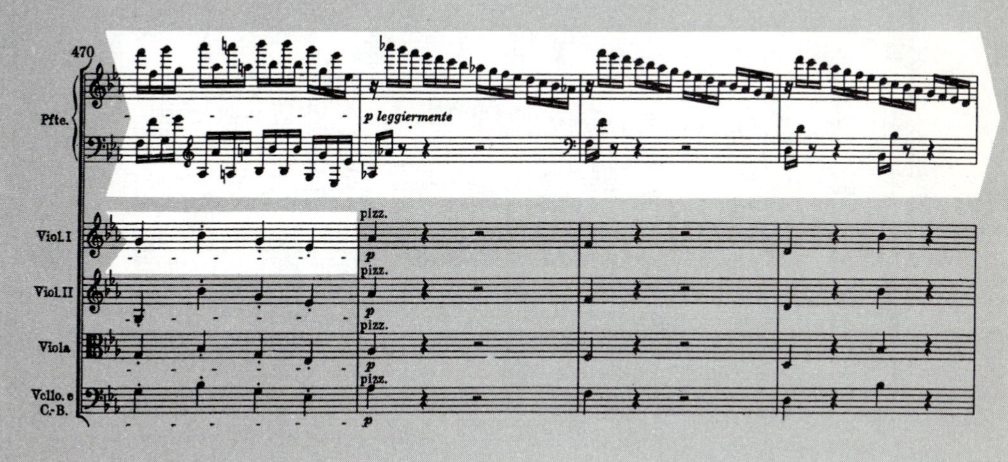

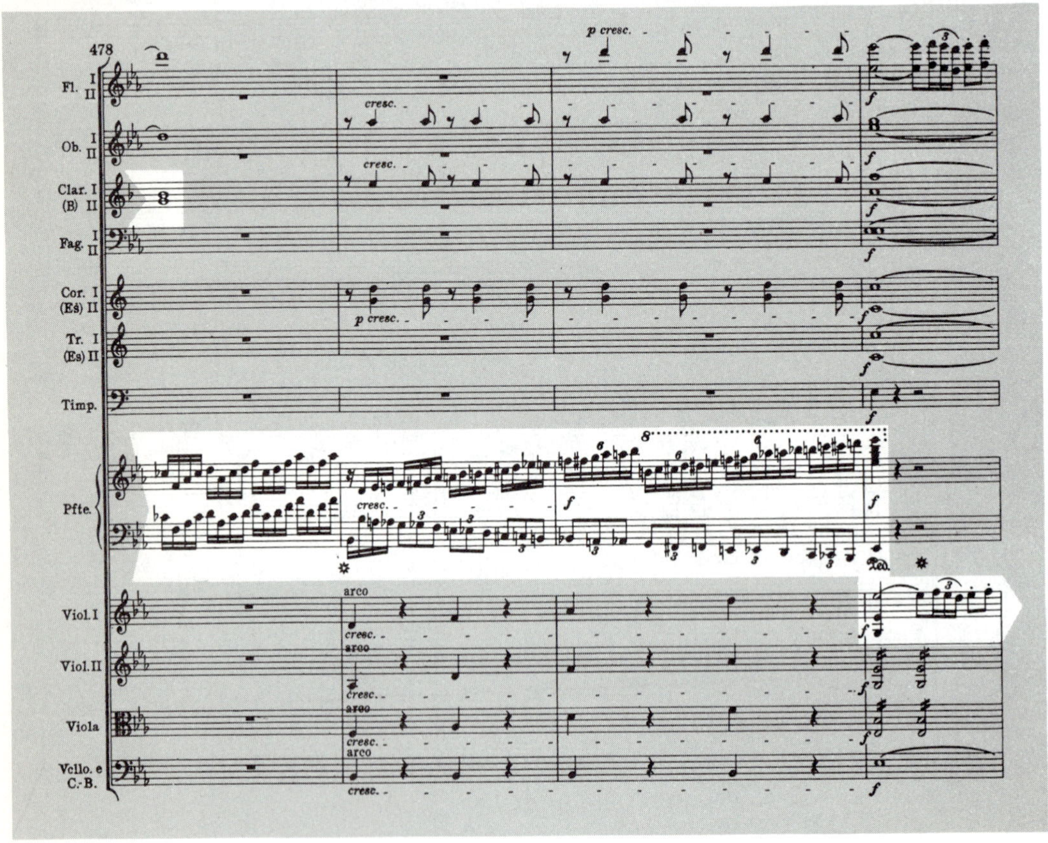

478
Fl. I II
Ob. I II
Clar. I (B) II
Fag. I II
Cor. I (Es) II
Tr. I (Es) II
Timp.
Pfte.
Viol. I
Viol. II
Viola
Vcllo. e C.-B.
p cresc.
cresc.
cresc.
p cresc.
f
f
cresc.
Ped.
arco
cresc.
arco
cresc.
arco
cresc.
arco
cresc.
f

482
Fl. I II
Ob. I II
Clar. I (B) II
Fag. I II
Cor. I (Es) II
Tr. I (Es) II
Timp.
Pfte.
Viol. I
Viol. II
Viola
Vcllo. e C.-B.
488
NB. f
NB. Non si fa una Cadenza, ma s'attacca subito il seguente

494
Pfte.
sf
498
502
dim.
pp leggiermente
511
Cor. I (Es) II
N
p
Viol. I
pizz.
Viol. II
Viola
Vcllo. e C.-B.
516

520
ppp
Fl. I II
Clar. I (B) II
ppp
Fag. I II
ppp
Cor. I (Es) II
ppp
Pfte.
pp leggiermente
arco
Viol. I
pp sempre
Viol. II
Viola
Vcllo. e C.-B.
arco
ppp
legato
524
cresc.
Fl. I II
Ob. I II
Clar. I (B) II
Fag. I II
Cor. I (Es) II
cresc.
Tr. I (Es) II
Timp.
Pfte.
cresc.
ff
Viol. I
cresc.
Viol. II
arco
Viola
arco
Vcllo. e C.-B.
ppp
cresc.

529
Fl. I II
Ob. I II
Clar. I (B) II
Fag. I II
Cor. I (Es) II
Tr. I (Es) II
Timp.
Pfte.
ff
Viol. I
Viol. II
Viola
Vcllo. e C.-B.
f
p
534
sempre f
cresc.

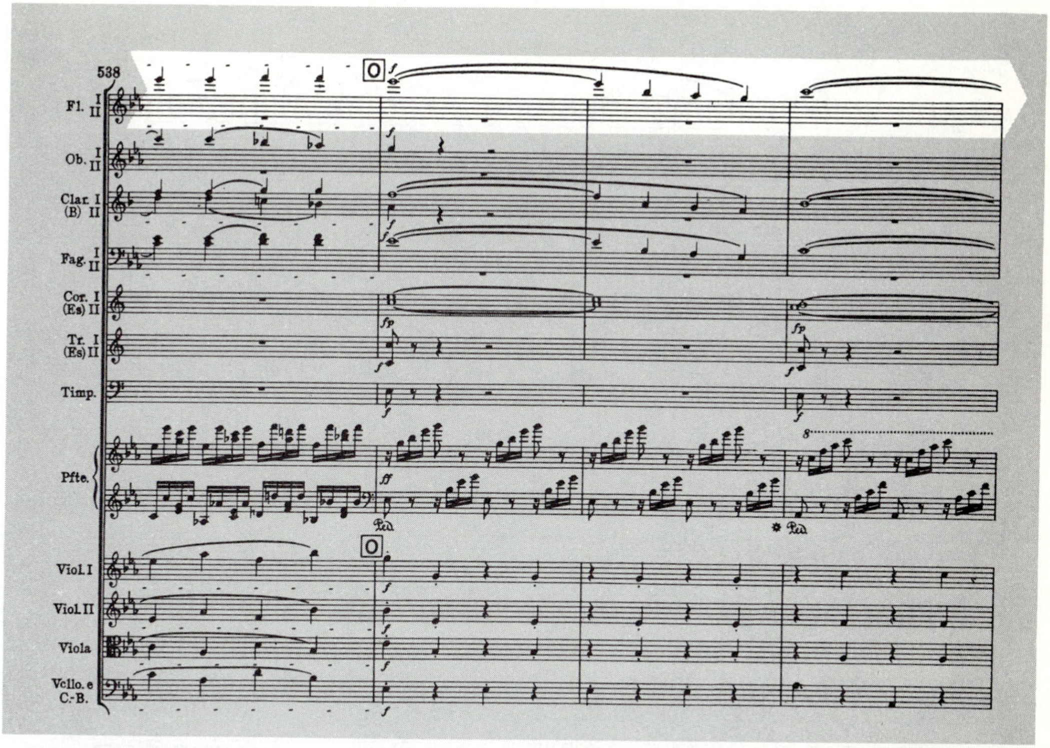

538
O
Fl. I II
Ob. I II
Clar. I (B) II
Fag. I II
Cor. I (Es) II
Tr. I (Es) II
Timp.
Pfte.
Viol. I
Viol. II
Viola
Vcllo. e C.-B.

542
Fl. I II
Clar. I (B) II
Fag. I II
Cor. I (Es) II
Tr. I (Es) II
Timp.
Pfte.
Viol. I
Viol. II
Viola
Vcllo. e C.-B.
dim.

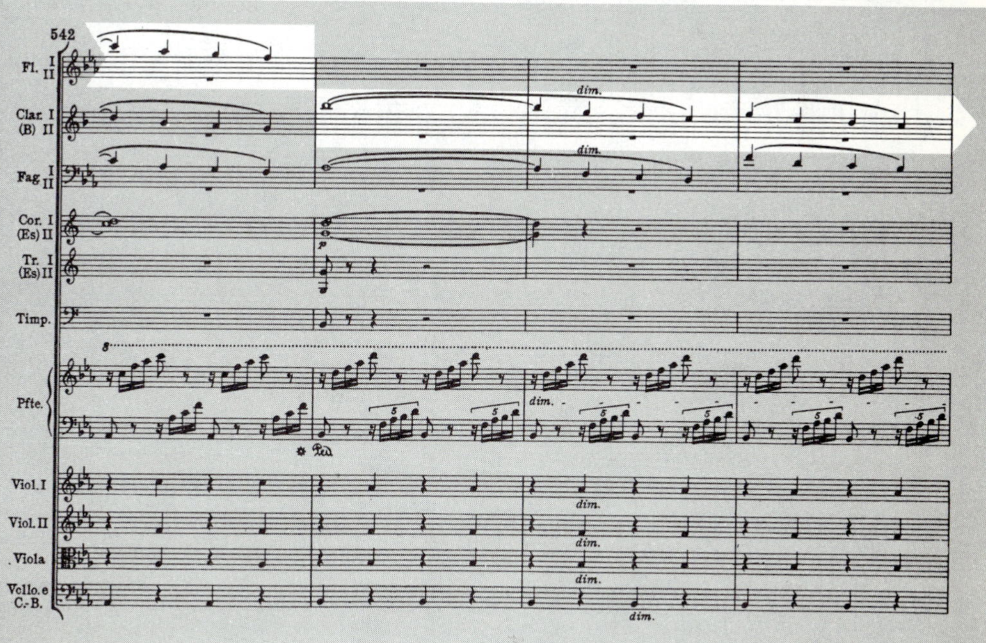

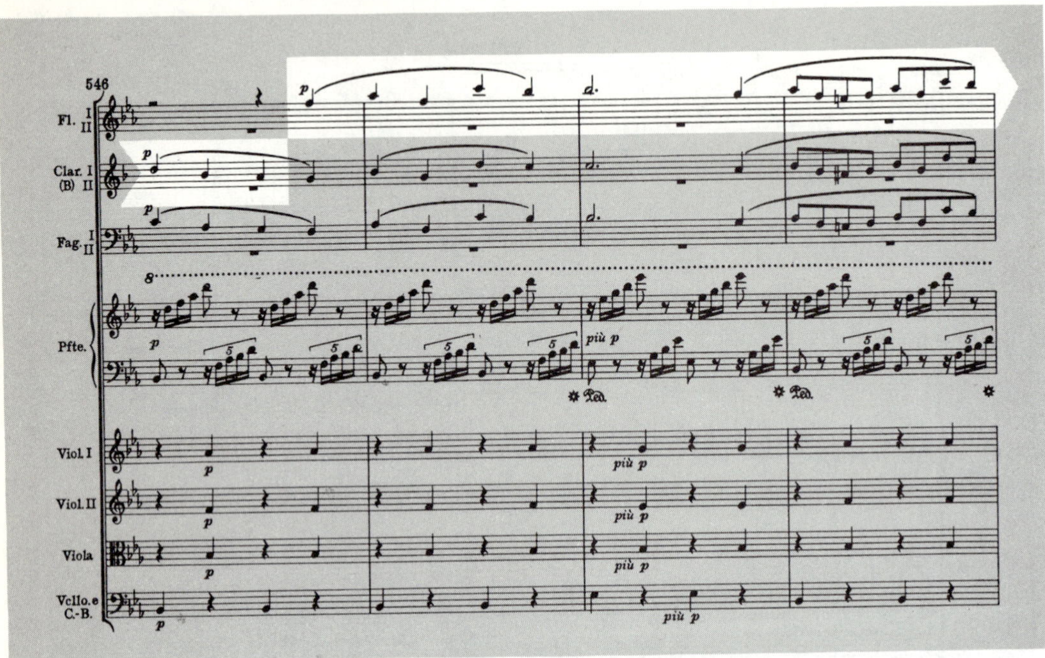

550
Fl. I II
Ob. I II
p
Clar. I (B) II
p
Fag. I II
Cor. I (Es) II
p
8
Pfte.
f
dim.
Ped.
Viol. I
f
Viol. II
f
Viola
f
Vcllo. e C.-B.
f

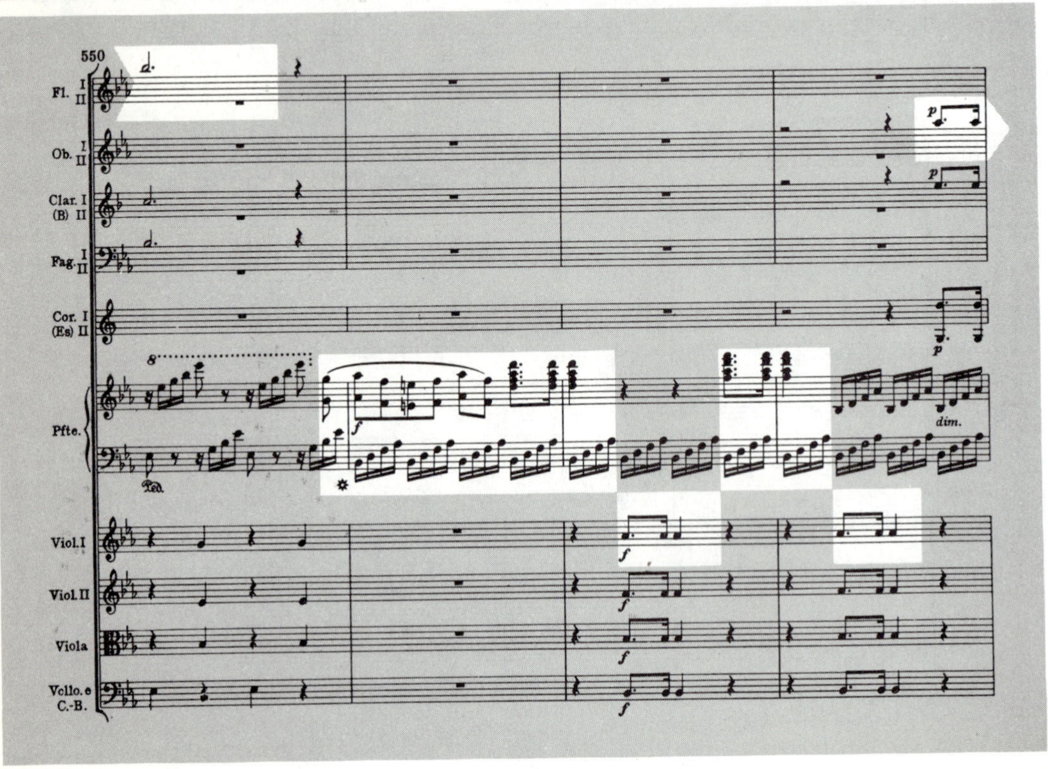

554
Fl. I II
Ob. I II
Clar. I (B) II
Fag. I II
Cor. I (Es) II
Pfte.
Viol. I
Viol. II
Viola
Vcllo. e C.-B.
p
sempre p
pizz.
558
più p
pp
Ossia più facile
II.

561
Cor. I (Es) II
Pfte.
leggiermente
Viol. I
Viol. II
Viola
Vcllo. e C.-B.
564
Cor. I (Es) II
Pfte.
cresc.
Viol. I
arco
cresc.
Viol. II
Viola
arco
cresc.
Vcllo. e C.-B.
arco
cresc.
567
Clar. I (B) II
cresc.
Cor. I (Es) II
cresc.
Pfte.
Viol. I
cresc.
arco
Viol. II
cresc.
Viola
cresc.
Vcllo. e C.-B.
cresc.

570
Fl. I II
Ob. I II
Clar. I (B) II
Cor. I (Es) II
Tr. I (Es) II
Timp.
Pfte.
Viol. I
Viol. II
Viola
Vcllo. e C.-B.
f
8

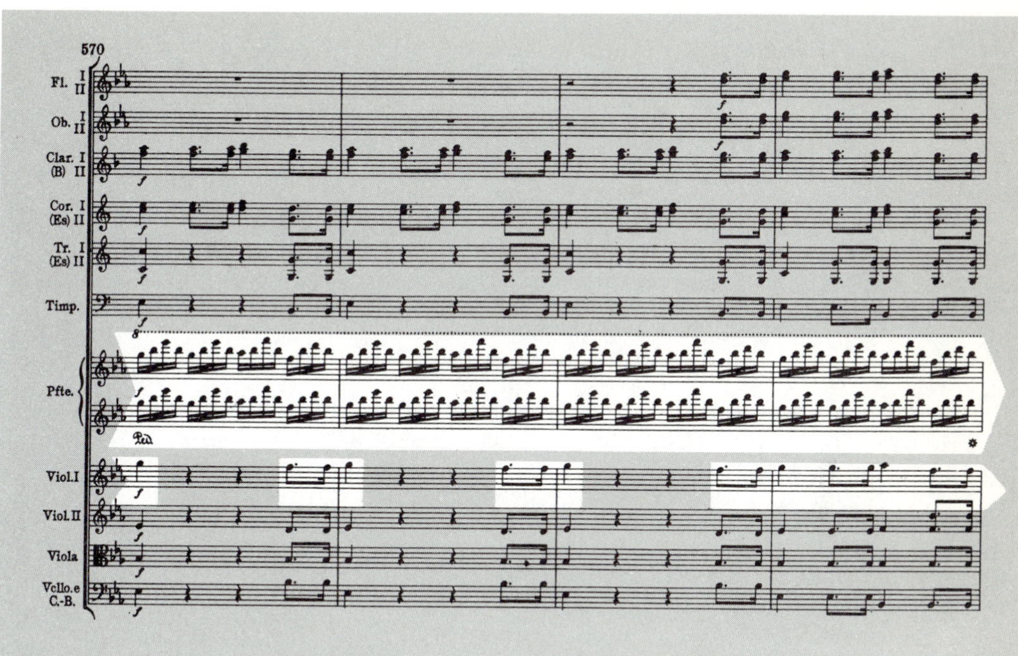

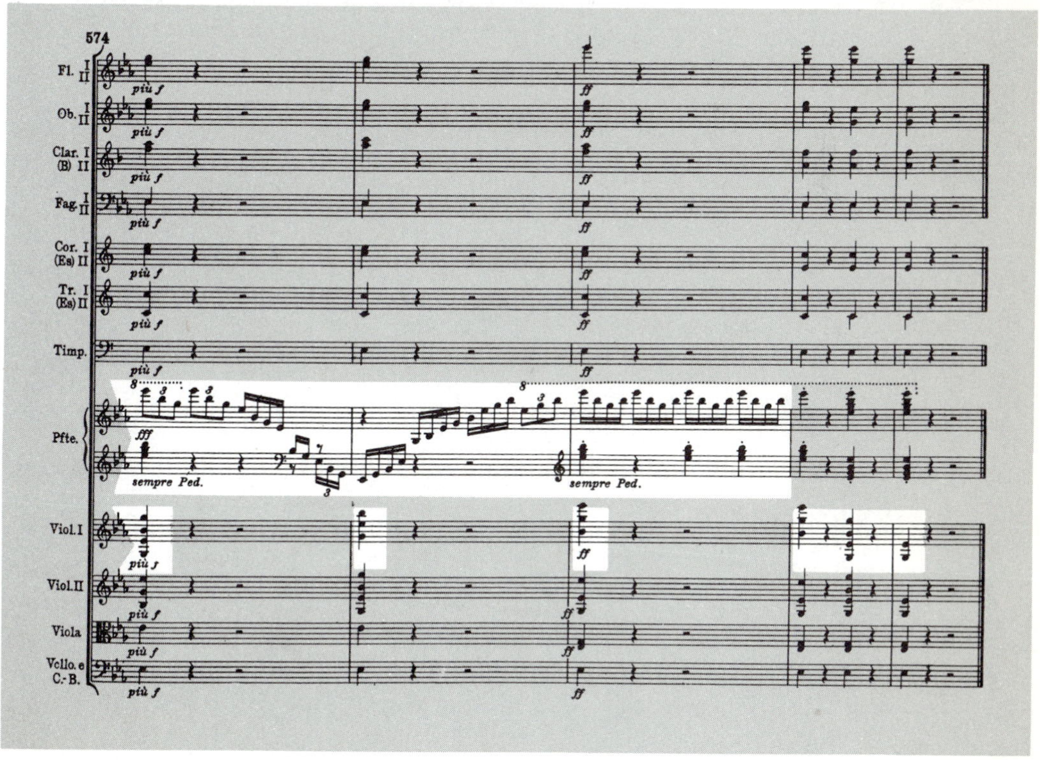

574
Fl. I II
Ob. I II
Clar. I (B) II
Fag. I II
Cor. I (Es) II
Tr. I (Es) II
Timp.
Pfte.
Viol. I
Viol. II
Viola
Vcllo. e C.-B.
più f
ff
fff
sempre Ped.
8
3

APPENDIX A

Reading an Orchestral Score

CLEFS

The music for some instruments is written in clefs other than the familiar treble and bass. In the following example, middle C is shown in the four clefs used in orchestral scores:

The *alto clef* is primarily used in viola parts. The *tenor clef* is employed for cello, bassoon, and trombone parts when these instruments play in a high register.

TRANSPOSING INSTRUMENTS

The music for some instruments is customarily written at a pitch different from their actual sound. The following list, with examples, shows the main transposing instruments and the degree of transposition. (In some modern works—such as the Stravinsky example included in this anthology—all instruments are written at their sounding pitch.)

Instrument	*Transposition*	*Written Note*	*Actual Sound*
Piccolo Celesta	sound an octave higher than written		
Trumpet in F	sound a fourth higher than written		
Trumpet in E	sound a major third higher than written		

Instrument	*Transposition*	*Written Note*	*Actual Sound*
Clarinet in E♭ Trumpet in E♭	sound a minor third higher than written		
Trumpet in D Clarinet in D	sound a major second higher than written		
Clarinet in B♭ Trumpet in B♭ Cornet in B♭ Horn in B♭ alto	sound a major second lower than written		
Clarinet in A Trumpet in A Cornet in A	sound a minor third lower than written		
Horn in G Alto flute	sound a fourth lower than written		
English horn Horn in F	sound a fifth lower than written		
Horn in E	sound a minor sixth lower than written	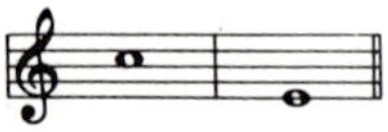	
Horn in E♭	sound a major sixth lower than written	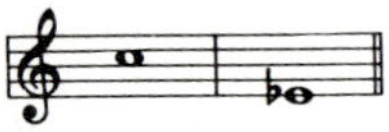	
Horn in D	sound a minor seventh lower than written		
Contrabassoon Horn in C Double bass	sound an octave lower than written		
Bass clarinet in B♭ (written in treble clef)	sound a major ninth lower than written		
(written in bass clef)	sound a major second lower than written	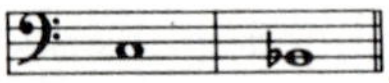	
Bass clarinet in A (written in treble clef)	sound a minor tenth lower than written	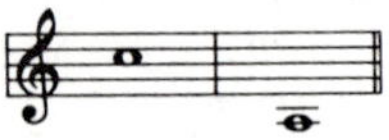	
(written in bass clef)	sound a minor third lower than written		

APPENDIX B

Instrumental Names and Abbreviations

The following tables set forth the English, Italian, German, and French names used for the various musical instruments in these scores, and their respective abbreviations. A table of the foreign-language names for scale degrees and modes is also provided.

WOODWINDS

English	*Italian*	*German*	*French*
Piccolo (Picc.)	Flauto piccolo (Fl. Picc.)	Kleine Flöte (Kl. Fl.)	Petite flûte
Flute (Fl.)	Flauto (Fl.); Flauto grande (Fl. gr.)	Grosse Flöte (Fl. gr.)	Flûte (Fl.)
Alto flute	Flauto contralto fl.c-alto)	Altflöte	Flûte en sol
Oboe (Ob.)	Oboe (Ob.)	Hoboe (Hb.); Oboe (Ob.)	Hautbois (Hb.)
English horn (E. H.)	Corno inglese (C. or Cor. ingl., C.i.)	Englisches Horn (E. H.)	Cor anglais (C. A.)
Sopranino clarinet	Clarinetto piccolo (clar. picc.)		
Clarinet (C., Cl., Clt., Clar.)	Clarinetto (Cl. Clar.)	Klarinette (Kl.)	Clarinette (Cl.)
Bass clarinet (B. Cl.)	Clarinetto basso (Cl. b., Cl. basso, Clar. basso)	Bass Klarinette (Bkl.)	Clarinette basse Cl. bs.)
Bassoon (Bsn., Bssn.)	Fagotto (Fag., Fg.)	Fagott (Fag., Fg.)	Basson (Bssn.)
Contrabassoon (C. Bsn.)	Contrafagotto (Cfg., C. Fag., Cont. F.)	Kontrafagott (Kfg.)	Contrebasson (C. bssn.)

BRASS

English	*Italian*	*German*	*French*
French horn (Hr., Hn.)	Corno (Cor., C.)	Horn (Hr.) [*pl.* Hörner (Hrn.)]	Cor; Cor à pistons
Trumpet (Tpt., Trpt., Trp., Tr.)	Tromba (Tr.)	Trompete (Tr., Trp.)	Trompette (Tr.)
Trumet in D	Tromba piccola (Tr. picc.)		
Cornet	Cornetta	Kornett	Cornet à pistons (C. à p., Pist.)
Trombone (Tr., Tbe., Trb., Trm., Trbe.)	Trombone [*pl.* Tromboni (Tbni., Trni.)]	Posaune. (Ps., Pos.)	Trombone (Tr.)
Tuba (Tb.)	Tuba (Tb, Tba.)	Tuba (Tb.) [*also* Basstuba (Btb.)]	Tuba (Tb.)

PERCUSSION

English	*Italian*	*German*	*French*
Percussion (Perc.)	Percussione	Schlagzeug (Schlag.)	Batterie (Batt.)
Kettledrums (K. D.)	Timpani (Timp., Tp.)	Pauken (Pk.)	Timbales (Timb.)
Snare drum (S. D.)	Tamburo piccolo (Tamb. picc.)	Kleine Trommel (Kl. Tr.)	Caisse claire (C. cl.), Caisse roulante
	Tamburo militare (Tamb. milit.)		Tambour militaire (Tamb. milit.)
Bass drum (B. drum)	Gran cassa (Gr. Cassa, Gr. C., G. C.)	Grosse Trommel (Gr. Tr.)	Grosse caisse (Gr. c.)
Cymbals (Cym., Cymb.)	Piatti (P., Ptti., Piat.)	Becken (Beck.)	Cymbales (Cym.)
Tam-Tam (Tam.-T.)			
Tambourine (Tamb.)	Tamburino (Tamb.)	Schellentrommel, Tamburin	Tambour de Basque (T. de B., Tamb. de Basque)
Triangle (Trgl., Tri.)	Triangolo (Trgl.)	Triangel	Triangle (Triang.)
Glockenspiel (Glocken.)	Campanelli (Cmp.)	Glockenspiel	Carillon

Bells (Chimes)	Campane (Cmp.)	Glocken	Cloches
Antique Cymbals	Crotali Piatti antichi	Antiken Zimbeln	Cymbales antiques
Sleigh Bells	Sonagli (Son.)	Schellen	Grelots
Xylophone (Xyl.)	Xilofono	Xylophon	Xylophone
Cowbells		Herdenglocken	
Crash cymbal			Grande cymbale chinoise
Siren			Sirène
Lion's roar			Tambour à corde
Slapstick			Fouet
Wood blocks			Blocs chinois

STRINGS

English	*Italian*	*German*	*French*
Violin (V., Vl., Vln, Vi.)	Violino (V., Vl., Vln.)	Violine (V., Vl., Vln.) Geige (Gg.)	Violon (V., Vl., (Vln.)
Viola (Va., Vl., *pl.* Vas.)	Viola (Va., Vla.) *pl.* Viole (Vle.)	Bratsche (Br.)	Alto (A.)
Violoncello, Cello (Vcl., Vc.)	Violoncello (Vc., Vlc., Vcllo.)	Violoncell (Vc., Vlc.)	Violoncelle (Vc.)
Double bass (D. Bs.)	Contrabasso (Cb., C. B.) *pl.* Contrabassi or Bassi (C. Bassi, Bi.)	Kontrabass (Kb.)	Contrebasse (C. B.)

OTHER INSTRUMENTS

English	*Italian*	*German*	*French*
Harp (Hp., Hrp.)	Arpa (A., Arp.)	Harfe (Hrf.)	Harpe (Hp.)
Piano	Pianoforte (P.-f., Pft.)	Klavier	Piano
Celesta (Cel.)			
Harpsichord	Cembalo	Cembalo	Clavecin
Harmonium (Harmon.)			
Organ (Org.)	Organo	Orgel	Orgue
Guitar		Gitarre (Git.)	
Mandoline (Mand.)			

Names of Scale Degrees and Modes

Scale Degrees

English	*Italian*	*German*	*French*
C	do	C	ut
C-sharp	do diesis	Cis	ut dièse
D-flat	re bemolle	Des	ré bémol
D	re	D	ré
D-sharp	re diesis	Dis	ré dièse
E-flat	mi bemolle	Es	mi bémol
E	mi	E	mi
E-sharp	mi diesis	Eis	mi dièse
F-flat	fa bemolle	Fes	fa bémol
F	fa	F	fa
F-sharp	fa diesis	Fis	fa dièse
G-flat	sol bemolle	Ges	sol bémol
G	sol	G	sol
G-sharp	sol diesis	Gis	sol dièse
A-flat	la bemolle	As	la bémol
A	la	A	la
A-sharp	la diesis	Ais	la dièse
B-flat	si bemolle	B	si bémol
B	si	H	si
B-sharp	si diesis	His	si dièse
C-flat	do bemolle	Ces	ut bémol

Modes

major	maggiore	dur	majeur
minor	minore	moll	mineur

Note on Baroque Instruments

In the Baroque works, certain older instruments, not used in the modern orchestra, were required by the composers; the following list defines these terms.

Continuo (Con.) A method of indicating an accompanying part by the bass notes only, together with figures designating the chords to be played above them. In general practice, the chords are played on a harpsichord or organ, while a viola da gamba or cello doubles the bass notes.

Corno. Although this term usually designates the French horn, in the Bach Cantata No. 140 it refers to the *cornett,* or *zink*—a wooden trumpet without valves.

Taille (Tail.). In the Bach Cantata No. 140, this term indicates a tenor oboe or English horn.

Violino piccolo. A small violin, tuned a fourth higher than the standard violin.

Violone (V.). A string instrument intermediate in size between the cello and the double bass. (In modern performances, the double bass is commonly substituted.)

APPENDIX C

Glossary of Musical Terms Used in the Scores

The following glossary is not intended to be a complete dictionary of musical terms, nor is knowledge of all these terms necessary to follow the scores in this book. However, as listeners gain experience in following scores, they will find it useful and interesting to understand the composer's directions with regard to tempo, dynamics, and methods of performance.

In most cases, compound terms have been broken down in the glossary and defined separately, as they often recur in varying combinations. A few common foreign-language particles are included in addition to the musical terms. Note that names and abbreviations for instruments and for scale degree will be found in Appendix B.

a The phrases *a* 2, *a* 3 (etc.) indicate the number of parts to be played by 2, 3 (etc.) players; when a simple number (1., 2., etc.) is placed over a part, it indicates that only the first (second, etc.) player in that group should play.
aber But.
accelerando (accel.) Growing faster.
accordato, accordez Tune the instrument as specified.
adagio Slow, leisurely.
affettuoso With emotion.
affrettare (affrett.) Hastening a little.
agitando, agitato Agitated, excited.
al fine "The end"; an indication to return to the start of a piece and to repeat it only to the point marked "fine."
alla breve Indicates two beats to a measure, at a rather quick tempo.
allargando (allarg.) Growing broader.
alle, alles All, every, each.
allegretto A moderately fast tempo (between allegro and andante).
allegro A rapid tempo (between allegretto and presto).
allein Alone, solo.
allmählich Gradually (*allmählich wieder gleich mässig fliessend werden*, gradually becoming even-flowing again).
alta, alto, altus (A.) The deeper of the two main divisions of women's (or boys') voices.
am steg On the bridge (of a string instrument).
ancora Again.
andante A moderately slow tempo (between adagio and allegretto).
andantino A moderately slow tempo.
anfang Beginning, initial.
anima Spirit, animation.
animando With increasing animation.
animant, animato, animé, animez Animated.
aperto Indicates open notes on the horn, open strings, and undamped piano notes.
a piacere The execution of the passage is left to the performer's discretion.
appassionato Impassioned.
appena Scarcely, hardly.
apprensivo Apprehensive.
archet Bow.
archi, arco Played with the bow.
arditamente Boldly.
arpeggiando, arpeggiato (arpegg.) Played in harp style, i.e. the notes of the chord played in quick succession rather than simultaneously.
assai Very.

assez Fairly, rather.
attacca Begin what follows without pausing.
a tempo At the original tempo.
auf dem On the (as in *auf dem G,* on the G string).
ausdruck Expression.
ausdrucksvoll With expression.
äusserst Extreme, utmost.
avec With.

bachetta, bachetti Drumsticks (*bachetti di spugna,* sponge-headed drumsticks).
baguettes Drumsticks (*baguettes de bois,* wooden drumsticks; *baguettes d'éponge,* spong-headed drumsticks).
bass, bassi, basso, bassus (B.) The lowest male voice.
battere, battuta, battuto (batt.) To beat.
becken Cymbals.
bedeutend bewegter With significantly more movement.
beider Hände With both hands.
ben Very.
bewegt Agitated.
bewegter More agitated.
bisbigliando, bispiglando (bis.) Whispering.
bis zum schluss dieser szene To the end of this scene.
blasen Blow.
blech Brass instruments.
bogen (bog.) Played with the bow.
bois Woodwind.
bouché Muted.
breit Broadly.
breiter More broadly.
brio Spirit, vivacity.
burden Refrain.

cadenza (cad., cadenz.) An extended passage for solo instrument in free, improvisatory style.
calando (cal.) Diminishing in volume and speed.
calma, calmo Calm, calmly.
cantabile (cant.) In a singing style.
cantando In a singing manner.
canto Voice (as in *col canto,* a direction for the accompaniment to follow the solo part in tempo and expression).
cantus An older designation for the highest part in a vocal work.
capriccio Capriciously, whimsically.
changez Change (usually an instruction to re-tune a string or an instrument).
chiuso See *gestopft.*
chromatisch Chromatic.
circa (ca.) About, approximately.
coda The last part of a piece.
col, colla, coll' With the.
colore Colored.
come prima, come sopra As at first, as previously.
commodo Comfortable, easy.
con With.
corda String; for example, *seconda (2a) corda* is the second string (the A string on the violin).
corto Short, brief.
crescendo (cresc.) An increase in volume.
cuivré Played with a harsh, blaring tone.

da capo (D.C.) Repeat from the beginning.
dal segno (D.S.) Repeat from the sign.
dämpfer (dpf.) Mutes.
dazu In addition to that, for that purpose.
de, des, die Of, from.
début Beginning.
deciso Determined, resolute.
decrescendo (decresc., decr.) A decreasing of volume.
dehors Outside.
dem To the.
détaché With a broad, vigorous bow stroke, each note bowed singly.
deutlich Distinctly.
d'exécution Performance.
diminuendo, diminuer (dim., dimin.) A decreasing of volume.
distinto Distinct, clear.
divisés, divisi (div.) Divided; indicates that the instrumental group should be divided into two parts to play the passage in question.
dolce Sweetly and softly.
dolcemente Sweetly.
dolcissimo (dolciss.) Very sweetly.
doppelgriff Double stop.
doux Sweetly.
drängend Pressing on.
dreifach Triple.
dreitaktig Three beats to a measure.
dur Major, as in *G dur* (G major).
durée Duration.

e, et And.
eilen To hurry.
ein One, a.
elegante Elegant, graceful.
energico Energetically.
espansione Expansion, broadening.
espressione With expression.
espressivo (espr., espress.) Expressively.
etwas Somewhat, rather.
expressif Expressively.

facile Simple.
fin, fine End, close.
flatterzunge, flutter-tongue A special tonguing technique for wind instruments, producing a rapid trill-like sound.
flebile Feeble, plaintive, mournful.
fliessend Flowing.
forte (f) Loud.
fortissimo (ff) Very loud (*fff* indicates a still louder dynamic).
forza Force.
fou Frantic.
frappez To strike.
frei Freely.
freihäng, freihängendes Hanging freely. An indication to the percussionist to let the cymbals vibrate freely.
frisch Fresh, lively.
furioso Furiously.

ganz Entirely, altogether.
ganzton Whole tone.
gedämpft (ged.) Muted.
geheimnisvoll Mysteriously.
geschlagen Pulsating.
gestopft (gest.) Stopping the notes of a horn; that is, the hand is placed in the bell of the horn, to produce a muffled sound. Also *chiuso*.
geteilt (get.) Divided; indicates that the instrumental group should be divided into two parts to play the passage in question.
getragen Sustained.
gewöhnlich As usual.
giocoso Humorous.
giusto Moderately.
glissando (gliss.) Rapid scales produced by running the fingers over all the strings.
gradamente Gradually.
grande Large, great.
grandioso Grandiose.
grave Slow, solemn; deep, low.
grazioso Gracefully.
grosser auftakt Big upbeat.
gut Good, well.

hälfte Half.
hauptzeitmass Original tempo.
hervortreten Prominent.
hoch High, nobly.
holz Woodwinds.
holzschlägel Wooden drumstick.

im gleichen rhythmus In the same rhythm.
immer Always.
in Oktaven In octaves.
insensibilmente Slightly, imperceptibly.
intensa Intensely.
istesso tempo Duration of beat remains unaltered despite meter change.

jeu Playful.
jusqu'à Until.

kadenzieren To cadence.
klagend Lamenting.
kleine Little.
klingen To sound.
komisch bedeutsam Very humorously.
kurz Short.

langsam Slow.
langsamer Slower.
languendo, langueur Languor.
l'archet See *archet*.
largamente Broadly.
larghetto Slightly faster than largo.
largo A very slow tempo.
lasci, lassen To abandon.
lebhaft Lively.
lebhafter Livelier.
legatissimo A more forceful indication of *legato*.
legato Performed without any perceptible interruption between notes.
légèrement, leggieramente Lightly.
leggiero (legg.) Light and graceful.
legno The wood of the bow (*col legno gestrich*, played with the wood).
lent Slow.
lentamente Slowly.
lento A slow tempo (between andante and largo).
l.h. Abbreviation for "left hand."
liricamente Lyrically.
loco Indicates a return to the written pitch, following a passage played an octave higher or lower than written.
luftpause Pause for breath.
lunga Long, sustained.
lusingando Caressing.

ma, mais But.
maestoso Majestic.
marcatissimo (marcatiss.) With very marked emphasis.
marcato (marc.) Marked, with emphasis.
marschmässig, nicht eilen Moderate-paced march, not rushed.
marziale Military, martial, march-like.
mässig Moderately.
mässiger More moderately.
même Same.
meno Less.
mezzo forte (mf) Moderately loud.
mezzo piano (mp) Moderately soft.
mindestens At least.
misterioso Mysterious.
misura Measured.
mit With.

moderatissimo A more forceful indication of *moderato*.
moderato, modéré At a moderate tempo.
moins Less.
molto Very, much.
mordenti Biting, pungent.
morendo Dying away.
mormorato Murmured.
mosso Rapid.
moto Motion.
mouvement (mouv., mouvt.) Tempo.
muta, mutano Change the tuning of the instrument as specified.

nach More.
naturalezza A natural, unaffected manner.
neuen New.
nicht Not.
niente Nothing.
nimmt To take; to seize.
noch Still.
non Not.
nuovo New.

obere, oberer (ob.) Upper, leading.
oder langsamer Or slower.
offen Open.
ohne Without.
ondeggiante Undulating movement of the bow, which produces a tremolo effect.
ordinario (ord., ordin.) In the usual way (generally cancelling an instruction to play using some special technique).
ossia An alternative (usually easier) version of a passage.
ôtez vite les sourdines Remove the mutes quickly.
ottoni Brass.
ouvert Open.

parte Part (*colla parte*, the accompaniment is to follow the soloist in tempo).
passionato Passionately.
paukenschlägel Timpani stick.
pavillons en l'air An indication to the player of a wind instrument to raise the bell of the instrument upward.
pedal, pedale (ped., P.) (1) In piano music, indicates that the damper pedal should be depressed; an asterisk indicates the point of release (brackets below the music are also used to indicate pedaling); (2) on an organ, the pedals are a keyboard played with the feet.
per During.
perdendosi Gradually dying away.
pesante Heavily.
peu Little, a little.
piacevole Agreeable, pleasant.
pianissimo (pp) Very soft (*ppp* indicates a still softer dynamic).
piano (p) Soft.
più More.
pizzicato (pizz.) The string plucked with the finger.
plötzlich Suddenly, immediately.
plus More.
pochissimo (pochiss.) Very little, a very little.
poco Little, a little.
ponticello (pont.) The bridge (of a string instrument).
portamento Continuous smooth and rapid sliding between two pitches.
position naturel (pos. nat.) In the normal position (usually cancelling an instruction to play using some special technique).
possibile Possible.
premier mouvement (1er mouvt.) At the original tempo.
prenez Take up.
préparez Prepare.
presque Almost, nearly.
presser To press.
prestissimo A more forceful indication of *presto*.
presto A very quick tempo (faster than allegro).
prima, primo First, principal.

quarta Fourth.
quasi Almost, as if.
quinto Fifth.

rallentando (rall., rallent.) Growing slower.
rapidamente Quickly.
rapidissimo (rapidiss.) Very quickly.
rasch Quickly.
rascher More quickly.
rauschend Rustling, roaring.
recitative (recit.) A vocal style designed to imitate and emphasize the natural inflections of speech.
rein Perfect interval.
respiro Pause for breath.
retenu Held back.
r.h. Abbreviation for "right hand."
richtig Correct (*richtige lage*, correct pitch).
rien Nothing.
rigore di tempo Strictness of tempo.
rinforzando (rf., rfz., rinf.) A sudden accent on a single note or chord.
ritardando (rit., ritard.) Gradually slackening in speed.
ritenuto (riten.) Immediate reduction of speed.
ritmato Rhythmic.

ritornando, ritornello (ritor.) Refrain.
rubato A certain elasticity and flexibility of tempo, consisting of slight accelerandos and ritardandos according to the requirements of the musical expression.
ruhig Quietly.

sans Without.
schalltrichter Horn.
scherzando (scherz.) Playful.
schlagen To strike in a usual manner.
schlagwerk Striking mechanism.
schleppen, schleppend Dragging.
schluss Cadence, conclusion.
schnell Fast.
schneller Faster.
schon Already.
schwammschlagëln Sponge-headed drumstick.
scorrevole Flowing, gliding.
sec, secco Dry, simple.
secunda Second.
sehr Very.
semplicita Simplicity.
sempre Always, continually.
senza Without.
sforzando (sf., sfz.) With sudden emphasis.
simile (sim.) In a similar manner.
sin Without.
singstimme Singing voice.
sino al Up to the . . . (usually followed by a new tempo marking, or by a dotted line indicating a terminal point).
si piace Especially pleasing.
smorzando (smorz.) Dying away.
sofort Immediately.
soli, solo (s.) Executed by one performer.
sopra Above; in piano music, used to indicate that one hand must pass above the other.
soprano (S.) The voice classification with the highest range.
sordini, sordino (sord.) Mute.
sostenendo, sostenuto (sost.) Sustained.
sotto voce In an undertone, subdued, under the breath.
sourdine (sourd.) Mute.
soutenu Sustained.
spiel, spielen Play (an instrument).
spieler Player, performer.
spirito Spirit, soul.
spiritoso In a spirited manner.
spugna Sponge
staccato (stacc.) Detached, separated, abruptly, disconnected.
stentando, stentare, stentato (stent.) Delaying, retarding.
stesso The same.
stimme Voice.
stimmen To tune.
strascinare To drag.
streichinstrumente (streichinstr.) Bowed string instruments.
strepitoso Noisy, loud.
stretto In a non-fugal composition, indicates a concluding section at an increased speed.
stringendo (string.) Quickening.
subito (sub.) Suddenly, immediately.
sul On the (as in *sul G*, on the G string).
superius In older music, the uppermost part.
sur On.

tacet The instrument or vocal part so marked is silent.
tasto solo In a continuo part, this indicates that only the string instrument plays; the chord-playing instrument is silent.
tempo primo (tempo I) At the original tempo.
teneramente, tenero Tenderly, gently.
tenor, tenore (T.) The highest male voice.
tenuto (ten., tenu.) Held, sustained.
tertia Third.
tief Deep, low.
touche Key; note.
toujours Always, continually.
tranquillo Quietly, calmly.
tre corde (t.c.) Release the soft (or *una corda*) pedal of the piano.
tremolo (trem.) On string instruments, a quick reiteration of the same tone, produced by a rapid up-and-down movement of the bow; also a rapid alternation between two different notes.
très Very.
trill (tr.) The rapid alternation of a given note with the diatonic second above it. In a drum part it indicates rapid alternating strokes with two drumsticks.
trommschlag (tromm.) Drumbeat.
troppo Too much.
tutta la forza Very emphatically.
tutti Literally, "all"; usually means all the instruments in a given category as distinct from a solo part.

übergreifen To overlap.
übertonend Drowning out.
umstimmen To change the tuning.
un One, a.
una corda (u.c.) With the "soft" pedal of the piano depressed.
und And.
unison (unis.) The same notes or melody

played by several instruments at the same pitch. Often used to emphasize that a phrase is not to be divided among several players.
unmerklich Imperceptible.

velocissimo Very swiftly.
verklingen lassen To let die away.
vibrare To sound.
vibrato (vibr.) To fluctuate the pitch on a single note.
vierfach Quadruple.
vierhändig Four-hand piano music.
vif Lively.
vigoroso Vigorous, strong.
vivace Quick, lively.
vivacissimo A more forceful indication of *vivace.*
vivente, vivo Lively.
voce Voice (as in *colla voce,* a direction for the accompaniment to follow the solo part in tempo and expression).
volles orch. Entire orchestra.
vorhang auf Curtain up.
vorhang zu Curtain down.
vorher Beforehand, previously.
voriges Preceding.

waltzertempo In the tempo of a waltz.
weg Away, beyond.
weich Mellow, smooth, soft.
wie aus der fern As if from afar.
wieder Again.
wie zu anfang dieser szene As at the beginning of this scene.

zart Tenderly, delicately.
zeit Time; duration.
zögernd Slower.
zu The phrases *zu 2, zu 3* (etc.) indicate the number of parts to be played by 2, 3 (etc.) players.
zum In addition.
zurückhaltend Slackening in speed.
zurücktreten To withdraw.
zweihändig With two hands.

Index of Forms and Genres

A roman numeral following a title indicates a movement within the work named.